Y0-BCN-162

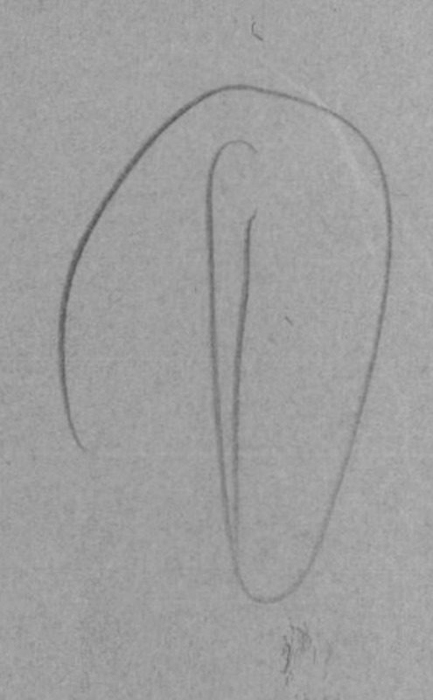

The Searching
Mind of Greece

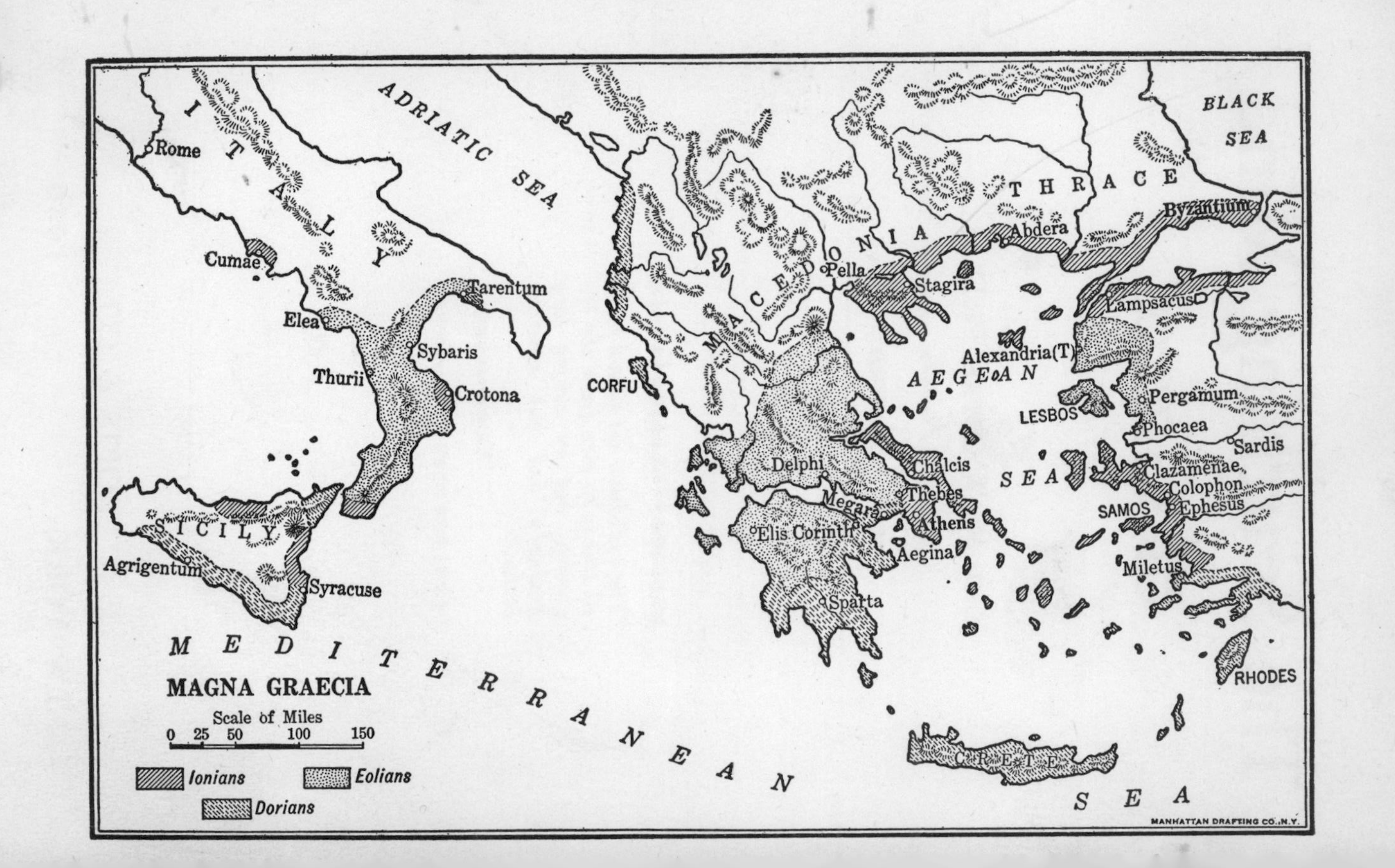

MAGNA GRAECIA

The Searching Mind of Greece

by

JOHN M. WARBEKE, PH.D.
Professor of Philosophy
in
Mount Holyoke College

"The gods have not shown forth all things to men from the beginning, but by seeking they gradually find out what is better."

XENOPHANES.

F. S. CROFTS & CO.
NEW YORK 1930

MANUFACTURED IN THE UNITED STATES OF AMERICA
BY THE VAIL-BALLOU PRESS, INC., BINGHAMTON, N. Y.

To my students, past and present,
at Williams, Mount Holyoke and Amherst,
who have climbed and still are climbing
on these trails with me.

PREFACE

This book was written that the pursuit which Plato called "The noblest of them all" might, if possible, be made more attractive to my countrymen. It is a daring book, because the quest appears to be an endless one and has elicited heroic efforts from most searching minds. But I hope it may be an inspiriting one as well. Philosophy has sometimes been compared to mountain-climbing, and its purest springs of joy are then said to flow from the most rugged heights of endeavor. The figure, however, is misleading. For it has helped to foster the idea that the few who scale these heights are undertaking an icy, futile, or even unearthly venture. This, indeed, is common opinion to-day. How many accidents to human minds is not philosophy held responsible for! Our very newspapers seem to take it for granted that any untoward personal event, from a runaway youth, to a divorce, an apostasy, or a suicide, is the product of some new "philosophy." What that is, is generally left unsaid—whereby the fearsome mystery becomes more ominous still. And yet our William James has characterized philosophy as "only an unusually obstinate effort at clear thinking."

It is time that a nearly universal desire "to see life steadily and see it whole" should be cleared from misunderstanding. We should no longer dishonor those gallant explorers, who (as a matter of history) have brought to our minds whole continents of what we call "modern" in our science, our religion, our conceptions of government, and ethical practice. They should no longer be esteemed altogether "foolish in their own conceits," dark, dismal, and dangerous men, because there have been such among them. Nor should the hazards of their new ventures, even on uncharted seas, be frowned upon. All things excellent are dangerous—from human love to human arts, and human life itself. If thought is dangerous, and no doubt it is, our hope for progress in every desirable thing that can be named, from happy marriage and the just conduct of a state, to the coordination of science and religion, as surely depends upon it—the most comprehensive and searching thought of which our minds are capable.

Now it is a matter of record that Greek thinkers have, again and again in the course of time, been a potent inspiration in this direction. Why this is true will later appear. But here we must note that the way is not one of imitation, but a more direct and vital one. These men are not authorities who did our thinking for us many years ago; the idea is itself a negation of the ever-progressive Greek spirit. Modern artists who realize the intuitions of an Alcamenes or a Praxiteles are not impelled to a copy, or a "barren rehearsal," but to creative expressions of their own. The same is true of modern poets. Mere imitation of Homer or Sophocles would produce only feigning and sentimentality. Neo-classicism is always a falsification. What Greek philosophy engenders is native to the mind of the student and brings to birth new and genuine creations.

Perhaps it is this exuberance of life which makes so much of Greek artistry and thought seem as natural, as spontaneous, and as generous, sometimes also as naïve, as the love of a youth. There could be no better introduction to the problems of philosophy. Greek ideas of morality, for instance, are not of a kind to "make you dreary"—as Stevenson characterized some others. On the contrary, they inspire to joy and fulfillment by conceptions of success and excellence native to every open-minded human. It was no Greek thinker who invented the sorrowful dogma of mankind's total depravity! Crime and vice they pronounced—not by word of power or authority, but by examination of the evidence—as the unnatural, unreasonable, and unhappy thing. At this point their so-called "pagan" liberality promises a new wholesomeness in ethical matters. And the same might be illustrated by the extraordinary influence of a new reality-sense which is developing in religion; or by the natural interpretation of the state as dissociated from any and every idea of mere power or sovereignty as such.

In this study of the Greek quest for enlightenment, I have aimed throughout to coordinate their conceptions and hypotheses with our own. Only thus can their significance be understood, and our own efforts toward the solution of these problems be furthered. It is of great value to know as a matter of record, that a group of important ideas was the gift of a certain man in a given period of history. We must preserve, and extend, exact and exhaustive data concerning things so precious. But ultimately they are tools to serve our own philosophic insight, lacking which our study of any sources, facts, and records, is without its reason for being. I have, of course, aimed never to violate the meaning and intention of the sources. Under the spell of great *aperçus* it is easy to read into them somewhat more than their authors contemplated. But there is equal danger of reading too little—which is no less a limitation and perhaps a more serious one.

It was my constant source of regret, in reading the originals, that the Greek language itself is numbered among the dead. Surely it is one of humanity's most remarkable creations, a vehicle lending itself to the utmost refinement and abstraction, yet with a robust directness and clear-cut precision which defy comparison. This language itself appears to be the work of a master-artist, thrilled by the possibilities of beauty. Yet I started the work with the determination, if possible, to bring our heritage of Greek thought home to those who have no knowledge of the original tongue. I regret nothing more than this "lost cause" in our present-day education. Yet I trust that for English readers the book will be more comprehensible than if it had been filled with foreign phrases.

These pages were written primarily for students taking courses in Greek Philosophy or Introductions to Philosophy in our colleges and universities. But the general reader may derive some help from the thought of men at once so rich, open-minded, penetrating, and disinterested, on subjects which are of so great import for the future of mankind. Should he desire to limit himself to a study of ancient Pragmatism (the Sophists), Plato's Communism, or his Interpretation of Art, the various conceptions of Evolution (Anaximander, Empedocles, Aristotle), Atomism, or Aristotle's Natural Interpretation of the State, and of Morality, etc., he will find it possible. But it is recommended that he "drink" at least as "deep" as the sections devoted to a given philosopher, or his period, in order to secure an adequate perspective.

Many colleagues and friends have freely offered me counsel and advice of a stimulating kind. Here I should, perhaps, acknowledge the courtesy of those who have taken the trouble critically to read parts or all of the manuscript. These were Professors James Bissett Pratt, William J. Newlin, Anna Cutler, Mary G. Williams, Sir Gilbert Murray, David Rogers, and Edgar O. Singer. To the penetrating judgment and unending kindness of Professor Singer I am indebted in more ways than words can express. My wife, as in all our pilgrimage so far, encouraged every step, even to the reading of the proofs together.

J. M. W.

CONTENTS

INTRODUCTORY:

What Manner of Men They Were

CHAPTER I

INTRODUCTION: THE GREEK SPIRIT

1

History very likely can show no greater contrast between two neighboring civilized peoples than that between Phœnicians and the Ionian Greeks in the respective times of their florescence. The story of the former is soon told. They were an amazingly skillful and prosperous folk whose dominant interests were business and money-diplomacy. Their wars, which seem to have grown out of trade rivalries, have little to interest historians. They were the master bankers, middlemen, manufacturers, ship and warehouse owners of antiquity. They had the swiftest vessels on the seven seas. They possessed trade-stations on the western coasts of Europe and Africa and even pushed beyond the Cape of Good Hope to the shores of the Indian Ocean. Their own country, north and south of the Lebanon, was, and still is, remarkably fertile, despite its long intensive cultivation. They lived on one of the most important overland trade routes, and doubtless profited by that. Yet the record tells of almost no poets, prophets, sculptors, scientists, composers, historians, or philosophers among them. The story, like that of their kindred Philistines, has little to amuse, instruct, or inspire.

The Ionian Greeks, on the other hand, were much devoted to what a typical Phœnician must have deemed a waste of time. They listened to stories told in verse by rhapsodes about the very market-place. They chiseled endless blocks of marble into statues merely intended to please the fancy of the passer-by—or perchance some god. They attended many dramatic contests in which the imaginary woes of legendary heroes were set forth with endless variations; and then they presented the victor with a worthless sprig of laurel. Cisterns were carved below their houses, and kitchen utensils molded, as delicately as though intended for royal palaces. They discussed endless and useless questions, metaphysics, psychology, abstract mathematics, as though these could be utilized for something more than mere talk. They assumed, in short, that new creations of their special invention called beauty, or the discovery of original ideas and interpretations of the universe, are what a human being should chiefly aim for in an unrestricted leisure. Yet the Phœnicians would also recall that these Greeks knew quite well how to carry on war; and that trade, although with them more a means to an end, was hardly unsuccessful.

Modern students when they come into possession of their heritage from the Greeks are often disposed to think of them in terms of a human Golden Age with its climax in Periclean Athens. And no wonder. Poets and artists in endless succession have exclaimed: Here were the happiest, most gifted, most vital, and resourceful men who so far have lived on our planet. Doubtless imagination has often colored such judgments. Modern poets, captivated by the dramatic quality of that life, set in a beauty which seems to epitomize all that land and sea can afford, have sometimes amplified their pictures. Shelley, when he wrote of "faultless productions whose very fragments are the despair of modern art,"[1] was perhaps unjust to modern art. Sometimes even historians, excited by the characters and events of an amazingly active and significant age, have not seen the picture as a whole. Not a few classical scholars have appeared to believe in supermen. So judicial and learned a student of law and government as Sir Henry Maine could write: "Except the blind forces of nature, noth-

[1] Preface to *Hellas*.

ing moves in this world which is not Greek in its origin."[2]

What manner of men were these, and what the products of their minds and hands that they should have aroused so much enthusiasm? Why do so many critical scholars say: If by some catastrophe the heritage from Greece and what it has engendered in the world were now to be removed, it would be equivalent to the destruction of Western civilization? A part of the record is very clear. They who have traced the origins of the sciences from pure mathematics, astronomy, and physics, to biology and psychology; or who have followed the course of liberal theories of government; or the development of European literatures, say they recognize the fathers of our spirits in that race. Its city-states are held to be the prototypes of our modern forms of self-government, and are still confessedly a forlorn hope to many who crave a more perfect democracy. Greek annalists first realized that history is an interpretation and not merely a chronicle. The scientific undertakings developed there brought into existence many of the fundamental concepts and principles by whose light our knowledge of the world in these later centuries has been so greatly extended. Their arts are so woven into the fabric of what we call liberal education—training towards the maximum richness of human existence—that we designate them and their fruits as *humanities*.

If we could remove all these interests we should probably revert to the mentality of superstitious barbarians, unacquainted with the freedom of common rights, submitting our ignorant fears to the sway of arbitrary satraps, going our way without any strong initiative toward disinterested knowledge, or creation for their own sakes of monumental works of beauty. Much that our typical Phœnician would have regarded as "too idealistic," weak, impractical, and "high-brow" would also have disappeared. For there is not

[2] Rede Lecture, p. 38.

a little in this heritage which has led to "Utopian" ideas. Boys and girls who have read even the political history of Greece can never again be brought to think of their fellows as merely merchants, doctors, politicians, or commodity-producers. The pages of Herodotus and Thucydides will have told them indeed of unscrupulous men and terrible events. But the dramatic issues there at stake reflect the course of persistent and spontaneous aspirations toward excellence, and events are traced to their sources in the characters of men. Hence the perennial appeal to ideals inspired by their history. No lad who has read so much as a speech of Pericles or Demosthenes will henceforward be wholly content with anarchy and license, or with arbitrary power wheresoever found. This is the tragic hope which Sir Henry Maine considered the mainspring of Western civilization—the Greek idea of progress.

The same marriage of real and ideal is consummated in Greek poetry. Where refinement is a condition of workmanship the besetting sin of an artist is easily over-subtlety, straining, and empty conceits. But Greek poets from Homer to Aristophanes have scarcely a tinge of Euphuism, romanticism, melodrama, sentimentality, or even form for form's sake. Whether it be in the stories of prodigious Polyphemus, the wizard Circe, and Nausicaä, she of the fair arms with her maidens washing the clothes, or in the very Cloud-cuckooland of Aristophanes, everywhere the sense of reality dominates. Homer is simple enough to delight the imaginations of children, and so penetrating in his knowledge of men and affairs that he holds us in our greatest maturity. Of overt sentiment there is none. Yet a passing observation speaks pages to feeling and reflection, a mere adjective among his wingèd words is often a poem in itself. The free, yet perfect form of the verse and the spontaneous narrative of his tales are fused into a unity of intuitions so rich that time increases their originality. Thus Hesiod, shepherd-poet of Helicon, writes of spades as spades and of ordinary work-a-day matters, sometimes indeed making up stories like Pandora's box, or imagining the life-histories of some ancient and almost forgotten gods, but with sentiment which is never falsified or distorted. The stories of heroic fate as told by Æschylus, Sophocles, Euripides, require no violent change of attitude, a retreat to some foreign world of high romance. The scene is generally near at hand though the heroes may be of old. And authentic poetry is found in the daily thought and actions, the rich variety, of men's lives, their destiny similar to all their fellows—from cicadas chirping in the shade to the very blessed gods, who might any one of them on occasion be disguised as a passing stranger in the street, or a playful shepherd on the hills. Restraint expresses itself with all the ease of natural law in these tragedies, though differently, of course, in the three writers.

By the time of Aristophanes the lesser comic poets had come to farces and strained absurdities. But the greatest of comedy writers, though he deals with the ugly, and often with what is contemptible, rarely stoops to exaggeration or mere stage effects, and constantly delights his audience by the beauty of his ideas and the exquisite forms of his language. Myriad fragments of lyric song from dozens of lesser poets bespeak the same love of reality and genuineness. To many of us moderns (as to Friedrich Schiller in his youth) Greek poets seem cold—as too restrained, or even factual. But what most Greeks abhorred was unnaturalness, unreality, sentimentality. And that is why their poetry was a part of life no less than other forms of speech. That is why the prose of a Plato, a Demosthenes, or Thucydides is robustly mundane and part of the day's work, even though it scintillates with intelligence and refinement.

In the other arts we find a similar union of reason with nature. For example, in sculpture, an art which so far is only on the periphery of modern life, the Greeks made an effort to show how the inmost spirit of a man is expressed in every line, surface, and form of his body. Was it mistaken? Or have we here another projected ideal? Let him answer who has studied the plastic art of the Golden Age beckoning us through the centuries to a glorified human life! The calm figures of men and women, whose very existence, whether in their grief or piety, war or love, presents to contemplation the unity of what is admirable in body and in soul, will summon him beyond the feverish nonentity of a life caught up in the machinery of livelihood, or unaware of its purpose! Whether in the serene severity of Pæonius and Phidias, or the tender grace of Praxiteles, or the restrained passion of Scopas, character always implies this integrity of the physical and spiritual, as well as an inner harmony, a living above the petty discords of life. Never during that brief florescence of almost miraculous sculpture does exaggeration, vulgarity, or uncontrolled passion assert itself. Never was more poignant embodiment of human perfectibility put into bronze and marble.

Or consider Greek architecture at its best which too is yet to be surpassed in refinement of design and significance as expression of human character. Not only can one say of the Parthenon: "There are no lies in this building." One must also say it is imbued throughout with exuberant imagination. So transparently honorable is the workmanship, so choice every block of marble, that one cannot even to-day find room for a needle between their uncemented edges where the walls have not been blasted apart. Such joy in labor is itself an interesting light on the sort of life even slaves enjoyed in Athens. It also points a practical ideal of perfection whose importance it would be hard to overestimate. From granite foundations to pediments and acroteria the honest blocks of the Parthenon embody pure serenity combined with strength that is perfectly poised.

Refinement and power are the two seemingly antithetical presuppositions of art! Here they are combined with formal grace, proportion, sensuous charm, and inner significance, into so rich a variety that study seems never to exhaust its originality. Even what was thought of as decoration in frieze and metopes is itself so full of significant intuitions of vital men and women, that the fabric, even in its mutilation, seems vibrant with spiritual energy.

One feels the pulse of Greek life in these arts of which the "lesser" ones—from that of the goldsmith to the glass-blower—might have provided even more striking examples. For there seems to have been no distinction between artisan and artist among them. Their most trivial possessions, from copper coins to wine-jars or kitchen-sieves, were assumed to be as much in need of charm as their frescoed walls, their language, or athletic contests, which last were spectacles intended for the gods as well as a joy to humans. The frescoed walls as well as the canvas pictures had great celebrity in antiquity. But to-day we can only judge of Greek painting from examples in the lesser arts, chiefly water and wine receptacles. Their music, which gave us our various scales, seems to have consisted almost entirely of melodies. If so, it is fairly certain that in our classical harmonic and contrapuntal music, we moderns have developed an art which greatly surpasses its Greek prototype in richness of form and sensuous quality.

2

One cannot say what might have happened if the peoples of Europe and their colonies had never come under the influence of Greek conceptions of government. But it is significant that when, as in the Middle Ages, that influence was obscured, autocratic social institutions prevailed, just as, before the advent of Greek democracy, they had characterized pretty generally the governments of the ancient world. It was also coincident with the later Renaissance, that representative or parliamentary systems developed. These were (and are) modifications of the Greek, or literal, self-government, under which each citizen took his turn by lot at the common business of the state. The latter form was obviously possible only under certain very remarkable presuppositions!

A number of institutions aiming for the common good which have come into being, or developed more fully, since the Renaissance, were also inspired by Greek prototypes. Among these should be mentioned: public school education, municipal theaters, and international associations for peace. One cannot, of course, forget the serious limitations of character presented by the all too common self-superiority of Hellenic leaders, whatever the basis for it in fact. The difference between "barbarians" and Hellenes was indeed marked. Again they were all too fickle and nimble in their loyalties. Like their neighbors, they practiced slavery, usually upon these "barbarians." But historic fact none the less constrains one to say, that those who have come under the influence of Greek conceptions of social life and government have developed a marked sense of personal liberty, both in thought and in action. Along with this individualism has also come a sense of form, or reasonableness in social life, which, as an ideal of natural, or common, law, has opposed the autocratic, the merely artificial, the hieratic agencies, wherever it has come into contact with them. The conception of the state as an ethical agency whose function is to provide its citizens with the richest opportunities of life, physically, æsthetically, and intellectually, is one inspired not only by Plato's *Republic*, and the *Politics* of Aristotle, but is inherent in the actual laws and constitutions which have come down to us.

3

The love of knowledge was another distinctive trait among these Greeks. Not that they were pioneers in gathering information or in keeping records and chronicles. The ancient Chaldeans long before had made painstaking observations of the heavens. Egyptian "learning," and the "wisdom" of the Hebrews, had collected very significant records for our knowledge both of men and of external nature. But a new and dramatic moment appears with the little question "Why?" one so characteristic of Greek minds. Egyptians knew very well that the square of the hypotenuse of a right-angled triangle is equal to the sum of the squares of the other two sides, and found this fact very convenient in their geometry, or "measurement of land." But they seem never to have asked why this is so, much less how one might *demonstrate* the Pythagorean proposition. "Come now and let us reason together" wrote the first prophet Isaiah. But his appeal was to exalted emotions and beloved traditions rather than to dispassionate inferences from observable facts. The Assyrians mapped the constellations and collected data with accuracy—for the sake of divination.

Greek devotion to "theory" was a baffling, incomprehensible phenomenon to their neighbors. The surprise which Solon awakened when he answered the question: Why was he traveling so far? by saying: "On account of theory," had its analogues in many other directions. There was no money in it for these "lovers of wisdom" (philosophers) or sophists as they were called at first. The pioneers of the new learning even refused fees from their students who, kindled to new intellectual adventure, also devoted themselves to theory for theory's sake. Nothing seemed too insignificant or remote, too large or too invisible, to exercise the ingenuity of these intrepid seekers. Curiosity led them to inquire what reason might discover concerning mere points and lines, and the properties of every imaginable figure, or a long array of abstract numbers. They wanted to know the structure and origins of plants and animals, their mechanisms, and whether they were kindred to those of lifeless things. They proceeded to analyze invisible minds, to discover, if possible, how their functions are linked up with other activities about us. They challenged even their own minds in the midst of the process by demanding: How can we know when we really know? When are we thinking straight? They made reason try its best to storm the very gates of death and project itself into the "dark backward and abyss of time." They tried if by seeking they might find out God. They projected the rational way for humans to live in the light of their character as men and of all possible sources of happiness. They boldly demanded reason in society; and with unflinching eye examined the shrinking form of beauty.

This insatiable curiosity to know how and why things are what they are, and act as they do, made Greeks the originators both of Western philosophy and of science. The former became the mother of all the special sciences. Originally physics, mathematics, biology, psychology, theory of government, literary criticism, astronomy and some other departments of knowledge were all included as part of the philosopher's undertaking. Specialization was gradually recognized to be the necessary condition of progress. Mathematics early set up an establishment of its own. In Aristotle's day the principle had become generally accepted. Yet from first to last these Greek investigators knew that the "body of human knowledge" is a living organism, whose functions, howsoever various, are all interdependent. They never expected a hand or a tongue to function cut off from that body. And although the later thinkers recognized the almost hopeless task of realizing this coördination—even Plato thought it worthy of Deity—they knew that willy-nilly every intelligence has *some* "vision of all time and all existence," the only question being: Is it crude and ignorant, or a more penetrating and enlightened one?

The intensely dramatic character of this search can be appreciated only as we see the individual actors. We may, however, divide the piece for our better understanding into three main "acts." The first is the Quest for Mechanism, which dominates all the early seekers. Their stage is a very wide one from Miletus in the east to Italy in the west, but Athens is not included. The second "act" is played almost exclusively on the stage of Athens and may be called the Quest for Purpose. The last unfortunately is a little anticlimax, for reasons which will appear in the sequel. But it has an interesting motive, the Quest for Practical Wisdom, and perhaps will be even nearer to the modern pragmatic "lover of wisdom" than are the earlier "acts." Be that as it may, Greek thinkers, sooner or later, will intrigue even those who "bear a wary eye," perhaps by some unimagined originality, it may be by the generosity of their adventure. Possibly their detachment will then make empires and world-commerce dwindle to some quickly passing incidental episode. Yet in their drama of "lost causes," the Tragic Story of Human Reason in Evolution, they will be found to act gallantly, directly, simply, humanly, even in their most persistent penetration.

4

Beauty, justice, truth—three master-passions—were combined in the genius of classic Greece to a degree never since equaled. How and why it was that this handful of people in two short periods of their florescence, one in the ninth, the other in the sixth, fifth and fourth centuries B. C., should have attained what they did, no historian has adequately explained. They inhabited a land of bold outlines and charming valleys, they enjoyed the constant challenge to imagination which nearness to the sea provides. Their harbors were mostly on the eastern coasts of the archipelago, a fact which would have tended to keep them in contact with the more ancient life of Asia Minor, even if their own colonies on those shores had not existed. At the same time their individuality was fostered by the degree of isolation which mountains and difficult navigation provide. Although fertile valleys and smiling plains relieved the rocky slopes, and commerce also brought in gain, the people must have been poor compared with the "standard of living" which seventh century Phœnicians enjoyed, or with our own resources. Their life was hampered by constant warfare, much of it against great empires whose armies and navies repeatedly tried to crush their institutions. But climate, environment, external resources, the challenge of great events, all these fail to explain an age of Pericles, as they fail to explain the torpor of mediæval Hellas. Perhaps one must, in the end, have recourse to vague terms: a certain quality of blood, a peculiar distinction of character (preëminently present in the Ionian race) by virtue of which Greeks faced the opposition of a world of enemies, carried out their purposes both ideal and practical, by willing to do them, notwithstanding all lack of precedent and aggressive obstacles, maintaining all the while a poise and genial harmony of life which in so many respects reminds one of their works of art.

PART ONE:

The Quest for Mechanism

CHAPTER II

EARLY NATURE PHILOSOPHERS

1

The question which first aroused the wonder and philosophical interest of thoughtful men in Greece, and especially in Greek colonies, was: Where did the visible, tangible world and its inhabitants come from? This was not a new question, for men everywhere and at all recorded times have sought to answer it. East Indians, Babylonians, Egyptians, Chinese, the Hebrews, and the Incas of Peru, all had their stories of creation, their interpretations of an ever-moving heaven. So did the Gnomic poets of Greece, and the Orphic Mysteries. Hesiod wrote a story of the Cosmos, and Epimenides explained how the egg-of-things-in-general came into being and what, in his imagination, resulted from its hatching out. Orpheus described the beginning of sun and moon and stars in their courses, while many a rhapsodist aroused general admiration by his grandiose stories of the Abyss and the Chaos of Night, before ever the first God had taken an interest in the order of things, before ever there was light.

In striking contrast with these stories of world-genesis and of ultimate world-destroying fire—a fire ordained by Fate against the time when human wickedness should have attained its maximum—were the ideas of a group of men who toward the middle of the sixth century B. C. set up a school in the Ionian colony of Miletus, the town on the coast of Asia Minor which still bears that name. This school, variously called the Milesian, or Ionian Physicists, seems to have continued upwards of a century. Its leaders invented a point of view which was to prove of extraordinary influence upon Western thought. By establishing scientific imagination beside the Muse of poetic fancy they paved the way for a new reality-sense which could no longer be satisfied with traditions of heavenly calves [1] or with Hesiod's *Theogony*—at least as accounts of truth and the basis of religion. Instead they looked to the simpler aspects of nature for explanations of the more complex, to real or supposed *facts* for their knowledge. They refused to be daunted by fear of the unknown. Quite unconscious of the significance of their method for later thought these pioneers looked to earth, to water, to fire, and even to air for their interpretations of the traditional wonders and mysteries. They began to inquire: What is the *Arché*, the original substance, out of which the universe developed? What processes were involved in the changes by which it became what it is? In short, they aimed to establish a natural interpretation of our world and all its seemingly miraculous transformations.

2

The distinction of having introduced this way of thinking belongs to Thales, whom Aristotle calls the founder of that school which regarded the nature of matter as the fundamental problem to be considered.[2] He seems to have been born about 624 B. C. and to have enjoyed a long and interesting career. Endless stories are extant concerning his dramatic life. Those which seem to be authenticated show us the Father of Philosophy as a merchant who traveled extensively, a statesman who was called upon to advise his government, as well as an astronomer and a mathematician "for theory's sake." What distinguished him from the other sages with whom he is frequently named was, according to Plutarch,[3] the fact that "the wisdom of Thales alone seems

[1] Cf. Breadsted: *A History of Egypt,* p. 54.
[2] *Metaphysics,* I, 983b 20.
[3] *Lives,* Dryden's Trans. Ed. A. H. Clough, Vol. I, p. 171.

to have extended far beyond the knowledge of necessary things. The others derived their name of sage from their practical wisdom." Thus he tried his hand at proving geometrically the Egyptian rules of thumb. He calculated the height of the pyramids by shadows and similar triangles. From Babylonian records he first and successfully attempted to *predict* a total eclipse of the sun (May 28, 585 B. C.). He even tried his skill at weather reports.

But what chiefly interests us here is his speculation that the primitive world-substance, out of which the solid earth, stars, trees and human beings had sprung, was water, or perhaps more justly, something fluid.[4] The details of his doctrine have not come down to us and, in the bald, meager form in which we possess it, the theory seems naïve enough—especially since in antiquity it was a very widespread belief that the (flat) earth either floated directly upon water or through elephants and tortoises eventually rested upon some water animal. Students of physical geography will note a certain resemblance between our "primitive nebula" and the *arché* of Thales in so far as *nebula* implies something like vapor. But it was the substitution of a given reality, something at hand and observable, for unseen dragons, spirits, or incredible eggs, which made the method rather than the results of this hypothesis significant. Henceforward students of nature were in possession of the idea of an orderly cosmos as alternative to the arbitrary and divergent purposes of Olympian or other miraculous agencies. Its changes were thought to be subject to what was inherent in things themselves taken as a whole, even though Thales and some of his successors also regarded "all things as full of gods." Part at least of these changes were thought to be predictable, and all to have a natural origin. This hypothesis, known in modern times as Naturalism, has remained a general presupposition of scientific investigation. Whether

[4] Cf. Aristotle, *Metaphysics,* I, 3, 983b 22.

Thales also taught, as certain later writers claim, that all things in the course of time return once more to their origin cannot with certainty be made out. Most likely this is to be classed with the doubtful tradition that the Sage who first preferred theory to practice lost his life by walking into a well while he was observing the stars!

3

Naturalism became more explicit in Anaximander (610–546 B. C.), the pupil and successor of Thales, a man of bold scientific imagination. He may be said to have given us approximately our present conception of a cosmic nebula or world-substance, out of which the universe through boundless time has come to develop into more specific forms. We know very little about him personally. Perhaps the external events of his life were few. But it would be difficult in point of sheer sublimity to surpass the voyages of his mind. Looking backward and forward, and into the farthest reaches of space, secure in his belief in the order and regularity of nature, he sought to bring his reason and imagination to some faint comprehension of the whole.

He called the material foundation of the world *Apeiron*, or "Boundless," and thought that from the beginning it must have contained in itself whatever has since developed in the course of world history. How could something come from nothing? Or how destroy anything utterly? Surely nothing can be spirited into the world or out of it! Aristotle, to whom we are indebted for a good deal of our knowledge concerning early philosophy, explains in his *Physics* [5] how Anaximander and other physicists who followed him argued concerning the *Apeiron*. It must be timeless, because it cannot be thought to have either a beginning or an end. It is

[5] Book III, 203b 6.

boundless in space because divisible into an infinite number of parts. Everything finite is bounded by something outside of itself; and there would necessarily be an endless series of such finite limits unless their common boundary is infinity. As the source of the ceaseless coming into being and destruction of particular things it must be an inexhaustible cause by which these changes take place. But the most decisive reason for such conceptions of infinity was thought to be the fact that, however large a given number or quantity might be, we are constrained to regard a larger one as possible. Hence Anaximander also used the word "divine" to express the deathless and indestructible character of *Apeiron*. . . .

The world which presented itself to his keen imagination was indeed one of amazing richness. Its very qualities are innumerable, just as its parts are beyond number. It contains within itself the sources of all motion. Thus early we have the hypothesis not only of an indestructible world-substance but of a continuous natural motion which having neither beginning nor end is also indestructible. Students of modern physics will easily see that these two ideas are closely related to the hypothesis respectively of the indestructibility of matter and the conservation of energy. Everything down to the most insignificant quality of the tiniest piece of our world has its roots in reality. And so, too, all motion. Nothing comes from nothing. This point of view whether in our day or any other seems to involve the idea of a *completed* world. Everything is already given. Nothing *new* can possibly come into being unless created by some outside agency, which, according to this scientific way of thinking, is a hypothesis running counter to the whole structure of mechanical science. Here again Anaximander laid the foundations. He explained the changes and apparent novelties which are constantly presenting themselves to our eyes, as nothing more than combinations or separations of parts already there. Whether in a vegetable, a star, or a man, *Apeiron* is bringing together or pulling apart pieces of its own hoary antiquity. But nothing is being created. The original qualities and materials are still intact. "Into that from which a thing originates it must of necessity return." [6] Individual existence as such seems to run counter to the nature of things. . . . The importance of this doctrine of combination and separation for later interpretations of the physical world hardly needs to be pointed out.

Although it is the everlastingness of the world-substance which dominates Anaximander's imagination, he also conceives of vast cycles of change very much like what we in modern times call Evolution. World systems arise, develop and progress to a certain point: and then fall apart and decay once more. Who knows how often this has happened or how many worlds have evolved and gone to pieces again in the far reaches of eternity? As regards our own earth and the heavens, they too are only one of the interminable series thrown up in *Apeiron* by a process of "differentiation" of the "cold" and the "warm" parts. Running violently counter to all apparent facts as well as to the established tradition of a necessary support for the earth (a foundation which common sense also seemed to demand), Anaximander for the first time in history brought his scientific imagination to picture it as unsupported. His astronomy, however, was not destined to be much of a contribution. Puzzled by the apparent flatness of the earth he was led to think of its shape as cylindrical—the known world being one of the faces. The direct evidence of his sense of sight also constrained him, apparently, to regard the earth as in a central position from which, by centrifugal motion in the world-mass, the sun, moon, planets and stars were "differentiated"

[6] Simplicius *Phys.*, 24, 13.

in times long past. All these heavenly bodies he took to be masses of fire inclosed in an envelop of air. Fire shines forth to us through apertures in the great dome of the sky made up of circles surrounding the earth above and below, and revolving about us ceaselessly. It is not very clear from his extant fragments how he conceived the sun and the stars to be related in their circles. He is known to have made efforts to calculate their distances from the earth and to have concluded that the sun was farthest away. He also in principle understood one natural cause of eclipses. Another he took to be the stoppage of the star's "aperture." His imagination faltered in conceiving of the stars. He could only liken them to "wheels" in never-ending revolution. Perhaps the naïveté of such conclusions (which were so largely the result of depending upon direct sense-perception) is somewhat offset by his explanation of hitherto miraculous winds and rains as produced by the action of the sun and evaporation from the sea. He also for the first time tried to make a map of the known earth and invented the astronomer's celestial sphere. Significant, too, is the fact that he first wrote a book in prose. It was entitled "*Concerning Nature*."

Anaximander may also be called the forerunner of biological Evolution. According to him, life, like motion and all recognizable qualities of *Apeiron*, is a permanent characteristic of the world-substance, and also goes through its cycles. Life is not something new, projected into reality from some (impossible) outside source. As part and parcel of the whole scheme it, too, has had its long history of "combinations" and "separations." Individual animals, like every other new combination, are subject to decay and separation, being nowhere permanent. Only *Apeiron* which is the source and destination of all life is "without beginning and ageless." Yet individual forms of life, both separately and collectively, go through a course of development and changes from one kind to another. Not only are we told [7] that living creatures were brought into being by the sun (in the slime of the seashore): man himself is declared to have descended from other kinds of animals. In fact, at one time he resembled a fish. . . . It is, of course, impossible to make out whether Anaximander was aware of the relationship which exists between man's uterine life and his racial heritage. But it is sufficiently striking that he should have spoken of a resemblance to *fish.* He was also aware of the survival of the fit. He uses the principle in his argument [8] to prove that man must have descended from other animals. For if (so it runs) man "had been at the beginning such as he now is, he would not have survived." Unlike other animals he has to be long cared for in his early days. Such conclusions concerning the origin, survival and kinships of men and animals were, to say the least, significant in the sixth century B. C., especially if one recalls with what difficulty the nineteenth century A. D. substituted similar ideas for the tradition of a special creation in the year 4004 B. C.

Even yet it is difficult to estimate the importance of Anaximander's contributions. His single thought of the uncreated *Apeiron,* forever alive and yet wholly "natural," the source of all being and all activity, is still a challenge to the most comprehensive thought of scientist, philosopher and prophet of religion. The same is true of his remarkable interpretation of the meaning of individuals and how their disappearance does not affect the material character or the life of *Apeiron.* His effort to explain all things in terms of their mechanism has remained to this day the prevailing motive of science. Its tendency is doubtless toward Materialism—the theory that ultimately everything is merely matter in motion. Yet Anaximander did not blink the ques-

[7] Hippolytus: *Refutatio omnium hæresium,* I, 6.

[8] Eusebius: *Preparatio evangelica,* I, 8, 2, quoting Plutarch's statement.

tion of life, which he regarded as spontaneous activity ready to blossom forth in individual lives under appropriate conditions (e.g. the sun's rays and moisture). This doctrine is known as Hylozoism (Matter has life) and has also figured largely in later thought. The six or more rudimentary principles which he set up for later physics, astronomy, and biology are still fundamental, and by many scientists regarded as axiomatic. But what is most surprising in this pioneer, and a standing challenge to later intelligence, is his successful "speculation" beyond the appearance of sense-perception into a deeper reality. Despite its occasional lapses into fancy the greater portion of that speculation must be called scientific imagination at its best.

4

Anaximenes, who seems to have lived during the second half of the sixth century B. C., a time [9] when the increasing domination of Persia was endangering Greek democracy and secularism in Miletus by its political and religious hostility, succeeded in extending the doctrine of his master at only one point. He was no genius like Anaximander. In some respects he was a reactionary. Going back to the traditional astronomy he reaffirmed a support for the earth and also went back to the old disc idea. Like Thales he tried to find a *particular* substance out of which all the content of our world could be derived, and took air to be such an *Arché*. He seems to have thought of air as encompassing and holding together the whole world—a theory which reminds one of the more modern ether. Through boundless space, air extends, the matrix so to speak, from whence all life and being in recurrent cycles have come and gone. Anaximander may well have asked his pupil how he could have derived the

[9] For historical evidence concerning his life see Burnet's *Early Greek Philosophy*, Sec. 23.

extraordinary richness of the world from a single, simple substance—a problem which, of course, also confronts those modern chemists who try to think of all things as derivatives of hydrogen. However complex such a problem may yet turn out to be, it was Anaximenes who gave us one simple and fruitful principle by which to interpret the process of cosmic development. This was the idea of condensation. Fluids and solids were produced by the gradual condensing of the *Arché*. "When it is very attenuated fire arises; when it is condensed, wind, then cloud, then, when more condensed, water, earth, stones; and other things come from these." [10] For all its simplicity of expression this conception of a heated and attenuated primary substance (if we combine with it Anaximander's *Apeiron*) is still the basis upon which our latest efforts to trace the origins of world systems have built. Condensation and rarefaction —such is the mechanism, according to Anaximenes, also the soul. As the "breath" of our soul holds us together, so, too, "air" in the universe. Whatever we may think of his reactionary tendencies we shall have to credit Anaximenes with an effort to extend the scientific method. His school probably came to an end with the conquest of Miletus in 494 B. C.

In our Western physical science we have so long taken for granted most of these presuppositions of the Milesian School that it is difficult to appreciate their one-time novelty or even their full significance. Naturalism has indeed had a long combat with traditional caprice and miracle. The idea of development has only gradually overcome that of sudden jumps from nothingness into being and from being into nothingness. The axiom of equivalence between causes and their effects long had to contend with fear of the unknown. But more and more the hypothesis of a definite order, of a truth based upon reality, has proved to be fruitful beyond

[10] Theophrastus quoted by Simplicius *Physics* 24. Diels: *Fragmente* p. 18.

the physical sciences. Naturalism as developed into a purely *mechanistic* interpretation was not to prove itself wholly acceptable to many later investigators. But in many ways, as we shall shortly see, it ushered in a new age for man.

CHAPTER III

FORMS AND NUMBERS IN NATURE: THE PYTHAGOREANS

1

Pythagoras about the year 529 B. C. started a movement at another Greek colony, Crotona in southern Italy, from which a very different but no less influential speculation developed. He seems to have had some contacts with the Milesians at Samos, his first home; but warmly as he accepted their scientific or natural view of the world, he tried to bring certain moral and religious conceptions into line with it. How find place for the fact of human aspirations in a wholly mechanical universe apparently oblivious of our actions and our fate? In trying to answer the question Pythagoras used a method which has been employed by most religious thinkers ever since. He looked for something unseen, intangible, something which occurs as a thought in the mind, reality "back" of visible objects, more fundamental than the mass and impact of tangible things.

The schools which derived their inspiration from him had a long and checkered history. As religious brotherhoods and in various Neo-pythagorean forms they persisted well into Christian times and included among their teachers a number of remarkable men. Unfortunately it is not always possible to give credit where credit is due. Some few doctrines can be traced to Pythagoras himself, who lived probably from about 581 to 500 B. C., others to Philolaus and Archytas, who flourished about 150 years later. But many important ideas were generally regarded as common property of the school. The original Pythagorean society is interesting to us not only as a school of philosophy but as a political and religious agency, a combination which was often attempted by Greek "colleges." Pythagoras and his followers, assuming that action has need of insight not only in individuals but in states, and that beauty of life and environment depend upon intelligent direction, proceeded to train themselves for such leadership. And, strange to say, they did succeed for a time in directing the affairs of Crotona, as well as those of a number of other cities in *Magna Græcia.*[1] In Plato's day, three or four generations later, Archytas did the same at Tarentum. Rarely, however, were such governments long-lived, and that of Crotona is an interesting example. The school required of its candidates for admission five years of study with severe moral discipline. Silence, simplicity of life, cleanliness, celibacy, vegetarianism, cultivation of the arts, especially music, as well as the study of science and philosophy, and extraordinary obedience to their chief (who is said to have dressed in white linen and to have worn a golden crown) determined their daily discipline. We do not know exactly how long it took for invidious distinctions between the "initiated," "educated," "superior men" and the "illiterati" to develop. But we do know that before many years the aristocratic rulers, howsoever high-minded or disinterested, were in part burned alive in the house of one Mylon of Crotona, and that those who escaped the fire and the subsequent butchery fled into exile. This project of "saving society" by superior insight and the cultivation of severe Doric restraint in life and art profoundly influenced Greek thought in other places, however, and later became more explicit in the political theory of Plato and Aristotle. Plato spent a good deal of time with Archytas at Tarentum.

[1] For historical references in ancient authors see Zeller: *Pre-Socratic Philosophy,* Vol. I, p. 341, 349.

2

Pythagorean philosophy may be said to center in the proposition that there is a mathematical definiteness, a given appropriate numerical relationship, between all the parts of the universe. Whoever discovered the so-called Pythagorean proposition in geometry may well have been surprised to find how numbers and relationships, about which he had reasoned in a quiet corner, turn out to be so widely applicable to material things. Pythagoras himself seems to have had his mind directed to such facts by noting the correspondences between musical intervals and various lengths of strings, as well as of anvils of different sizes. Perhaps we shall better understand the importance which they attached to Number in nature, if we consider the reflections of a modern man in trying to explain why it is that the sepals, petals, stamens, and pistils of a flower are arranged on the scheme say of 4, 4, 8, 4, respectively. A religiously disposed mind might think of some antecedent plan or design. The Weismannian evolutionist might conceive of certain "determinants" in the plasm of the seed. But whatever the interpretation, the number four would seem to be the significant factor in the situation as giving us a clue to the operation of whatever intelligible cause may be back of the flower. Without it our clues would clearly be less definite. This was once expressed by Philolaus [2] as follows: "It is the nature of number which makes every piece of knowledge possible, not only in the finding of what one is seeking, but also in the discovery of what one does not yet know. For nothing would be clear, either in things themselves or in their relationships if it were not for the nature of number." No modern man would probably go the length of saying that the number four was of the essence, or the

[2] *Fragmente* collected by Boeckh: *Philolaus des Pythagoreer's Lehren,* 139 *Vors. St.* 243.

cause of the flower. Nor did Philolaus. But all would agree that the mathematics of any given piece of reality is a very significant part of its interpretation.

Now the earlier Pythagoreans, impressed by their discoveries of widespread mathematical relationships, did not hesitate to draw the conclusion that the nature of number is also the nature of reality. Aristotle[3] reports that they supposed "the first principles of mathematics were the first principles of all things that exist." "They supposed the elements of numbers to be the elements of all things, and the whole heaven to be a musical scale and a number."[4] Aristotle also found it impossible to coördinate Pythagorean Numbers with his own ideas of cause and effect.[5] How could number be a cause? Yet he intimates[6] that the "elements"—which he had previously said were also elements of numbers—were "ranged under the head of matter." Under the circumstances it is, of course, impossible for us to make out exactly *how* they conceived numbers to be related to material things, or in what sense, if any, they were thought to be causes. We ourselves are not quite clear, even yet, as to what relation exists between mathematics and the "real" world. Our interpretations of ether, electrons, space, chemical relationships, etc., are in large part mathematical. In astronomy when we try to conceive of the universe as *one* we are clearly implying law, similarity, continuity, etc., as *qualitative* aspects of a real world. We assuredly do not suppose that calculation concerns only our minds. There would be little significance in the study of mathematics if it were merely playing with abstract quantities—a phantasmagoria of imagination—however nice its logic.

[3] *Metaphysics* I, 5, 985b 23.
[4] *Metaphysics* I, 5, 986a 1.
[5] *Ibid.* 986b 5.
[6] *Ibid.* 986b 6.

So it was perfectly natural that the early Pythagoreans should have conceived mathematics as a key to the treasures of the cosmos. It was they who first used the word cosmos, or order. And no wonder they indulged in poetic, as well as in scientific, imagination. The properties of the five regular geometrical bodies and all sorts of linear figures were studied for the purpose of finding clues concerning nature, for example, the distances separating the various planets from one another.[7] They even looked to geometrical explanations for the structure of the particles making up water, air and earth. Because they thought that the number one could be regarded as representing a point, two a line, three a plain, four a cube, etc., they proceeded to work out the relationships between arithmetic and geometry by thousands of calculations. Music they quickly perceived to be dependent upon numerical relationships. Had they been in possession of our modern harmony in addition to their own melodies (of which Greek music seems to have consisted) they would doubtless have wondered even more than they did. For notes which are concordant, or most please our ears when sounded together, are related to each other in the proportions of small integers, e. g., 2 to 3, 3 to 4, 3 to 5, etc., a fact which suggests a numerical basis for the activity of the mind itself. In Plato's *Phædo*,[8] Simmias, a Pythagorean of his day, actually contends that the soul is a kind of harmony. Virtue as harmony and proportion of life also suggested mathematical analogies; and beauty was seen to be dependent upon laws no less definite in character. Their treatment of diseases by music was an interesting practical application of the theory. So far indeed did they look to mathematics for the meaning and relationships of everything, that they tried to apply it to such matters as

[7] Kepler, it may be remembered, successfully calculated the planetary orbits by a study of ellipses.
[8] Sec. 85, E, fol.

marriage, justice and human opinions. Except in a vaguely metaphorical sense, the conceptions of justice as "square," of marriage as "five" (3 + 2), of opinion as two, or of ten as the symbol of perfection (because of its decimal qualities) are for us almost meaningless.

Much more significant is the question of how order and unity are related to variety and plurality. How can there be so many different things and yet all work together as a unit? What is logically implied by the idea of order? The Pythagoreans tried to solve the problem which we raised in connection with Anaximenes: "How can something absolutely simple be differentiated or ordered?" Their method was to assume that nature is everywhere characterized by opposites. Rest and motion, good and evil, light and darkness, one and many, odd and even, limited and unlimited, and other seeming contrarieties make up the mixture with which we are acquainted. These ideas will perhaps be clearer if we illustrate by some concrete examples. Suppose we try to think of the primitive world nebula (or better still, hydrogen) as perfectly homogeneous, the only existing thing in space. Obviously there could be neither right nor left, rest nor motion, light nor darkness, nor any other "difference" in such a world. It could not be called a unity. Neither could it be called a plurality. Order, the idea upon which unity is based, itself presupposes plurality. Hence this statement: Harmony is a "unity of the manifold and accord of the discordant." [9]

But what is this order, harmony, or *form*, which binds together so astonishing a bundle of contradictions? Is it some special particle or group of particles, some particular portion of the whole? Certain Pythagoreans seem to have been convinced that it could not be anything *material*. Here again perhaps an example will help us to understand their answer. When we inquire: "Does a human being consist of

[9] Boeckh: *Philolaus,* p. 61.

a certain number of organs, so many blood-corpuscles, so much oxygen, nitrogen, phosphorus, so many mental states bundled together?" we seem to be constrained to say that, however necessary such "ingredients" may be, not one of them can be said to produce the coördination of all these parts. In the seventeenth century the pineal gland near the center of the brain was thought to bring about such order. But scientific psychology has since discredited every effort to locate special pieces of matter as centers of "life" or of organization. From the air we breathe to the activity of the blood corpuscles, everywhere there is organization according to definite laws—but it is not the air itself, nor is it the blood-corpuscles or anything else to which we can point. . . . Was it a wonder then that some Pythagoreans thought of invisible, intangible *Forms*, especially because of their mathematical definiteness, as no less significant than the matter which they appear to organize?

However vague such conceptions as aspects of the real world or our means of understanding it, the discovery of *Forms* was one which was destined to play a great rôle in mathematics and philosophy. A study of the properties of numbers and figures is indeed no longer regarded as a direct means of revealing the nature of things. But the nature of things is revealed in the mathematical definiteness which they display. And back of that definiteness is *Form*—in more than one sense of the word, as later philosophy will show. Ultimately it was faith in a rationally ordered cosmos which led the Pythagoreans to attempt a synthesis of the many contrary aspects of our world. For them to have found in that variety itself the very *condition* of possible order was a brilliant *aperçu*. Neither we nor they have heard the "music of the spheres" which they believed attested a cosmic harmony—since the heavenly bodies in their motions are no less regular than the vibrating strings of the lyre. But howsoever faint our hearing (to which they attributed our inability to hear celestial music) or imperfect our vision and reason, we have continued to discover ever more precise relationships in the minutest as well as in the most far-reaching aspects of our world.

3

The Pythagoreans applied their scientific imagination to astronomy with some very remarkable results. They early conceived the earth to be a sphere and not only unsupported but in motion—no longer at the center of the universe. Together with the other planets, the sun, and the moon, it was held to revolve about a "Central Fire." By what course of reasoning they came to such conclusions we have no very definite data, but not improbably it was mathematical. They can scarcely be thought to have had any intimation of stellar distances—Who could without a telescope?—and naturally enough at first attributed the apparent regular motion of the stars to their revolution about the Central Fire. In this way the universe itself came to be thought of as a sphere, with Hestia, a great Hearth, the source of heat, light and life, at its center. Farthest from the Central Fire they placed the circles or rings of fixed stars, then in order Saturn, Jupiter, Mars, Venus, Mercury, the sun, moon, earth, and finally the "Counter-earth," a body between the earth and the Central Fire, which Aristotle said they invented to complete the number ten for their scheme. Why do we not see this Counter-earth? The Pythagoreans assumed that the earth itself kept one face constantly toward the Central Fire —just as we know the moon does toward the earth. The sun, no less than the moon and the planets, was at first regarded as shining by *reflected* light and heat.

Obviously the problem of the early members of the school was how to explain the rapid motion of more distant stars together with the regular but seemingly different motions of the planets, the sun, and the moon. By assuming that they all revolved about a central body at various distances they were clearly on the right track. But it required the discovery of the rotation of the earth upon its axis to make further progress. A later Pythagorean, Hiketas,[10] actually made this discovery. How the school developed the nucleus of modern astronomy is, indeed, an amazing record. Once the earth was known to rotate upon its axis the "Counter-earth" became, of course, the western hemisphere. The "Central Fire" retired to the interior of the earth. By 281 B. C. Aristarchus of Samos demonstrated that the earth revolves about the sun.[11] The stars were thought to be at incredible (by some even infinite [12]) distances away. Eclipses both lunar and solar were correctly explained, and the inclination of the earth's orbit to the ecliptic had been ascertained. They even went so far as to speculate about the kinds of life that may have developed upon Mars and Venus. The fixed stars were seen to be far beyond the solar system and to have their individual motions or "vortices." The Milky Way was regarded as a circle of fire on the outer boundary of the universe beyond which extends unbounded space.

It is interesting to note that even in antiquity it was heretical to question the geocentric conception. Cleanthes, a Stoic, charged Aristarchus with *impiety* because of his conviction that the earth revolves about the sun! And when after more than 1800 years the truth once more reaffirmed itself, it came through the influence of the Pythagoreans. Copernicus [13] attributed his inspiration to a reading in Cicero about

[10] Cicero: *Acad.* II, 39, quoting Theophrastus, the successor of Aristotle at his Academy.

[11] Vid. Th. Bergk: *Aristarchus von Samos.*

[12] Seleukus—about 150 B. C.—The account is given in the *Placita philosophorum* of the pseudo-Plutarch II, 1, 13, 24; III, 17.

[13] For a further account see: Ludwig Ideler in *Wolfs und Battmanns Museum für die Alterthumswissenschaft* II, 1810, pp. 393–454. "*Uber das Verhältniss des Copernicus zum Alterthum.*"

Hiketas and his theories. Had those ancient scientists been taken more seriously by men in command of material resources, the voyage of Columbus might well have taken place before 250 B. C. and the western hemisphere have been colonized by Greeks.

4

The religious doctrines of Pythagoras and his followers are of peculiar interest as a kind of mediation between science and Oriental faith. Pythagoras is himself known to have taught the doctrine of Transmigration, a tenet which is still an important belief for perhaps one half of the human race. This dogma, or hypothesis, conceives of all animal life as belonging together in a scheme of ethical development. Man is one with the animal kingdom in body and in mind. The purpose of his life in the "House of Clay," however, is to rise to higher degrees of excellence. To that end he must "purify" himself and strive for inner harmony of soul which is the "greatest possible likeness to God." Eventually he may attain to the life of God himself, serene in a similar perfection and ecstasy, no longer fettered to a body. But this progress is by slow degrees; and it is easier for the brute in man to drag him down than for the divine to inspire him. Yet one of the "Golden Words" which have come down to us from the school, says, "*Can* dwells nigh to *Must*." Some by the "simple, cleanly, mode of life," by judgment, "setting best thought over all as a charioteer," by gentleness, reverence and cultivation of beauty do succeed in climbing the steep ascent to the "free ether," where they are no longer mortal.

But what happens to imperfect humans when they have reached the judgment of death? According to the dogma they are given new bodies suitable to the degree of perfection attained. The soul of a man brutish, sensual and selfish, reappears after the trial of death in the body of a new-born swine or hyena, while a soul of greater promise finds its way into the body of an infant suitable to its level of culture. The obvious motive of such speculation, as indeed of most religious thought, was, and is, to discover a moral order in the universe, a justice in the light of which our striving for a "higher life" may be vindicated as against appearances to the contrary. And in all fairness it must be said that Oriental metempsychosis is a doctrine of evolution applied to life in general on its ethical, or value, side with the added hypothesis of immortality. With us in the West biological evolution, even in psychology, has mostly followed the lead of the physical sciences. That is to say, evolution has rarely been thought of as an ethical process making for greater excellence in man or beast. We have generally preferred to interpret the changes we observe as due, not so much to purposes as to mechanical causes. The essential difference between East and West in this matter is that one theory finds *life* the permanent reality while the other emphasizes tangible, visible, *matter* as the most significant item in our world. Both have elicited great creative imagination to "save the appearances of things." Divested of its concrete, and to us somewhat fantastic, features of reincarnation the theory of metempsychosis is simply one of progressive development which operates naturally and through the whole range of living beings according to the laws of an impartial moral order. Human souls (since they are undisturbed by death) may expect to attain their high purposes and to be measured by the standards of an ideal justice. The school seems commonly to have thought of Deity as a kind of cosmic harmonizer (of natural contrarieties and cross-purposes) who has also put justice into human souls. Yet along with this incipient monotheism, the Pythagoreans, like some other religious devotees, found room for the more ancient traditional concepts. Heroes and "powers beneath the earth" still enlivened their imagination and they "honored the gods immortal as by law disposed."

However much of the fanciful, the mystifying, or exaggerated side of Pythagorean teaching we may reject as without significance, we shall always be indebted to it for the hypothesis of *Forms* whose presence points to a cosmic order representable in terms of mathematics. A notable mathematician [13] writes: "The history of the seventeenth century science reads as though it were some vivid dream of Plato or Pythagoras. In this characteristic the seventeenth century was only the forerunner of its successors." Science would have made small progress without the development of mathematical theory. No more brilliant evidence of this can be found than the bold pioneering in astronomy to which it led. So long as men attempt to solve the deeper-lying problems of the one and the many, good and evil, or the destiny of human minds, they will honor the Pythagoreans. Nor is their hypothesis of a universal natural justice without significance for all future religion and the attempt to evaluate human life.

13 A. N. Whitehead in *Science and the Modern World,* p. 48.

CHAPTER IV

NATURE IN CEASELESS CHANGE: HERACLITUS

1

That an early religious upbringing frequently gives initiative and interest in the larger problems of men and things has often been observed; and nowhere, perhaps, is there a better example of it than in the life and philosophy of Heraclitus of Ephesus. He was born about 535 B. C. of a noble family whose hereditary privilege it was to preside at the sacrifices in his home city. This implied descent from Androclus, the founder of Ephesus, and bespeaks the conservatism with which in all probability, the young nobleman was educated. Yet philosophic doubts concerning the use and genuineness of the temple practices and dogmas of his day seem early to have taken hold of him. Concerning the sacrifices of animals he thus expressed himself: "Men seek in vain to purify themselves from blood-guiltiness by defiling themselves with blood; as if, when one has stepped into the mud, he should try to wash himself with mud. I should deem him rather mad who should pay heed to a man who does such things. And, forsooth, they offer prayers to these statues here! It is as if one should try to converse with houses." [1] The same questioning attitude is obvious from his remark concerning the procession for Dionysos: "Is Hades then the same thing as Dionysos that they should go mad in his honor with their bacchanalian revels?" [2]

So penetrating and honest-minded a man could not long

[1] The Fragments quoted are mostly from the Collection of Diels—*Fragmente der Vorsokratiker Band I*—and except where otherwise indicated will hereafter be referred to by his numbers. Diels, 5, Herakleitos.

[2] Diels, 15, Herakleitos.

retain his post as presiding officer at the sacrifices, and we are informed that he resigned the privilege in favor of his younger brother. Whether this also implied disinheritance we are not told. Later he certainly led an extremely simple, John-the-Baptist order of life. How he despised luxury is attested by his letter to King Darius. The great monarch had desired his company at the palace, but Heraclitus replied: "I hold in contempt the vanity of a court. I live as I please." Truth was his passion, a quest which might well have appeared to the great majority of his contemporaries a "weeping" business, and himself the "weeping philosopher." Yet with even greater disdain he observed the sheep-like quality of the masses, "oblivious of truth," who "being present are absent," [3] even as men in their sleep are unmindful of the beauty and significance of things. "One is as good as ten thousand to me in case he is the best" [4] is a fragment well expressing the fearless temper and independence of the man. The heretic of polytheism was, however, to become the prophet of one of monotheism's most remarkable doctrines.

2

The central thought or axiom of Heraclitus is one which has awakened, perhaps, as much poignant questioning as any which so far has entered the mind of man. It has also been the nucleus of a very great deal of philosophic thought. Most briefly stated, it is the hypothesis of eternal flux, the presupposition supported by so many apparent "facts" that everything in the universe is in a state of continuous change. "One cannot step into the same river twice." [5] One animal grows from another, and has its origin among the dead, so that life comes from death and death from life.

[3] Diels, 34.
[4] Diels, 49.
[5] *Ibid.* 91.

Everything flows; nothing abides. "Man is kindled and put out like a light in the night-time." [6] It is quite impossible to put one's finger upon anything and say: Here is a thing which is permanent. For time will change it into something different, something not itself.

But if everything in the world were like old man Proteus of the Sea, continually eluding our grasp, how would it be possible to *know* anything, especially if our mental states are subject to the same continuous change? Such a "fact" would seem to involve the negation of every fact, including itself. What, for example, are *we* our "selves," whether physical or mental, regarded as something permanent? Is a human being the two original organisms with which his body began, the infant in arms, the mature man of power, or the meditative gray-beard with poor memory? Or is he, perchance, a heap or halo of chemical ingredients—so much carbon, so much phosphorus, nitrogen, water and the rest? Yet every second of life we breathe in new material for our bodies and exhale a part of what we were before. This is not, of course, an example of Heraclitus, but it will serve to make clearer the meaning of the supposedly dark words of the master: "The immortal are mortal; the mortal, immortal; each living in the other's death and dying in the other's life." [7] Another philosopher (Empedocles) with whom we shall soon be concerned, proposed the idea of permanent elements, or roots, whence things are derived in all their complexity. But were Heraclitus alive to-day, he might still point to the significance of his own doctrine. For it is by no means made out that the very elements with which we are acquainted are absolutely permanent. Transmutation of elements definitely takes place, according to modern chemists, in the transformation of radium into helium, a process which possibly goes on to the formation

[6] Bywaters' Collection, No. 77.
[7] Diels, 62.

of lead. And our Electron Theory brings into question the stability of all but one of the supposedly permanent elements.

But however obvious a "fact" this process of becoming might become, the question would remain, What is it which changes? The human mind has not been able so far to escape the conclusion that more than a process is involved. It seems to be a common aspiration of the religious consciousness to look for "something far more deeply interfused." It is the aim of every philosophical investigation to help discover what is "real," or what is abiding, genuine, permanent, verifiably back of the conflicting (i. e., changing) appearances of the world. To answer this question completely would greatly extend the sphere of science and clarify many philosophical issues. It would have a vital import for religion, as determining how the individual "real" being (myself, for example, if it should prove true that I am a really permanent being) is related, or to be subsumed, under the larger "real" (i. e., whatever is permanent in the universe taken as a whole). The answer of Heraclitus to such questions was the proposition that this ever-active, mobile, self-transforming, "something" is a divine Fire which has always existed and always will be operative according to "fixed measures" or a definite order.

Its ceaseless activity, fire "down" into water and earth, and earth "up" into water and fire—both being really one process—suggests our modern idea of *energy* and its transformations. So does the greater or lesser degree of its activity—which is relatively latent in earth, more active in water, and most of all in fire. Heraclitus, in fact, is the father of those who have looked upon the *dynamic* aspect of things as their essential (even if passing) character. At the same time he gave expression to the principle of conservation, which is so important for every effort at mensuration, in the following terms: "This universe, the same for all, no one either God or man has made, but it always was, and is, and shall be, an ever-living fire, fixed measures kindling and fixed measures dying out."[8] Every individual thing, according to him, must be considered a part of the Deity; every man is a "spark" of the great world-force.

The last-named doctrine has been called Pantheism: God is all and all is God. But Heraclitus recognizes higher and lower in the scheme of things. Material objects, as among the Pythagoreans, are seen to be dependent upon something more ultimate than the shifting, changing content which our senses perceive. Reality is not ephemeral waves or particular shapes. It is a world-energy building up and destroying, producing now the invisible from the visible, now day from night, now the beneficial and again the destructive, but all in accordance with the "fixed measure" of reason. Heraclitus called the Reality, or all-embracing divine Fire, an everlasting Word, or the Logos—a concept which was destined to play an important rôle in European thought. Whether he meant by this term to designate a universal "divine intelligence" cannot be said with certainty. We shall later, in studying Anaxagoras and the Stoics, see how the idea of the Logos gradually developed into the conception of a divine Reason either separate from things (Anaxagoras), or part and parcel of the visible universe. Students of the Fourth Gospel will also recognize how its author made use of the Logos idea. It is there identified with Deity manifested in the life of Jesus. But Heraclitus most probably meant something like our impersonal "order" or "cosmos." Everything happens in accordance with the the Logos. Moreover it is something "common to all men," though much higher than the "private wisdom" which most men follow. "Private wisdom" allows men stupidly to close their eyes to reason and to forget what they are about. Not so conformity with the Logos by which men attain true in-

[8] Diels, 30.

sight. All of which certainly implies an intelligible, cosmic regulation, and a community of the Logos with our reasons; but not necessarily a *conscious* World Intelligence. It is possible, of course, that Heraclitus may have had in mind something like a *personal* God in his idea of eternal wisdom manifest in every process of change, ever-living, and present in our own souls. He does not himself, however, use such language in the fragments which have come down to us.

Heraclitus identifies the Logos with the great World Process by which all things are what they are, and in which human beings find their origin and destiny. Man's fate is continued existence (since life comes from death), but it may be an unconscious existence. When our philosopher was speaking figuratively and when literally is sometimes difficult to make out, as when he described the most active, mobile, living condition as fire; the sleeping, as fluid water; the dead, as earth. Yet in earth itself the Cosmic Process is bringing into activity, even through dead matter and sleeping water, souls of men endowed with insight, themselves parts of that divine Fire. Because they suffer change, however, they also share the fate of sleeping water and inert earth in their time. How very true on such a hypothesis that "you cannot find out the boundaries of the soul; so deep a measure hath it!"[9]

3

The World-Logos is also beyond our ideas of good and evil, according to Heraclitus. Such evaluations are, indeed, held to be real distinctions and valid for us; but we must not suppose that good, which is relative to us, i. e., dependent upon our own particular advantage or disadvantage, is good in any universal sense. Something very good for us might be quite the reverse for others differently situated—

[9] Diels, 45.

not to speak of the good of the whole. Here is the key to some of our philosopher's most epigrammatic sayings. "Sea-water is both the purest and the most abominable water; it supports the life of fishes, for men it is undrinkable and deadly." [10] "The way up and the way down are one and the same." [11] (A saying which we can, perhaps, better appreciate if we think of the antipodes. But for Heraclitus it probably referred to constructive and destructive changes.) *Our* distinctions, whatsoever they may be, are declared to depend upon varying conditions. Thus early we have a doctrine of Relativity. If there were no injustice men would never have known the name of justice. "The most beautiful ape is ugly as compared with the human race." "The wisest man compared with God, is like an ape in wisdom, in beauty, and in everything else." [12] "To God all things are beautiful and good and right; men deem some things wrong and some right." [13] Hence our distinctions are comparative, and lose their significance from the standpoint of God. What we call evil or good are both part of the active work of the Logos. Were we in possession of an all-embracing Reason, we too might see all things as beautiful, or, perhaps, characterized by something transcending beauty in more ultimate value. It may have been some such possibility the Logos-philosopher had in mind when he wrote: "There await men after death things they do not expect or even dream of." [14]

4

We can hardly speak of Heraclitus as a man of science. He continued, to be sure, the Ionian tradition. But his general point of view, so largely determined by religious

[10] Diels, 61.
[11] *Ibid.* 60.
[12] *Ibid.* 82, 83.
[13] *Ibid.* 102.
[14] *Ibid.* 27.

considerations, does not tend toward emphasis upon the tangible world which for him was a passing and everchanging appearance. That which he conceived to be back of all these transformations, lends itself more to mystical contemplation than to measurement by instruments of precision or mathematical reasoning. And so it was natural that the wonderful acumen of this thinker should have turned in the direction of ethical and psychological study, rather than to speculation concerning the heavens or physics. There would be little profit in rehearsing the details of his orthodox world-combustion ideas, or his conceptions of star-vortices, and exhalations. Here we may apply his own fragment to himself: "They who dig for gold dig up a lot of earth and find a little." [15] Significant, however, for the sciences having to do with the interests and aspirations of men is his doctrine that the operation of natural forces is essentially one requiring both the negative and the positive, one which is a never ending opposition—action and then reaction. As he expressed it, "All things have their birth in strife, and out of discord comes the fairest harmony." [16] Hence the way up and the way down are both a continuous warfare; hence the seething maelstrom of contending forces, the divisions among men; hence the divisions in the breast of the individual. "War," he said, "is the father of all." [17] "Justice is strife" [18]—an idea which suggests Darwin's "survival of the fittest." Very epigrammatically he said: "The bow (Biós) is called life (Bíos) but its work is death." [19] So beauty must forever overcome and do battle with the ugly; so wisdom must contend with self-interest; "so weariness makes rest pleasant." And if, for a time, quiet and peace be our portion—something which he seems to think is attained

[15] *Ibid.* 22.
[16] *Frag.* 8.
[17] *Frag.* 53.
[18] *Frag.* 80.
[19] *Frag.* 48.

in art—then "hidden harmony is better than that which is obvious." [20]

The scientist of matter in motion who has followed the lead of the Ionian Physicists may find little profit in the doctrines of one "who sought to understand himself." But the religious consciousness of men will always be interested in that view of God which finds him everywhere in nature the governing principle, an ever-living "Fire" which has kindled whatever of insight and reason we possess, a God who "assumes various forms, just as fire when it is mingled with different kinds of incense is named according to the savor of each," [21] yet is also an eternal Reason, a Reality abiding through all changing appearances. If on the other hand it be the function of both scientist and philosopher to "save the appearances of things," then the flux—which has been more and more confirmed as fact in the outside world no less than in human minds—remains a central problem. That problem is in short to interpret what the universe *does* in large and small. And if, back of this dynamism of change, order, law and reason are increasingly being discovered are not these more specific and refined expressions of the Heraclitean Logos—or perhaps Logoi? The alternative, at any rate, seems to be to describe a mechanism. Relativism may also be said to present a challenge to us of the twentieth century, especially to those who think of right and wrong in terms of changeless fixtures and unalterable decrees.

[20] *Frag.* 54.
[21] *Frag.* 67.

CHAPTER V

IS THE UNIVERSE A UNITY? THE ELEATIC SCHOOL

There is much of poetry in early philosophy. One feels a liberal, disinterested, and, as it were, timeless spirit pervading the thought of these fragments. Oftentimes they are written with a beauty of diction which we of a later age regard as a limitation in a scientific writer. But so far we have met no professed poet. Xenophanes, a wandering composer of elegiacs, and possibly a rhapsodist, who was known in a good many Greek settlements east and west about the Mediterranean, was more interesting as a poet than as a philosopher. But his fragments in dispraise of the current religions are very significant taken in conjunction with our other sources of information. He was born at Kolophon in Asia Minor about 570 B. C. Driven out of his native city by the invading Medes in his twenty-fifth year, he "went out west," but not, it would seem, until he had enjoyed the instruction of Anaximander at Miletus. Plato[1] implies that Xenophanes was the earliest of the Eleatics, a group of thinkers who held all things to be one in nature, and Aristotle[2] calls him the first of the monists and the instructor of Parmenides whom he regards as a more important member of the group. The Eleatics were so called because they had a "school" at Elea, a town not far from the snowy peaks of Calabria. Greeks founded it in 540 B. C. and the event appears to have been celebrated by a poem

[1] In the *Sophist,* 242d.
[2] *Metaphysics,* 986b 22.

from Xenophanes. But we know little of his associations with the place except that after his "careworn soul had been tossed up and down the land of Hellas for three score years and seven" he died there.

The Eleatic School cultivated metaphysics, that bugbear of many a modern man, a discipline often esteemed to be a foolish futility of over-sanguine minds. But whatever else may be said, metaphysics is a persistent effort of human reason to penetrate to the roots of things. Confidence in the processes of thought which have led to the magnificent structure of mathematics has also led men of the more vital periods of human culture to attempt interpretations in other terms than those of *quantity*. To-day we are witnessing another renaissance of metaphysics in the realization of scientists generally, no less than of religious thinkers, that the deeper aspects of their subjects are none other than metaphysical problems. The physicist interpreting the nature of matter, or of ether, or of space, the psychologist interpreting minds, or heredity, or evolution, just as certainly as the mathematician interpreting his invisible points and lines, when they press far enough are called upon to reason beyond the evidence of their senses. Metaphysics is simply the effort to reason as far beyond the evidence of the senses as our logic and mental power permit us to do; and, perilous or fallible as the effort may be, such facts no longer condemn it with intelligent men, any more than the difficulties and problems of art or of virtue are the condemnation of art and of virtue.

1

Xenophanes approached metaphysics from a standpoint of religion. His great question was: Is it reasonable to suppose with all the conflicting ideas of gods and heroes among men, especially in different tribes and nations, that all can be true? Is there a common valid basis of something genuine and real back of all these conceptions? Are men the dupes of their particular, established forms of religion? Or is there a universal basis, a ground in reality for all these faiths—stripped of their personal and racial idiosyncrasies? Very likely the scientific idea of a unified and orderly world, the common world-substance of Anaximander as well as other early conceptions implying unity, constrained him to attempt such a synthesis, a comprehensive interpretation, or incipient science of religion.

The primary facts with which his thought in these matters started are set forth in a few extant fragments. "Æthiopeans make their gods black and snub-nosed, Thracians give theirs blue eyes and red hair. Mortals fancy gods are born, and wear clothes, and have voice and form like themselves." It would appear that, "if oxen and lions had hands, and could paint with their hands, and fashion images, as men do, they would make the pictures and images of their gods in their own likeness; horses would make them like horses, oxen like oxen." [3] The difficulty with such conceptions of gods is not only their number and differences. According to Xenophanes [4] it is just as impious to say that a god is born as it is to say that a god dies. For it follows from either view that at some time or other the god did not exist. We must not suppose therefore that our petty characters and the short span of three-score and ten apply to Deity. "Homer and Hesiod have ascribed to the gods all deeds that are a shame and a disgrace among men: thieving, adultery, fraud." [5] A first principle in thought about religion takes account of anthropomorphism, this projection of our little selves as the index of the universe. When we consider how in time men will vanish from the

[3] Diels, p. 49, No. 16, 14, 15 respectively.
[4] As set forth in Aristotle's *Rhetoric,* II, 23, 1399b 6.
[5] Diels, 11.

earth altogether, leaving only their bones in the fossils of the rocks, just as now in the quarries of Syracuse and Malta imprints of all sorts of sea-creatures are found, we shall see how inappropriate it is to apply such analogies to Deity.[6] "There is one God, supreme among gods and men; resembling mortals neither in form nor in mind. The whole of him sees, the whole of him thinks, the whole of him hears. Without toil he rules all things by the power of his mind." [7] Such propositions seemed to force themselves upon him as the starting point of consistent thought in these matters. And yet he regards the quest for God as a tentative and progressive one just as we think of scientific hypothesis. "Let these opinions of mine pass for semblances of truth!" he exclaims.[8] Perfect knowledge and ultimate truth he does not expect to acquire nor does he think it will ever be attained.[9] But as time goes on by searching we may discover more and more.[10]

Thus early, Xenophanes set up a principle in metaphysics and in religion which, had it been heeded, would have made impossible not only the finalities and dogmatisms in which some metaphysicians have indulged, but also any creed of a sole correct and authoritative faith. Aside from its ignorant bigotry, an almost incredible amount of human misery is to be traced to this conception of tribal or literary monopoly with its final word on the deeper interests of human minds. Yet it is only with the twentieth century that a general recognition of the significance and value of religious aspirations and records other than Christian has come to us in the Occident. This is not unlike the rediscovery of the heliocentric astronomy in the fifteenth

[6] Hippolytus *Refutatio* I, 14 gives further geological conclusions of Xenophanes. Fossils are explained in the sense of modern geology.

[7] Diels, 23, 24, 25 respectively.

[8] Diels, 35.

[9] Diels, 34.

[10] Diels, 18.

century, and even more momentous in its significance for human destiny. What a tribute it is to Xenophanes that more than 500 years B. C. when tribes and nations thought of themselves as chosen folk, and sometimes as the depositories of authentic and exclusive revelations, he should have seen religion as a progressive, a universal, and above all a *human*, matter! Each people thinks of Deity in terms of its own degree and form of intelligence. By searching we may hope for more adequate knowledge of nature, duty, and destiny, but our present limitation bids us be charitable to all. Here surely was a genuine brotherhood of man based upon natural principles and growing out of a scientific attitude. When we, after these two thousand four hundred years, shall have understood more generally the point of view of Xenophanes, religion will not unlikely come to a new florescence, a renaissance based upon appreciation of Reality and aspiration toward an ever-beckoning higher human life.

2

Parmenides, who flourished about 470 B. C., a pupil of Xenophanes and also of some Pythagorean teacher, was not a poet; but for some unknown reason he put his philosophy into verse. Bad poetry, however, has not beclouded the significance of his thought, which may be characterized as an argument for Monism, the hypothesis that the world is of one piece. This may be contrasted with the doctrine of Pluralism which maintains that there are separate, even unrelated, portions or systems of reality which go their own way quite independently, or even lawlessly. Not only religious interpretations, but scientific ones as well, have their roots in this issue—since both depend upon some degree of uniformity and rationality in nature. For Parmenides the way of "Truth and Conviction" lay in a single, all-embracing, scheme of things which admits of no breaking up into unrelated pieces, no dissociation, or "getting loose" from the universe.

Perhaps we shall best be able to understand him if we interpret his thought first of all in terms of space. When we divide any given object which "fills space" into two or more portions have we separated those parts absolutely? Or to make use of the conception of atoms (which, as we shall shortly see, developed in another Greek school), what are we to think of the interstices between the atoms? Can these be sheer emptiness? Suppose we reply in terms of some modern physicists—that what fills up all such interstices, whether in the minutest portion of matter or in the farthest reaches of the heavens, is an extremely elastic medium called ether, through which incidentally the light of the sun and of other heavenly bodies is transmitted to us, and by whose means some other phenomena are interpreted. Then suppose we ask: Is the ether also made up of atoms? And if so, how are we to interpret the interstices between its parts? Must there not be *something there* making possible the connections and going together of these parts? The answer of those who maintain the ether-hypothesis is that atomic structure does not characterize ether. It is a perfect fluid having no divisions. All things are held together, as it were, in one immense world-jelly, perfectly elastic, but everywhere continuous with itself. Such a continuity is also presupposed in mathematical thought. How can space suddenly break off? How indeed is it possible to deal with it in thought except as something continuous? So that whatever other qualities the mathematician or the physicist may find in their world, they generally think of it as a continuum. Whenever we think in terms of matter we seem constrained to postulate "something" there even in the apparent holes and vacuums which we discover. In other words the universe is one and solid, in the sense of being nowhere empty.

Now Parmenides, so far as we know, made use of no such examples, and put this in very much briefer form: "Being is, and non-Being is not." [11] Whatever *is* shares Being with every other real thing and there is no place for non-Being. The latter simply has no standing, and they who suppose that one can come from the other, something from nothing, are only muddling their wits. Wherever you turn you find some portion of Being whether you confine your attention to some little piece, or look at the sum-total of things. And whoever stops to consider for a moment will realize that Being is really indivisible. It is a unit, aboriginal, and indestructible. It cannot be spoken of in the past tense, nor in the future, but only in the eternal Now.[12]

But if it be a mark of clear thinking to start with the axiom, "Nothing comes from nothing," what are we to think of the data to which Heraclitus has called our attention? How can Becoming and Destruction, that is to say any *real* change, take place when the decisive question confronts us, "Is it or is it not?" [13] And if one cannot think or put into language a process of nothingness becoming something, it must be that change itself is illusory, the "knowledge of a visionless eye" or of "an ear full of ringing," the confusion of "those who, lacking judgment, make Being and non-Being the same thing." The truth about reality therefore depends upon reason. Reason alone enables us to penetrate to the stable, the real foundations of things behind the confusion and transformations which our senses present us.[14] A *real* change—something into nothing—is a stultification of our minds.

Moreover the same thing must be true of motion. Obviously in the sense of moving through empty space, ab-

[11] Diels, 6 Parmenides.
[12] Diels, 8.
[13] Diels, 6.
[14] Parmenides in Sextus Empiricus VII, 111, fol.

solute motion cannot take place—if there be no empty space! What we call motion is only pushing something into the place of something else. We should say the ether-jelly yields at one place and flows in at another. But there are other good reasons why absolute motion is unthinkable. When anything moves it does so with relation to something outside of itself. If the universe as a whole were to move it would only be in relation to something outside! But what is outside of the infinite sphere which constitutes our world? Of course Parmenides, like every other sane person, recognizes relative motion. In the second part of his poem where he deals with human illusions he explains the apparent changes of day and night, of generation and death, as due to motions. But at the same time he is aware of how deceptive even relative motion is. We shall shortly see this in greater detail when we take up the mathematical arguments of Zeno in support of his great master.

Thus Parmenides and Heraclitus present the first antinomy, or seemingly fundamental contradiction in Greek philosophy. One regards the world as absolutely stable, identical with itself, unaffected by the "changes" of time, and certainly without "degrees" of reality. How could something both be and not be—as it were partly existing? Yet Heraclitus, keenly aware of the apparently destructive changes going on in every part of the observable world, defies one to point to what is tangibly or visibly permanent. "Everything flows, not a thing abides." Everything in the course of time seems to get new qualities. It is visible, then invisible; you hold it in your hands, soon there will be nothing to hold. True that Heraclitus also agreed that "something" is "there"; and Parmenides in his turn could not accept the sense qualities which we experience as belonging to permanent reality. But how in reason could one expect a thing to become that which it was not before? And how can one repudiate the evidence of one's senses?

Our reason, Parmenides observes,[15] always has something which *is* for its content, while sensations disclose a variable world. We become aware of a flux or a process by our senses. Who would know of a change of color without seeing it? And what but a "necessity of thought" would ever lead us to suspect that the change in color did not affect the "reality" of what we see? Even Heraclitus, as we have noted, questioned the evidence of his senses and based his conclusions about the everlasting Logos upon the deeper insight of reason.

From that time even to the present, the question as to the validity of our mental processes, chiefly that of sensations as related to our more "inward" thought processes, has remained a central one for science, philosophy and religion. Where does the deception come in, by these flagrant contradictions of "appearance" and "reality"? How put change and permanence together? How account for something *new* if all is already given? Parmenides' answer, which is that of most mathematicians and metaphysicians, runs: "Thus I have reasoned it out; thus it must be in the world." It is also represented in the thought of the religious thinker, who, for example, makes use of the "ontological argument" to prove the existence of God. "I find that my conception of a perfect, righteous, omnipresent Being," so the argument may run, "coincides with the rest of my information. Therefore the hypothesis of a perfect Being is rational." Such a method is called Rationalism because it depends so largely upon the operations of reason, more or less independently of observable facts. It is contrasted with Empiricism which aims to build upon sense-perception and, so far as possible, not to trust interpretations for which there is no warrant in so-called "facts." Exact science as theory and mathematics

[15] Diels, *Frag*. 5. "For to think and to be are the same" —which we can safely interpret: Every proposition involves the assumption that something exists as identical with itself.

is, of course, Rationalism. The physicist reasons that, since the ether fulfills the requirements of his thinking and does violence to no calculations or observable phenomena, it probably exists, despite the fact that it has never been perceived by his senses. The same is true of ions, electrons, atoms, absolute zero, ids, and many other scientific concepts and interpretations. If one were to limit one's thought to observable "facts," as the naïve empiricist would have us do, there would clearly be very little science. On the other hand, so many have been the demonstrably false conclusions of "pure reason" that thought has come to sit in judgment upon itself; and metaphysicians who have learned this lesson are chary of pressing their conclusions when sufficient evidence has not been forthcoming.

3

No one better illustrates this difficulty of "pure" or even mathematical reason when it comes to interpreting certain assumed fundamental realities, than Zeno, the pupil of Parmenides. Concerning his life we have only the scant information that he was about 25 years younger than his great tutor and shared his interest in the political affairs of Elea. This would make the date of his birth about 485 B. C. He died in mid-career, a martyr whose fortitude was much lauded in antiquity, the victim of a military campaign against some unnamed usurper. Aristotle later called him the discoverer of the art of drawing conclusions (dialectic) and Plato compares him with the great wrestler, Palamedes, for his mental agility.

Zeno has been of peculiar interest to modern thinkers by the supposedly fundamental contradictions which he discovered in every idea of motion, even of relative motion, and in numerical ideas as applied to space. Perhaps his problems arose out of Pythagoras' attempts to correlate arithmetic and geometry with the "real" world. Perhaps he meant to defend his master against the ridicule of those who charged him with thinking the world into a dead lump of motionless matter, bare Being with ghostly qualities, such as colors, and weights, and tastes, to deceive us. But whatever his object, he set himself with the whole persistence of his nature, against the conceptions of a many-pieced universe as well as against the assumption that thought can comprehend motion. Against those who presumed to an intellectual (i. e., mathematical) grasp of motion he argued somewhat as follows: Let us think of a body in motion as passing along a line A—B. How many different positions are there in such a line? The only possible answer is: an infinite number. Nobody can prevent my thought from taking a point between any two which may be chosen. But however near together such positions, *some* time will be required to get from one to the next one. And since the number of these is infinite, an infinity of time seems to be required to move from A to B or through any distance whatsoever. An infinity of moments is infinite time. Or again, suppose one succeeded in getting over one half the distance and then proceeded to advance over half the remainder, then a half of its half, and so on indefinitely. Would there not be a tiny fraction left over even to the very outermost half? How can Achilles ever hope to overtake the tortoise— in the strict logic of mathematics? The whole conception of motion seems contrary to certain "necessities of thought" if one assumes that space is indefinitely divisible into discrete, numerical quantities. One can never reach unity by an addition of fractions in the series ½, ¼, ⅛, etc. To one who might ask, as did Aristotle,[16] "Why must time be thought of as made up of moments of time?" Zeno might well have replied, "In what other way can one apply arithmetic to time? And is not the same true of the different

[16] *Physics,* VI, 2.

positions along a line? Indeed how can one avoid regarding *every* line as infinite in extent—if it have an infinite number of positions? Nor does the supposition that the points traversed are to be regarded as zeros help the situation. For if motion is to be represented by an addition of zeros, then one must say it is zero motion though an infinity of points be traversed."

Other arguments point to the same necessity of continuity as applied to space and time. Suppose an arrow one cubit long goes through a room ten cubits long in which every cubit has been marked off. When can the arrow be said to be in the space of any one of these sections other than the first and the last? Common sense would be inclined to say that at a given instant the arrow is in the space between 3 and 4 and at some other instant precisely in the section between 8 and 9. Yet if at a given instant it were to be precisely "there" it would be *at rest.* And how can one get motion by any adding of such instants at rest? [From the standpoint of modern psychology as applied, for example, to motion pictures we know that the *illusion* of motion is due to after-images on the retina. If our eyes were perfectly instantaneous, what we should have would be merely a succession of *pictures*—no motion.] The answer once more seems to be: at *no* specific instant is the moving arrow in a given position! Every motion is *of one piece,* absolutely indivisible. Motion as motion has no units of measurement, just as extension has no parts.

Or again, suppose we imagine our world built up out of discrete *pieces*—molecules, atoms, or, if we prefer, electrons, or the nuclei of electrons—an infinite number of them to make up the seeming infinity of space. How large are these particles? We naturally think, of course, that they have a mensurable size. Our physicists give us amazing fractions to help us realize the approximate dimensions of the particles with which they are dealing. But they go on finding still smaller ones and there seems to be no good reason why they should stop their efforts to analyze still further. But the trouble again is mathematics! Zeno inquires: Have these particles a size large enough to take up any space at all? Then an infinite number of them makes the world infinitely large. Are they without magnitude—since mathematics and physics seem to know no good reason why division should stop at a certain point? Then even an infinity of them would leave the world infinitely small. And surely it cannot be both! The upshot seems to be once more that we cannot take such divisions seriously. Whatever the universe consists of, including "space," must all be of one piece. We are deceived by the apparent multiplicity and plurality of things. All their varieties and contrasts do not prevent them from forming *one* inevitable system. Everything has a common matrix.

The relativity of motion was also a favorite problem with Zeno. An object appears to move very rapidly with relation to some other object. But a third object is moving just as rapidly in the opposite direction. What then is the real rate of speed in the first? We can perhaps make this more significant for ourselves by an astronomical example. The earth clearly moves about the sun. But what would be the motion of the earth if the sun itself also moved in an (hypothetical) orbit exactly compensating the movement of earth? Of course we can in turn calculate the sun's motion in relation to the stars. But what if they too are in motion? Or who is to say *which* is at rest? . . . Thus on every hand matter, motion, space and time bristle with difficulties when we try to consider them as pieces or take the experiences of our senses as the source of knowledge.

4

Melissus, another interesting Eleatic from Samos, seems to have combined the functions of sea-captain, statesman, and speculative reasoner. It was probably at the height of his career that he commanded the fleet of his native city when in 440 B. C. the Samians defeated the Athenians. His was surely a mind resolute in denying what did not agree with the logic of his convictions, even though in so doing the very substance of things became "appearance" and illusion. As such he is both a stimulating example to those who are "trying to think things out" and a warning to make sure of one's presuppositions before logic is pressed to its limit.

Melissus agreed with Parmenides and the Ionians that Beginning, Nothingness, Creation and such conceptions have no place in science. He took it to be axiomatic that nothing comes from nothing. There can be no end to the world in time. But he seems to have argued from temporal infinity to spatial infinity, a piece of thinking which Aristotle characterized as "uninstructed" and "clumsy." [17] Another extraordinary result of his logic was the inference that absolute self-identity and uniformity must characterize the world-substance. If it be *one* (in any thoroughgoing sense of that word) it must be *simple*, i. e., without complexity and differences of kind, which seem to spell multiplicity. Something *absolutely* one is surely not divided against itself! And since he assumed that such absolute unity was forced upon our thought, he was prepared to deny the obvious differences of his senses. The impossibility of *change* (taken in the same radical meaning of producing something from nothing) also supported this conviction of perfect homogeneity at bottom. Since no such real change is possible, the fundamental unity of the world must not be expected to yield a real multiplicity (again, of course, taken in the radical sense of two or more *incomparably different* things). For this once more would be "creating" something from what did not exist before.

[17] *Physics,* I, 3.

Such reasoning, like that of mathematics, howsoever cogent it be, has to face the further question as to *where* such simplicity or invariability is to be found outside of thought. Granted that we have, for example, certain qualities assumed to be known about angels, we can draw some other conclusions. But it surely remains a significant matter to know what evidence there is for the existence of the angels. Unfortunately (from the standpoint of exact reasoning) we are acquainted neither with absolute simplicity nor absolute change, but only with relative unity and relative variety. In other words, our world seems *in some respects* to be unified, in other repects to be an indefinite variety and full of kaleidoscopic changes. Had Melissus been a more thoroughgoing metaphysician, he would hardly have repudiated variety because of the difficulty of understanding it.

5

And yet we are deeply indebted to him and the other Eleatics for attempting, with all the precision they could muster, to think certain assumptions and inferences through, by means of strict definitions after the manner of the mathematician. Since all philosophy and science is an effort to provide by words and symbols a mental representation or understanding of a part (ultimately the whole) of the world, every exact means of interpreting by precise concepts as far as those concepts will permit is a contribution to such intelligence. To have shown what results from thinking of the universe as *many*—a variegated and disconnected pile of changing contradictory "things"—was no mean effort. Their analysis in terms of a single substance, taken seriously as unified and hence simple and unchanging, resulted in a breach between reason and direct sense-perception. But the progress of physics, just as in that of Pythagorean astronomy, depended upon a penetration of thought deeper than external appearances of sense. Science and philosophy have continued to show us ever since that things are not what they seem. Yet the acumen of the Eleatics in trying to set forth what is (or, more strictly, what ought to be) meant by such conceptions as change, motion, novelty, creation, variety, and so forth, did not succeed in making out that the Heraclitean idea of process finds no place. They craved, as every scientist does, a simple, fundamental, lasting, elemental basis for their interpretations. But like some of their fellow explorers since, they found their problem too complex for the instruments at their disposal. There is, we think, a static, a spatial, a material, and an unchanging aspect of our world. This was and is the beginning axiom of exact science. But there is also a dynamic, an active, an evolving, even humanly purposive side. Only as the metaphysician does justice to these, and all other significant aspects, can his thought be called adequate, comprehensive, or true.

Greater honor will yet be accorded these bold sailors upon seas which most men even yet consider too perilous, or impossible of navigation. With the ever-deepening penetration of the sciences, new continents of thought are beckoning our imaginations to enjoy and interpret them through the guidance of sufficient reason. Already we realize that no single "fact" (at our feet or among the stars), no idea or aspiration of religion whether our own or the gift of another, but depends upon a general view of reality, upon the mathematical, metaphysical and psychological conceptions in whose light the interpretation is made. With the renaissance of the human spirit to more comprehensive thought, we shall be grateful even to erring metaphysicians for our greater maturity of judgment.

CHAPTER VI

NATURE AS "ELEMENTS." THE PROBLEM OF "MIND." EMPEDOCLES AND ANAXAGORAS

1

Some new and important interpretations of nature which both extended the ideas of the Ionians and mediated between Heraclitus and the Eleatics, appeared in the thought of Empedocles of Agrigentum, a half-legendary figure whose name still casts a spell over the people of his native Sicily. He seems to have been born of a distinguished family about 490 B. C. At least the importance of his father, Meto, in the councils of Agrigentum (the modern Girgenti) attests this reputation. His grandfather was able to take four horses and a chariot to Olympia and win the chariot race in 496 B. C., which also supports the tradition. He himself was definitely offered the kingship of his native city and refused it. Why we can only surmise; but we know that he combined the functions of poet, physician, statesman, philosopher and "holy man," and that nearly to the end of his life of 60 years he enjoyed somewhat more than human fortune. He seems himself to have claimed extraordinary powers as a physician, which indeed his countrymen regarded as miraculous. Stories were told of how he had awakened from catalepsy or death a woman who had been for thirty days "without pulse or breath." He freed the city of Selinus from the pestilence by draining the surrounding district. He improved the health of Agrigentum by an engineering project which gave the north wind better access to the city. No wonder it was said of him that the winds and the rain obeyed his voice! The disconcerting part of the story is that he was worshiped as a god, himself accepting and even claiming the honor. In a poem to his native town [1] he says: "I am honored as an immortal god, which is seemly . . . in passing through the flourishing town men pray to me. . . ." Yet perhaps we do not here get all of his meaning. It is only fair to add another fragment: "But why do I speak so much of this as though I had done great things? Am I more than they, these mortal men dedicated to manifold corruption?" [2] Whatever the mixture of gold and tinsel in his character we know that he lectured to his dazzled countrymen in robes of purple with laurel in his hair and a golden girdle at his waist. But we must interpret Empedocles in the seething, vivid life of his day among a people overflowing with dramatic imagination, in contact as it were, with the interior fires of the earth. Although he died as the result of an accident in the Peloponnese, the legend-makers saw him ascend in Ætna's clouds of fire on his way to Paradise.

Under the circumstances it is difficult to make either a consistent picture of the man or an adequate account of his philosophy. We shall here try to consider those theories and principles which are significant for our own thought. It would profit us little to set forth a multitude of reflections vaguely expressed and based upon meager information or mistaken conclusions. Such an undertaking may be necessary in a chronicle. But it only hinders progress in philosophy.

Empedocles found what seemed to be a way out of the flagrant contradiction between Heraclitus and Parmenides by supposing (as has often happened since) that the antagonists could each claim a measure of truth. Why may not both Becoming and permanent Being obtain in our world if we assume that a certain number of elements are permanent? May not the combinations and separations of such elements in varying proportions explain the manifold variety

[1] Diels, *Frag.* Empedocles No. 112.
[2] *Ibid.* No. 113.

and change in things? The "roots" (as he called these elements) would then provide the stable background of genuine Being, satisfying the scientific axiom that nothing can come from nothing, while the heterogeneity with which our senses acquaint us is the result of their mixture in different proportions. Thus we might still agree that the substance of the world is a continuum, being everywhere filled up, and at the same time not be constrained to think it all one kind of substance. These permanent "roots" he regarded as four—earth, water, air, and fire—a very crude observation, but one making use of a principle, which together with that of proportionate combinations, has had important influence upon the development of chemistry in later times. From another point of view he regarded the elements as six in number, for he could not see how water and air, or any other substances, could combine or separate of their own accord. Attraction and repulsion, two other elemental facts, must be explained.

As was natural for a physiologist who regarded his body as part of the world-substance and its activities as an expression of the cosmos, Empedocles thought of the attractions of the various elements for each other as Love, an idea which survives in our phrase "chemical affinities." Even what we should call cohesion (water for water) was by him explained as the operation of such a force. He does not, however, seem to have had a definite idea of energy as differing from a substance in space, and hence speaks of Love as a fifth element or "root." Likewise for repulsion, which he called Strife. Both Love and Strife are everywhere present operating in varying degrees, now one and now the other having ascendency. Attractions and repulsions determine now a new individual in his mother's womb, now a star; and then in turn bring about their separation, disintegration, or what we call death. Yet "No wise man in his senses will dream that only so long as we live . . . are we present, experiencing good and evil, or that we were nothing before we were put together as mortals." [3] Nor will an instructed man suppose that water becomes mere nothingness by its attractions and repulsions, its building up or disintegration. But *what* Love or Strife might be apart from material body he seems to have been unable to imagine. His difficulty was probably parallel to our own when we try to conceive of energy apart from spatial relations.

It was thus by a new anthropomorphism—an analogy similar to that which discovers Reason in the universe because *we* reason and are parts of that larger whole—that Empedocles came to regard a cosmic Love and cosmic Strife as impersonal, elemental facts (we should say energies) determining the course of events. They hold the universe together and resolve it into chaos. The tiniest individual plant no less than the starry heavens and a drop of water is determined by their activity. Sometimes there are cycles during which one or the other of these opposing agencies has the upper hand—a thought which is reproduced and extended in Herbert Spencer's nineteenth century conception of Evolution. According to the latter the world-building force (Evolution) and the world-destroying (Devolution) have alternated through long periods of time. So for Empedocles in earlier ages the universe was more homogeneous and less differentiated, more harmoniously under the sway of Love. But Strife broke up the concord, stirred things up, differentiated, and tore down. The future may again see Love's hegemony. Meanwhile the two are nearly balanced—a contest of good and evil, as Aristotle interpreted Empedocles' conception "according to its meaning and not to its lisping expression." [4]

Whatever we may think of such anthropomorphism, we are constrained to say that it aims to be scientific in so far as

[3] Diels, *Frag.* 15.
[4] *Metaphysics,* I, 985a 3.

the agencies in terms of which earth's changes as well as human aspirations are interpreted are cosmic rather than local, universal rather than individual. Individuals are but passing phases, temporary aggregations; yet their roots are implicated with the destiny of worlds. That is why, in turn, with the passion of an inspired prophet, he bade men look to their own mortal frame to discover that by which the universe is held together or resolved. "And do not sit there with astonished eyes," he exclaims, in speaking of the cosmic Love, "rooted in your own members, it vouches for itself." [5] Unfortunately we have little information as to how he put together his idea of transmigration with the six impersonal roots and their natural processes of change. That we as individual beings are separated out from the whole and find our "salvation" by a worthy return to the great Source of our being is consistent enough with his general doctrine. By what "Justice," however, Love or Strife condemns a delinquent human to some new sojourn in the "prison-house" of particular individual existence is not clear. Of course we have only a portion of his book "*On Nature*." And it is possible that he found a way of coördinating the elements and their activities with his idea of God and a moral order. Concerning the Deity he wrote: "We cannot bring God near us so as to reach him with our eyes, or lay hold of him with our hands—whereby the chief highway of persuasion leads into the mind of man. For he has no human head attached to bodily members, nor do two branching arms dangle from his shoulders; he has neither feet nor swift knees nor any hairy parts. No, he is only mind, sacred and ineffable mind, flashing through the whole universe with swift thoughts." [6]

A great many of Empedocles' efforts toward scientific observation and experiment were crude and sufficiently naïve. Yet it is interesting to note that he should try by means of a

[5] Diels, *Frag.* 17. l. 20.
[6] *Ibid.* 133, 134.

klepsydra, or water-clock, to demonstrate how all space is filled. This experiment took the form of showing that two things, water and air, could not be in the same place at the same time. He anticipated Harvey to the extent of arguing that the systole and diastole of the heart keep the blood in motion for the purpose of bringing air to the interior of the body, which, like the "pores" of the skin, was also held to "breathe." Blood he conceived to be a finely proportioned mixture of the elements, the more delicately balanced its constitution the more capable the individual. Even thought depends upon blood, especially that about the heart. He also tried to work out the mechanics of sense-activity. Vision he interpreted as the meeting of "emanations" or "effluences" from objects seen with other emanations originating in the eyes themselves. This seems to have been his way of saying that vision is not exclusively the result of outside agencies, but depends no less upon "inner" activity. Yet what we know of his incipient psychology is throughout naturalistic. It never so much as suggests occult, hidden, or supernatural agencies. Taste, together with smell, he explains as due to minute particles of substances which penetrate the sense organs. The theory that only like can perceive, or be attracted by, like was a curious assumption on his part, but one destined to have no small influence in later science. It was derived no doubt from the fact that only love can know what love is, or the hater realize hate. Good reason therefore why the blood should contain all the six elements if man were to experience his world!

The emanation-theory of light, a hypothesis which has played quite a rôle in physics, seems to have been developed, if not originated, by Empedocles. According to it, light is the projection of little particles or effluences coming from the pores of glowing bodies, and bombarding, so to speak, all eyes and all visible objects. Light was assumed to require time for its passage through space. But the emanation-theory fits in better with a hypothesis of empty space (the Atomists' idea) than with that of a world completely filled! Very likely this was one reason why Newton later clung to it, and also why more recent believers in empty space think in terms of emanations or corpuscles of light. Yet Empedocles' view on this matter of space is not clear to us; nor his view concerning the "pores" through which the corpuscles pass into the eyes. Of course the question here again is, Are the pores *empty?* And if not, how can anything pass through them, except by pushing something else out of the way?

2

A longer account must be given of his peculiar evolution hypothesis because of certain philosophical parallels with more recent theories. Taken as the effort of a modern thinker, it might appear to be a parody on the Darwinian "survival of the fittest," the Weismannian Ids and Biophors, as well as de Vries' "chance mutations." Perhaps if we think of Empedocles' theory in some such light we shall be able better to appreciate some of the scientific difficulties which confront us in any dependence upon "chance changes," corpuscular (chromosome) heredity or even "determinants" in our current speculations. Empedocles maintained that from the evolving earth in the early day came plants, and later animals of every conceivable absurdity of form and structure. There were eyes without heads and futile tails, there were inconceivable mixtures of spontaneously generated arms, hair, and feathers. Apparently everything was being tried out separately and the result was many monstrous, chance forms. But Love soon began a better order by bringing together organs that were suited to get along together, and "mingled sex with them" to insure the future of the kind. The many chance forms which were not adapted to this life, "men with heads of oxen" and "oxen with heads of men" disappeared in time; olive trees overcame their erstwhile chance habit of laying eggs, and definite order became established in the reproductive plasm so that even the sex of each new generation could now be regarded as determined by mechanical factors such as heat or cold. Empedocles clearly asserted, therefore, the "chance" origin of organic structures and of their coördination into bodies—there being no prearranged plan in their adaptation; he interpreted the "kinds," or species, of plants and animals in the earth as due to the survival of those best fitted to survive. The ridiculous character of his "separatist" theory, according to which particular organs were conceived to have gone their own way originally, may, perhaps, put us on our guard against a similar breaking up into parts of the "germ plasm" with its invisible, and therefore less easily ridiculous, "determinants." This last doctrine Empedocles would, of course, recognize to-day as an extension of his own.

3

The ethical side of his teaching, he tried, not wholly successfully, to correlate with his scientific theories. Since he regarded man as organic to the universe and one of many forms of evolving life, it was natural for him to think of human purposes as related to cosmic ones, and of evolution as an ethical fact—just as it had been in the Pythagorean metempsychosis. If life is a permanent reality and death only a change of form, then evolution as an ethical fact presents us with higher and lower degrees of life. All living forms are related to the greater whole. The lower animals have a common origin and common destiny with ourselves. All are rising or falling in the scale. So convinced was Empedocles of this that he thought he recognized the voice of a dead friend in his dog. That is why, holding all forms of life to be sacred, he deprecated the "murder" of slaughterhouses as well as sacrifices, and restricted himself to certain forms of vegetable food. (Which, we do not know. The problem must have been difficult since he regarded plants as sensitive and only less vaguely animated than other forms of life!)

But whatever his solution of this difficulty was, he held that it behooves us always to support the Love in our natures which not only harmonizes ourselves as individuals but unites us with the whole creation, by just proportions balancing the ever-present Strife. Strife and warfare are, indeed, part of the very being of the world-order. But they are also guilt in humans. For men break loose from the community of Love in which they might enjoy harmony, beauty and happiness, and besmirch themselves with blood and tears. They might sacrifice myrrh and incense, pouring golden honey upon the ground, but instead they must kill the noble lives of animals and shed human blood. They even think highly of a father who raises aloft his beloved son, one bearing his own image, and, who, terrible fool, slaughters him while he prays. Such crimes do men commit in their perjuries and killings that one can imagine how the power of the wind drives them, banished and homeless, into the sea, and the sea spews them back upon earth, and earth with equal detestation hurls them toward the sun. So far removed are men from what they might become by cultivation of the elemental Love in their natures.[7] Salvation from evil is impossible without overcoming sin. "Oppressed by your sins you will never free your heart from hopeless grief." [8] Only knowledge provides a way. "Blessed are they who have gained a treasure of divine thoughts." [9] Their souls become poets and physicians and princes among men. And they go hence to a divine life rich in honor.

[7] Cf. Diels: *Frag.* 117, 136, 137.
[8] *Frag.* 145.
[9] *Frag.* 132.

So the individual man like every other individual thing is fragmentary. He finds a richer life by contact with the larger whole which is possible through intelligent love. Man has the prerogative of intelligence over other individual objects in nature—not that of sensation, which he shares with other living beings, and which gives only a fragmentary knowledge depending upon proportion in the adjustment of sense-organs—but the intelligence of divine thoughts produced by a harmonious mixture of the heart's blood at the center of one's organism. This more inward knowledge alone brings about man's freedom from the evils of cosmic Strife and individual isolation.

To estimate justly the thought of this true poet, physician, and scientist, is difficult. But it will always be significant for the light which it throws upon the question (for it is still a question!) of elements, or how a plurality of true elements can have the unity and permanence demanded by Eleatic and mathematical axioms. It was no less strategic an *aperçu* to have conceived of variety and change as *proportional* combinations or separations, i. e., spatial rearrangements in the parts making up a body, a hypothesis which has proved extraordinarily fruitful in chemistry. At the same time he challenged the theory of spontaneous motion and attributed movements to elemental causes no less fundamental than bodies themselves. Because of the major oppositions of attraction and repulsion, Love and Strife, good and evil, he thought he could interpret the course of evolution in terms of a preponderance of them on one side or the other. Hence arose the conception of chance, which, as among certain modern evolutionists, seemed to force itself upon him by so many unexplained variations—even challenging the conception of an ordered cosmos. Yet as a believer in cosmic values, he interpreted all life in evolution as purposive, and man's place in the scheme as intelligible only in his natural setting among other animals and in the light of general causes, physical, geological, and psychological. He can hardly be said to have combined his mechanical view of the physical universe with monotheism or with cosmic good and evil. But neither have we been successful in such undertakings. His ideas are still challenges both to our scientific and to our ethical imagination.

4

Another interesting nature-philosopher, the first of these early thinkers to make his home at Athens, was Anaxagoras (B. at Clazomenæ, flourished 460 B. C.), the intimate friend of Pericles and Euripides. He seems to have been the first philosopher who suffered for heresy in Greece. The charge brought against him was one of "irreligion" and was probably connected with his observation that the sun is a great ball of fire. He also aroused some resentment by calling the much venerated stone at Ægospotomos a meteorite, or piece of detached rock which had fallen upon the earth from some space beyond. But it cannot be made out definitely for what specific doctrine he was brought to trial. The procedure may also have been an indirect political blow at Pericles. Be that as it may, Anaxagoras, who for his philosophical insight was by Aristotle called a "sober man among the drunk," found it prudent to retire from Athens to Lampsacus, where he founded a school and continued his writing. The school was secular in character and he wrote in prose. There seems to have been considerable strength in the orthodox reaction which took place toward the middle of the fifth century B. C., yet this explorer resolutely held to the method of natural investigation which had been set up by the Ionian philosophers, and even tried to extend it to another sphere.

The distinction of Anaxagoras in the history of human thought rests chiefly upon his reasoned conclusion that there are two fundamentally incomparable realities in the world, namely, matter and mind. This is the doctrine known as Dualism and is to be contrasted with a Monism which finds, for example, only that which occupies space, or matter, to be real, everything else being a passing product or phenomenon of matter. We have already seen how near Empedocles came to this dualistic point of view. His fragment concerning "ineffable mind flashing through the whole universe" implies it, and, of course, Love and Strife as cosmic realities are not far removed from the idea of spiritual entities. But Anaxagoras first made the doctrine explicit and tried to demonstrate it. The arguments which he employed have been much in the minds of men since, especially among those who have tried to prove the "soul" immortal, or who have tried to discover God in nature. Strange fate for one of his temper to have been persecuted for irreligion!

More specifically, that which brought Anaxagoras to conceive of two absolutely contrasted kinds of realities seems to have been the question concerning the origin of motion. Matter does not start itself going when it is in a condition of rest. How then could it have become ordered out of the great original "sphairos," or primitive nebula, to use the modern equivalent? Following the analogy of Empedocles in turning to his own inner experiences, Anaxagoras reasoned: It is a mind (*Nous*) which started the ball rolling, just as it is mind which controls my bodily motion. Over everything which lives, be it great or small, mind holds sway. Mind also has power over the entire cosmic revolution, and must be regarded as its great Originator, that which gave it a starting impulse. This incipient revolution must in the beginning have been confined to a small area; now, he said, it extends over a wide space; in time it will extend still farther.[10]

In this way Anaxagoras came to attribute to mind a real-

[10] Simplicius in his *Physics,* 164, 24, gives us a summary of teachings of Anaxagoras. It is found in Diels: *Frag.* p. 318.

ity coördinate with that of matter. Neither could have come from something-not-itself, therefore both matter and the Nous are uncreated, and can never come to an end. Mind is an eternal cause of order, an *intelligent* energy more and more widely determining the motions of the world. Anaxagoras still regarded it as something corporeal. The same difficulty which beset Empedocles in trying to conceive of Love as a real existence made him speak of this cosmic Mind as "the thinnest of all things," the "purest," somehow "unmixed" with the matter in space but causing, ultimately, its motions, growths, and complex shapes. But his efforts to describe mind are in this respect parallel to our descriptions of intangibles, e. g., electricity, as "currents" or "fluids." "Something," we say, is "there" and usually we think in terms of a corporeal thing if it is supposed to have reality. Our imaginations are still troubled by anything "incorporeal" just as his was!

The great original mover, Nous, back of all world changes, is not, however, everywhere operative. Aristotle [11] held it against his predecessor in this, which we call the "cosmological" argument for the existence of a "Prime Mover," or God, that he did not go the full length of his argument. If mind started the motion of things then it must have been from all time and at this moment everywhere operative. And one should be able to find mind not only working as the cause of motion, but as the creator of purpose and of beauty in things. For that reason he characterized the mind which Anaxagoras discovered as a "*deus ex machina*," an idea coming in conveniently when you have reached the end of your tether in a natural explanation. Plato too argues thus.[12] But let us note that Anaxagoras found a wholly mechanical motion, as in the case of a falling body, impossible to interpret as the direct result of anything mental. Following the Ionians (and

[11] *Metaphysics,* I, 984b 16; 985a 18.
[12] *Phædo,* 97c.

in entire agreement with the presupposition of modern science) he tried to interpret nature mechanically just as far as he could, assuming, probably, that such was the really significant explanation of things. But he also reasoned that more ultimately, i. e., somehow back of the mechanical order a mind is implied as the primeval source of all activity.

Concerning the nature of mind as contrasted with matter, Anaxagoras had the following to say: It is simple, because similar throughout, whether one find it in great or in small; matter, on the contrary, has widely different kinds. It is "unmixed" with matter and, therefore, independent. As independent it has self-initiative, and so is not bound by mechanism. Rather it obtains power over matter by knowledge.) Obviously it was assumptions of this character which later very naturally led to the psychological doctrine that mental states are essentially similar, and that the "soul" is indivisible into separate parts or "faculties." It was also the first dawning awareness of the idea that mind is not to be interpreted in terms of mechanics when Anaxagoras insisted that the "soul" is "unmixed" with matter. Wherever mind is present—and Anaxagoras found it in all plants and animals—he ascribed to it the activities which we should call life. Indeed it is Nous which "ordered everything as it is to be in future, as it was but is no longer, and as it is to-day. So, too, the rotatory motion of the stars, the sun and moon, with that of the thicker atmosphere and higher ether which are gradually being separated out, their separation being due precisely to this rotatory motion." [13] Mechanical motion seems, therefore, to be derivative and secondary to the original act of mind, which, it should be noted, also foresaw whatsoever was to come to pass. But mind is not directly operative among inanimate things. Apparently our difficulties about the relationship between the living and the lifeless also beset

[13] Diels, *Frag.* 12, p. 331.

the thought of Anaxagoras. He was an evolutionist, maintaining that life originated in the moist earth under the influence of the sun's heat, but he urged that the seeds of life came from a source outside of our earth probably through the agency of the many bodies which, he said, were falling through the atmosphere.[14] Of course this last doctrine once more makes material things the carriers of mind!

Concerning Empedocles' elements he reasoned: They cannot be only four in number if the great variety of things is to be explained. Nothing could have come from nothing; no new quality comes by the combination and separation of things which we call change. "How can hair be made of what is not hair? Or flesh from what is not flesh?" [15] Hence there must be indefinite numbers of "roots" or "seeds" if the great variety of things is to be adequately interpreted. These roots were by Aristotle called *Homoiomere*, ultimate "simples" or things having identical structure in all their parts—a concept similar to Empedocles' roots. But the difference, and from our modern point of view perhaps the advance, in the thought of Anaxagoras lies in the fact that he seems to have regarded these very elements themselves as abstractions and to have denied that one could obtain one perfectly pure, and unmixed. There are always portions of other "seeds" mixed in with all material things, a hypothesis which he illustrated by the example of colors. Something white is only relatively so. There are other colors commingled with it. Snow, for example, is partly black. An absolutely pure white no one has ever obtained. In the same way all material particles, howsoever small, are complex, and we name them by their predominant quality. Flesh is a new combination of food substances taken into the body, but the qualities of the grain or cheese, etc., did not vanish by being taken into the

[14] Irenæus *Against Heresies,* II, 14, 2.
[15] Dìels, *Frag.* 10, Anaxagoras.

body; they are still there but subordinate to other qualities. And except in the instance of mind (which is "unmixed") one can never get two things absolutely alike.

Thus it was the apparently infinite variety back of all similarity which most impressed this thinker. He could not conceive how anything, even a so-called quality, could come from nothing. Therefore all must have been in existence from all time. The changes which the ordering of the cosmos entailed, were, and are, only new mixings and separations. By the cooling of the primitive world-substance, which the imparted motion brought about, the denser portions were separated from the lighter, the dark from the shining, the cooler from the hotter, etc. But this did not mean that the *Homoiomere* got piled together into particular places. They became somewhat less commingled than they were before, but only relatively so. We get no absolutely pure elements of anything. In the original chaos before the incipient activity of *Nous*, everything must have been "through-other" to such an extent that one would have been aware of no quality whatsoever. Anaximander's "Boundless" in space and time is thus thought of as boundless in qualities as well—varieties elicited in cosmic history. If Anaxagoras were alive to-day, he would very likely regard the allotropic forms of our elements—the very radical changes which they undergo under varying conditions—as further evidence for his theory. The simple after all turns out to be indefinitely complex.

Interesting observations were also made by Anaxagoras concerning the application of mathematics to nature. The following fragment has come down to us without its setting, consequently without its full implication. "For there is no least of what is small: always there is a still smaller. For it is impossible that what is should cease to be. On the other hand, there is always a still larger than the large. And it is as full as the smaller. In itself everything is both great and small." [16] Whatever else may be here implied, infinite divisibility and spatial relativity are clearly in his mind. In point of size, therefore, as well as in its qualities nothing is separated from other things "by a hatchet."

One is willing to grant the justice of Aristotle's high praise when one considers the various contributions of Anaxagoras. The conception of a world-ordering mind planning a progressive universe is one which was destined to play no small part in Plato and Aristotle. It is a central concept of religions to-day. We do not know by what reasoning he was led to conclude that the two world-agencies of Empedocles were in reality one, a knowing, ordering, purposive, foreseeing *Nous* of cosmic powers. In the famous twelfth Fragment the separateness of mind from material things is argued as a necessity growing out of its power over things, which suggests a kind of ontological argument—what is necessary for mind is true in reality. If we possessed more of his thought, we might know how he came to this amazing conclusion; also why he made use of mechanical interpretations everywhere as far as he could. His analysis of the idea of elements remains to our day a challenge to the physical investigator. With all our refinements of experiment we have not yet found simplicity in the particles with which we deal. Remarkable, too, is his doctrine of relativity. That in itself anything is both great and small—or as we should say: that no measure is absolute but depends upon circumstances—is an elementary postulate of our relativity doctrines. And yet Anaxagoras, like most thinkers since, was limited by tradition. Despite his observations on meteorites, his descriptions of the sun and stars as highly heated matter, and his efforts to establish how the moon shines by light reflected from the sun, he stuck to the geocentric astronomy of his master, Anaximenes.

[16] Diels, *Frag.* No. 3, p. 327.

CHAPTER VII

A WHOLLY MECHANICAL SCHEME: THE ATOMISTS

To find an interpretation of things in terms of one fundamental substance, something common through all apparent differences, has from the beginning been an important motive in the quest of science, philosophy, and intelligent religion. We have seen this in the efforts of the Ionians to find the *Arché*, in the Eleatic effort to think of God as a cosmic being and of the universe as a single piece. We have observed it in the unity of process, the "fixed measures" according to which Heraclitus conceived the activity of the *Logos*, as always working according to universal law. It was less explicit in the *Forms* of the Pythagoreans; yet they conceived their mathematics as obtaining not only upon the earth but in the outermost reaches of space with "all the choir and furniture of heaven" belonging to one system and harmony. The human mind seems to find it difficult to accept disorder, chaos, lawlessness! Even when constrained to realize the contrasts and antitheses of good and evil, mind and matter, or the various kinds of matter, as in Empedocles and Anaxagoras, it reaches for some hegemony, some central or organizing factor, which serves, either permanently or temporarily, as a basis of unity.

This monistic presupposition, whether in its extreme form as Eleatic absolutism (unconditioned unity) or the Variety-in-unity hypothesis of those who find some measure of apparent chance, or contrasting differences, or opposing processes, to be accounted for, has from the start bristled with difficulties. We are familiar with those of Zeno and the mathematicians. But they are also present in the relative Dualism of Anaxagoras. He posited the eternal existence of both mind and matter; but since the latter was thought to be dead, inert, without initiative, and in itself thoroughly "mixed up," while mind is intelligent, creative of order, unity and purpose, the greater reality, or at least the hegemony, was found in cosmic mind. Then, however, the problem of space arose in another guise. For the activity of mind was supposed to begin at a point, whence it expanded and continues to expand mechanically. Whereby, as Aristotle pointed out, Anaxagoras tended to revert again to the unity of a mechanical scheme.

We have before us now the interesting effort of the Atomists to think out the hypothesis of Pluralism—the universe consists of an indefinite or infinite number of really separate particles, so many self-contained pieces, or atoms, in constant motion. The founders of Atomism were Leucippus and Democritus who are usually mentioned together by Aristotle. Concerning Leucippus very little is known. Some scholars (e. g., the German, Rohde) have even denied his existence. But he is referred to in antiquity as the "comrade" of Democritus (Aristotle) and as a contemporary of Anaxagoras, as well as the pupil of Zeno and Melissus. In reality his work seems to have suffered eclipse by the more popular style and expositions of Democritus. A book of Leucippus was called "*Diakosmos*." Democritus called one of his own books the "*Great Diakosmos*," which title seems to tell a story, since we know that his book became a classic. At any rate, Aristotle was clearly determined to give honor to both these men.[1] Democritus was the son of a banker at Abdera, a city on the coast of Thrace, and seems to have been born about 470 B. C. He is said to have squandered his patrimony; but in turn

[1] For a discussion of all extant references to them see Karl Goebel, *Vorsokratische Philosophie*, pp. 257–317.

to have reëstablished a reputation among his townspeople by reading one of his books aloud. In Abdera, so the story runs, whoever came to poverty by his own neglect was denied a grave in the homeland, a fate which Democritus triumphantly forestalled by his "*Great Diakosmos.*" He is said to have received enough from the book to have made him once more a rich man. His popularity is further attested by a bronze statue erected in his lifetime, and a funeral at public expense. His power of mind and self-control were so great that he is said to have postponed his own death for three days by sheer will-power, in order not to interfere with his sister's plan to participate in the festival of the Thesmophoria (celebrating the return of Demeter from the underworld). He lived to be 90 or more and achieved fame as a mathematician, a writer of treatises on ethics, music, physics, medicine, agriculture, tactics and even reminiscences of travel. His happy disposition is indicated by his unique epithet, "Laughing Philosopher."

Following the precedent of Aristotle, we shall here discuss Atomism as the joint labor of Leucippus and Democritus. In general it may be characterized as an effort to analyze matter on the supposition that there are discrete and independent particles separated from each other by *empty space.* By the latter conception which is one of their fundamental contributions, they thought some of the difficulties of Parmenides might be avoided, especially the vexatious problem of motion. They agreed that for real motion to take place, it must be more than just the process of displacing something else. Real motion requires a vacuum. Why not then assert the real existence of nothingness (i. e., space without content) in which it is easy to conceive motion as well as to explain the "pores" into which some things take up, or absorb, others. For example, a glass of water receives into itself a considerable amount of salt without a corresponding increase in bulk. Where could it have gone if not into the empty spaces *between* the particles of which the water is made up? With empty space and atoms free to move about in it, a good many problems might be simplified and new means of interpreting nature be discovered.

So the Atomists posited a Plenum and a Vacuum. The former is space filled by atoms, the latter is space absolutely void. But both are *realities*—a proposition which is as difficult for us to understand as it was for Zeno. Leucippus and Democritus also argued (Mathematics to the contrary) that nature as a matter of fact would not admit of infinite divisibility in the Plenum. A point would be reached in the process at which one would have absolutely simple, homogeneous, indestructible masses which hold their own through all the changes which we observe. Indeed change is itself combinations and separations, condensations and rarefactions, rearrangements and motions of these ultimate particles. They surely must be permanent otherwise we could not assume the universe to be permanent. We should be getting something from nothing, which all agree is impossible.

How large are these atoms? The answer was: of a size much too small for human eyes to perceive. Everything we can see is still further divisible. We cannot even see "pores." How much less likely then that we should see what goes into them! Yet they are of varying sizes and shapes—for we can assign no reason why this should not be so. And assuming that they are different in these respects, we can explain a good many different qualities which visible things possess. Some atoms being smooth and round would account for the free motion which the parts of some substances possess. Others which hitch together because of their shapes, or have jagged edges, and so resist easy motion, would explain why some bodies hold together more rigidly. Where the atoms are thicker one would, of course, have a harder, less easily penetrable, body. Lighter bodies have relatively smaller numbers of atoms and greater spaces between them. From the beginning these atoms have been in motion. Not even the cosmic mind of Anaxagoras was necessary to start their activity. Like the atoms themselves, motion is eternal.

It need hardly be pointed out that Atomism is an extension of the principles set up by the Ionians and Parmenides with an addition of the Vacuum and a division of reality into multitudes of discrete pieces. The atoms fulfill the requirements of Eleatic Being in so far as they are *simple* and indestructible, without complexity and change, hence the basis of elemental reality. They and their motions account for the character and qualities of things in large and small, no less in the flower than in the sky. Pythagorean "Forms," Anaxagoras' "*Nous*," or anything else which might be conceived to superimpose itself upon the universal mechanism, this play of infinite numbers of atoms, becomes superfluous. "Only the atoms and the void are real." [2]

At first thought such a division into independent little bodies, all going their own way except as they get caught up or rebound from contact with others seems equivalent to chaos, absolute Pluralism, mere haphazard chance. If there is nothing to determine the direction of motions, no intelligible purpose to be discovered, how can we say there is order, regularity, system anywhere? How interpret, for example, any growing thing as an assemblage of atoms brought together by chance and each still going its independent way except as others prevent it? Such a Pluralism obviously has its difficulties no less puzzling than the perfect unity of the Eleatics.

But the Atomists, as a matter of fact, were far from the Pluralism of chance and disorder. The only surviving fragment of Leucippus runs, "Nothing happens without a cause, but all for a specific reason and under the pressure of

[2] Sextus Empiricus, *Adversus Mathematicos,* VII, 135, quoting Democritus.

necessity."[3] Like other philosophers, they too conceived of the world as unified, all the parts somehow necessarily co-ordinated. The movement of every individual atom is definite, necessary, reasonable, grounded in the total situation. One is tempted, indeed, to suppose that Leucippus here had something like universal mind in his thought especially since the passage is quoted from a book or chapter "*On the Soul.*" But however that may be, the supposition does not fit in well with a scheme which recognizes only atoms and the void; and Democritus expressly denies the cosmic mind, at least as related to the origin of motion. Another good reason for a unified world is found in their assumed fact that the atoms are qualitatively all the same. They differ indeed in size and shape but not in real character. All of the qualities which we ascribe to different things are explained as due to the way in which their atoms move and are put together. The material particles themselves merely fill space and have different weights according to their sizes. They are neither sweet nor red, neither hot nor cold. So that, from the standpoint of matter at least, the universe is identical in its ultimate parts; the empty spaces between them do not affect these indestructible "simples."

So even Atomic Pluralism turns out to be a spatial one. Unity is still found in a common substance and a world-wide system based upon necessity. To be sure, the conception of order based upon necessity is an extension of "Whatever is has always been" so as to include the *operations* of the atoms as well as their existence. *Some* sort of order would necessarily be given by the mere presence of the atoms in motion; in other words, there is no possibility of disorder. Whatever occurs is *the* order. There is no contingency. Yet atomic processes were also thought to have made history; that is to say, regroupings and separations—by a sort of cosmic weather—have produced and destroyed

[3] Diels, *Frag.* 2, p. 365.

new worlds in large and small. Our own earth was formed by a vortex motion in the course of which the heavier atoms were drawn together as earth, while those of the air formed a layer about it and beyond the air a "shell of ether" developed. So long as the given conditions are favorable such a system must survive. But under other conditions it might break up, its multitudinous atoms being caught up into other systems, new vortices in the making. This evolution—if we may use that term in connection with Atomism—is not only wholly natural, it is absolutely mechanical, based on the attraction of like for like. Atoms of the same general shape and size (as in air) tend to be drawn together quite as the winnowing process of the farmer makes lentils gather with the lentils, and barley with the barley. Such organizations are not "superimposed" or planned in advance. A world-system or a man simply grows by the give and take of inherent causes.

These spatial rearrangements and combinations of atoms are the prototypes of some modern theories of physical chemistry. In the abstract they also suggest the geometric forms of the Pythagoreans. Atomic configurations depend upon their size and shape, as we have already illustrated. But order of arrangement is also an important factor. To make use of Aristotle's illustration:[4] if A and N are atoms, the nature of the substance which they build up is dependent upon whether the (linear) order is AN or NA. In their angular relations the same thing is true. Turn an N around so as to make it a Z and AN will differ from AZ. If you take account, therefore, of motions, sizes, shapes, orders, and angular "turnings" of atoms, you have, according to these philosophers of materialism, a complete account of your world.

How do we know this? one immediately inquires. By our reason, rather than by our senses, is, of course, the answer

[4] *Metaphysics,* I, 985b 14.

of Democritus. Yet it is not a cock-sure, dogmatic answer. An account of things which denies so fundamentally the evidence of our senses could not but leave some questions over. Consider how many primary perceptions the Atomic Theory (both ancient and modern) relegates into "appearances"! Most objects seem to us continuous and with their parts at rest. But theory shows that both impressions are mistaken. Many objects have color. But atoms have none; it is their arrangement or motion which gives us that impression. Objects may be hot or cold. But atoms do not suffer change; it is only their motions and figures which change. Fluids may seem "sweet' or "bitter." But atoms are neither one nor the other. "'There are two forms of knowledge, the genuine and the obscure. To the obscure belong all of the following: sight, hearing, taste, smell, feeling. The other form is the genuine and quite distinct from this. (And then distinguishing the genuine from the obscure he continues:) Whenever the obscure way can no longer see, hear, smell, taste or touch what is smaller, and the investigation must be carried to a finer point, then the genuine way of knowing which has a finer organ of thought takes its place." In these quite specific words, the skeptical physician, Sextus Empiricus,[5] who flourished about 200 A. D., quotes Democritus.

The distinction between what in later times came to be called primary, as opposed to secondary, qualities was thus explicitly made by Democritus. Primary qualities are those upon which the very existence of the atoms depends; while secondary qualities are only the way we perceive the various combinations, motions, figures, etc., of these atoms. Another fragment [6] runs, "By convention sweet is sweet, by convention bitter is bitter, by convention hot is hot, by convention cold is cold, by convention color is color." In other words, if

[5] *Adversus Mathematicos* VII, 139. Diels, p. 407.
[6] Also from Sextus Empiricus, *Ibid.* VII, 135.

most people suffered from jaundice, honey would be called not sweet but bitter. A slight difference in people's eyes would transform "green" objects into yellow, or red ones into gray, or transparent ones into opaque. Our senses, in fact, fail to respond to minute particles such as make up our world. When we divide beyond a certain point, color and all other secondary qualities simply disappear. But that, according to these philosophers, would not be true of primary qualities. They belong to the very nature of atoms. To assume that atoms could exist without occupying space would be to identify Being with Not Being.

On the other hand, it is difficult to blink the "facts" of our senses! They too are at least a natural process. Hence Democritus was at some pains (as many psychologists have been ever since) to explain their mechanism. Curiously enough he had recourse to a brand-new *deus ex machina.* Objects when perceived give off "images" or effluences which imprint themselves, so to speak, upon our senses. He called them *Eidola,* presumably meaning some kind of atomic structures which are produced by objects and which dimly represent them in miniature. The theory reminds one of some later efforts to interpret the sense of smell as awareness of atomic structures which are given off by odorous objects. Democritus, however, was concerned chiefly with vision, and thought of images as constantly impinging upon our eyes and as being carried there through a medium. Despite his vacuum, like most other physicists he found it difficult to think of *actio in distans.* How can one thing affect another if there is no bond connecting them? To use a modern example, how could light be transmitted from the sun without ether in the intervening space? So the ancient psychologist thought of images as propagated by contacts through the air and suffering somewhat in the process. But eventually *Eidola* are impressed upon our eyes somewhat after the manner of a seal upon wax. Most readers will be inclined to smile both at his naïve disregard of the vacuum and his conception of air. We know so much more about the latter! But Democritus' effort to mechanize a mental process is not a whit more naïve than corresponding ones by later psychologists. Even to-day we hear of "images" and "ideas" as mechanisms or properties of certain cells, and of memory as spatial contacts (even new contacts) between nerve cells. Materialism, of course, has its difficulties in interpreting whatever by hypothesis is non-material, be it a vacuum or a mental fact.

Democritus, however, also thought of souls as matter. There are soul atoms. They are very fine, round, smooth bodies, kindred to fire, which all living things are constantly breathing in and giving out. Souls, therefore, are as permanent as atoms—a theory which at first thought might lead one to hope for immortality. But not so the Atomists. They conceived individual forms of life to be structures dependent upon the give and take of soul atoms. So long as the delicate adjustment lasts, for example, in a human being, he continues to live. But when the balance is no longer possible the individual body breaks up and the little soul atoms join other systems. Some bring life to a tree, to grass, or to worms; others perhaps help to constitute the life of beings higher than ourselves.

Again one naturally expects to hear that all these atoms, taken collectively as the animating life of the universe, will be called God. But the Atomists looked for their interpretations not to comprehensive systems or cosmic organizations. For them knowledge lay in the structures and activities of numberless independent atoms. Consequently their problem became: How explain the commonly accepted ideas and images of gods and heroes in terms of atomic figures and motions? For everything that happens has a real cause. We cannot imagine a thing we have never seen. Even hallucinations are built up out of sense experience. Gods and heroes must, therefore, be genuine "*Eidola*" which have impressed themselves upon human eyes. But whatever remarkable men or other beings may have given off these images, and so been responsible for the confused and obscure knowledge which we possess, they were real, even if temporary, deities. Thus Democritus preserved them, at least for imagination, and successfully avoided ulterior problems—as most of his scientific successors have done even to this day.

One does not expect to hear of purposes and ethical ideals in a world of mechanisms which together and singly go their way by inevitable necessity. How could choice or initiative arise, a human design be imposed upon nature, when "only atoms and the void are real"? Have we not ruled morality and responsibility out of court when we regard human actions, like drifting sands on the shore, as determined by the concourse of atoms? Yet Democritus apparently did not think so. He must have written voluminously on ethical subjects for most of the fragments we possess (approximately 300) concern themselves with the conduct of life. He was famous throughout late antiquity and among early Christian writers as an ethical teacher. The "Golden Sayings" do not, unfortunately, concern themselves with basic problems, being more of the nature of maxims. We do not learn how he reconciled Materialism and ethical purposes. We can only guess that he may have conceived of soul-atoms (which were also thought to be atoms of *reason*) as enjoying some special control under certain conditions, because of their peculiar shape and mobility. But even that assumption has obvious difficulties.

However uncoördinated with his science the ethical choices and purposes recommended by Democritus, they are exalted as well as incisive ones. One naturally expects to hear from such a man that we "should rejoice as much as possible and grieve as little as may be." True joy, however, is found in "goods of soul," not in gold or in the pleasures of the body. Such desires tend to overthrow the balance and harmony of life. Happiness is "uprightness and fullness of understanding." No ignorant man knows how to enjoy himself, for this comes only by knowledge. Not fear, therefore, but quest of the right should restrain a man from sin. Quite in the spirit of the Sermon on the Mount, Democritus wrote, "He who does wrong is more unhappy than he who suffers wrong." [7] Whoever loves things spiritual loves the divine and the permanent; whoever loves the body, a mere envelop of the soul, loves the human and the temporary. Unselfish devotion to the common good of one's city and state is a constant spring of joy. "When the state is in a healthy condition all things prosper; when it is corrupt, all things go to ruin." [8] Freedom, health, and joy go along with intelligent right mindedness while "dying long drawn out" is the bitter portion of the foolish and the irreligious.

One cannot but regret that the religious thought of a scientist so acute, and an ethical teacher so noble, should not have come down to us, if it was ever written down. That so keen a mind should have kept his ethics and his science in separate compartments seems hardly credible.

The influence of the Atomic Theory upon the development of physical science has been continuous and decisive. Since the renaissance of the sciences in the fifteenth century most of the major discoveries and interpretations in physics and chemistry have been in the light of its concepts. We realize this when we ask ourselves where chemistry would stand to-day without the Atomic Hypothesis. Its rudimentary form in antiquity already pointed the way to not a little secure knowledge. Differences in volume which material things undergo by different states of aggregation (as expanded or contracted) were finally made comprehensible. The rela-

[7] Diels, *Frag.* p. 418, No. 45.
[8] *Ibid.* p. 450, No. 252.

tive weights and impenetrabilities of substances were no longer so great a puzzle. Growth and decay no longer did violence to the idea of permanence. The contrasting qualities which a single element may have under different conditions, as well as the new ones produced by combination of two or more substances, were, *in principle*, interpreted as they are in chemistry to-day. Qualitative differences were already construed quantitatively. The principle of atomic weights was dimly apprehended. But most remarkable of all was the inflexible determination of the ancient Atomists to interpret every aspect of nature in terms of abstract figures, weights, positions, shapes and angular relationships, attractions, movements and contacts.

Modern science has greatly extended and refined the methods and observations of these men. But it has not seriously modified their principles. The ideal of a *mechanism*, and of the smallest possible size, as a key to the secrets of our world has continued to inspire not only the physical sciences, but even biology and psychology. The atoms of the various elements, once thought to be so many "simples" of their kind—but not by Leucippus and Democritus—have been "broken up," or found to be complex. The analysis of their structure has led to hypotheses of still smaller units, with much more rapid motions than these men probably dreamed of. The ancient idea of atomic configurations has been exchanged for rings and orbits of lesser units within the atom itself. The energy which the ancient Atomists conceived in terms of motion has been further analyzed into other forms of "action" including charges of electricity. These latter as negative charges, or electrons, go their rapid and incessant way about the nucleus, or central mass of the atom. The many more elements with which we are acquainted are now assumed to vary chiefly by the number and arrangement of the electrons and the size of the central nucleus. Yet electrons are all of them taken to be identical as unit charges. Physical chemistry for mathematical reasons also holds to the hypothesis of an identical substance (hydrogen) as constituting the source of all our elements. In this way qualitative differences of all kinds—not only the "secondary" qualities of Democritus but also his "primary" one of filling space—are now referred to geometrical configurations which in turn depend upon *how many* identical tiny units are acting together as a system. In this reliance upon distances (larger and smaller rings of electrons), velocities (relative to that of light), angular relationships and bare *numbers* of identical units, to explain the varieties which our senses experience, modern physics has extended and improved upon the mechanical abstractness of the Atomists. Curiously enough, the vacuum (whose "place" was long securely held by the ether) has been reinstated in some recent theories. No small part, therefore, of the development of modern physical science has depended upon extensions of the Atomic Hypothesis. Whatever its limitations may be as a radically mechanical interpretation of organic structures, or of actions which seem to be the expression of purposes, the theory has given us an amazing vision of infinitesimal nature. It has, perhaps, more than any other source of insight, put intelligence on guard against the naïve acceptance of the superficial aspects of things. Surely nothing could be more surprising than the discovery that most of the qualities commonly accepted as making up the nature of objects are in reality the motions and configurations of identical units! But whether atoms and their mechanisms in large and small, or some non-material cause, will turn out to be more illuminating as an explanation of events remains for future consideration.

CHAPTER VIII

FROM GODS TO ATOMS: A RÉSUMÉ

The first act in the drama of Greek thought may be said to have had a prologue among the gods. We paid little attention to these stories of war and peace, of the begetting and bringing up of divine children, of the Mother and Maid of Eleusis, Zeus, Poseidon, Hades. Our primary interest has been to interpret the thought and motives which led to the work of science. And yet it must be admitted that the religious stories of Homer and Hesiod, which in some measure characterized the usages and customs of the gods and so implied at least some regularity in their government of men and nature, are linked up with the fundamental idea of Naturalism. That regularity is also implied in the Orphic Wheel of Birth which determined the reincarnation of men to new lives—a conception familiar to Pythagoras and Empedocles. Zeus as the father of gods and men was somewhat more than an arbitrary creator *ex nihilo,* absolutely "on his own." And Fate too, whose age is still uncertain, played a very important rôle in the days of the tragic poets, as superior to the volitions of Father Zeus himself. Even the goddess Chance suggests that the determinate and the indeterminate, the willed and the unwilled, were early in the minds of religious men.

Yet this extraordinary plot of Greek thought turns rather abruptly after the Prologue. For the burden of the first act—roughly from about 600 to 425 B. C.—is emphatically to discover what *mechanism,* rather than what *will,* determines alike the revolution of the heavens and the order of mundane affairs. For all that Thales and the others down to Democritus have to say about the gods, the primary motive of early philosophy is the scientific one of finding out all that may be discovered about our world without special recourse to their assistance.

The stage setting was also remarkable. Perhaps we shall more vividly appreciate the meaning of this search if we envisage some of its dramatic political events and personages. Adequately to do this would take us back to the early migrations centuries before, and the secret of that happy blending of Dorian and Mycenæan peoples by which the Ionian stock was produced. It would trace the development of the Ionian cities in Asia Minor—Miletus, Ephesus, Colophon, Clazomenæ and others—torch bearers of Hellenism already in the ninth century B. C., the age of Homer and Hesiod. It would exhibit the checkered course of other Greek colonies along the coasts of Sicily and Calabria in the following century—Tarentum, Leontini, Crotona, and Syracuse. And then the interesting but turbulent seventh century when so much of anarchy and tyranny succeeded each other in nearly all the Greek states, when none the less the new elegiac and iambic poets—Archilochus, Tyrtæus, Alcman, Simonides, Sappho and Alcæus—were about in the land, and when the new plastic arts were groping in many places through poignant archaic forms toward the splendor of a later time.

But to envisage all this would exceed our scope. If we picture the Milesians of Thales' and Anaximander's day we must, first of all, think of them not as primitive pioneers, mere economically minded traders. They were more than that; they were proud of an ancient civilization, of an artistic and religious tradition which could claim even Homer himself. The "tyrants" of the seventh century had maintained "courts" whose cultural interests vied with those of Athens. They enjoyed cosmopolitan relationships which linked them with three continents. When we recall that in the pre-philosophic period men generally thought of the earth as a disc it hardly occurs to us that the disc included the major continents. But there could be little doubt that, for all their limited knowledge of astronomy, traders and travelers from Ormuz and Ind came into contact in the busy streets of Miletus with others who hailed from the far northern lands, even "Hyperborians" from the region of Cimmerian darkness and the midnight sun.

One difference must be noted as between these Ionian Greeks of Asia Minor and those of the homeland—a difference which has some bearing upon the history of philosophy. All Ionians were, of course, markedly independent in temper and lovers of liberty. But while the aristocratic republic of Athens was already well established in the early seventh century, and suffered relatively less from tyrants, the coastal citics were constantly harassed by the great power of Lydia, and had to compromise their status. For decades there was armed independence, then years of alliance, then overlordship until in 568 B. C. Crœsus succeeded in subduing the whole of Ionia. Twenty-two years later, howevcr, he and all of Lydia in turn fell under the power of Cyrus the Persian, to whom Miletus acknowledged allegiance. The story of how the Ionian Greeks, instigated by Athenians and others, plotted their independence (and sometimes tyrannies abroad), thus creating an impossible situation as between the Persian monarchs and the Greek republics, is known to every schoolboy. The challenge of the allied expedition to Sardis and the destruction of that city by fire led directly to Marathon, Thermopylæ and Salamis.

What is of peculiar interest to us here is the fact that these struggles brought about the scattering of many refugees to distant parts of the Mediterranean. Thus when Cyrus in 546 B. C. became overlord of Ionia, and Phocaea came under his heel, a group of resolute men and women fled his power and made their way to Italy, to try once more for liberty. There the town of Elea arose, founded by these refugees among whom the philosophers Parmenides and Zeno were soon to be born. Leucippus was also associated with Elea but we do not know whether he was born there. In a similar way the survivors of Teos, driven out by Cyrus, proceeded to found the new city of Abdera over in Thrace—Abdera which later gave birth to Democritus, and Protagoras with whom we shall shortly be concerned. Xenophanes of Colophon, it will also be recalled, was driven out by the conquering Persians in 546 B. C. and carried his poetry and philosophy of religion to far-away Calabria. As to the motives of Pythagoras in emigrating from his native Samos about 532 B. C., we have inadequate information. But it is very likely that Crotona had to thank these wars for his coming. And when eventually in 494 B. C., Darius with terrible vengeance overwhelmed the allies, the torch of liberal studies no longer shone at Miletus.

Empedocles was a native of a Dorian colony in Sicily, Acragas, or Agrigentum; and Pythagoras migrated to an Achæan one. Perhaps these facts explain how so much that is foreign to Ionian Naturalism should have become incorporated in their thought. None the less (however one explains it in Empedocles) the dominant motive, without exception, in the whole pre-Socratic philosophy from Thales to its dramatic climax in Atomism, was mechanism. This will shortly become more evident when we coördinate the thought of these men in résumé. And however surprising this may seem, when one considers their remoteness from one another, the complimentary fact is no less so: Persian armies helped to effect the dissemination of science. They did not entirely expel it from Ionia, however, as the life of Heraclitus in Ephesus attests.

We must now try to picture Athens whither Anaxagoras has led us and where the next great scene is laid. At first it seems anomalous that the mother-city with its ancient and cultivated traditions, which long anticipated its colonies, should not have been the first home of philosophy and science. But however the fact be explained, it is quite definitely true that Anaxagoras was the first to introduce such ways of thinking at Athens, and that he was invited thither by Pericles, probably not earlier than 462 B. C. Moreover it was a full century later, when Aristotle was a young man in his twenties, before the real significance of Ionian Naturalism was appreciated there. This is extraordinary when one considers how close were the common interests of Ionia and Athens (as kindred against Medes and Persians), and how relatively remote Abdera, Elea and Acragas were, when compared with the distance between Athens and Miletus.

The genius of Ionians in the homeland was clearly other than scientific during the sixth and most of the fifth centuries. When Pythagoras was plotting the heavens and Anaximander coördinating the various forms of life, the Athenians were intent upon "goat songs" and dialogues at the festivals of Dionysus, which later led to the florescence of tragic poetry. This passionate interest in poetry was very marked in the time of the "tyrants," Pisistratus and his sons (560–511 B. C.), when Athens symbolized her cultural leadership by monumental new editions of the Homeric poems and by taking charge of the temple of Apollo at Delos, where from of old "the long-robed Ionians gather with their children and their wives, beings . . . whom a stranger might think were ever free from death and eld." Such public festivals, religious dramatic performances like the Dionysia, dramatic processions like the Panathenæa bringing the "peplon" to their Virgin queen with all the pomp that fastidious restraint would permit, or the Elusinian and later Orphic Mysteries, staged around marble temples—these engaged the imagination of the town. Music, painting, and the other fine arts, were more than meat and drink to them. Their passionate interest in new intuitions of beauty extended from the black (and later red) figured jars and other kitchen utensils, to the myriad statues of men and gods which adorned alike the pediments of temples and the market-place. Everything these Athenians touched they tried to shape into something pleasing, as a hundred museums of Europe still attest. It is fairly certain that artistry was a vivid interest with them even before suitable media of expression or the various arts were developed. But our record exhibits their progress from about the middle of the sixth century.

How rapid that florescence was may be seen from the succession of world-names that followed. Æschylus was born at Eleusis 525 B. C.; Sophocles, at Colonus 495; Euripides, at Salamis 480—all very near to Athens. Phidias was born there about 500; Myron in Eleutheræ (Attica again); Thucydides at Athens in 471. The history of the period, and of the Periclean Age which was soon to follow, is too full, on its literary and artistic side alone, to be interpreted here. Remarkable too is the fact that in these days poets could also be generals and statesmen; sculptors and musicians mere men of affairs. Thus Sophocles commanded fleets as well as composed music, which he himself helped render as accompaniment to his plays. Euripides had no small political influence. Herodotus read his history to the Athenean Assembly, which thereupon voted him the extraordinary sum of ten talents. Perhaps the dominant influence in the life of Pericles was that of Damon, the master-musician. Thucydides was an army general. Examples might be multiplied. But we are here primarily concerned with Athenian life as related to philosophy and science. And our general conclusion must be that artistry and practical statecraft were its dominant interests until the wane of the Periclean golden age. Pericles died 429 B. C.

There are indeed many reasons why fifth century Athens

should have aroused the enthusiasm of later times. There is probably little exaggeration in the words which Thucydides in his *History* attributes to Pericles: How in his noble city "the claim of excellence is recognized." "We are lovers of the beautiful, yet simple in our tastes, and we cultivate the mind without loss of manliness. Wealth we employ not for talk and ostentation, but when there is a real use for it. To avow poverty with us is no disgrace. . . . I say that Athens is the school of Hellas and that the individual Athenian in his own person seems to have the power of adapting himself to the most varied forms of action with the utmost versatility and grace. This is no passing and idle word, but truth and fact; and the assertion is verified by the position to which these qualities have raised the state. For in the hour of trial Athens alone among her contemporaries is superior to the report of her."

All this the record seems to confirm. Yet it cannot be said that philosophy was at home in Athens before the Periclean Age itself (461–431 B. C.) Socrates was born there probably 469 B. C. We have the reports of visits by a number of philosophers to the "school of Hellas," notably that of the aged Parmenides toward the middle of the century. The practical sophists were very much in evidence. But strange to say the work of the Ionian Naturalists seems to have been little appreciated there until the time of Plato (428–354 B. C.) Both Socrates and he seem to have known very little about Democritus. At any rate, Plato never refers to him. When eventually Athenian philosophy came to its own it was of a very different temper. It opened a new era, a new act in the drama, which we shall soon endeavor to report.

It remains for us now to summarize what we have called the first act, by showing the inner connections of the plot. The beginning axiom of Naturalism was: There is one single *Arché* or world-stuff, unbegotten and thoroughly regular in whatsoever takes place in it. This "*Physis*," or Substance, at first particular (Thales), was generalized by Anaximander, so as to include all observable characters or qualities, all the various activities of our world as part of his "*Apeiron*." One might express this axiom in various other ways. It would certainly include the idea that nothing comes from nothing. It assumes a wholly natural, or regular, dependable, system in the course of events. It assumes a unity even in the succession of worlds upon worlds in time—which after all are thought of as one world in evolution, combined and recombined in endless new arrangements. But this world-stuff of Anaximander is emphatically more than what we call matter. Indeed the distinction between physical qualities and mental ones was not made at all by the Milesians. They assumed that life was a fact among other facts, part and parcel of the world-order, and subject to the same laws which determine the activities of other things.

One must, therefore, avoid identifying this Naturalism with Materialism. From the first the Milesians were interested in the mechanisms of the "*Physis*," its combinations, separations, motions, changes. But they also conceived its parts as not only law-abiding, but "just" or somehow inevitably right, and "balanced" in relation to the course and nature of the whole. Their axiom—the rock upon which so large a portion of religious, scientific, and metaphysical structure has since been built—was, however, quickly subjected to the most searching and distracting questionings. Parmenides enters as a marplot. We can imagine him saying: It is all very well to speak in popular terms of how animals, or perhaps world-systems, "evolve" and "change" into this or that by "combination" and "separation" of parts or (Anaximenes') "condensation" and "rarefaction." It is very impressive to deal with "infinities" and the prodigious "variety" of qualities in "*Apeiron*." But my difficulty is in knowing what, more precisely, is meant by these terms. I have no small suspicion that all of them, applied to Reality or Being as it is, will not bear investigation.

You say a thing "changes"? Does this mean into something new which did not exist before? And if not, does not the more comprehensive view of the particles "combined" or "separated" show them to be exactly what they were before? Surely it is very important not to confuse what is real with what is not real, what *is* with what is *not*, in one's ideas of things. And if "Evolution" brings into being what was not in being before, it is clearly giving you something for nothing. Out of nothingness into being—how preposterously inconceivable! The way of truth and knowledge must avoid such deceptions of rabbits out of empty hats, and other tricks which reason should discover in time!

Again Parmenides inquires: Is one the same as two or a hundred? And if not what meaning can be attributed to the axiom about the unity of the world? You answer: common sense tells me it is *both* one and many according to the way you look at it? But ponder a moment! Is it non-being separates one part of being off from another? And non-being is nothingness? Again this seems to me very like deceptive magic. Nothingness it is which gives character to your somethings! You derive rabbit A from nothingness, then evolve rabbit B from nothingness, and finally tell me that what distinguishes A from B is nothingness! Nonsense, friend, the way of science is to banish this nothingness and deal with what really is.

But Parmenides found no less difficulty in the contradictoriness of what, at least apparently, really is. Our senses show us an immense variety of things. They are heavy and light, sweet and sour, white and black. Yet since all these differences come and go, can they be said to characterize true being? Suppose the immense variety, the contradictory qualities of things and their multiplicity to be a passing deception of the senses, then we could characterize real being, permanent being, as *one* in a way which would not do violence to our intelligence. Away then with what is passing and hold to what is permanent! . . . Thus arose the perennial ghost which science even yet cannot down: *Appearance*, or what seems to be but is not. Parmenides found too much in heaven and earth to admit as "there." His problem was not what is yet "undreamt of in our philosophy" but rather the ephemeral riches of an impossible dream, the apparitions, passing shadows and empty deceptions of our senses. If we think of true Being as one with itself, not subject to birth and decay, not characterized by contradictory qualities, such as heavy and light, visible and invisible, audible and inaudible, and other suicidal proclivities, then in the name of science we can speak of a unified and permanent Reality without stultifying our reasons.

Every thoughtful man will see how this conception of unchanging, simple Being is related to later developments, all the way to Empedocles' elements and the atoms of Democritus. Indeed it still challenges our latest efforts toward rationality—howsoever we may joke about the abstract "isness" of Being. Our modern Zenos, intrenched in the most obvious mathematics, are bowled over by the absurdities presented in the tiniest movement of a finger, conceived as divisible into parts. Time, Space, Reality, Being—these are inseparably one, we still hear old Zeno's logic proclaim in the effort to make the beginning axiom of Naturalism rational.

Yet an even more formidable challenge to that axiom came in the conclusions of Heraclitus, backed as they were by so great an amount of seemingly direct experience. We need not again point his arguments. Change, whatever its problems, is not to be gainsaid either within or without us. And when Heraclitus made his "*Physis*" a dynamic, self-transforming Process, but none the less permanent as divine Fire, "fixed measures kindling and fixed measures dying out," he too threatened the whole visible (or otherwise sensible) universe as such. For whatever the ostensible qualities of a thing, all of them are manifestly in flux. You and I as conscious beings pass on from state to state. The very Reason which Parmenides set up as arbiter of true being shares the movement of a ceaseless river.

Despite all these poignant and baffling considerations, both Parmenides and Heraclitus furthered the traditions of Naturalism on the side of its assumed regular system of law, its single, unified, cosmic Something, Being or Logos, which not only makes it a system, but rational as well, and within the scope of our intelligence. In other words, they hoped in science, despite the contradictions presented by a Reality whose qualities could be expressed only as "not this" or "not that" and a Process whose nature was likewise neither this, that, nor any other particular one. Empedocles found a temporary *modus vivendi*, a half solution, in his theory of elements and their proportionate combinations. Part of his "roots" took on Eleatic stability, others were supposed to provide dynamic power—which obviously makes at least two fundamentally contrasted realities and once more challenges any thoroughgoing idea of unity! "Chance," which also began to figure in Empedocles' interpretations, was clearly another absurdity in the naturalistic program. How could what is haphazard, irrational, and subject to no law, become part and parcel of a scientific explanation?

One might easily underestimate, however, the contributions of both Empedocles and Pythagoras to the cause of Naturalism. Both, in their scheme of moral evolution as expressed in transmigration, embraced something foreign to mechanism. And Empedocles' biological evolution (like modern theories which depend upon chance) was quite extraneous to it. Yet he made all the use he could of Anaximander's "separating out" by warm and cold, moist and dry, to which he added the notions of attraction and repulsion, and pressed his mechanisms as far in the direction of physiological and mental activities as he could—thus drawing upon himself the special shafts of Aristotle. You will recall how sensations were explained as effluences of particles from the six elements or roots in the external world, which fit into their appropriate "pores" in our organs, and are picked up by corresponding "roots" in our bodies, on the principle that "like perceives like"; and how the various human temperaments, thoughts, and capacities were traced to the particular "mixtures" of roots (we say secretions) which enter into the blood. All this is as mechanical as Behaviorism.

The Pythagorian "Opposites" of the "Unlimited" and "Limited," "Darkness and Light," the "Hot and the Cold" and others—which, in part, were inherited from Anaximander—do not indeed suggest a unified world in the sense of Eleatic simplicity and self-identify. Action and reaction, good and bad, like Empedocles' Love and Strife would seem to indicate a world divided against itself. Yet the Pythagorian concept of Form which gives definite "figures," even with the precision of mathematical patterns, to what is otherwise "unlimited," was perhaps the greatest of all supports to the theory of Naturalism. For these Forms not only "harmonize" the utmost variety and contrariety of things—just as order is brought to the notes of a lyre by tuning them to a scale, or "temperance," health, balance, to a human being by a "blend" of the "opposites" in him —they have a *definiteness* which before was lacking in order to establish natural law. This was, of course, due to the proposal to apply mathematics in every situation.

These Forms were destined to complicate matters (as we shall see in Plato) when it became clear that patterns, numbers, or "blends" in themselves are not really "parts" of any tangible, visible thing—and hence suggest something more than mechanism. Yet apart from this consideration, the definiteness or inevitableness, which only the discovery of mathematical norms in nature could demonstrate, was, and is, a powerful incentive to the work of exact, or mechanical, science. Perhaps the Pythagorian astronomy was the best fruitage of their quest for a "harmony of the manifold and accord of the discordant." On the other hand, they seem to have taken lightly the problem of the "one and the many," or the more precise sense in which the many aspects of our world can be reduced to a single system (whether "mechanical" or "moral" or something else). In fact they simply incorporated both horns of such dilemmas.

The climax of Mechanism came, of course, with the Atomists, who exploited and brought to a focus all the principles developed by the earlier Ionians. The first presupposition of every such scheme, Parmenides' idea of a Being which *is*, i. e., really, permanently, exists, they found in unalterable, individual atoms. Unity, which is also a requisite for it, they placed in the qualitative identity of the atoms. All phenomena, including those of the mind itself, whatever their apparent variety or contrasts, were referred to the motions, shapes, and combinations of these "simples"; so that from the standpoint of Pythagorian system and arrangement the same unity was assumed as axiomatic—the world is a cosmos, even without the latter's "opposites." Mathematical patterns, built up by spatial forms, sequences, and angular relationships, were held to account for things both as they are in the external world and as they appear to the mind. These "*Eidola*" are, of course, Pythagorian *Forms* conceived as built up, not of points or counters but of atoms, which, as such, originate nothing. Their motions have been from all time, unimpeded in absolutely empty space. Despite all their collisions and the more or less definite forms which they assume, these motions continue undiminished. (Cf. Newton's first law of motion.) Nor is there any irregularity or chance in all this. Every motion, whether of soul atoms or of less easily mobile (say viscous) material, is determined absolutely by the necessity of the system as a whole. Thus "nothing happens in vain," there is a cause for every event. All these inevitables taken together constitute the "order" of the whole.

Thus by the combination of Pythagorian "patterns" and Parmenides' "not-being" conceived as the void or empty space, they made the apparent mixture and variety of things quite congruent with the conception of a single element. Their method, which was essentially that of explaining in terms of concealed structures, and motions in all directions, seemed to provide a definite solution for the differences of hard and soft, hot and cold, which had so baffled the earlier naturalists. Heavy and light, it is interesting to note, never once occurred to any of these thinkers as finally characteristic of anything. Leucippus and Democritus thought of "weight" simply in terms of impacts, to which larger atoms and those of irregular shapes are exposed. Vortex motions, the natural results of motions in all directions among atoms of endless shapes and sizes (an idea of Anaxagoras which the Atomists developed), bring about the segregation of so-called "elements." The homogeneous or concentrated distribution of atoms in given volumes also accounts for the hard-soft (solid-liquid) character of things. Heat and cold they likewise attributed to geometrical, i. e., spatial, factors.

All this seems like perfection itself as an abstract mathematico-physical, or scientific, method. All later efforts toward a mechanistic interpretation of nature have followed most implicitly the principles of the Atomists. The smallest number of dimensions, the minimum of size, concealed structures, concealed motions (since Descartes), and latterly motions independent of space (Quantum Theory), continue to offer themselves as keys to the knowledge of the universe. Almost incredible results have crowned this method wherever it has been successful. But the difficulty in Democritus' day, as well as in our own, has been to interpret living, or apparently purposive phenomena, in terms of mechanism.

Democritus did not hesitate to assume that sensations should be explained in terms of the motions and configurations of atomic structures which succeeded in getting through certain "pores" of our sense-organs. These *Eidola* (or images, material objects it must be remembered, though of finer grade than the objects from which they emanate) are stored up in our bodies—an assumption by which their retention in the mind was explained. Forgetting is, of course, the disappearance of *Eidola;* recollection, their (mechanical) association. We are not told whether this association was thought of in terms of Empedocles' principle of like attracting like (similarity), or of Anaxagoras' principle of contrast as the basis of attraction. Emotions must have been an interesting controversial subject in the school at Abdera—interpreted as configurations and motions of atoms. But we still have the close association of emotions and motions in our current psychology; indeed it extends to every mental fact as coördinated with structural changes and motions in the nervous system. Thoughts themselves Democritus conceived as atomic structures, very fine *Eidola*, which somehow, independently of our sense organs, succeed in penetrating our bodies. Thus, consistently with a strictly mechanical theory, the highest as well as the lowest mental facts and functions were all included.

A further problem presented itself in the distinction which Democritus made between "true-born" and "bastard" knowledge, the latter being confused and untrustworthy, while the former gives us genuine truth. This we found to correspond in general with the later distinction (of John Locke) between primary and secondary qualities. Sight, hearing, smell, taste and touch were called "bastard" by Democritus. For, of course, they do not give us genuine knowledge of the atomic figures and motions which are the foundation of reality. *Eidola* entering through the sense organs are not only suspect; they are "quite apart" from the true-born ones. Unfortunately we have in our records no accounts of what marks were supposed further to distinguish the true-born kind of knowledge. But the same difficulty which has since confronted every mechanical interpretation of the mind presented itself in Democritus. He, for consistency's sake, was compelled to attribute all mental facts whether true-born or bastard, false or true, what is merely apparent or deceptive, as well as exact thought about atomic structure, to the same inevitably definite course of the mechanisms. But if every thought—an absolutely false one as well as one which "corresponds" with atomic structure—is the product of *Eidola* working by fixed necessity, then truth and error would seem to demand some other means of distinguishing one from the other.

Anaxagoras of Clazomenæ was quite certainly an older man than Democritus. But we mention him last in this chapter because he represents a transition from the first to the second act. He was an Ionian indeed, and his mechanical interpretations went far enough to arouse to the danger point the opposition of conservative religious leaders in Athens. His contributions from the standpoint of an indefinite variety of elementary units (*Homoiomere*) are also very significant for every mechanical theory. But what chiefly interests us here is the fact that he, the first Athenian philosopher, for the first time seemed to appreciate the independent significance of mind as a factor in the order of nature. True that it was only hesitatingly affirmed as "at the beginning" and in a very restricted area. But it gives the key to the plot of the new philosophy in the second act, namely, the quest for *purpose*, a search which was destined to make immaterial mind, rather than atoms, the central fact of the cosmos. This we shall now follow upon the stage of Athens.

PART TWO:

The Quest for Purpose Dominant

CHAPTER IX

THE PROPER STUDY OF MANKIND IS MAN: THE SOPHISTS

1

In the richly variegated life of ancient Greece the Ionian stock was distinguished, not only as the originator of Western philosophy and science, but for its many world names in art. We must not forget, however, that the other two great races, the Æolians and the Dorians, were also remarkable for their artistry. Lyric poetry, as represented in Alcæus and the marvelous Sappho of Lesbos, was a glory to the Æolians. So were the chorals of Alcman and Simonides to the Dorians, though the latter was Ionian by birth. Pindar too, by his fertile and often sublime imagination, lent poetic and musical splendor to many Pan-Hellenic athletic games. (All Greeks seem to have taken it for granted that the alliance of athletic contests with religion, music, sculpture, and poetry was a wholly natural one. The extent to which taste and intelligence in matters of art were characteristic of them may be appreciated in one direction if we realize how 20,000 people in the Theatre of Dionysus at Athens received and judged new plays by such writers as Æschylus or Sophocles. The various schools of sculpture, also, in Crete, Sparta, Selinus, Argos, Ægina, and Acarnania were only less remarkable than the Ionian ones at Samos, Chios, Melos, Paros, and Samothrace. Even Athenians preferred the Doric order for their Parthenon; and the Corinthian style, though somewhat overornate, is none the less a distinctive one. Plato, who was a connoisseur in these matters, preferred Dorian music to all other modes. In short, the life of the classical Greeks in all of the three chief races was an abounding one artistically and intellectually, even though the Athenians remained unsurpassed in their eventual achievements.

Again one must not think of the Hellenes as dreamers—men who required others to give them guidance in their everyday affairs. Such ideas are quickly dispelled by a study of their political history and institutions, their scientific agriculture and stock-raising, their ship-building. It was no group of over-enthusiastic dreamers who, in heroic devotion to their free institutions, by sheer military technique beat back the armies of Datis and Artaphernes! They were not "foolish geniuses," those men, women, and children, who rebuilt the old town walls, or constructed the long ones to the Piræus under Themistocles! The fact of the matter is that they were quite as "practical" as they were "theoretical," even when they assumed that action is best guided by intelligence. And this fact also helps explain why a "practical" philosophy was early in the field among the Greeks of the homeland.

Those who first undertook to apply theory to everyday affairs were called Sophists. They proposed to bring the most expert information to bear upon every trade and occupation. As early as the sixth century, when the development of democratic ideas was sharpening individual initiative and competition for all forms of success and prestige, these itinerant teachers were in great demand and had an excellent reputation. In Æschylus and Herodotus the Sophist is a master of his craft, a man wise in action, a "knower," a "lover of wisdom." And during the greater part of the fifth century, his learning remained in very general esteem. The number of those who aimed to further the cause of such education was extraordinary. Democritus, our Atomist, wrote handbooks on agriculture, on painting, and on military tactics. Hippodamus wrote on building and architecture. Simo brought philosophy to earth by applying his learning to horse-training. Sophocles wrote a handbook for the stage. The list could be almost indefinitely extended.

During the course of the fifth century, however, another type of Sophist arose, men who brought out very sharply the ever-familiar antithesis between those who cultivate theory for its own sake, and those who look to practical objects for which such learning can be made a tool. The latter of these became more and more dominant, as the true or characteristic Sophists, in Greek cities generally. They poured no small contempt on the inconsequential efforts of the cosmological speculators in our first "act." And their popularity is most strikingly attested, even toward the end of the century when Aristophanes, and other writers of comedy, so successfully entertained, and warned, Athenian audiences by pointing to the futilities and dangers of metaphysical inquiries. Thus Aristophanes' *Clouds* (produced in 423 B. C.) pillories Democritus by the line "Long live King Vortex, who has dethroned Zeus!" The same play has Socrates sit aloft in a basket where he may sniff the purer intelligence of air undefiled by earthly considerations.

Even at this time, however, the lines were not clearly drawn. Socrates was himself called a Sophist by many, and yet he detested the name more than that of barbarian. Where then did the lines of cleavage lie? In the first place, the Sophists, early and late, had no use for natural science, or mathematics, or any form of "speculation." They held it to be far more to the point for human beings to concern themselves with their own affairs and not to be troubled by what is beyond their reach. Hence the question, "What's the use?" became a very characteristic one. If no human advantage could possibly be derived from a study of evolution, or of atomic theories, why should one be bothered by them? Let these new-fangled philosophers (like the Milesians, Democritus, and now Anaxagoras in the very circle of Pericles) forego their pretensions to the invisible, the distant past, the silly *homoiomere* and the "music of the spheres"! Such idle projections are both useless and dangerous. If only they would turn their attention to things nearer at hand, they might still be redeemed. They could teach young men how to speak well in the law-courts and advance themselves in life. They might write books on grammar, rhetoric, *How to Get on in the World, Essentials of a Good Memory, How to Win a Case,* and other worthwhile subjects. If level-headed, practical men could only overhaul their "think-shops" they might even yet be made into good, useful citizens.

Now the characteristic Sophist of about 400 B. C., so persistently condemned by Plato, and later by Aristotle, was one who had learned this lesson. He professed a practical sort of philosophy which avoided the preposterously futile and contradictory imaginations of the physicists. Cannot any one see that atoms are an illusion, and evolution a metaphysician's dream? Who can believe that colors are motions? Or that Achilles can fail to overtake the tortoise? The pitfalls which such theories present from the standpoint of unsettling, even undermining, the ancient established faith of the fathers would also be avoided (not, however, by all Sophists as we shall presently see). A truly human philosophy need consider only the best interests of men. It will teach them how to get on with all sorts and conditions too. So well had the Sophist learned this lesson, according to Plato, that he had no need of definite convictions on any subject. He could make the worse appear the better reason. He was not necessarily a radical or a conservative; he could be either or both if he were sufficiently tactful. He was a vain pretender who, by good advertising of his royal roads to learning, had succeeded in the unworthy financial venture of extracting money from students. In this connection it must be recalled, that, except for the Sophists, many of whom amassed fortunes, the philosophers of Greece generally received no fees for their instruction.

If the type we have just described included all Sophists, we should not be justified in studying them here. Many there were, no doubt, of those who traded in these doubtful wares and found purchasers. The record tells of wealthy and unprincipled ones in abundance. But there were also mixed types. In fact they founded no "school" at all and had not even a common understanding, professionally speaking. Moreover, not a few of those who really belong to the "opposition," including Anaxagoras and Socrates, were condemned as Sophists. Under the circumstances we shall be more likely to do justice if we consider characteristic individuals and their positive contributions.

There was not only a superficial, but also a profoundly significant, aspect to this Humanistic movement which the Sophists did most to bring about. Many of them merited contempt as seekers of the main chance through such means as a little knowledge might supply. Others discredited more disinterested studies by their emphasis on the externally useful. A few were anarchists of what we should call the bomb-throwing type. Most of them were brilliant little schoolmasters who, while making a "successful career" externally, stimulated popular thought and imagination to an interest in debating, grammar, argumentation, memory-systems, legal technique, history, sociological and ethical problems. It is true that they made philosophy "bake bread" so far as that could be done. But their anthropocentric interest very strikingly brought out the "human equation" in our every undertaking, including knowledge. Clever wits might and did ridicule philosophy by pointing to Thales, who, star-gazing fell into a well, when a Thracian handmaiden might have told him to watch his step!

But there were also more important questions; for example: Does the *value* which human beings attach to their ideas of nature or themselves have anything to do with the "truth" or "falsity" of them? To challenge each and every theory as personal "opinion" and prepossession was a smart and easy attack upon science. But it also served to bring out the relationship of knowing to feeling and willing. Even those who claimed a hearing for every whim and caprice of judgment served to give point to the issue. Both they who professed to recognize no authority, bidding each man do that which was right in his own eyes, and those who proclaimed the sovereign authority of convention or custom, in this way helped more thoughtful citizens to reflect on the relation of the individual conscience to natural law and the prospects of a better human society.

Such questions, when they engaged more penetrating thinkers (including Socrates), led to conclusions no less important than the Atomic Theory or Evolution. They are still in the focus of interest in twentieth century thought. As we shall shortly see, the doctrine known as Pragmatism is a modern extension of the "better sort" of Sophistic.

2

The most significant thinker of the group was Protagoras of Abdera, a fellow-townsman of Democritus, born at approximately the same time, probably 481 B. C. The "Great Sophist" (as Plato calls him) must have had a varied and interesting life. In Athens, where he enjoyed the friendship of Pericles and Euripides, he was famous as an inspiring teacher. Plato's Dialogue *Protagoras* gives us a picture of what he meant to keen-minded young Athenians for whom the news, "Protagoras has come," was exciting enough to get them up before dawn to attend a lecture in the courtyard of his house. There they found the magnificent man already taking a walk in the cloister while "a train of listeners followed him; the greater part of them appeared to be foreigners, whom Protagoras had brought with him out of the various cities visited by him in his journeys, he, like Orpheus, attracting them with his voice and they following." Plato is exquisitely ironical of the exaggerated sense of form and dignity as well as the dilettantism of other Sophists who, superficially and *ex cathedra*, are discussing all manner of subjects. But he overshoots the mark somewhat, and our other sources of information show that Protagoras was a man of penetrating mind. In 443 B. C., when the Athenians founded the colony of Thurii in lower Italy, he was chosen to write the constitution and laws of that brilliant community. We know of twelve books written by him. One of them was on *Truth* or *The Throwers* and must have been an important work; another called *On the Gods* was the source of litigation and ultimately the cause of his death. He seems to have read the latter publicly one night at the house of Euripides, much to the scandal of a certain army officer, Pythadorus, who forthwith had him indicted for impiety. The public authorities, doubtless ready enough for heresy hunting in the distracting events of the Peloponnesian War, sustained the charge, confiscated and burnt all copies of the book which could be found. Protagoras himself escaped the net but was drowned by a shipwreck on his way to Sicily.

His teaching centers about the proposition, "Man is the measure of things; of things that are that they are; and of things that are not that they are not," [1] one of the most arresting statements in the history of human thought. Since man is made the center of the universe, the dictum may not inappropriately be called the corner stone of Humanism. In other words, the Knower himself determines the character of the universe. With each new experience of it he recreates it to that extent. My knowledge of a thing must necessarily be as *I* perceive it. Who or what I am, is, therefore, a prior question to what it is that I perceive. Reality revolves about

[1] Diogenes Laertius: *Lives and Opinions*, Protagoras, III.

my own mind which, as the Knower, is the center of the world.

The *homo mensura* doctrine first explicitly called attention to the fact that what we know is a product of our experience. Because I have eyes many things become related to my mind as they certainly should not if I were blind. Additional senses on the other hand would doubtless also enrich the content of my world. In what way this could happen, only new senses could show me. The same is true of whatever *meaning* is discovered in sense-perception. It clearly depends upon the kind of minds we possess. Not every one realizes the deeper significance even of simple "facts." To "know ourselves" is therefore to know the conditions of knowledge itself.

Protagoras here laid down the foundation principle upon which Idealism builds. Idealism, as a theory of knowledge, holds that we do not "get outside of ourselves" when we know. We have only something "going on inside," mental facts in whose light the whole world gets its character. "To be is to be perceived" is perhaps the briefest form in which it has ever been stated. Unless I somehow experience an object, it does not exist for me. . . . At first thought this scarcely seems in need of saying; but its self-evidence becomes less obvious when one goes on to draw the entirely logical inference: Then the existence of all things so far as we know depends upon minds to perceive them. If there were no minds, there would be—nothing. This is probably more than Protagoras meant to imply, but it serves to make more explicit the meaning of the second half of his proposition: "Man is the measure . . . of things that are not that they are not." It is the absence of any perception on our part which leads us to say, Nothing is there; the Being or not-Being of anything depends upon a man's mind.

"Who then is Man," one hastens to ask, "upon whom all things in heaven and earth depend?" Whereupon the Sophistic complication arises! For Protagoras undoubtedly meant the single, individual person. The world is as it appears to *me*. I can see by nobody else's eyes. Nobody else can use my mind. Each man really lives in a world of his own. To which some joker may have objected: "But suppose you collide with someone else in the dark, aren't you forced to grant the existence of 'something there' quite apart from the previous lack of perception?" Yet Protagoras might have replied: "None the less, all I know is the pain, the touch, the resistance to my muscles, perhaps the thud as heard, and my interpretation of these sensations. How could any one claim more?"

A doctrine which makes the *individual* man the only knower, and hence the measure of what is or what is not, is known as Solipsism. Protagoras as represented by Plato [2] was undoubtedly a Solipsist but not consistently so. Plato in his most facetious temper writes, "So the best of the joke is that he (Protagoras) acknowledges the truth of their opinion who believe his own opinion to be false; for he admits that the opinions of all men are true." Probably this is exaggeration, for in the same connection Protagoras is represented as holding by the most expert knowledge available—his own included—since "some were wise and excelled others." Possibly the inconsistency arose from the conviction that every man's opinion is true *as far as it goes*, being a product of more or less limited experience, but *as experience* never false. In that event Protagoras was tackling the problem of error: How can any perception as such be *false?*

However that may be, Solipsism, taken strictly, admits of no comparison of my experience with yours. For aught anybody knows, my own or that "of a pig or a dog-faced baboon" is as true as yours. Hence the logical upshot of Solipsism is Skepticism: Nobody can be said really to know in case of a difference of opinion. There being no com-

[2] In the *Theætetus*, Sec. 152 fol.

mon basis, no standard of comparison by which to measure the "truth products" of the various "doctors," it cannot be said that any one of them is right. And this is equivalent to saying that universal truth—correct knowledge which "forces" itself upon human minds—is impossible. Truth is indeed coming into being in various centers but only as it appeals to those individual minds. As Plutarch [3] put it long ago, "Nothing is such rather than such." And the quizzical aspect of the thing comes out when I profess to know this of other minds as well as of my own!

In Plato's opinion there were still other reasons why such cavalier Skepticism was severing the roots of knowledge. If Protagoras, following Heraclitus, applies the doctrine of eternal flux to the mind itself, it would hardly seem possible for him to be sure even of his own individual "measure" for a day, much less for a year! "Knowledge" is the particular impression of the particular moment. It need not "hold together." Such arguments are probably overstatements of Protagoras' position; but they show conclusively how the most thoroughgoing skeptic cannot be sure that he will remain one for very long!

Protagoras certainly raised these fundamental difficulties. But we know that he also held both individual and collective knowledge to be possible. His use of the word "measure" in the famous dictum shows this pretty conclusively. For in his day mathematicians and others were perplexed by the strange surds, or *incommensurable* quantities, with which it seemed impossible to deal. How amazing that we cannot measure by one unit the side and diagonal of a square, or the diameter and circumference of a circle! Does it mean that the mind is incapable of dealing with things? Protagoras' axiom, on the contrary, reasserts the possibility. Not things but minds are the measure. They set the conditions,

[3] *Adv. Col.* 4, 2. Cited in Ueberweg-Heinze, *Gesch. der Philos.* I, p. 111.

mark off the units, even determine the very existence of the objects themselves.

But even though one granted so much, another question would remain. Is it the mind *as a whole* or some particular "portion" which is the measure? Are imagination, feeling, preferences, pain, thought, and other aspects or parts of the mind equally good measures? The answer of Protagoras, as rather too briefly set forth by Plato,[4] is that our *senses* constitute this measure—a point of view which will be clearer if we bear in mind Parmenides' mathematical necessity of thought, or Democritus' argument for atoms, as a contrasting theory. Such reliance upon sensations was, again of course, striking at the roots of a great deal of scientific knowledge. Naïvely to take all our sense perceptions as measures of the qualities and reality of things would be not only to repudiate, for example, the Atomic Theory and mathematics, but to separate the various moments of sensations themselves, since they are so variable. But whether Protagoras did so or not, Plato argues against his choice of the least stable and most contradictory portion of experience, namely, sensation, for his measure. Perhaps we must make allowance again for the prevailing reputation of the Sophists in Plato's day.

What chiefly contributed to that reputation was, of course, the outcome of individualism in practice. If individual men are measures of truth, they, no less than cities and other groups, are judges of right and wrong. "General experience," or the "common opinion of mankind," need be no deterrent for the superman. In short, moral Skepticism, the denial of any natural or common standard of action, was an easy step from Solipsism. And with individual sensations as "measures," passing pleasures or pains would become the criterion of "good" or "value." Here again, however, we

[4] *Theætetus,* 156.

know that Protagoras was "not guilty." For he was an advocate of the standard or "conventions" set up by particular *states* rather than of the "laws" of particular individuals.[5]

From the book *On the Gods* we possess one tiny but significant fragment: "With regard to the gods, I cannot feel sure either that they are or that they are not, or to what they are like in figure; for there are many things that hinder sure knowledge, the obscurity of the subject and the shortness of human life."[6] This frank statement is interesting not only as a religious confession but as reflecting an honorable open-mindedness. Its suspension of judgment clearly implies some common criterion of knowledge. If (as seems to have been the case) he also found no evidence in sensation for the existence of souls, he not only limited his knowledge to sense experience, but took a negative attitude toward other sources of insight. For that reason he has been called the first radical Empiricist—the one who first consciously professed the language of "facts and facts only." Yet, like some others who have followed in his footsteps, he seems also to have recognized that all facts are ultimately "men's measures." Perhaps the very difficulty of combining this Empiricism with the relativities of the *homo mensura* doctrine was one reason for the great success which Protagoras had in awakening the minds of his pupils. For new problems and difficulties stimulate to more comprehensive efforts, and his were more than enigmatic sophistries. They were strategic issues which still challenge our intelligence.

3

In order to illustrate other aspects of the Sophistic movement by personal examples, we shall briefly pass in review several other characteristic figures.

[5] *Theætetus,* 167c.
[6] Diogenes Laertius: *Lives and Opinions,* Protagoras, III.

Hippias, a contemporary of Protagoras, seems to have professed no end of knowledge, which he was also willing to impart for a competence. But, somewhat modernly, he depended upon advertising. On one occasion he appeared at the Olympic games for an ocular demonstration. He announced that his garment had been spun and woven, his sandals cobbled, his hat designed, his ring molded, by himself. As to psychological offerings he cited his memory-system which he "demonstrated" by repeating, after a single hearing, fifty nonsense syllables in the order in which they had been given. He also distinguished himself as rhetor, or "public orator." As to the *content* of his thought we have the sentence imputed to him by Plato, "Law is the tyrant of men."

Prodicus, another contemporary, was chiefly a teacher of Sophistic ethics. The famous allegory of Hercules at the Parting of the Ways is attributed to him. The two forked roads, are, of course, virtue and temporary pleasures. Yet the hero is promised possessions and other financial advantages if he chooses the path of virtue, so that still another "useful" aspect of knowledge is proclaimed. Prodicus was also the first conscious pessimist: he taught that the evils of life greatly outweigh its benefits. Death is therefore a Friend and not to be feared. He never vexes the wise either among the living or the dead.

Other Sophists argued after the fashion of supermen, that might is right (Callicles [7]) and that the tyrant, who is the happiest of men, should allow his desires to grow to the uttermost (Thrasymachus [8]). Critias maintained that religion is a happy invention of statesmen to insure obedience to their rule.[9] Some tried to make out that every opinion, or piece of "knowledge," is a policy, a convenience, an in-

[7] Plato's *Gorgias,* 483–492.
[8] Plato's *Republic,* I, 338, fol.
[9] Plato's *Laws,* X, 889.

strument for the advantage of a person or a party.[10] Ideals of common law, of action, or of excellence of any sort are inventions having no further warrant than human desire or consent. Such tendencies help explain the negative attitude of Socrates, Plato and Aristotle toward Sophistic.

4

A longer account must be given of Gorgias, who, along with Protagoras, made a distinct contribution to the theory of knowledge. He was a pupil of Empedocles and we hear of his coming to Athens in 427 B. C. as the ambassador of his home town, Leontini in Sicily. He was then past middle life, but must be considered as belonging to a later generation than Protagoras, since, like Nestor, with whom Plato compares him, he saw three generations of men and lived until approximately 375 B. C. His teaching may be described as absolute Skepticism, or the doctrine that it is impossible to know anything with certainty. This was, of course, the logical conclusion from the teaching of Protagoras that the "measures" of all men are "true." With such a presupposition there seems to be, indeed, no possibility of error. But, without error, truth has no distinction, no mark of identification. The Skepticism of Gorgias, however, is based upon the question of exact communication. Suppose you or I were in possession of some knowledge, how could either of us *communicate* it to another person? We have no guaranties that the sense perceptions of two people are identical or even similar when they look at some "red" object. How then compare them as "true" experiences? The same is true of concepts, or words. With their constant flux and many shades of meaning, in all sorts of contexts, with each man's peculiar use of them, how can one suppose that any proposition means identically the same thing for any two

[10] Aristotle's *Politics,* 110.

people? . . . But even supposing this difficulty did not exist, we are confronted by the fact that a man's mind "measures" not only what is real but what is unreal. We think of chariots on the sea as well as on the land. We say the vacuum *is*. In dealing with anything imaginable we say: it *is*. Now if language were a reliable means of getting at the truth, we should not be compelled to say What is *not*, *is*. In short, we cannot distinguish between what is and what is not. Therefore *Nothing is*.

This is dramatically summarized by Gorgias [11] in three propositions:

1. Nothing exists.

2. But supposing something to exist, it could not be known.

3. Even supposing a thing to exist and to be knowable, knowledge of it could not be communicated.

Such arguments, in so far as they are based upon linguistic facts, are hardly adequate to support Nihilism, the skeptical denial of all knowledge of what is real or unreal. But, even as such, they helped to foster a critical examination of our "meanings" and to show, how much more than we generally suppose, our pictures of the world are of our own creation. In Heraclitean terms the arguments are still modern. With minds that change like the "stream" of outside "things," can we be sure of anything but a *process?* Heraclitus saved himself from such Nihilism by his theory of a great, permanent World Energy or *Logos*, which *exists* even though we pass on, and which *knows* even though we have but passing and private wisdom. But supposing one asks: How did Heraclitus with his passing and private wisdom find that out? the problem becomes less simple. Once more we realize with Parmenides that the central problem of science and philosophy is to discover *that which permanently is*. And to this day, it must be confessed, we have had

[11] Reported in Sextus Empiricus, *Adversus Mathematicos,* VII, 65.

no little difficulty in distinguishing what really *is* from what appears to be or is *not*. Even in the crucial case of matter whose qualities we usually take to be "there," and which most people regard as really existing in the way that we perceive them, the modern physicist has mostly denials. Hardness, color, taste, weight, and even the extension, or mass, of physical bodies are in reality states or activities of invisible points of force, little charges of electricity, incessantly in motion. Even they who are tempted to hold to atoms as permanent realities are met by another denial. Individually atoms give and take electrons and modify their "qualities" by new arrangements. Only their *sum-total* can be said to exist permanently! And the psychologist faces the same question with mental "states" and "actions." Individually they pass. In what sense, then, can they be said to exist? . . . So much, not by way of additional arguments for Nihilism but to illustrate the bearings of the theory. The absolute Skepticism of Gorgias cannot in fact be so much as stated without refuting itself. It professes a real piece of knowledge in the very effort to repudiate knowledge. Even the relativities and flux of words, or meanings, cannot be discovered except by some standard of comparison. Absolute Skepticism imposes perfect silence.

5

In general, however, the Sophists, even by negative studies of language and meanings, were doing an important service, despite their sophistical and sometimes anarchistic conclusions. Putting men at the center of knowledge involved all the dangers of liberty. The field was opened to any opinion, any caprice of temperament. The sciences, whose progress depends upon painstaking observation and the collaboration of many minds in common understanding, were effectively thwarted. Not until Aristotle's day did natural science return to its sphere as a fundamental basis of knowledge. Energy which might have been put into investigation was dissipated into "methods" of investigation. An almost exclusive study of the machinery of knowledge prevented the use of the machine itself. It was like the self-consciousness which stands in the way of effective action. And for all its emphasis upon the "practical" as "working" toward certain advantages, it thwarted the truly practical purpose of knowledge which, after all, is to know.

Yet the discovery of the *subject* as the creator of knowledge and arbiter of action was a great one, however dangerous it proved to be. The individual conscience, now seen to be the ultimate "measure" of action, could also exploit the superman. It might, and did, question all values. But to have the question of values raised was important if progress was to be made toward deeper insights. It was unfortunate that the value of knowledge was interpreted in terms of external benefits, including trade advantages and physical or social well-being. This left out of account the more essentially human interests, the higher values, of disinterested knowledge. Surely the heroic efforts of speculative scientists toward a comprehensive interpretation of our world are more genuinely "human" than the "applied" knowledge of a recipe-inventor, though he make a million thereby. Emphasis upon the useful, the workable, the practical, in ancient Humanism thus *dehumanized* knowledge in so far as it failed to include intellectual insights and interpretations among the measures of a man's mind.

One could hardly find a better means of estimating modern Sophistic than an objective study of the Greek Sophists. The later-day movement is variously known as Humanism, Pragmatism, and Instrumentalism,[12] and, like its ancient prototype, it has many aspects or varieties. Those which in-

[12] The names preferred respectively by its three chief sponsors, F. C. S. Schiller, William James, and John Dewey.

terest us here are the common roots. And among these the chief one is the doctrine that knowledge must serve a purpose other than knowing. It must be useful, must work as an instrument to attain some non-intellectual value or purpose. "Intellectualism," merely understanding or trying to understand for its own sake, is "otiose," an unjustifiable expenditure of human resources. Metaphysics in general, because it leads to no "practical consequences," is a futile undertaking. Only where the problem makes a "difference" in men's living (as contrasted with their thinking), is it worth attention. Most problems simply "evaporate" under this acid test. The measure of good philosophy and touchstone of truth must be answers to the questions: How are men benefited by the doctrine? How will the theory affect their conduct? For thinking is merely a stage in the business of living, it is not a "survey" or an interpretation of our world, but a means of helping us find our way about, or of rectifying human ills. Its verification process is the practical one of measuring "fruits," "profit," and "cash rather than credit." As ancient Sophistic abandoned natural science, so modern Pragmatism would forego all problems which have no immediate relevancy, no value in "adjusting life to forward-moving action."

Clearly the *homo mensura* theory is still a doctrine to be reckoned with! In Protagoras, though not in Hippias or Callicles, the measure was still an intellectual one. But in modern Humanism, *homo* has become so perfectly the center of the universe that his sensations, "satisfactions," sentiments and "demands," not merely reflect, but actually "create," the character of that universe. Real knowledge makes an actual difference in the course of the stars. Man "demands" a certain kind of world—and gets it. The modern pragmatic demand is said to be "biological" rather than "intellectual." That is to say, if mathematical reasoning derives certain conclusions about matter, or the intellect concludes that God has ethical character, the supposed "truth" remains unverified until it has been practically tried out in the "business of living." Only as such "leadings," or "cues," can be acted upon by humans, and discovered to be beneficial biologically, can they be called true. In this way modern Humanism recognizes the rights of temperaments, as well as of practical advantages in the measure of "truth," and, with Protagoras, ignores the difficulties of Solipsism and Skepticism growing out of the indefinite variety of personal measures. One of its exponents has recognized the truth both of the geocentric and of the heliocentric astronomy. Another has proposed to demonstrate logically the negative of any proposition which may be set up. Somewhat as Protagoras is said to have recognized the truth of those who asserted his own doctrine to be false so modern Sophists profess to recognize "Intellectualism," even the "impersonal logical machine," when it is convenient to do so. The end justifies the means. Many people are too timorous in the construction of "frame-ups" which might bring them real advantages. The supposed controls of external nature have blinded men to the possibility of adventure in the "physical adjustment of forward moving action." Even the supposedly fanciful "demands" of traditional theology can be made to do service as creators of our world, when we fashion it more nearly to the heart's desire, and thus insure a "continued functioning of the organism." Presumably when all organisms function most continuously we shall be in possession of most truth.

Perhaps it is still more important to note that, in modern as in ancient days, Sophistic is a "method," a famous introductory chapter. The sequel, in the form of its own "fruits," "workings," biological and social advantages, remains "unverified," and even unspecified. When, measured by the demand for "cash" or valuable results which the method makes, its own promises are not even speculative "futures." We do not know whether the biological benefits by which a true interpretation is verified include an improved circulation and emotional stability, or whether a new "physical adjustment of forward moving action," for example, the cure of a heart disease or rheumatism, has particular kinds of theories to verify—other than the medical ones. In short, the utilitarian assumptions of the method, the demand for external usefulness, thwarts and demoralizes the cause of science and philosophy, to-day as in antiquity. And the reason is not far to seek. Philosophy by its very nature is disinterested, and, whatever the benefits of its pursuit may be, it has no ax to grind. Whoever seeks to make it a tool, a means to an end, transforms it into something else, and foregoes its "practical" benefits as well. Fortunately for the cause of knowledge, Socrates, Plato, and Aristotle, realizing both the human character of knowledge and the claims of Intellectualism, saved the day and vastly extended the work of disinterested intelligence.

CHAPTER X

SOCRATES

The personal influence of Socrates upon the development of occidental thought has been well-nigh incredible. One must say personal influence because he left no writings; we know of him only through his disciples. And this seems all the more surprising when one realizes how far from the Greek ideal the personality of Socrates was. He might almost be regarded as an ancient prototype of street and market-place evangelist, one who regarded himself as divinely ordained to confound the wisdom of men and to teach them the ways of righteousness. And he did this less by positive construction than by conviction of ignorance, an ignorance in which he professed to share. In a beauty-loving and fastidious city he embraced a care-free poverty, and flaunted public opinion by going barefoot and shirtless. Though his father, Sophroniscus, was a sculptor, and he himself was apprenticed to that art, he seems to have had slight sense of form, and to have esteemed the arts in general chiefly because of their external usefulness or for their moral lessons. In his person there was little to suggest the "never overmuch," so important a demand in Hellenic feeling. He was repulsive in features, thick-set, snub-nosed, with protruding eyes, a Satyr or Silenus in body, as one of his warmest friends (Alcibiades) informs us.

Yet Plato's *Dialogues* and Xenophon's *Memorabilia*, the two chief sources of our knowledge, are full of superlative praise for the "best, most just, and wisest of men," one whose spirit was a source of light and liberality. His moral fervor, his temperance in food and wine and every other physical pleasure, his capacity for going without, his tact and charm of manner, his mastery of language and penetration of thought even when professing ignorance, his bravery on the field of battle are many times extolled. He seems to have gained attention on street corners from old and young, from friend and foe, not only to questions of every day right and wrong and politics, but to the more abstruse problems of psychology and theory of knowledge. Spontaneously such groups seem to have become common seekers for whatever he had a mind to suggest, so much was he a genius at adapting himself to all sorts and conditions of men. Unsuspected he taught them, the genial charm of his humorous self-depreciation usually disarming criticism and giving him personal ascendancy over his foes. Thus he would playfully claim to be the handsomest man among the handsome, or, since he was aware of his ignorance, the wisest among the wise. On occasion he could adapt himself to Sophists, beating them even at their own game of making the worse appear the better reason.

Whatever the secret of such influence, a power which made the most exaggerated eccentricity serve his purpose, it is a matter of history that Socrates was the acknowledged master of all who founded schools of philosophy during his lifetime or in the years immediately following. Cynicism, Cyrenaic Hedonism, the School of Megara, Platonic Idealism —all grew out of his teaching. And through Plato, Aristotle, and the Stoics he has influenced the practical, i. e., ethical and theological course of men's thinking ever since. Justin Martyr, one of the Church Fathers (fl. 150 A. D.) called him "a Christian before the coming of Christ," so similar are many of his ideas to those set forth in the Gospels.

The course of his life (469–399 B. C.) was spent almost entirely at Athens. Far from being a "traveler in the interest of theory," he preferred death to banishment from his unique city and confessed that he was bored in the country. He seems to have been absent from Athens chiefly to consult an oracle or to fight in the campaigns at Potidæa, Delium, and Amphipolis. He enjoyed the usual education of his day, which emphasized athletics, a knowledge of the arts, especially poetry, and mathematics. He also had abundant opportunity to hear the Sophists and other independent teachers, and we are told that in youth he familiarized himself with the extant science of his day, having been particularly interested in astronomy. One of the pleasing pictures which Plato gives of this period shows us the logically inept young Socrates measuring his strength with the aged and kindly Parmenides. Of his work as a sculptor we know little beyond the attribution of work to him by Diogenes Laertius [1] and the description of such a piece by Pausanius in his *Description of Greece.* This in his day (*cir.* 150 A. D.) stood at the entrance to the Acropolis and represented the three Graces. We may assume, however, that the heart of Socrates was not in sculpture. If the Chiaramonti Graces now in Rome are copies of Socrates' work (as some archæologists hold) we can understand why the philosopher gave up this art.[2]

His early self-dedication to philosophy is connected by Plato with a visit to the oracle at Delphi, on which occasion the inspired priestess is said to have proclaimed Socrates the wisest of men because he knew his ignorance. The desire to test this saying, if he could, led him to measure the knowledge of politicians, Sophists and artists, by questioning them concerning the theory of their work. From the beginning to the end of his public career he regarded these conversations as divine commands and seriously tried to make them contribute to the intellectual and moral improvement of all with whom he came into contact. Why, then, did he volun-

[1] *Lives and Opinions,* Socrates IV.

[2] See Frazier's ed. of *Pausanius,* Vol. II, pp. 268–272.

tarily embrace poverty when he became a teacher? Doubtless that he might be completely independent of fees and free to discuss any subject disinterestedly. So simple was his external manner of life that a Sophist is reported in the *Memorabilia* to have said: "A slave whose master compelled him to live as you do would run away." We may assume that this was sufficiently perplexing to his wife, Xanthippe, and their children; but contemporary writers show little sympathy for her, and she still serves in many literatures as the classic type of shrew. Perhaps the mission of the God presented issues for the husband's mind too great to exchange for household problems. Be that as it may, the picture of Xanthippe suddenly drenching Socrates with a basin of cold water to cut short his meditations, or of his indulging in solo-dancing at home in order to get concentrated exercise, illustrate the predicaments of resolutely philosophical temperaments.

Whatever important action Socrates undertook was, in his belief, made clear for him by the guidance of an inner voice, attendant spirit, or daimonion, which, he maintained, invariably gave him authoritative advice what not to do on important occasions (Plato), or both what to seek and what to avoid (Xenophon). This belief, so similar to the early Christian and mediæval conception of conscience, formed the basis for one of the charges brought against him at his trial. "To have introduced strange divinities" is an indictment whimsically unique in the liberal history of Athens, and can hardly have been the count on which the jury by a vote either of 253 to 247 or of 280 to 220 pronounced him a public malefactor. It is true that with all his respect for traditional piety and ritual, there was in Socrates no little heterodoxy. He did not favor long advisory prayers, and recommended simply a "Thy will be done." His conception of Deity is in many respects identical with the Christian idea of Providence. The Supreme Being as intelligent and beneficent Creator of the universe, everywhere manifested in the wise adaptations of nature, could not act as did the jealous, petty and immoral gods of the Homeric story. A being so powerful and so knowing could not be inferior to man in moral insight and purpose. But in the light of all that we know concerning this period of history, it is inconceivable that, for such conceptions as these or for his guiding inner voice, an Athenian jury would have condemned him to death in the fourth century B. C.

It is more likely that he died a victim of politics. In the unsettled times which followed the close of the Peloponnesian War it was natural to look for scapegoats among radical leaders of thought especially if they had had any relationships with blundering generals, and autocratic, dissolute or atheistic leaders. Socrates was undoubtedly a radical innovator, and some of his followers and pupils figured later as tyrants (Critias), or even as traitors to their country (Xenoption). He opposed the old system of education with its established traditions and tried to introduce one in which the critical examination of all ideas and institutions was fostered. By fearless questioning he tried to discover the fundamental axioms of his pupils and then got them to draw independent conclusions if he could. This he conceived to be the object of the whole process of education. Such a point of view exposed him, of course, to public attacks from men who, like Aristophanes in his *Clouds*, were very much concerned to see the good old order maintained. Along with Protagoras he was an easy mark for politicians who recognized individualism as the root of anarchy. But however persistently he maintained that a man can act morally only in so far as he attains insight, and warmly as he commended open-mindedness on every subject, he was far from being a Protagorean Sophist or a Skeptic. On the contrary he was convinced that by the collective efforts of thinking, and especially by what he called dialectic, men progressively reach more complete knowledge, much of which, especially knowledge of right and wrong, is already on firm foundation. He attacked, it is true, the science of his day which, because of its inconsistencies, he regarded as made up of more or less improbable conclusions. But he also maintained both that truth must be sought by coördinated effort as a community purpose, and that distinction must be made as between those who are, and those who are not, in a position to understand. The work of the educator is, therefore, to elicit a choice of judgments most in conformity with the individual learner's insight and at the same time in agreement with the general body of accepted knowledge. The freedom of such a questioning process is generally dangerous, however, because it seems to assume that everything is open to question. It becomes not only ridiculous to men like Aristophanes, who imagined Socrates going up in a basket to pursue his questions among the clouds; it very easily assumes the form of treason or impiety when the state or the gods are under discussion. The Socratic method always makes for a certain number of atheists, anarchists, philosophical skeptics, and moral libertines. In his day it undoubtedly helped to produce the profligate Alcibiades, the atheistic Critias, and Antiphon, leader of the four hundred oligarchs.

It was no wonder, therefore, that Socrates incurred the hatred of conservatives who clung to the established faith, the good old times, the traditional interpretations of Homer and Hesiod. Oddly enough the accusers were: a forgotten poet, Meletus, who is said to have been offended because Socrates questioned his rules of poetry; Anytus, a wealthy business man, whose son the philosopher had advised to get a higher education; and Lykon, who "opposed Sophists on general principles." But many liberal politicians were also opposed to him, and, it would seem, for the opposite reason. Socrates consistently maintained that affairs of state could not be managed by everybody but called for special knowledge, expert training, and good standing in the city. This doctrine, to certain "democratic leaders" for whom "all men are equal" and none superior in value, was a blow at democracy itself. Such men regarded his attacks upon the choice of officials by lot (which then obtained in Athens) as reactionary, even dangerous to the republic. Very likely he drew upon himself the hatred of many an unnamed man from the lower strata of society by his proposed qualifications for voters.

It was not so much Socrates the heretic, "introducing strange divinities," as Socrates the bringer of a new ideal of education and culture, the radical political reformer, who was condemned by the dicasts. The incalculable good effected by his life work was overlooked in the discovery of a certain amount of evil. The most precious things are often the most dangerous, the greatest good is strangely near to evil. In ancient and in modern day the liberator is charged with license; the teacher of an exalted morality, with disobedience to established social habits. And yet, even on the final day of his trial, it is likely that Socrates might have got off easily had he shown more deference to the court. When, after the initial vote, a small majority had found him guilty and he was asked what punishment he himself thought suitable, instead of showing submissiveness or attempting to placate the jury, he boldly claimed that his services to the state might well be rewarded by a pension—maintenance at the Prytaneum for the few remaining years of his life. Instead of suggesting banishment or some milder punishment, he declared that only death could banish him from his beloved city whose institutions he had indeed questioned, but whose laws he had never willingly disobeyed, and that he could not change the manner of his life without being disobedient to God. The jury, now more hostile than ever by this sublime independence, thereupon voted the penalty of death. But even this sentence failed to perturb him.

Calmly he warned those who voted against him that "the difficulty is, not to escape death, but rather to escape wickedness." He, a slow runner in old age, had been overtaken by death, but they even in youth had been outrun by wickedness. To his friends on the jury he explained that death is a blessing, whether the alternative be a night of perfect sleep or a journey and a recognition. In the latter event he would have new opportunities for dialectic and conversations with the heroes of old, but, even should death mean forgetfulness, the providence of God would be good. The thirty days intervening between the trial and the execution of the sentence (owing to the absence of the sacred ship at Delos) were unperturbed and cheerful. The discussion of subjects important to him in life was continued. All efforts to make his escape easy were frowned upon. He would continue to obey the laws of his native city. When finally inch by inch the hemlock benumbed his limbs, he described the experience for his friends.

What were the philosophical contributions by which Socrates became significant in the course of human thought? Strange to say, these are very uncertainly known because so closely interwoven with the philosophy of his pupils, notably that of Plato. One cannot with complete assurance say that a speech of Socrates in any given *Dialogue* is an unelaborated report of his point of view. Certain doctrines are definitely ascribed to him by Aristotle; Xenophon, who was in no sense a constructive thinker himself, imputes others; but Plato, the creative artist, though he certainly built upon Pythagorean and Socratic foundations, cannot be regarded as historian of their thought. Perhaps the safest and at the same time most nearly just method (though there is much admirable scholarship to the contrary) is to credit Plato with his written contributions except where he, or some other credible witness, definitely ascribes a doctrine to other sources.

Aristotle[3] would have Socrates honored for two things: first, his inductive method, and second, for having fixed thought for the first time on definitions. That there are definite meanings, or concepts, and that they remain constant for the purposes of common discussion, not being subject to time or the caprices of individual quibblers, is the initial assumption of the Socratic dialectic. This postulate he urged as against Sophists like Gorgias, who, as we have seen, denied the possibility of meaning the same thing in two different contexts, or that two individuals with necessarily different backgrounds of experience could mean the same thing by the same word. Many a delightful passage in Plato shows him eliciting the various meanings of Sophistic amphibolies and putting their impossible logic to the alternative either of silence or of definite concepts consistently used. To some of us this may seem an extremely simple or even self-evident matter; but there is point in it even to-day as against the modern disciples of Protagoras who look to a future logic in which definition and determinate concepts will apparently be no longer necessary.

The inductive procedure which Aristotle attributed to Socrates is not what is now generally understood by induction, e. g., the inferring of general conclusions from particular facts or supposedly objective evidence. To contrast these two conceptions of induction one might compare the conclusion reached by a scientist after working with his reagents, with that of a religious thinker, who, after examining a number of men's minds and finding them in agreement, also reached a certain conclusion. Of course the Socratic dialectic could not help ultimately referring to objective facts, but it was primarily interested in discovering what intelligent men commonly and consistently believed to be the facts and why. Conversely it may be observed that the modern inductive procedure also looks to a confirmation in other men's

[3] *Metaphysics,* XIII, 1078b 30.

judgment. But it must be confessed that the influence of a purely dialectical method has sometimes militated against the progress of both science and philosophy.

There are good reasons for supposing [4] that the doctrine, usually ascribed to Plato, which maintains that eternal archetypes, *Forms*, or *Ideas* are active as causes in the being and operation of all nature, was already more or less explicit in the teaching of Socrates. His efforts in the direction of definition are by Aristotle characterized as "seeking the universal in ethical matters" which Aristotle also regarded as an extension of the Pythagorean quest for "*Forms*." [5] The same author, however, expressly differentiates between Plato and Socrates by saying that the former "accepted his (Socrates') teaching (concerning universals, definition, *Forms*) but held that the problem applied not to any sensible thing but to entities of another kind, i. e., something not subject to the Heraclitean flux.[6] This certainly implies that the Platonic interpretation of the *Forms* was not only more elaborate but in an important sense different from the Socratic. On the other hand, Plato in his *Phaedo* intimates that the theory of *Forms* was long familiar to his great master. So that in the absence of more specific data we can only say that this thought-revolutionizing hypothesis of cosmic *Ideas* was developed through a series of indefinite steps from Pythagoras through Socrates to its classic elaboration in Plato.

A general proposition which can with assurance be attributed to Socrates is the doctrine that theory and practice are one and indissoluble. Ethically this means that knowledge of the right is not only a prerequisite of moral effort; it is the very act of doing the right. This seems to assume that "pure theory" dissociated from the character of men is impossible, and that thought processes (as distinguished from

[4] See Burnet: *Greek Philosophy,* Vol. I, p. 154, fol.

[5] *Metaphysics* XIII, 1078b 18.

[6] *Ibid.* I, 987b 4.

emotions) are the determinants of men's wills. It also implies that the choice of good in preference to evil is natural to men and in accord with the general course of nature. Intelligent men naturally choose that which makes for their happiness; and happiness is human good. "What man willingly is wretched or against his will is blest?" To be immoral is, therefore, to be ignorant. If men only knew the good there would no longer be any evil.

This remarkable doctrine, which seems to find no place for the divided self, or the sin which holds us despite our better judgment ("The evil that I would not, that I do!"), shows the character of Socrates to have been one of singular integrity, or inner unity. He would clearly have been baffled by our modern divisions against ourselves. For him selfhood implied unity and could have brooked no Sunday belief or practice which on Monday was discredited or abandoned. Nor could he conceive how anyone who really intended to do a thing could fail to undertake it. The fact must have been that he never so intended; that he never really believed. Thus integrity was made the heart of morality just as self-consistency was regarded as the test of knowledge. The truth even of many minds, if it be genuine, can never be a house divided against itself. A man's idea of right and good cannot fail to be expressed in his action. Evil is therefore merely ignorance.

Such interpretations seem to imply that the normal course of nature makes for human good, integrity and happiness. And this is exactly Socrates' doctrine. He assumed that everything is teleologically, that is, purposively, intelligently, arranged. The scheme of the universe presents not only a coördinate whole; it is anthropocentric in being an order which makes for the good of man. To support this view he did not appeal to inductive evidence from the external world. He was convinced that the special sciences would never provide such evidence, and preferred to rest his case (as has many a religious mind since) upon reasoned arguments starting with assumed axioms, intuitions, inner satisfactions, the requirements of our moral natures, or the consent of past tradition. And conversely he assumed that whatever provides satisfaction (happiness) is true knowledge.

The end or final purpose of the universe being man, and man's happiness his highest good, it is no small matter to know what is understood by happiness. But on this point, despite the fact that Socrates professed to concern himself with human affairs rather than with external things and urged self-knowledge as the beginning of practical wisdom, he gives us very little that is specific. The man of insight will realize that just thought and action will always bring useful results. So too will bravery, piety, temperance; all are mensurable by their usefulness, not necessarily in relation to external gain but for lasting and intense satisfaction of the mind. And not only the good but what we call the beautiful constitute one common class. With this in mind we can easily understand how it was possible for Socrates to declare that a dung basket which fulfills its purpose is more beautiful than an unserviceable shield of gold, and also why he insisted that every genuine work of beauty must have its more or less obvious moral lesson. Physical pleasure he seems at times to have identified with mental pleasure, and to have made that of self the prior consideration. Yet the richness of such pleasures seems also to have been limited by the dictum that he is most godlike whose needs are smallest. Whether this refers to physical needs and satisfactions or to mental ones as well is not always clear. But very certainly Socrates esteemed the expanding and refining of moral insight as the greatest human satisfaction. For purely intellectual or æsthetic needs he had little more sympathy than for mere gratification by what wealth might provide. And the reason seems to have been that all of these fail to make for the happiness of moral insight. Friendship, concerning which we have in reported speeches of Socrates some of the most beautiful accounts in existence, is declared to be the mutual effort of good men to attain ethical improvement. The standard of criticism by which states, professions, industries, arts, and the means of education are to be judged is the answer to the question: What measure of fitness have they as contributing to the welfare (happiness, moral improvement) of mankind? Since by intellect alone this practical end can be understood and carried out, it follows that moral experts, and not mere politicians with their "policies," should be the rulers chosen by a society. Although Socrates had faith in democracy he founded his hopes on aristocratic leadership.

Summarizing, we may characterize the first martyr to philosophy as a thoroughgoing Optimist who believed that the only hindrance to man's complete happiness is ignorance. He was a Eudæmonist in maintaining that happiness is the sure result of virtue, and a partial Utilitarian in regarding usefulness sometimes toward the gaining of physical pleasure as the criterion of what is good. In as much as he made reason rather than emotion the arbiter of our choices he must be called an Intellectualist—wisdom, insight, understanding, being the common center of the virtues. His anthropocentric teleology was supported by geocentric astronomy, and he was content to reason with considerable independence of science, whether that of Anaximander, Pythagoras, or Democritus. It may be said that he universalized the Humanism of the Sophists by projecting a common measure to take the place of the individual one of Protagoras; but he omitted some of the most significant evidence when he took a negative attitude toward the natural philosophers, an attitude which seriously limited even his own inductive method. With all his opposition to the Sophists he remained a "practical" thinker—one who was inclined to regard the influence of any theory upon human good as the criterion of its importance. With modern Pragmatists he was disposed to regard the advantageous aspect of a theory as one measure of its truth. A Naturalism which conceived the world to be independent of human concerns, a physical, mathematical, self-sustaining mechanism, was for him ethically evil and hence anathema. The intuition of his inner voice counted for him more than external sense-perception, a doctrine which we shall find strongly emphasized in Plato. In his communion with a Spirit unseen, and, in general theistically conceived, he sought to realize one important aspect of the Mystic's doctrine. If he was properly called a "Christian before Christ" because of his conceptions of God, he was not one in respect to the ethics of forgiveness, vicarious pain, or self-sacrifice. He believed in a hearty hatred of enemies, in expecting no better reward than you deserve, in a consciousness of personal worth and in duty to one's self. But we can safely say that he was no Egoist, despite the fact that we have no very definite discussion by him of the problem of collective, versus individual, norms of action. He accepted the institution of slavery and not, so far as we know, because it made for the slave's happiness. But he anticipated a higher status for women, and vigorously fought class distinctions based upon manual labor. Values were for him in his own sense of the word inevitably moral, and for that reason not only was "art for art's sake" for him unintelligible, every piece of art must be finally judged from the standpoint of its being a handmaiden of morality. Thus he was throughout the serious, though genial, and even in death [7] jocularly ethical philosopher who saw his world in terms of human good.

[7] His last words were: "Crito, I owe a cock to Asclepius; will you remember to pay the debt?" *Phædo,* 118.

CHAPTER XI

THE FOLLOWERS OF SOCRATES

1

The wealth of Socrates' teaching was itself a source of misunderstanding. He who brings much may indeed bring something for many. But the character of the gift is often determined by the recipient. And just as the jurors at his trial interpreted the man in terms of his pride, not realizing his equally fundamental humility, so lesser minds among his pupils adopted more or less subordinate doctrines and made them central or even exaggerated them in the schools which they set up under inspiration of his example.

One of our most remarkable of these pupils was Aristippus (*cir.* 435–360) who while still a young man, attracted by the fame of Socrates, came over from his pleasure-loving Cyrene, a city on the high terraces of the African shore, to study at Athens. What impressed the sanguine Aristippus and probably confirmed his natural bent was the Socratic joy of life. Socrates was then past middle age but one for whom living seemed ever a feast and worry non-existent. What greater good than such a life as his, full-vibrant to the wealth of agreeable stimulus, alert in every sense! A glad welcome then to the warm sun, to colors, fruits and wines, and the normal functioning of our appetites! Sensations are the basis for vividness of life. There are other sources of agreeable feelings, but wisdom bids us seek first the keener, physical pleasures.[1]

And so with Aristippus came the first conscious Hedonism, the doctrine which maintains that pleasure provides a norm

[1] Diogenes Laertius: *Lives and Opinions.* Aristippus, VIII.

by which to judge the value of life or of any particular act and experience. How much satisfaction of eye and ear, and taste and motion—this is the question for one who is truly alive! At his home in Cyrene, where the disciple set up his school, he taught that of pleasures there could never be a surfeit, that not one could be regarded as evil, that all indeed are of one kind, the only differences being that the pleasures of the body are more fundamental. Pleasures of art, memory, friendship—these are good but less intense. Yet this frank embrace of every agreeable experience did not blind the cultivated Aristippus to the necessity of estimating for a lifetime and not merely for the passing moment. Physical pleasure is indeed of the present; but there are different after-effects, intensities, and purities of pleasure. He would be a fool who plunged into every agreeable stimulus without a look before and after. Their proper measurement then is the art of living, and he who gets most in the long run has the fullest existence.

But sensations are more than a primary source of agreeable feeling. They are for Aristippus our one source of truth. We cannot reach beyond the stimulus; that to which a sensation refers or what the source of the various stimuli might be, we have no means of finding out. It is therefore impossible to discover truth by reason or find any satisfaction outside of sensations and their memories. Thus for a double reason the cause of science and philosophy had slight interest for the "practical" teacher. For him the purpose of science was to direct men in the satisfaction of their wants. And because each man can rely only upon his own sensations, he must be a judge unto himself.

The somewhat tragic history of this School in its later development is accentuated by its setting in so lovely a place as Cyrene, where life was easy and nature lavish. Aristippus himself, who seems to have realized the value of Greek self-control, was far from being unhappy as the manager of his considerable resources, a patron of the arts, and the friend of many cultivated people east and west about the Mediterranean. He found no reason for supposing that "wealth could ever be like shoes which, when too large, cannot be worn." But very likely his artistic refinement combined with easy means of self-gratification made his experience exceptional. For his pupils fared less successfully and some of them came to rather melancholy ends. So that ever since we have heard of the "Hedonistic paradox"—to get pleasure one must forget it. Many a Cyrenaic, failing to understand or to apply the dictum of Aristippus, "Never to be overmastered by pleasure," found it difficult to discover a sufficiency. The daughter of the founder (Arete), and the grandson (Aristippus II), seem indeed to have successfully continued instruction and practice of the pleasure-arts. But other followers, men like Hegesias the "Death-persuader," preacher of suicide, after trying the Hedonistic art of mensuration came to the conclusion that the many ills of life combined with the after-effects of sensuous gratification make a balance on the side of pleasure impossible. Be indifferent then to so meager a world or, better, end it for yourself! Men like Theodorus, dissatisfied no less with the quality than with the quantity of pleasure, and, contrary to the dictum of Aristippus, reasoning thence to something back of their experience, concluded that any idea of Providence must be a contradiction. But in addition to atheists and disappointed connoisseurs there were Cyrenaics of the type of Anniceris, a man who, turning his attention to the pleasures of others, succeeded in discovering new sources for himself. Such teachers, however, were clearly reaching out for something other than physical gratification, and in so doing brought into question both the idea of qualitative similarity of pleasures and that of individual standards as well. Their thought will later be discussed in connection with the Epicureans, who continued and modified the Cyrenaic tradition.

Both in ancient and in modern times the school of Cyrene has been summarily condemned as atheistic and pessimistic. So crudely pragmatic a criticism, however, overlooks the fact that many a scientific hypothesis is implicitly or overtly atheistic and yet not disproved thereby. Nor can one argue that indifference is the necessary outcome in the practice of this theory. Too deliberate a consciousness of *any* object sought defeats its full attainment. Moreover such criticism implies that pleasure is something to which one should not become indifferent. But if one assumes that the problem of ethics is to determine values which shall be generally valid, it is clear that Cyrenaicism provides no basis for such knowledge. The *homo mensura* doctrine in its extreme form is Solipsism. By hypothesis no man's sensation need have anything in common with the sensation of another. From the standpoint of scientific knowledge, or a valid interpretation of external things, such an assumption becomes Skepticism. In ethics it also becomes Skepticism and for a similar reason. For there is, by hypothesis, no convention, custom, history, or consensus which can stand before any individual's private bodily satisfactions. Nor can any "self-mastery" doctrine help us, unless it provides objective sources of insight. And unless Sextus Empiricus and Aristocles were mistaken such a basis of common reference is just what the theory repudiates.

2

Among other followers of Socrates was a man of more lethargic mind, a Megarian, of whom, in general, Athenians were wont to make sport on account of their plodding heaviness and slowness. This man, Euclid (not the mathematician), was, however, a serious, persistent, thoroughgoing, somewhat Germanic grubber who came over to Athens from time to time at great personal risk. He seems to have been greatly impressed by the Socratic idea of Providence. And being convinced by Eleatic arguments that all things constitute a unity he raised an issue similar to that which they had urged concerning motion: Evil must be something non-existent, because incomprehensible, if the universe be one and goodness its attribute. Since when the so-called problem of evil has remained a source of perplexity to the thinking mind no less baffling than that of understanding motion in terms of geometry.

Euclid seems to have made brave efforts to resolve the knot by penetrating to the meaning of the concepts themselves. What do we mean, for example, by our assertion that anything *is?* Is it an affirmation of *existence* or merely of a *relationship* between a subject and a predicate? With the keenness of a Zeno and by methods similar to his, he examined an endless number of affirmative predicates in which the meaning seems now to imply existence and then a most dubious "nothingness." But we should gain no great advantage here in discussing the many eristic difficulties encountered by those who were perplexed in their use of terms. The problem is indeed still with us. Despite the development of logic since Plato and Aristotle we still have difficulty with our meanings. But many of them, like those of modern eristic Pragmatism, are hardly better than dust-raising. In the familiar example of Euclid: "When a man says he is lying, is he telling the truth?" it is easy to see that he is doing both. He is telling the truth with reference to himself and presumably what is false concerning the matter referred to; but in neither case could one trust his judgment—or language. A different problem, however, emerges for one who declares the universe to be (in some sense) good, and then is called upon to explain in what sense *not*-good *is*. Can reality, or being which *is*, include what *is not?* Or do any of our meanings give assurance of a use which will not involve contradiction in terms? To have raised such questions was something. To this day it has compelled every thoughtful man to have respect for Skepticism, even though no living man can rest content with it. Microscopic exactitude in our use of the word "impossible" certainly involves omniscience, and something like it is implied in the strict use of almost any term. Yet a Skepticism of this type urges one to expect greater knowledge with more experience and penetration.

Alexinus, Diodorus, Stilpo and other members of the school at Megara would doubtless have had more significance for us if their works had been preserved. And especially interesting would have been their criticism of Plato's Idealism and of Aristotle's conception of Potentiality—both of which we know were severely handled. Megara, however, paled and dwindled in the greater light of Athens.

3

Still another type of pupil was Antisthenes, who in mature life and after various contacts with Sophists, came to admire the simplicity and radical reasonableness, the imperturbability and heroic self-discipline of Socrates. Antisthenes, who was to become the founder of Cynicism, concluded that indifference to external things, not only as the capacity to go without the so-called means of livelihood, conveniences, protection, and comforts, but as a resolute living of one's own life independently of the habits and conventions of society, was the secret of Socrates' life. He, indeed, had learned the lesson from Nature herself. For man alone of the animals must give nearly all his time to the production of means of livelihood; man alone is enslaved by the ignorant opinions of his fellows. Reason does not lead to this. Reason challenges a man to be strong, to conquer comforts by activity, to resist the elements by sufficient strength, to be the slave neither of beauty nor of duty, conceived as some outside command. Reason pampers not. Let a man harden his body by little clothing and, like Socrates, he too will enjoy the snow barefoot. The wise man will require little food—and no medical attendance. He will do no mourning over present, past, or future ills and thus avoid the killing worry. The pleasures of sense will not entice him since he does not wish to becloud his reason. Why indeed be solicitous about any earthly concern: the family, government, city-building, are not these disturbers of the simple life? So, too, the dogmas of religion. Fear God, but do not be perplexed. Let no doctrine of the origin and fate of worlds, no Elysian Fields or dark forgetfulness, no theory of knowledge or of history, be a robber of the soul's independence.

Another famous exemplar of this radical "reasonableness" well illustrates the destructive possibilities of the "simple life," or the "dog's life," according to one derivation of the word Cynic. Not only clothes and food, but tools and utensils, shelter, art, cleanliness, were by Diogenes (d. 323 B. C.) reduced to a minimum. He, a pupil of Antisthenes, charged his master with a failure to hear the trumpet he was himself blowing, and willingly adopted the nickname Dog, adding that he bit not his enemies but his friends, and for their own good. Diogenes even dared to tell the great Alexander what he thought of the prerogatives of a king's life. The future conqueror had looked him up in a grove near Corinth, where he was discoursing, radiant with health and vigor. Alexander, when he was about to go, asked what gift or other kindness he might bestow as a little tribute to the teacher in a tub. To which the Cynic replied: "Only to get out of my light," an answer which so much astonished Alexander that he is reported to have said he would gladly have been Diogenes had he not been born a king. His contempt for the ordinary decencies and honesties of men is illustrated in his famous quest with a lantern by daylight, and how he repelled with scorn anyone who thought himself honest when he had so much to hide. "Socrates grown mad" was a dictum applied to him. At the same time he was the beloved tutor of the sons of Xeniades in Corinth. He was tolerated even when uninvited he came to Plato's party saying: "Thus do I trample on the pride of Plato." The latter only remarked: "With greater pride, Diogenes," and bade him stay.

Since the days of these early simon-pure Cynics there have been multitudes of them with less marked personalities. All lovers of the "simple life," all who "consider the lilies of the field" somewhat literally and look askance at the senseless wants of their fellows, they who construe conventions as insincere, and find hypocrisy in the refinements of life are mentally kindred to them. The influence of such men has clearly worked against any such crystallization of life as characterized, for example, the three thousand years of ancient Egypt. But when one recalls how Roman emperors were addressed between acts at the theatre and all sorts of motives were (and are) challenged in the interest of an assumed abstract reason, it becomes clear why the very word "cynical" came to mean primarily a negative, suspicious, even audacious, attitude of mind. At the same time their refusal to admit the sacro-sanct character of any tradition has undoubtedly made for progress when it has itself had a better objective—which unfortunately Cynicism has often lacked.

When one compares the positive values which they sacrificed with those which ancient Cynics tried to foster in their effort to find a more perfect life, one realizes how bad a bargain they made. Like the ethics of the primitive Christian saint (with which it has closest kindred) Cynicism committed æsthetic, intellectual, social and economic suicide, and forewent even the consolation which the early Christian derived from his hope of the resurrection. The religious values generally were forfeited in the interest of such peace of mind as carping criticism can produce. The family, the state, libraries, the intuitions of imagination on canvas, the speculations of science and all their practical fruits are not to be found in Diogenes' tub. Nor are cleanliness, and other amenities of human life. It is open to question whether work of any kind is likely to thrive there. Cynicism at its fountain is thus "back to nature," but not to human nature. It is a witty effort to return to a far distant semi-human past.

CHAPTER XII

PLATO: THE MAN AND HIS WORKS

There could hardly be a task at once more difficult and more delightful than to evaluate the genius of Plato. His thought brought to a focus innumerable rays of light emanating from earlier philosophy. Pythagoras, Parmenides, Heraclitus, Protagoras, Anaxagoras, and, above all, Socrates, lived again in him. Yet the radiant interests of his own mind so transfused their thought that it was changed to something rich and new. Though, like every other thinker, he depended on the work of his predecessors, the "many-splendoured thing" which he evolved made him the crowning glory of his age. But how shall one be just either to Socrates, through whom he speaks in so many of the Dialogues, or to himself? Plato, the poet, exquisite in artistry, sees his work as a thing apart; Plato, the philosopher never disillusionized in the love of truth, forgets himself in the search. Nowhere does the author appear in all these dramatic conversations; only three times does he mention his own name, and then quite casually.

The same difficulty confronts us when we consider Plato, the prophet. For he anticipated many interpretations by which philosophers of a later age have achieved renown. More specifically his own best pupil, Aristotle, seems by his criticism to have limited the scope of his master's thought, and himself to have obtained credit for what is implicit—and sometimes explicit—in Plato's own work. In our account we shall endeavor to evaluate the Dialogues as such. It is doubtless the way their author would have had us read them, as world thoughts which rise superior to individuals, however dramatized in vivid character. Plato was a seeker who permitted all manner of hypotheses to be presented in the most cogent possible way, that out of their contest there might come new insight. By our objective method we run the risk of giving or withholding more credit than is due. But Plato would have been the last to care.

Nearly all of his published work seems to have been preserved to us, a fact which symbolizes the extraordinary good fortune of their author. Plato was a child of the gods in more ways than one. Born from two of the noblest Athenian families, he was by nature endowed with a strong body and exquisite taste. He had a career replete with dramatic interest, not without danger to himself, and throughout concerned with matters of great import. He lived at a time when Athens, though already past her prime politically, and weakened by the great war, was none the less mellow with the fruitage of a golden age, the home of unrivaled beauty and cultivated intelligence. He traveled widely about the Mediterranean, east and west, and learned from other peoples and times. He had the privilege of carrying out a great educational work, perhaps the most influential one so far in the history of Europe and America. He enjoyed his own "peace, health and harmony of soul" to such a degree that he might almost stand as the spiritual, as well as physical, embodiment of classic antiquity. He came to his death in happy and vigorous old age. The Academy, or school of philosophy founded by him, maintained itself while empires waxed and waned, until 529 A. D. when Justinian, in the interests of the faith, destroyed the centers of "heathen" education.

More explicitly, Plato was born either at Athens or Ægina in May 428 or 427 B. C. His father, Ariston, was a descendant of Codrus, the self-sacrificing last king of Athens. His mother, Periktione, belonged to the family of

Solon, the Law-giver. As a child he was called Aristocles, but his gymnasium master, noting the sturdy shoulders of the lad, gave him the nickname which he has borne ever since. We know the names of several of his early teachers, but unfortunately these tell us little concerning his training. The curriculum in Athenian schools then included most of our elementary subjects, the chief exceptions being foreign languages and grammars. But, in addition, they included training to enjoyment and creative efforts in the liberal arts, especially poetry, and a balanced education of the body (gymnastic). No wonder that the high demands of excellence which artistry requires were imbued in Greek young men and women! Plato from early years had the mind of a poet, as his verses in the *Anthology* testify. His lifelong interest in music and the other arts—despite the moral questions which they aroused in his mind—also bear witness to the inspiration which he derived from them.

This development of imagination, so vividly fostered by Athenian education, did not destroy his sense of reality. Our so-called "practical" tendency to brand the quest of ideal excellence as "Utopian" has misled not a few into supposing that the author of the *Republic* was a dreamer of dreams. It is interesting to note in this connection that before he came under the influence of Socrates [1] his plan was to devote himself to active political leadership. Nor did this interest in men and affairs abate throughout his long career. He seems to have been in his twentieth year when the dedication to philosophy took place, and Socrates henceforward became the dominating influence in his life. Through Cratylus, his instructor in philosophy, he also became acquainted with the earlier schools, notably that of Heraclitus. Whether or not his literary efforts began during the eight years when

[2] See John Burnet: *Greek Philosophy,* Part I, pp. 205–206, concerning the authenticity of the *Epistles.*

he studied under Socrates' direction cannot be made out with certainty. In general, Plato seems not to have introduced living characters into his Dialogues. But Socrates may have been an exception.

After the death of his friend and guide, an event which illness prevented him from attending (as we learn from one of the three references to himself, *Phœdo,* 59 b) he went to Megara, where undoubtedly he learned much from Euclid. He must have enjoyed even the latter's discussions which ended nowhere, if we may judge by his own "dialogues of search." In his early thirties Plato seems to have spent some time in Egypt especially at Heliopolis among the sacerdotal class. For many things Egyptian he shows great admiration in his writings, but we can only conjecture what knowledge he may have sought there. Cicero thought he went to study mathematics and astronomy. But if this was so, it does not seem likely that he could have profited very much. What he commends in the Egyptians is their stable, practical character, their sense of form, and permanent traditions. And it is curiously significant that, in his latest work, he should have recommended the Egyptian way of teaching arithmetic and geometry by concrete objects, games and figures.[2] Elsewhere he wonders what influences of climate, soil, or food, have made the Egyptians, like the Phœnicians, chiefly tradesmen.[3] Of inspiration to philosophy from them there is no hint in all his works. Either going or returning from Egypt, he appears to have spent some time at Cyrene with Theodorus. For the ten years following the death of Socrates we have, unfortunately, very little definite knowledge of his activities.

About 390 B. C., or when Plato was approaching 40 years of age, we learn of his leaving Athens for his first trip to Italy. His ancient biographers give various reasons for his

[2] *Laws,* VII, 819b.
[3] *Laws,* V, 747c.

interest in the Greek colonies there which were then a very important part of the Hellenic world. Olympiodorus in his fragment conjectures that "since it is requisite for a philosopher to be fond of seeing the works of nature, he sailed to Sicily likewise, to view the craters of fire that are in Ætna."[4] Aristides even conjectures that it was for the sake of a "Sicilian table."[5] But whatever other motives may have been present, Plato was primarily interested in coming into first hand contact with the Pythagorean school, especially with the ethical and political experiment of Archytas at Tarentum. And he seems to have regarded Syracuse as a possible field in which to try his experiments in statecraft. He had there a young pupil and friend, Dion, who was brother-in-law to Dionysius, the tyrant of Syracuse. Through the former Plato actually got so far as to give instruction in ideal commonwealths to this Dionysius, but only for a short time. The tyrant, evidently no lover of humanitarian principles, soon wearied of the "senile"[6] reformer. But Plato is here said to have retorted to this charge of dotage by declaring Dionysius arbitrary and tyrannical. Whereupon the latter threw him into chains. Dion alone saved him from death and got the sentence commuted to slavery. Thereupon follows the picture of a Spartan ambassador (Pollis) selling Plato to the highest bidder in the slave market of Ægina! And not the least title to fame of Anniceris, whom we have already met as an altruistic pleasure-philosopher, was his kindly act in ransoming the distinguished slave, and refusing afterwards to be compensated. He thus helped to make possible the Academe or Garden (now said to be part of the Athenian Botanic Gardens), where Plato taught from this time to his death in 347 B. C.

[4] *Life of Plato.*
[5] *Orat. Platon,* II, p. 376.
[6] Diogenes Laertius: *Lives and Opinions.* Plato XIV.

Twice, however, he interrupted his work in the interests of the Sicilian commonwealth—or at least better conditions in Syracuse. A younger Dionysius, son of his former unwilling pupil, again through Dion, was brought into touch with Plato. But the experiment again failed. The fickle tyrant banished his uncle, and the philosopher advisedly withdrew (367 B. C.). A third time risking his life (361 B. C.), Plato made another trip to Sicily and was saved from Dionysius only by the good offices of his friend, Archytas of Tarentum. Whatever one may think of the political acumen of the great Idealist, his efforts, even at great personal risk, to get ethical norms applied, show that he was more than a theorizer, though with Socrates he realized that theory is back of all intelligent practice.

In the Academy his teaching was of a kind to stimulate imagination to bold hypotheses, as will later abundantly appear. But a thorough going exactness and severity of proof also accompanied his intuitions. We know this, independently of the great Dialogues, from his emphasis upon mathematical studies in the Academy. No candidate was admitted who had not mastered geometry. The still very difficult question of the relationships between mathematical concepts and the real world was one which also received a good deal of attention there. Plato early recognized that scientific interpretation depends upon knowledge of quantitative relationships. No greater mistake could therefore be made, than to assume that the teaching of Plato was pure inspiration unrelated to the cogency of analytic thinking. At the same time the Academy, like most things Greek, had a marked religious character. There was a chapel in the garden; there were sacrifices and processions, which under such leadership doubtless had something of the satisfaction of art as well as of stimulus to thought. We know too that the manner of life which teachers and pupils enjoyed was one of extraordinarily democratic fellowship, but within the limits of aristocratic, or, perhaps better, refined, purposes. Olympiodorus in his fragment writes of how he (Plato) did not frequent the work-shop and public meetings which Socrates had visited, but how at the same time he exhibited himself "more like a citizen to all" than had the distant and haughty Pythagoreans. We may surmise that meals in common did not endanger recognition of persons, and that pride was hardly based on precedence.

We have [7] the names of certain outstanding pupils. One is surprised to note how they came from Macedonia and Pontus, no less than from Athens, the Peloponnese and Sicily, women as well as men, students of philosophy, orators (including Demosthenes), artists and statesmen. If only we could know more about a method of education which trained at once great political leaders, scientists and philosophers! As it is we have only the bare implication of Aristotle, quoted by Aristoxenos, that there were lectures in continuous discourse to supplement informal discussions. How the studies in biology, astronomy and geology were carried on we do not know. But it is interesting to note that Plato in his account of the economic life of Attica [8] correlates correct geological observations with economic facts. Of mechanical experiment as distinct from observation, we have no record. It would be only just to add, however, that his primary interest was in men, minds, the knowledge processes, art, government and religion, rather than in tangible things, and that, however significant as principles the scientific hypotheses which he expounded may be for us, for him they were subordinate to the problems of human good.

When the Dialogues were written, in what order, and for what purposes have been problems of a painstaking scholarship for generations. Its results are not as conclusive as one might wish. Schleiermacher (d. 1834) assumed that Plato

[7] Diogenes Laertius: *Lives and Opinions.* Plato, XXXI.
[8] *Critias,* 109–111.

had a didactic purpose, and for that reason regarded the *Phædrus* as his earliest work, the most elementary of all. But Hermann (d. 1848) for the same reason placed it at the beginning of his third and last literary period. Similarly the *Apology* was by Munk [9] placed among the later Dialogues, since he conceived their general purpose to be a dramatic idealization of Socrates. But Lutoslawski [10] who studied 500 Platonic phrases and their distribution, puts the *Apology* first in his list. Lewis Campbell [11] investigated the occurrence of hiatus (two vowels together in successive words or syllables), finding it quite absent in some Dialogues and very frequent in others. And since we know that Plato learned to respect Isocrates, a fellow teacher who set up a stylistic rule against hiatus, many scholars have since put the works in which hiatus abounds into an earlier group, and those without it later. Burnet [12] traced a cycle beginning with dramatic sketches, which are succeeded by others in narrative forms characterized by more elaborate *mise en scene*. With the coming of a more critically scientific temper, Plato returned, according to Burnet, to the simpler dramatic presentation.

Fortunately our understanding of the Dialogues themselves is not too seriously limited by uncertainty about their exact order. Converging lines of evidence, especially linguistic studies, have now made it fairly probable that those in which Socrates as the central figure discusses the meaning of certain concepts belong to Plato's earlier works. Thus the little dramatic piece called *Euthyphro* raises the question: What is Piety? Euthyphro proposes various answers, but can satisfy neither himself nor Socrates. Piety cannot

9 Ed. Munk: *"Die natürliche Ordnung der platonischen Schriften."* Berlin, 1856.

10 *The Growth and Development of Plato's Logic,* 1897.

11 The *Sophistes* and *Politicus* of *Plato*. Oxford, 1867.

12 John Burnet: *Greek Philosophy,* I, pp. 234–5. 1914. Natorp's *Platon's Ideenlehre,* 1903, is another important study.

be "attending" to the gods, for attending implies that we do something to better them. But how can man benefit the gods? Piety cannot be a "science of asking and giving," a "doing business between gods and men," for what can we give? Even giving, however, turns out to be no answer as to the essence of piety. For we do not know how such honor could be acceptable to them. In *Charmides* we have the charming youth of that name attempting to answer: What is Temperance? He suggests "quietness," "modesty," "doing one's own business." But Socrates quotes Homer: "Modesty is not good for a needy man," and shows that one can be temperate in other men's business, that quickness, too, is a desirable quality. And when still another answer is ventured, this time by Critias, that temperance is "self-knowledge," it turns out that a special knowledge of temperance is impossible, for it is shown to involve an understanding of good as a whole. In the *Laches* the same turns out to be true of Courage. It cannot be defined when taken in isolation. The *Protagoras* discusses in what sense Virtue is Knowledge and how it can be taught, Protagoras insisting upon teaching without a fundamental theory of what is taught, and Socrates holding to theory as our source of knowledge and norm of action, but curiously unwilling to grant its teachableness! In the *Meno* this matter of teaching is made more specific by contrasting what one finds in one's own mind (anamnesis), or has thought out for oneself in all its bearings, with that casual, popular, rhetorical sort of "knowledge" which was the object of teaching among the Sophists. The *Gorgias* attempts, as against the Sophists, to determine a positive meaning for the term good in its most comprehensive sense—a science of good, as opposed to rule of thumb. Socrates here meets Callicles the superman, worshiper of power and pleasure, as well as other "men of the world," and convicts them of unwittingly aiming for something less than their own good, which is "an order," an inner harmony of life, rather than pleasure, power, or any isolated experience.

In these Dialogues, as in the *Apology* and *Crito*, which are accounts of Socrates' trial and last conversations, we probably have the earlier work of Plato, when he was still under the influence of his great master. These works are by no means immature either in artistry or in thought, but are chiefly concerned with Socrates' inner life, experiments in definitions, and methods of awakening youth. They have a vividly dramatic setting. Somewhere in the early list also belong the very lovely though inconclusive conversation on Friendship entitled *Lysis*, and the skit upon the rhapsodes called *Ion* in which their innocent naïvété and induced inspiration are wittily exposed. Here, too, very probably belongs that half-comedy called *Euthydemus*, in which Socrates with relentless irony—and sometimes making the worse appear the better reason—tries to confute two Sophists, who, being on the lookout for boys, promise, for a consideration, to teach them virtue in a very short time and in the best possible manner.

In these conversations and narratives we meet with many tentative drafts of what is later elaborated and criticized. Concepts and more accurate definitions are being gradually transformed into Ideas, and, notably in the *Gorgias*, into a system of Ideas by which the mind can deal with things, Ideas in the light of which, and by which, all nature must be thought to operate, if we are to understand her within ourselves or without. This is clearly an extension of the Pythagorean conception of Form, as well as of the Socratic concept; and where the contribution of Plato begins is hardly to be made out. In self-effacing modesty he has compelled us to take account of thought first, and persons last. Truth is for him without epoch or school, above all reputation and advantage. Yet with an increasing clarity and emphasis upon Ideas as not only mental, but cosmic realities, one cannot, in the middle Dialogues, fail to recognize a more independent Plato. One observes this strikingly in the *Symposium*, that masterful, penetrating, and at the same time facetious, discussion of Love, by six men differing as widely from one another as the bantering, myth-making, somewhat carnal, Aristophanes, and Socrates, who finds Love a cosmic agency, in its higher ranges an impelling force by which the human lover may become a "spectator of all time and of all existence," and experience absolute beauty. Here Ideas become Ideals which guide thought toward its goal; they are also discovered to be active causes, and therefore an essential aspect of our world wherever we find it intelligible.

In the *Phædo*, where Socrates is made to express his reasons for hoping in Immortality, the Doctrine of Ideas is further elucidated. When we *think* we are dealing with something very different from objects seen or heard. The Idea of a man is not a picture of him, or the sound of his voice, or anything which can be sensed. And though we make use of these sensations as instruments, none the less our thought more and more gets away from his body when we think of the *essence* or ultimate reality, that is, *Idea* of a man. Moreover a perfectly realized Idea would have nothing of accidental deformity, temporary existence, or limitation of character —a thing we never see, but which none the less constitutes the criterion of our knowledge. To make sure that such ideals are not mere words, Plato seems about this time to have devoted a good deal of attention to words as such. At any rate the *Cratylus* is chiefly a lexicon of etymologies, most of them fanciful. But while he concludes that there ought to be a natural connection between names and what they designate, he insists that the true nature of things is not to be apprehended from names. Ideas must be realities, if knowledge is concerned with truth.

This conviction becomes so strong in the *Phædrus*, a work in which Plato again discusses Love as inspiration to knowledge and noble character, the "madness" or enthusiasm for Ideas, that he writes as a poet rather than as logician. The sources of knowledge are projected into some higher world, not subject to the changing vicissitudes of our limited vision. Truth must be permanent, unchanging, serenely self-harmonious. It cannot be the contradictory half-errors, the shifting scenes on our tiny stage of sense. It must be something above and beyond all that, something of which our intelligence gets only faint intimations, when in its higher reaches it becomes conscious of knowledge fixedly sure, pure, perfect—perhaps the thought of some divine mind. In a parable we see Reason, a charioteer, driving the unequal steeds of Concupiscence and Practical Morality up the steep ascent to Heaven where this high knowledge dwells, the "colorless, formless, intangible essence, visible only to Mind, the Pilot of the Soul." [13] That Dome of Truth is never reached with all the plunging and agony of the winged steeds. The soul must still "feed upon opinion." Yet "those who have once begun the heavenward pilgrimage may not go down again to darkness"; even distant vision, a mere "dream" of the divine, impels to noble action.

To this middle period also belongs the *Republic*, that ever-fresh discussion of Justice, as related first to the proper balance of a man's functions physical and mental, the peace, health, and harmony of his soul, and then to that collection of individuals called the State. Its many practical suggestions for education to a superior race, and equal opportunity for men and women, an education to begin before birth, and throughout life connecting man's purpose with the greater cosmic good, have made it the most popular of Plato's works. His "Utopian" proposals in politics, notably equality for men and women, have in many instances become accepted commonplaces of modern life, despite the fact that he himself thought they could never be realized. But for

[13] Sec. 247.

the student of psychology, ethics, logic, metaphysics, art, no less than that of government, the *Republic* is a mine of thought. And the lover of literature finds it mostly a grateful experience. One should read it bearing in mind the history of the Sicilian adventures, as well as his more successful school for philosopher-statesman at Athens.

Some time seems to have elapsed between the *Republic* and the more critical Dialogues, whose style is distinctly more scientific, "academic" and æsthetically less spontaneous. The *Theætetus* with great penetration discusses the problem: How do we know? Is knowledge something impressed upon us from without, a product of sensation, or is it something we construct for ourselves by an activity of the mind itself? Neither of these alternatives is an adequate account, for sensation belongs to the fleeting world of Heraclitus and the isolated individuals of Protagoras, and right opinion with all its reasons fails to tell us what a wrong opinion is. Nor can Plato see how any combination of the two can adequately solve the problem. In the *Parmenides* he seems to sit in judgment upon himself. At least he tears utterly to pieces a doctrine of Ideas which Aristotle imputed to him, and which is certainly found in the *Phædo* and the *Republic*, if we read them literally. Perhaps it was meant as his own defense against those who interpreted him literally. However that may be, a "young Socrates" quite unsuccessfully defends the supposition that Ideas are things. Anyone who supposes that an Idea of anything is a model of that thing existing somewhere off in Heaven does not realize that the model would itself require a model to make a common standard possible, and so *ad infinitum*. Nor could one model cover the innumerable, varying, things which are said to be like it, unless a model is both like and unlike itself! And this leads to the problem: How can we, if we follow Parmenides—and all who think must aim for a world-interpretation in some sense *unified*—how can we explain the manifold varieties and incongruities which seem inevitably to creep into our thought? An Idea of anything seems to include its opposite as part of its very essence. The Idea "Man" includes both slave and free, good and bad, body and not-body. How can these all "participate," or be part of the Idea, and make up a unity? This difficulty comes out even more sharply in the *Sophist* where, among other logical problems, that of error seems to be central. How can there *be* such a thing? Error, we say, is appearance. And if appearances are really *not*, then we seem to be treating of nothingness, and the thought of nothingness might well be considered no thought. What then is the distinguishing mark of something which *is* from something which is *not?* Plato's conclusion is that the distinction is not one of body versus what has not body; being is rather what has power of acting and being acted upon. But we must not think of "*is*" or "*is not*" as standing for anything. They have meaning only in connection with a judgment. So that we can, in thought, deal with "not-being," without, however, looking for something to correspond with it outside in space.

To the end of his life Plato had a predilection for political science. This is clearly shown by the fact that his *Laws*, a more conservative and somewhat less interesting *Republic*, is his last and longest work. But he also dedicated the *Statesman* (which follows the *Sophist*) to setting forth the relationships of laws and men in different types of states, and how to distinguish and train the few who can become leaders, in the true science of politics. The latter work especially has many interesting observations, as when he shows that commercial nations are lacking in political science, or that government exclusively by law is a form of tyranny, or how aristocracy, whether the number of rulers be one or many, alone develops spiritual dignity in the citizens.

In this latest period belong finally: a fragment called *Critias*, in which the strange myth of the submerged continent, called Atlantis, is embedded in a framework of observations on how civilization depends upon soils and climate; also two important pieces called *Philebus* and *Timæus*. The *Philebus* discusses pleasure as an ingredient in a well-balanced life. However important and necessary that ingredient may be, it is shown to be low in the scale of values, just because it lacks "right measure." Beauty and reason are set forth, not only as measures of pleasure, but as the very condition and basis upon which they can be experienced by humans. In the *Philebus* we also meet with perhaps the most direct statement of why Mind and its Ideas are forms of energy, active causes, not only in my consciousness, but wherever intelligence is manifested. The highest of these Ideas, or Laws, is that of Good, or Purpose, by which alone a system of Laws is possible; and everywhere such Laws can be mathematically expressed. In the *Timæus* finally, the imaginary story of the creation of the world and of man, we have the conception of a good Power, who organizes the infinite chaos of space according to definite mathematical norms. It is intended wholly as a speculation, "God only knows if it is true," but it is possible and even likely; investigation may make it certain. Here Plato's faith in mathematics is exemplified, even to the application of geometry as an explanation of the differences between the elements. Thus water is thought to be made up of icosahedrons; air, of octahedrons; fire, of pyramidal shapes. This suggests *in principle* the Democritean and modern arrangements of small particles as explanations of the different qualities of elements. But Plato's tendency in his later years was to ascribe a mysterious quality to numbers as such, and to associate mathematical forms with Ideas. We have no intimation why he did this, except in so far as he over-emphasized the importance of mathematical concepts in scientific hypotheses.

Taken as a whole, the works of Plato are thus seen to grapple with Ethics, Political Theory, Logic, Scientific

Method, Religion, Theory of Art, Education, Psychology, and Speculative Cosmology. In each of these fields, as we shall see, his contribution has proved to be fundamental for western thought. There is more than the fact of penetrating insight involved in this influence. The vision of the prophet, combined with scientific insight and artistic intuition, makes these works perennially young. It is natural that with the progress of science many of his tentative theories should by now have been superseded. There are parts of the Dialogues which are tedious, because for us the issues have become clarified, or even made irrelevant. But a selection of passages from Plato on subjects which are still in the focus of our philosophy would include much of the most significant matter to which expression has thus far been given.

CHAPTER XIII

IDEAS AS BASIS OF SCIENCE. PLATO'S THEORY OF KNOWLEDGE

To interpret the thought of Plato in terms intelligible to ourselves, we shall have to bear in mind that he tried to hold together what for us has often been divided. The reader of the Dialogues is at first confused by the ease with which their author turns from a discussion of justice to a psychological problem, thence to one of logic or natural science, before he returns to his original question. We separate our political theory from natural science; our religion from physical geography. We have learned the advantage of specialization for research. Plato, on the other hand, conceived all knowledge to have a fundamental unity. And when he turns from his discussion of justice to describe the make-up of particular human characters there is a point involved, and generally a deeper one than casual reading discloses.

But this is not the only difficulty. Plato, the poet, gives his intuitions wings when he deals with scientific matter. Not only is this true of the *content* of his imagination, for, so perfect is the *form* into which he casts his thought, that one has the sense of dwelling apart in a world of art. Yet his scientific interpretations strike the center of the various problems involved. Abstract thinking was no less native to his mind than the tangible figures of flesh and blood, in whose dramatic characterizations he chose to express that thought. And so his appeal is indeed to knowledge, but no less to the *love* of knowledge. Personal relations are involved. No one can be indifferent, howsoever cold and abstract the matter of discourse, either to Plato, or to the characters whose life-blood pulses in their opinions.

The same is true of visible and invisible aspects of our world. When Plato speaks of minds, they seem to be tangibly before us. We know, of course, in our day of duly segregated departments that one cannot speak of minds as though they occupied a foot of space or had an upper left-hand corner. It seems to us mere poetic imagination to follow the steeds of concupiscence and modesty (mere mental qualities) guided by the reins of the charioteer Reason—a "crooked lumbering animal put together anyhow," and the other "white, with a lofty neck and aquiline nose," until the charioteer wins a "truly Olympian victory." Our brass instruments and exact numerical tabulation of dreams, memories, and movements of the larynx, seem to be far more pertinent to science. And yet through all his "partly true and tolerably credible mythus."[1] Plato succeeds in giving us numerous conceptions of the mind and its functions, which bear the test of refined experiment and analysis.

Logic and mathematics thus go hand in hand with poetry; science entertains religion. And all the human drama of opinions, aspirations, love and death commingles with the cosmic fate. Abstraction, either in the sense of segregated compartments, or of formulæ involving no relationships to human minds, seems to have been impossible for him, however highly he also commended the "long and difficult language of facts." He could reverence mathematics and despise the mere mathematician.[2] Hence his intuition of cosmic good as key to the structure of science. Hence his political theory, taking account not only of economic goods, but of music, drama, procreation and philosophy, in his most nearly human and intelligent—and therefore to him most natural—form of commonwealth. Hence, too, the freshness and hu-

[1] *Phædr.* 265c.

[2] *Rep.* VII, 531.

manity of his work, which bids fair to live for many decades to come.

The Theory of Ideas in its various aspects is, of course, the index of Plato's philosophy. It had in his day, and at his hands, a long and checkered history. But we must not suppose that he sometimes maintained, and at other times, repudiated, it. His was a mind that tried to examine hypotheses from every possible angle. He was his own best critic. The most damaging evidence that can be adduced against the theory is what he himself presents. Yet it has internal coherence, from the earliest efforts to derive adequate moral concepts, to his latest speculations on numbers as related to cosmic Ideas. That Pythagoras was right in positing the real existence of non-material agencies, whose operations may be observed in the myriad organizations of things, he could never doubt—howsoever many the problems growing out of such a hypothesis. Nor did he question the Socratic axiom that adequate concepts are the key to knowledge. They alone enable us to deal with sense-experience intelligently. Putting together the Pythagorean Forms and Socratic Concepts, he aimed for a scientific method by which to realize interpretations that could resist both the Heraclitean flux in the outside world and the Gorgian slipperiness of language.

We have seen how unsuccessful were his (or Socrates') efforts to find the essential meaning of such terms as temperance, courage, justice, which are generally taken to be so simple! Yet these early failures succeed in showing how, as a matter of method, if and when you succeed in discovering what is back of these words in reality, you will have organized your concepts into a system. To know what courage is you will have to know what is just, and justice involves a knowledge of what is good. In order to understand the nature of beauty you look for its essence as displayed in beautiful things; but then you try to realize how it is related to symmetry, unity, balance, truth and so on. The same is true of anything that can be named. You know what it is, when you discover its essence, and how it fits into the scheme of things. In short: definite concepts, organized into a system of natural laws, is the ideal of science.

All this is simple enough. Of course real knowledge must be internally consistent with itself! We must try to avoid double meanings and to use our terms as precisely as we can! But the difficulty begins when we inquire: With what are we dealing when we reason in terms of language? Are we concerned with structures of our own minds, figments perhaps, which we build for ourselves? Or do we somehow deal with Reality when we discover and coördinate genuine Ideas? Do concepts copy, imitate, express, or stand in some direct and dynamic relationship to the essences of things, so that when we reason clearly, our language may be said to "stand for" what is actually there? Or, on the contrary, must we suppose that our language and what it stands for are merely convenient tools which enable us to manage our practical actions—somewhat more effectively than birds do by twittering or swine by grunting? Ontology, the science of Being, together with other sciences which profess to deal with *what is*, must in the latter event, be curiously naïve self-deceptions!

In the *Cratylus* Plato faces the issue of how words are related to things. Can they be said to *copy* what they stand for? And he answers, that even as combinations of sounds and letters, they sometimes appear to imitate. There are many interesting aspects of language, and proprieties in the use of words. But he who studied them with the expectation of finding reality there would surely be a foolish person. The true nature of things is to be apprehended not from their names but from themselves.[3] Terms, symbols, words, enable us to hold together in thought what we are dealing

[3] *Crat.* 439b.

with. But, unless we can suppose that we are thinking about something more than words, we are assuredly getting no knowledge. What then are the *objects* of our thought?

Ultimately it was faith in the possibility of knowledge (in the sense of dealing with Reality itself) which led Plato to propose the axiom: in Ideas coördinated into an adequate, self-consistent order, our minds are concerned with Reality, the true nature of what is. Ideas are not mere letters, breath, convenient structures of the mind to stand for the way we are affected by external things, or propose to deal with them. They are essential nature itself, the inner Being of things, back of all our concepts, pictures, or other devices, which we might use to represent them. If we cannot assume that this is true, then science and philosophy are fictions of human fancy.

But common sense interposes here: Have we not a knowledge of things in our direct awareness of them? Do I not see and feel the object before me to be what it is—this inkstand and the fluid inside? Does not sensation rather than thinking show me what it is? Plato's answer to this naïve Realism is a many-sided one. In various places, but especially in the *Theætetus* [4] he shows how the dictum of Protagoras, "Everything is as it appears to any man's senses," breaks down. The simplest test disproves it. Sweet tastes are not sweet to a jaundiced tongue. A wind may be warm to one and cold to another. The colors attributed to objects are really motions in the medium between the object and the eyes. So that color, as such, is clearly not a quality of things, unless we are ready to say that everything is made up of more or less rapid motion. And this is equivalent to saying, there is nothing that can be known: All is in flux. Only he who supposes that nothing anywhere is stable can admit that objects are made up of so astonishing a bundle of contradictions as they appear to our senses. Even a madman's hallucinations

[4] 152–186.

would be part of the picture, one key to reality, and Protagoras no wiser than a tadpole when the knowledge of both is reduced to sensations. But no man really believes that "what *seems* to a man *is* to him." Even the author of that statement himself undertakes to teach men having excellent sense organs, while experts are in demand in all professions. It is not by simple sensations, given at birth to both men and animals, that truth, or the knowledge of being, is attained. Such knowledge clearly involves comparisons, discrimination, thinking, which are slowly and hardly gained, if ever they are gained, by education and long experience.

This does not imply, of course, that Plato repudiated sensations as *instruments* of knowledge. He tried to realize the fullest significance of the "long and difficult language of facts." [5] But he also maintained with equal acumen that reality reveals itself in our *interpretation* of perceptual experience. Our bodily organs provide the occasions or tools of knowledge; an inner activity of the mind giving intelligible form to these sensations reveals Ideas back of them. And the latter Plato holds to be the "real thing," giving us the essence, the permanent being, *what is*. Perhaps some examples of our own may succeed in making the argument clearer for modern readers. For our loose use of the term "Idea" as designating almost anything from a hobgoblin to the taste of salt obscures the issue. So, too, the common supposition that, as such, Ideas are nothing, a passing breath, or at best a *process* in the brain. Unreflecting common sense never stops to ponder that the pressure, sight, or smell of "things" is also such a process.

Plato's argument in such terms as these merely regards the more elaborate process (which involves the simpler ones) as the source of deeper knowledge. Let us apply it to some examples. The process of vision brings us experience which we characterize as "red," "square," "continuous," "at rest"

[5] *Statesman,* 278.

—a little block of redwood. The physical chemist by a process of reflection has experiences which he characterizes as "molecules," "in very rapid motion," "rotating on their axes," "discontinuous" as "atoms," and again as "protons" and "electrons." Both concern the same little block of redwood. Which reveals the "true facts," the "real thing"? Modern science clearly stakes its faith on Plato's hypothesis. But "mere ideas"? we exclaim. Are not the secure results of laboratory work more than the ghostly, unreal, and arbitrary nothings we concoct for ourselves in words? The answer, holding ourselves rigidly to the "language of facts," is that all the above scientific terms are first of all Ideas. No one ever knew of an electron (much less tasted, touched or saw one) before it was projected in J. J. Thompson's hypothesis. As a matter of history these are all cases of terms gradually taking on the character of something real. How did it happen? Clearly by fitting in with other Ideas which we have derived in a similar manner, meanings whereby sense-experience is also coördinated into an intelligible order.

What makes us hesitate to accept Ideas as realities is, of course, the large number of fictitious ones, from angels and occult qualities to phlogistine, which marks the history of all thought. But the distinction again between the true ones and the false—just as between waking and sleeping—is whether they fit in with our interpretations as a whole and make our senses intelligible. Are electrons actual realities? They will pass as such so long as they can make all pertinent observation, experiment, and reason hold together. And just because a "real thing" so often appears as what we can handle and see, electrons will be grouped with objects which we could see or handle—if our eyes were better or our touch more refined. In other words, we have a strong tendency to think of "real" Ideas as external things. And it takes a penetrating effort of thought to realize that anything can be genuinely "there" without being (at least potentially) visible or tangible.

This may be illustrated in another way by mathematical Ideas. When we reason about the nature of circles (or, for that matter, three-dimensional bodies) are we dealing with the circle drawn before us, or the tangible figure (say a cone) which we may use as models? A moment's reflection makes it clear that geometrical reasoning is concerned with ideal points, lines, surfaces, solids—Ideas which no one has ever seen, or otherwise experienced through his senses. The center of the circle has no dimensions, lines have no breadth, even the visible cone is not the one dealt with by the mathematician. His reasoning would not be strictly true concerning any figure which could be made. And conversely he never *measures* the bodies or designs before him. They are but imitations, approximations to the real Ideas which he has in mind; the measurement of visible circles or cones is not mathematics. Moreover when the physicist establishes any law, or interprets his electrons, he does so by just these ideal mathematical means and is content to have his actual measurements approximate what he conceives to be reality. The latter are relatively rules of thumb.

Perhaps certain Ideas are, after all, more real than the tangible things we associate with them! Thought at any rate appears to constrain us to accept what (so far as our sense-evidence goes) exists only in the mind as a better index of what is "really there" than sense-perception itself. Scientific laws and relationships as well as entities (ids, atoms, protons) illustrate the same fact. It would be absurd to attribute any *law* as such to taste, vision or hearing. Yet we take it to represent the real situation. And all the way from gravitation to molecular rotations the data of our senses again give us only approximations to what we consider the true law. A cause, as such, has absolutely nothing among perceived objects to correspond to it. One billiard ball strikes a second one and sets it moving. We say the first was the cause of the motion. But did we see, or hear, or taste, what passed into the second when it began to move? What is true of causes is also true of similarity and equality, in fact of all relationships. Plato's own example of beauty may be taken as illustrative of qualities in general—which we also regard as "there." Unless we are prepared to say that beauty is a mere word—so much breath that we hear, as the nominalists later maintained—we seem to have no alternative to regarding it as "there," in somewhat the same sense in which we accept electrons or gravitation as real. Moreover, our visible, audible works of art can no more be identified with beauty than the figures we draw can be identified with the mathematical ones. A statue helps us realize by way of beauty what the model of a cone does for conic sections—and always imperfectly. Not even the sum-total of all works of art which have ever existed, or all the beauties manifested in nature taken together, can be identified with beauty, any more than all the lines which have ever been drawn can be identified with a mathematical line. Beauty continues to manifest itself whatever the fate of particular songs or paintings. The relationships expressed in mathematical laws do not depend upon individual figures, or even upon the understanding of them by particular students. Plato's description of such Ideas as essences manifesting something common in a number of particulars and, from the standpoint of our minds, non-sensuous (colorless, odorless, intangible, invisible) is a most precise statement of fact.

Even when, with unreflecting common sense, we try to deal directly with external things, forgetting that we have a mind at all, we are brought to the same conclusions. The most simple-minded person realizes that something is present in a seed by virtue of which it produces, say a poppy, not a mustard plant. Efforts have been made to locate this X in some part of the seed. In great numbers of eggs stains have been employed to count chromosomes in order to find the "determinants" of particular forms of life. But no one has thus far touched, or seen, or heard, or smelt, whatever determines the course of any given development. The number of chromosomes and their configurations suggest laws (Ideas); energy (another non-sensuous Idea) is said to be released and reorganized; ids and biophors (undiscovered, invisible particles or points of force) are set up as causes; and again we find ourselves dealing with—nothing, so far as our senses are concerned. But is it nothing?

The crudest mind here agrees with biologist and philosopher that something definite and real is "there," whether it be called by one name or another. A poppy seed will not produce petunias howsoever various the climates or the soils in which it grows. And if, by cross-fertilization or other means, we modify new generations of plants, we are only superimposing other X's, no less definite, no less active causes, no less imperceptible. Whether we take our examples again from living things or chemical elements seems to make no difference. "Something" determines the configuration of electrons entering into an atom of chlorine, making it fundamentally different from hydrogen, although both elements appear to be built up of similar protons and electrons. We may call this X a "form," an "energy," an "Idea," or, if we prefer, invent another name. But in any event we do not (or have not) found it in the matter which it organizes, though we also seem constrained to think of it as somehow present there.

With these examples in mind we may find it easier to understand why Plato wrote of Ideas as unchanging, indestructible, timeless, supersensible essences discovered by intuition, creative imagination, and reason, under the stimulus of sense-experience. They are "common notions,"[6] "pat-

[6] *Soph.* 240a.

terns" which exist in the mind [7] distinct from things which "partake" of them,[8] but almost unintelligible to human apprehension unless expressed by examples or translated into the language of facts.[9] We do not realize them in material things as such—and yet objects of sense are steps by which we are able to mount to the vision of perfection which they provide.[10] Every law of nature is an example; when we discover intelligible causes we realize Ideas.[11] The imperfect order and proportions manifested in particular things are reflections of a universal, ideal order which the mind discovers for itself, e. g., mathematics,[12] or in the contemplation of beauty. He who is instructed eventually perceives "a nature of wondrous beauty . . . not growing and decaying or waxing and waning, not fair in one point and foul in another . . . or existing in every other being, as, for example, in an animal, or in heaven, or in earth, or in any other place; but beauty absolute, separate, simple and everlasting which . . . is imparted to the ever-growing and perishing beauties of all other things." [13] In Ideas we discover purposes by which the rationality of the world is revealed to science. By them we synthesize, coördinate, unify our otherwise disordered perceptions. "Can anyone have a more exact way of considering or contemplating anything than the being able to look at one Idea gathered from many different things?" [14]

Thus we are said to have two kinds of knowledge: one fragmentary and particular, having to do with sensory experience; the other, form-giving, unifying, discovering causes, generalizing, making intelligible in terms of pur-

[7] *Parm.* 132.
[8] *Parm.* 129.
[9] *Statesman,* 277.
[10] *Symp.* 211.
[11] *Phædo,* 100.
[12] *Rep.* VI, 510–11.
[13] *Symp.* 211.
[14] *Laws,* XII, 965c.

poses, having therefore to do with non-sensuous Ideas, yet "occasioned" by perceptions of the senses. Despite their important differences both kinds of knowledge are interdependent. Many interpreters from Aristotle until late in the nineteenth century have assumed from Plato's language that he meant to distinguish "two worlds" corresponding to these two forms of knowledge. The "world of Ideas" exists apart in some transcendent "empyrean," uncontaminated by the dust and dirt of "this world"; the timeless, spaceless abode of pure "archetypes" reduplicating in some "divine" and "heavenly" manner our imperfect, changing world of everyday experience. Thus for every book there is a more perfect book "laid up in Heaven." There is an "absolute" bed in the "empyrean" far more glorious than ever man's hands constructed. Every man has his invisible double in the skies. Every act we perform is done over again up there among the "non-material" men, whose nature provides "patterns" for us to "imitate" if we can by "participating" in Ideas. This empyrean double of everything we know is the only "true" world; and we "ascend" to it when we cut loose from the "bondage" of our senses.

How any one with incipient intuitions of poetry in his soul could have failed to recognize the poet-philosopher's figurative language is, indeed, hard to understand! The phrases, of course, are all correctly reported. Ideas are non-spatial, non-material, invisible, they form a "cosmos" (order) among themselves when one reasons clearly and adequately, they are perfect archetypes, absolute standards by which we measure (cf. mathematics). Particular examples of any Idea (a particular "man," or a certain "just" act, or a drawn figure) are all "imperfect copies," imitations, yet have something in common, "participate" in their standard of reference. But was it a wonder that Plato should have broken into figures of speech when he realized the meaning of the scientific ideal, the conception of perfected knowledge manifested in laws and causes, mathematical relationships, purposes, and definite orders discovered by Ideas? Such a vision of perfection might well have seemed to him "heavenly" without any dogma of a Heaven beyond the skies; "divine" without theological implications; belonging to the "empyrean" because it raised one's mind from narrow, earth-bound isolation to an expansive and comprehensive view of things. The glory of the world as revealed to the mind of a philosophical scientist surely challenges him to language other than that of the market-place, or of superficial observation! Is not the "true world" in large and small, literally "beyond" what we perceive, immeasurably more beautiful, purposive and mathematically coördinated than what "appears" to us? He who finds more in heaven and earth than e'er was dreamt in our philosophy is not necessarily projecting "another world," a ghost of the one we live in.

In the first part of the *Parmenides*, Plato himself considers somewhat more literally this supposition that Ideas constitute a "world apart." "Young Socrates" (who, as we have seen, may possibly have been Plato's critic, Aristotle) is troubled not only by the question of how these "two worlds" are related to each other, but how there can be Ideas —so heavenly, divine, perfect, etc.—of dirt and such-like things. Plato's answer seems to be: There are ideas of ignoble and insignificant things as well as of beauty and what we cherish highly. Science considers all aspects of our world, whether great or small, noble or ignoble. "Young Socrates" will realize that there are laws and essential aspects of things in the commonest and pettiest facts, when he penetrates a little more deeply into philosophy. As to the "participation" of external things in the Ideas, e. g., actual men in the Idea of man, it cannot be taken literally. The Idea isn't like a sail that can be spread over a number of objects to hold them together in a unity, or even like this day of the month in which we are all said to "participate." "Copying" is also an inadequate figure. Even "resemblance" can hardly be imagined between Ideas and objects. For suppose a given object resembled a given Idea, it would be a *new* Idea of resemblance by which it would be realized! And so the process might go on forever. There seems to be no way of imagining things and Ideas as two worlds literally "copying," or "participating in" or "causing" one the other. These are figures of speech.

Why should we not then simply say: Ideas exist only in the mind; there is nothing "corresponding to them," "like them," "related to them" in the external world anywhere? Thus we should have done away with all the misunderstanding about a double world and the bother of trying to think how they are related. There are Ideas in the mind, and there are "things" outside; they have nothing to do with each other. Plato considers this too, but he finds it quite impossible to assume that knowledge is a fiction of our minds, a more or less agreeable dream without relation to reality. Even the simplest piece of knowledge assumes that it "represents" reality. And if we cannot believe that Ideas and things have some "common order," "relationships," "interdependence," "correspondence," we are reduced to a Skepticism that cannot so much as express itself. It was apparently to reinforce this point that Plato, in the second part of the *Parmenides,* drew a series of *verbal* conclusions proving diametrically contradictory propositions by Ideas which seem to be cut off from reality. But whatever his object may have been here, he shows conclusively that figures of speech all fail to present a consistent interpretation of how Ideas are related to things—but that on the whole symbolical language succeeds better than Skepticism here. So there are various aspects of the Ideal Theory, some indefinite and poetic yet based upon the fact that "something of the kind must be true"; others more specific and absolute, as in mathematical theory; some psychological, as when Plato shows how Ideas are the product of anamnesis—what the mind elicits by its own inner activity; others metaphysical, when he endeavors to comprehend how Ideas can stand for reality. But for all the difficulties he encountered, his thought, properly understood, is nowhere self-contradictory. Even the "transcendent existence of Ideas," about which so many have been troubled in the earlier works, fits in with the discussion of whether they are merely mental. For even as such they would be "apart from" reality! In the *Philebus*, *Republic*, *Theætetus*, *Sophist*, *Statesman* and *Laws*, Ideas are referred to in the same terms by which we—side-stepping, perhaps, the problem of what they really are, and how they give us knowledge—refer to natural laws, causes and general concepts.

Plato could not side-step such a problem and realized how all knowledge is dependent upon it. Nor could he satisfy himself that he had found an adequate solution. But he had faith that our various moments and variegated experiences, the maze of evanescent and conflicting particulars by which we are confronted, can be consistently ordered by the mind's own forms into a means of realizing the essential, the common, the permanent in that experience. How these mental constructs could give us natural laws, relationships, qualities, the fundamental being of what is, he could only surmise in figures of speech. The fact seemed incredible—yet none the less a fact! Ideas *are* the standard of reference by whose means we realize reality. (Cf. our examples from physical chemistry.) We hold by them even when particular measurements only approximate them (Mathematics). The absolutely pure or perfect Idea, whether of unity, cause, or beauty, or of anything else, is never manifested *in things*. Yet our hope for knowledge lies in making an orderly system of just these mental constructs by which the flux of tangible things may also become intelligible. So much Plato took to be the Thinker's axioms.

Have we any cues as to what this order is? Can we arrange Ideas on the scale of their importance or discover their hierarchy? Plato answers: The more we deal with dialectic—the art of correlating Ideas—the more we realize not that *some* order obtains among them but that the most potent Idea with which we are acquainted is that of *good.* "That which imparts truth to the known, and the power of knowing to the knower, is what I would have you term the Idea of good, and this you will deem to be the cause of science." As the eye alone makes intelligible the light of the sun, so the Idea of good is the "lord of light" for the "things of mind." [15] This suggests once more a poetic, or perhaps a theological, figure of speech. But Plato undoubtedly also meant it to be a literal scientific hypothesis: the goal of every explanation is teleological. Perhaps a modern example will help to make the hypothesis clearer. When we interpret the structure and functions, causes and activities, of any organic thing, what, in the last resort, are we aiming to do? In studying an organ of the human body for instance we dissect, count, describe, observe its motions, secretions, how it is controlled by nerves, how nourished. But the counting, the dissecting, the secretions by themselves are of little meaning until we coördinate movements with organic structure, secretions with other organs of the body, food with the organ's functions, etc. In other words, our object is to answer the question: What is the *good* which the organ serves, and how successfully is it attained? When, as so far with the vermiform appendix, we fail to discover that good purpose, we acknowledge the absence of real knowledge. Now the Platonic hypothesis is the more general statement that the final term in our knowledge of anything is the effort to discover how it contributes to the functions of the larger whole, how it forms a harmonious part of that whole.

The most difficult aspect of the theory is this conception of

[15] *Rep.* VI, 508.

Ideas as *causes*. From the standpoint of knowledge it is simple enough to realize that they are the *ground*, the basis upon which, and by which, knowing becomes possible. Without Ideas there would be no knowledge. They are agencies by which the mind attains insight. Even "Cause" is one of them. We discover causes first of all as Ideas. But Plato also thought of movements and activities of all sorts in the outside world as brought about by the same agencies which manifest themselves in our thinking. The intangible, invisible, A's (or X's) giving form, for example, to a living being, are Ideas as understood by the mind—and also external agencies, if our knowledge be supposed to have real and not fictitious objects. Thus the order of our Ideas not only "represents" (as we say) external reality. It *is* reality itself (which includes both our minds and external things), actively at work. The true objects of our thought, in short, when we think adequately of causes, are forces like those in our own minds.[16] This, whether consciously or unconsciously, is, to be sure, our modern hypothesis—and not only in psychology when we deal with "Ideo-motor action." In the illustration used above, biology endeavors to "represent" mentally the causes at work in the activities say of blood-corpuscles or muscles, calling them by various names and coördinating all of them under the Idea "Life." It assuredly thinks of them as genuinely active A's and B's (or X's), and of life as an objective, unifying agency. Now Plato thought of the Idea Good in some such way as we think of life in an organism—a coördinating force in the universe as a whole. And so, in a lesser way, every genuine Idea, howsoever insignificant or evil, is said to have an active part in the scheme, just as we think of a blood corpuscle's motions as related to the activities of life. In short: Ideas dialectically coördinated and adequately interpreting all the facts are the very agencies and forces back of all movements

[16] *Soph.* 248e.

and changes, as well as of the evanescent appearances of things.

Plato confesses his inability to think this out in detail. The "mythos" of creative imagination, incipient intuitions of knowledge, opinions inadequately accounting for all the facts, troublesome problems of dialectic itself, permit only "intimations," hypotheses, of how Ideas of evil, and chance, and the seemingly irrational can figure in an orderly, coördinated, intelligible scheme. But he holds to his ideal of science, the beckoning of omniscience, despite all dissatisfaction with its slight fulfillment. He sees how complicated that ideal is: and yet its purpose is clear, its tools are at hand, and one can measure progress toward the goal! It is a challenge both to clear-cut reason and to artistic intuition. Bare enumeration or description is its starting-point. The mind from the first provides forms, categories, patterns, by which to classify the items of experience. Thus it discovers essences, qualities, types by which to make intelligible what otherwise would be chaotic. Finding the universal in particulars, or the permanent in evanescent things, involves relationships, understanding contexts, above and below, earlier and later—or what we mean by "natural laws." But natural laws in their turn are more than "right points of view" or coordinations of a static system. They mean causes, functions, dynamic forces—and yet more, for numbers are included in that ideal. Natural law means mathematical regularity. All the arithmetical and geometric designs which in the *Philebus* and *Timæus* Plato constructs by way of trying to make more intelligible the causes he observed in things are confessedly hypothetical projections to realize the demands of mathematical accuracy. Hence his characterization of mathematical concepts as mediating Ideas between sense-experiences and the deeper knowledge of reality.

Granted however, that one had correctly described, found all qualities, categories, essences, understood their relationships, functions, laws and causes, even to the minutest mathematical perfection, still the ideal of science leads on to the question: To what good or purpose? And until we succeed in interpreting in the light of a reason for being, our object remains unfulfilled. The Idea of Good thus stands higher than that of Being itself as the key to knowledge. Yet all these demands, as well as their means of fulfillment, Plato regards as creations of minds inwardly realizing reality by intelligent use of the "long and difficult language of facts." Objectively Ideas are for the great Idealist also the basis of whatever is intelligible in nature. In short, thought governs the world as far as we understand it.

CHAPTER XIV

PLATO'S PSYCHOLOGY

The mind of man and whatever seems to be like it in nature was undoubtedly Plato's major interest. But he did not segregate his interpretations into a special book, or discuss them systematically. His "psychology" therefore is in constant contact with his conceptions of nature, of ethics, social theory, and dialectic. Yet his observations and conclusions, organized as we shall here undertake to study them, form a respectable and influential nucleus of that science. They are especially interesting as throwing light on the points of view which we are inclined to take for granted, because they have become habitual, and as showing how fanciful many of our own (as well as the Platonic) conceptions are. To illustrate by a single example: The persistent wax-tablet simile, according to which memory is the "impression" and retention of sensations upon a more or less abundant plastic material in the body, which can be either too hard or too soft for the purpose, is Plato's figure of speech. "Impressions," "plasticity," "resistance" (or inhibition), have to this day become the commonly accepted terms, though a moment's reflection shows them to be purely analogical.

Plato recognized the close relationships between body and mind, and localized various mental functions in particular organs and parts. He conceived the quasi-mental activities of lower forms of life to be analogous to our own functions, which latter he did not hesitate to call partly vegetable—though a part of the human "soul." He characterized our functions in general as different kinds of inner motions, some going smoothly, as a body in circular motion, others back and forth irregularly, as though in jagged lines. Yet the soul is not merely functions of the body—a kind of "harmony," or what music is to the lyre.[1] It is a substantial reality which must not be confused with the body as such.[2] The latter is too often a drag upon its activities—as well as being the organ by which it realizes itself.

To consider first of all this remarkable conception of mental activity as a form of *motion*, we should note that Plato probably came to this conclusion (as also did Democritus) by the analogy of motions in the external world, which, he observed, always accompany sensations. No sensation without these motions impinging on the various sense organs! What more natural than to assume that an *inner* motion somehow coördinates with the external one, the effect being propagated through the body to the "seat of consciousness," [3] where the soul becomes aware of color, sound, or warmth, as the case may be! Parallel analogies were at hand for all the various functions of the mind: pleasantness is regular unhindered motion; pain, unnatural, thwarted motion; harshness is incisive, angular motion; desire (will), prospective or uncompleted motion; reasoning, symmetrical motion.

What characterizes mental motion in contrast to that of the external world is spontaneity. Self-activity is the index of soul life and must not be confused with merely mechanical motion. There are various kinds of motion. Beginning with change of position by outside agency (mechanical), one rises to the more complicated motions of growth and decay (physiological), and eventually to self-active, and then purposive, motion. The activity of "soul" is, of course, not found in "motion by other" at all; it is vaguely present in

[1] *Phædo,* 93.
[2] *Laws,* X, 892.
[3] *Tim.* 45c.

vegetable or physiological appetite, which seems to be partly the result of "motion by other" (stimulus), and partly desire; but its highest form is in spontaneous action directed towards some end.[4]

This interpretation of mental life—which is still reflected in our "nervous impulses," "reactions," "reflex arcs," "currents," "molecular changes," "movements of thought," "neural connections," and elsewhere—places soul activity well within the course of nature (cf. supernatural interpretations), and also regards that life as having *degrees*. Even mental diseases are held to originate in the body by the commingling of the latter's (unhealthy) motions with those of the mind.[5] The conception of degrees or "parts" of the soul is elaborated in terms of a "rational," a "feeling," and a "desiring" part, having their seats respectively in the brain, the upper half of the spinal column (thorax), and the lower part (abdomen). These have characteristic motions of their own, but are none the less bound together in a unity, so that even at its best the rational activity of the mind is limited by its relations to feelings and desires. On the other hand, the activities of reason help to determine those of the lower centers. The influence of the cranial part of our life extends over all the vital organs. It is "reflected" in the liver, so that desires becoming unruly and indiscreet in sleep are checked by movements from above. So, too, with those movements in the heart known as courage or fear, which are modified by the activity of ideas.

Yet Plato also regards this close connection of body and soul, and of their three parts as not to the advantage of the highest, or thinking, soul. We are "mixtures." "As we now behold her the soul is marred by the union with the body and other miseries." Clear-cut, rational purposes are confused by irrational desires. We are subject to the play of external

[4] *Phædr.* 245e; *Tim.* 89a; *Laws,* X, 894–6.
[5] *Tim.* 87.

motions, not only in sensation, but also in feeling, and are pulled hither and thither by vague, unintelligible movements from within. Reason can only rarely attain the perfection of the dialectic. It must feed upon confusion, faith, the play of shadowy opinion, and conflicting notions, before it attains clarity. Free, spontaneous, purposive activity expressing a harmonious motion, which is also the quest of excellence, beauty, goodness, Plato regards as the central function of human life; but it also depends upon the peripheral, the irrational, the confused and confusing. We are all of us like that old sea-god, Glaucus, "whose original image can hardly be discerned because his natural members are broken off and crushed and damaged by the waves, in all sorts of ways, and incrustations have grown over them, of seaweed, of shells and stones, so that he is more like some monster than he is to his own natural form." [6]

On the other hand, Plato did not countenance the view which, even in his day, destroyed the fundamental unity of mental life. "No one can suppose, my boy, that in each of us, as in a sort of Trojan horse, there are perched a number of unconnected senses, which do not all meet in some one nature, the mind, or whatever we please to call it." [7] And this is true of reason, feeling, and desire as well, each of which implicates the others. Life, in other words, from nutrition and reproduction to the most exalted visions of truth, belongs organically together, however unfortunate that mixture may be from the standpoint of our higher functions. Nor can mind be separated from body "as we now behold her"—even though at times Plato doubts whether the brain is truly the organ whereby reason deals with ideas.[8] In fact there is no sharp line of demarcation between the whole organism, body and mind, and external nature. We are a

[6] *Rep.* X, 611.
[7] *Theæt.* 184.
[8] *Theæt.* 185.

part of a larger whole, not only physically, but mentally. A complete account of soul would therefore involve the whole of the cosmos.

Though every sensation has its specific organ, with a specific form of motion, and the three main divisions of the soul are also widely different, Plato makes the effort to think of them all as similar. "Soul," indeed, for him (as for Aristotle), is equivalent to "life" and includes much of what we classify to-day as physiological activity. Thus appetite is classed with desire, and emotions are sometimes called physical, sometimes "of the soul." Energy of the body is correlated with mental motion. So that Plato would not have been content to define psychology as a "science of conscious states," though he does not have anything corresponding to "subconscious." Nor could he have accepted a "science of behavior" as adequate, since purposive self-activity, and not mechanism, is the most characteristic function of soul. The problem of the "one and the many" presented difficulties which he could not overcome. How can reason and appetite, for all the "direction" of the former and the "impelling force" of the latter, be unified in a single system? How can bodily motions and emotions be conceived of as the same? Yet Plato's difficulty remains our own as well.

To consider sensations more in detail: they are dependent, one and all, as we have observed, upon external motion, but there is also a requisite inner order without which no sensation takes place. This is coördinate with physical development. Until the specific organ is there with its proper motion, the soul is without a particular sensation. Granted the proper adjustment, however, the perceived differences, or qualities, are to be explained in terms of different forms of motion appropriate to the organ. And though sentient parts transmit these motions, it is neither the sense-organ nor the matter between it and the "center of consciousness," mind, or whatever else you prefer to call it, which does the sensing.

Rather it is the mind itself acting through its connections and the particular organ, using it as an instrument. Sensation is, therefore, more than merely passive reception of external stimuli. It is inner activity, meeting the outer, as it were, halfway.

Vision, Plato conceives as a light or gentle fire in the eyes, which becomes active under certain conditions, and is projected from them to meet that which in daylight is reflected from objects. Night lacks this gentle fire of the sun and thus the eyes' own light becomes futile. Color is a sort of "flame" from bodies, which is perceived when the currents from the eyes are symmetrical with it. To explain the variety of combinations of color Plato has recourse to the different effects, especially dilations and contractions of the visual current, produced by outside motion, an explanation which he also tries to corroborate by reference to parallel effects in other senses, e. g., taste and temperature.

In taste the "vessels" of the tongue are contracted or relaxed by the four fundamental stimuli: bitter, salt, acid, and sweet. These and their qualities (astringent, pungent, earthy) he explains as varieties of motion, parallel to those of vision. In the case of acid he described these changes in terms of what we to-day call chemical action. Smell, due to contacts of "half-formed substances" (vapors), is assumed to be unanalyzable: but the differences in the "contacts" are supposed to explain the various qualities. The organ of touch is flesh all over the body. Touch is a kind of "general feeling" which he associates with hot and cold, hard and soft, heavy and light, rough and smooth—for all of which he attempts an explanation in geometric terms, or according as they resist or yield to pressure.

Hearing, Plato regards as the most important sense in the education of youth, for it can attain and regulate disorderly motion of the soul by communicating harmony and rhythm through sound. Hearing is made possible by shocks in the air, communicated by it to the ear, thence to the brain and blood, till it reaches the soul. Differences of pitch, he explains, are due to the swiftness or slowness of these "blows," and harmony to the similarity or dissimilarity (discord) of the motion aroused in us by them. It is uncertain whether or not vibrations are implied by these beats. Such an analysis of tones became a current explanation in Plato's day.

What is very surprising in this account of sensation is the connections of the sense-organs with most unexpected parts of the body. All conduct to the soul and at the same time are the instruments of the soul. Sensation in general is a communion of body and soul in relation to external objects.[9] Yet (apparently after announcing themselves to the "center of consciousness") the motions go on: in the case of sound, to the liver; of taste, to the heart; unpleasant smells irritate "all the cavity of the body that is between the head and the navel"; vision "affects the whole body up to the seat of consciousness." All of this implies an awareness of the close relationship between the vital organs and sensations, on its pleasant or unpleasant side. But he thought it necessary to conduct these effects thither by the blood vessels, which along with the flesh transmit such motions or impulses. To what place—as the "seat of consciousness"—he found it difficult to decide. So much of the body is involved in the pleasantness of sensation! Moreover, "seat of consciousness," with him as with us, covered a multitude of obscurities. How can an immaterial anything have a seat at all?

Pain, Plato regarded as the opposite of pleasure, thus initiating the long error which persists even to the present. Unrestrained, suitable, or natural motions of the soul, he interpreted as pleasant; while pain is generally impeded or diseased activity. This does not imply a standard of con-

[9] Cf. *Phil.* 34a.

duct, however, because pleasure is without rational measure.[10] It can be at once "the greatest incitement of evil," [11] even a disease,[12] and positive good.[13]

Memory he distinguishes from recollection, the former being the preservation of sensations in consciousness, retained, as we observed above, by a sort of "wax-tablet." (We say "traces in the nervous system.") But recollection presents another problem, which Plato makes doubly vivid by another famous simile. Suppose we liken our store of retained impressions to birds in an aviary. We may always be said to "possess" them, because in some sense they are ours. We certainly have in our minds a great number of these "birds," some in small groups, some solitary, flying anywhere and everywhere. And yet they have to be caught over again every time we *really* possess them. Oftentimes we catch a ringdove when we want a pigeon—and perhaps this gives us the cue as to why we make errors in general.[14] But how do we manage to catch any at all?

Plato's answer is: Association helps us. Like birds of a feather, similar impressions somehow flock together. If they were contiguous bodies moving under the same conditions, naturally they would appear every one with its neighbor. But we should be mistaken in assuming that these impressions go together mechanically, or come back to us without an act of our own minds. Recollection is self-activity and involves ideas, which cannot be interpreted as sensuous or as having anything in common with bodies. The proof of this will be recalled from the previous chapter. Recollection, *bringing* to mind, *associating* anything, as well as thinking, would have no physical analogues, even if impressions themselves turned out to be physical. It is the very basis of con-

[10] *Phil.* 65b.
[11] *Tim.* 69c.
[12] *Phil.* 46b.
[13] *Laws* V, 733–4.
[14] *Theæt.* 197 ff.

scious life. Sensations are *perceived* by a relation to past experience: *meaning* is only thus made possible. Thinking is, of course, the most obvious case of selective, spontaneous, self-activity. But recollection is its foundation. That is why Plato based an argument for immortality on recollection. He could not derive it from any but its own specific activity. Hence, like Bergson in modern times, he could not think of it as the function of a body, coming into being or disappearing with a particular organism.

Imagination also illustrates this principle of selection. It is a reinstatement, not of "images," or reduced copies of things,—as the reader will recall Democritus had said—but of sensory motions when the stimulus (external motion) is no longer there. It can be merely mechanical, the echo of what has passed. But we have not only a "secretary of records" but a "painter" within us who, using the records in his own way, correlates and creates spontaneously.[15] Thus creative imagination leads on to thinking and depends both upon memory (retention) and recollection.

Thinking, in its turn, is distinctive as selectively dealing with concepts. But it is more or less "mixed up" with all the lower functions, from nutrition and reproduction up. This is interestingly illustrated by the various degrees of knowledge, from conjecture and belief, to understanding and dialectical thought. "Fantasies" are given to us in sense experience with the minimum of recollection. One man may "fancy" a given wind cold; another will fancy it warm. Knowledge reduced to mere sense terms would be not only devoid of meaning but a chaotic flux. Opinion, however, utilizes sensations around the meaning made possible by recollection (which associates ideas with sensations), and thus begins the work of knowing. But in its simple stages it merely deals with shadows, with becoming rather than being. On a slightly higher level opinion becomes belief, or a kind of persuasion

[15] *Phil.* 39a.

which has convictions without knowing why. Higher still is the knowledge based upon hypotheses and the practice of the arts. This he calls understanding. But it is tentative still, as lacking the principles of that with which it deals. Absolute knowledge comes with the realization of perfect ideas so completely coördinated that reasons and principles are organized into a unit.[16] Thus there is a scale of knowledge from the lowest to the highest, and though the process "rises above" sensations it also depends upon them. Plato assuredly kept his eyes and his ears open as persistently as any naïve Realist!

At its best this "love" (urge, desire) for knowledge is restricted in us by our carnal nature. Sensations involve emotions; so does even the highest urge of knowledge. And emotions are physical as well as mental. They grow out of physical needs and appetites, and can be cranial as well as abdominal. Indeed Plato maintained that emotions associated with ideas (sentiments) can influence the abdominal organs and their appetites.[17] Of course this also takes place in the inverse direction. But how, he was at a loss to explain, confessedly using conjectures and mythological hypotheses which, God knows, are only probabilities.[18] Yet among them is the supposition that affections may be classified according as they belong to the soul, or to the body, or to both at once. There is, for example, purely mental, unmixed pleasure (intellectual); or the body may be in pain while the soul has pleasure (mixed); again the soul may itself be moved in two directions (tragedy's "pleasing horror"); even the body may suffer pain from cold and also pleasure in getting warm.

The three-part soul corresponds in the main to our cognitive, affective and conative division, though *will*, with Plato,

[16] *Rep.* VI, 511; VII, 534.
[17] *Tim.* 71b.
[18] *Tim.* 72e.

figures chiefly as unfulfilled desire. When rationalized, however, desire (eros) becomes the quest of excellence itself,[19] and once more illustrates how interconnected are all the portions of our mental life. This is also the key to Plato's conception of education, which looks to the training of spirit and desire as well as of reason, and of the body as appropriate instrument and expression of the soul. Man's noblest development is, of course, alone made possible by the wisdom of reason, justly apportioning and developing his functions in the light of the ideal essence, or Idea of a man. But this is also more than empirical knowledge, even that of the most penetrating science. It is the urge of desire rationalized, the divine love of excellence.

For all the poetic license of Plato's psychological interpretations the reader will agree that they still provide light for the shadowy portions of an incipient science.

[19] *Symp.* 209–211.

CHAPTER XV

PLATO'S ETHICAL IDEAL: SUCCESS AND THE MEANS OF ATTAINING IT

1

We already possess the key to Plato's conception of morality in his estimate of human nature. The happy development of all our functions to a balanced whole as determined by reason, is, of course, its central motive. How to attain effectiveness, to manage one's affairs, privately as well as publicly, in the most efficient manner, to be as much of a success as one can, is the problem. Morality is knowledge of what makes for the maximum richness and satisfaction of life, one "sound" physically and mentally. It is the path to inner health and lasting happiness increasingly made possible as one grows wiser. It is the means of overcoming the commonplace by making life itself an art. Far from being the tiresome old saws and arbitrary propaganda which modern times associate with the word, morality, for Plato, is a voyage of discovery, a golden journey in search of what every normal man in his heart of hearts most ardently desires. Nor does our "immorality" remotely suggest (as a foil) the positive content of his ideal.

It is an open-minded, unbiased attempt to answer the question: What do we include (or what exclude) in our picture when we paint a human life realizing the qualities of a thoroughbred? Or if we prefer "gentleman," what are the qualities we admire in him and why? Thus the word "good" for Plato has none of that "moralistic" quality which makes it distasteful to so many moderns. It means "successful," "happy," "effective," "well-balanced," "rich in content"—

in short what no man can possibly help desiring. It is this good concerning which Socrates quotes Simonides: "No man willingly is wretched, or against his will is blest." It is never a counterfeit, an appearance, a make-believe. No man would choose these for himself. And when he does choose evil for good he has simply mistaken one for the other. "Goods," therefore, whether "material" or of any other sort, can be grouped together as "What men desire."

This might at first seem a very easy way of solving one's ethical problems. Try to fulfill all your desires! Follow each impulse as it comes! Plato replies: Well and good if a man knows what he is choosing. But knowing is exactly what will prevent him from being pulled hither and thither by his impulses. Insight will enable him to choose the greater good in preference to the lesser, and spare him bad bargains with himself. So that reason is central in the picture, whatever a man may set his heart on. He has to know what he wants and why, he has to organize his possible "goods"; otherwise he gets what he doesn't want. No man in his senses chooses unhappiness, disease, or failure. And he will avoid the impulses leading in that direction—unless he mistakes appearances for reality.

From whatever other angle you look at "goods" you come to the same conclusions. One man desires money. But until he knows how to use his resources they are of little good to him. With the miser money is a source of anxiety, loss of sleep, suspicion, friendlessness, dishonor, unhappiness. The same is true of external power, authority, gifts of fortune, strength of body, indeed, of anything one might desire. Real possession means intelligent use. The man who *enjoys* a painting, rather than he who *merely* possesses it, gets the "good of it"; the skilled performer on an instrument, rather than the dealer. Even the possessor of a sound physique and excellent mental powers cannot avail himself of these without their *intelligent* use—which means fitting them into a general scheme of good. Thus it becomes apparent as a fundamental axiom that every particular, specific good, whatever else it may be, is first of all the mind's intelligent awareness and use of what it possesses, and what is harmonious, or fits in, with a *plan* of one's desires.

The earlier "dialogues of search" repeatedly illustrate this unity of the good. When we look into the meaning of "fine" (greater Hippias), "temperance" (Charmides), "courage" (Laches), "friendship" (Lysis), "pleasure" (Protagoras), the discussion generally ends with the disappointing realization that we know extraordinarily little as to the meaning of such terms taken by themselves. We call an act of courage, and also one of justice, a "fine" act. There are fine girls, fine horses, fine musical instruments, fine pots and pans. What is the common quality? Perhaps we answer: "Fine" is "becoming," "fitting," "appropriate," "beautiful," "pleasant." Or we characterize courage as "persistence," "endurance," "resolution." But every time you find the earmarks of a particular "good thing" in this way you discover that you need a further qualification. Courage, for example, is not just endurance under any and all conditions. There is surely nothing courageous about soldiers who hold on to an impregnable position. Nor is foolish endurance courage. You must have wisdom in your courage. The "finer" the art of justice the more wisdom it displays. And wisdom in its turn implies balance, poise of mind, persistence, as well as insight, a "fine" sense of values, tact, judgment and so on. In short, whatever is admirable or desirable belongs to a system which includes the *whole of good.*

Now there are several surprising corollaries which follow from these propositions. One of them is this: When a man desires "success," "efficiency," "happiness" he is really aiming for everything good, if he knows it! Only ignorance could stand in the way of his cultivating courage, temperance, whatever is "fine," the wise thing to do, and all the rest. So that the real problem in this connection is "tending one's soul," overcoming the ignorance which thwarts what everyone most desires. When a man "goes wrong" he stupidly "throws a monkey-wrench," as we say, into the operations of his organs, physically and mentally, for they go along together. Moral conduct, the quest of excellence, is ordinary prudence therefore, in "keeping after" what you want, avoiding evil in every form. But it is very much more than that. It is "blessedness"—an inner "success," a harmony of mind, a happy health and integrity of soul by which, indeed, external values (wealth, power) can alone be of any good.

And so the highest Idea, which Plato regarded as "like the sun" in illuminating the way of science, also makes intelligible the meaning of right and wrong, duties, commands, loyalties and laws. The final term, in whose light every desire, right, action, or institution is measured, is human good. What destroys our life or thwarts our healthy functions, by standing in the way of an inner harmony of purpose, is evil. Divorced from the Idea of Good, laws, duties and all other ethical ideas dissolve into mere arbitrary commands, "conventions" as the Sophists say, or sanctimonious nonsense. But illumined by good "the soul perceives and understands, and is radiant with intelligence." The harmonious order and rationality of our little human cosmos is then coordinated with that of the world as a whole. Our good is seen to be part of the universal order whose greatest perfection is revealed in the symmetry of its parts, its rational laws and harmonious functions. Thus one discovers anew that good is not an isolated advantage or desire. It is involved ultimately in all the undertakings of the sciences.

The specific problem of human good, however, is to attain such a harmony of mind that all our desires and purposes may make for the perfect functioning of our "parts," and thus also bring about the happiest use of our possessions —all the way from money and power, to friends and health of body. From a psychological standpoint Plato describes the perfecting of the irrational, or appetite-side of our nature, as the development of self-control or temperance. It is a result which, of course, cannot be achieved by appetites in themselves, since it depends upon their *rational* control. None the less it is the excellence which even the irrational part of our nature shows in its balanced functioning. In other words, one does not *suppress* the vegetative in man. It too must come to its florescence in the symmetrically developed person.

The distinction of the emotional ("spirited") side of our natures is courage. It consists of an awareness of what is really to be feared, loved, pitied, admired, combated, etc.—again a certain emotional (and volitional) *balance*. Without it both our healthy desires and the operations of our reasons are thwarted. Wisdom, the virtue of our rational nature, implies something more than knowledge, howsoever much it depends upon it. Above all it means judgment, the ability to *evaluate* in proper proportion. Upon it depends primarily the possibility of justice to all our functions. It has to check even the activities of thought when they do damage to our "spirit"—making us cold-blooded pedants, for example. But each of these "cardial virtues"—Temperance, Courage, Wisdom, Justice—is really a phase or aspect of the others, thus again illustrating the unity of good. Temperance is a kind of justice to conflicting impulses and appetites. Courage is wisdom in the control of emotions. Wisdom is justice that can "know itself," not overdoing even wisdom.

Plato's picture assuredly gives us that "unity in variety," which Greek artists prized so highly in a work of art! The central dominating figure is Reason, without which no order or intelligent judgment of any kind of value is possible. But Feeling, Will, Desire, Nutrition and every other human function has its appropriate place. For Plato was no ascetic. However much he regretted the sorry pictures of disease, senselessness, misery, worst of all the mess so many a man and woman makes of life by ignorance, he never advocated the "rooting out" of any part of ourselves. The problem is one of keeping in its proper place what is peripheral, or merely an episode, while developing all our various organs and functions to their normal part in the scheme.

"The just man does not permit the several elements within him to interfere with one another, or any of them to do the work of others—he sets in order his own inner life and is his own master and his own law, and at peace with himself." As a lyre of several strings rightly tuned finds use for all the notes and is one in many, so in the treatment of the body or our appetites, such action or thought is just, which brings about and preserves an active and harmonious condition. Its opposite is when a part of the soul rises up against the whole.[1]

It is true that Plato is sometimes oppressed by the thought of how strong a power the irrational parts of the soul can be. And then in poetic metaphor he speaks of the "prison-house" which hems in the aspirations of reason (*Phædo*). Again in the *Symposium* we hear how Love which demands beauty, and yearns to give birth to beauty, finds that "habits, tempers, opinions, desires, pleasures, fears, never remain the same in any one of us, but are always coming and going." If only Love's vision might be a permanent reality and our inspired moments could remain in contact with their object! Then a man might live the life of the gods! His soul might well give birth to fairer offspring than any mortal children. "Who, when he thinks of Homer and Hesiod and other great poets, would not rather have their children than ordinary human ones? Who would not emulate them in the creation of children such as theirs, which have preserved their memory and given them everlasting glory?"[2]

[1] *Rep.* IV, 443–4.
[2] *Symp.* 206, 209.

In such visions Plato even welcomes the prospect of a possible existence free from the cloying limitations of the body.[3] But these panegyrics of the higher functions cannot be said to swerve him from his fundamental idea of justice, which is to give the lesser as well as the greater its proper place in the whole. Nor is some other worldly existence the object of his ethical discussions. It is life as we know it, we creatures of fire and clay.

2

In the more specific application of his general points of view Plato comes to grips with many everyday problems. How can one specify *what* in particular cases the "good" course is? What sort of knowledge is it, and can it be imparted to another person? Wisdom, judgment, balance, do not seem to be qualities which one could directly *teach* another person. How then is good made available for one who seeks it? And this difficulty in turn suggests another: Is the unity of mind, or integrity based upon the just apportionment of our functions—an inner peace and satisfaction—either attainable or desirable? Is it not the very nature of the irrational part of us to be irrational, to resist "measure, proportion, balance," and hence to be in need of suppression rather than of development? But if we did that, ruling pleasures and appetites out of court, would the game itself be worth the candle? In fact are not pleasures nearer the center of satisfaction, as of more fundamental value to normal human beings, than the wisest judgment and most penetrating knowledge? Who would care for the latter *by itself*, unless he were a shriveled mass of bloodless categories?

Plato meets the various difficulties resolutely and without an ax to grind. Whenever he can, he gives the advantage of an argument to his opponent—thereby of course enhancing

[3] *Theæt.* 176.

the dramatic outcome when he makes his point. As to knowledge of the good, despite the fact that we are daily and hourly concerned with it, despite its fundamental importance for science, it is a specific kind of knowledge. Ethics is not likely to be of much value in the technique, say of writing a "good" speech, or of being "successful" as a physician. The good sought by morality is more ultimate than these, though to be a good physician may contribute to an ethical good. The latter concerns a *quality of soul*. It is more ultimate, because eventually everything we possess or do is determined by it. Without inner satisfaction the most brilliant professional success is without its good. Obviously self-knowledge is its center. For even the poor man who "tends his soul" is at bottom more successful than the distracted plutocrat.

But granting all this, can one maintain that there is a "science of good" which can be taught? This is an important question in many of the Dialogues but more particularly in the *Protagoras* and the *Gorgias*. At first thought it might appear as though the Sophists were correct in maintaining that the "goods" and "rights" cherished in various communities were the result not of any *thought* about principles, but of mere customs, habits, particular "knacks" of doing things, which developed under peculiar conditions. These are matters of convention. Success in any particular city means adaptation to the "times," to the "tastes" of the community. Hence the good of an Athenian, say artistic cultivation, might spell disaster to a militant Spartan.

Socrates admits that most people do not take much stock in teaching goodness to anybody. The Athenians seem to assume that everybody has (or ought to have) such discrimination as a natural gift, since every citizen takes his turn at government by lot. The superior power which leaders attain in the assembly and elsewhere would seem to be due not so much to "tending their souls" as to watching which way the wind may be blowing among the whims of the "general." There could be no doubt whatsoever concerning the great variety of standards, or how children imbibe what passes as virtue in a community much as they learn its language. But the curious fact is that the Sophists, who declare the good to be so various and merely conventional, should yet be *teaching it!* Protagoras professes to teach young men "prudence in the management of their private affairs and capacity to speak and act in the affairs of the city," "making them better than when they came," and showing them, in short, the basis of "statesmanship." How does he manage to do it, going from city to city where the natives of the place presumably would know more about local conditions than he? Gorgias also pleases all palates by a sort of "confectioner's art" in the communities to which he goes. Must not the reason be that there is something common to the various "goods" recognized in different places, and that men in fact do get similar satisfactions from them?

In the end Socrates convinces Protagoras that, despite all social habits, natural aptitudes, imitations, tastes, and varying traditions, which undoubtedly help to determine everyday opinions of right and good, he, the expert, is aiming for principles and common qualities. In contrast to the popular rule of thumb, his method is more scientific as aiming for greater exactness and as dealing with essential aspects rather than with accidental ones. The great Sophist himself is brought to realize that "goods" implicate each other. The just man cannot be impious, nor the temperate man unjust. He who cultivates courage is training himself all around. . . . At the same time Socrates realizes that this science has no such exactness as one finds in mathematics, and that the wisdom of the "general" is no small asset to the investigator. The latter cannot even examine specimens; his best discriminations have to include not a little "musical guesswork." Indeed, when it comes to saying what the *essence* of the Idea of Good is, we find ourselves face to face with

Reason's greatest problem and can only have recourse to the "visions" of intuition. The term (as applied to the cosmos) is perhaps impossible of being explained in other terms, just because it is the highest.

But to return to specific human goods, is it correct as a matter of psychology to say that he who cultivates courage also cultivates the rest of the virtues? The average opinion as combated by Socrates in the *Protagoras* and elsewhere agrees with that of most people to-day. The soldier excellent in courage may lack self-control; the ruthless politician may yet be gentle to his wife; the lover of his country, a boastful liar. Of course the answer of Socrates to all such instances is: Appearance is deceptive. *Truly* courageous soldiers will exercise self-control; the true lover of his country will not find it necessary to lie about her, etc. However various the aspects of excellence you always come back to the realization that wisdom is their common root and happiness their florescence.

This is interestingly brought out in the "greatest surplus of pleasure" doctrine as discussed in the *Protagoras*. All men would admit that he who lives a life of downright pain and misery is not living well, and that he who enjoys a happy life is. Does this imply that good and evil are simply other names for pleasurable and painful? Protagoras assents to the proposition but stipulates that the pleasure must be in worthy objects since there are bad pleasures and good pains. And of course it is the bad pleasures which people generally have in mind when they maintain that, despite all our better knowledge, we are overcome by them. The "general" do not put much confidence in knowledge as influencing conduct in the face of tempers, lusts and pleasures as a whole. But what does this really mean? Suppose one chooses a pleasant but evil course. Is it not implied that this pleasure eventually leads to painful consequences—while "*not* being mastered by pain" means enduring it for the sake of pleasant results?

So that even what is called "being overcome by pleasure" turns out to be in fact *making a false estimate!* The very assumption of Hedonism that the "greatest possible balance of pleasure over pain" is human good presupposes some art or science of measuring. The only way of avoiding mistakes is by an intelligent choice of the various "lots" of pleasure, so that a man doesn't get what is really painful when he thinks he is choosing a promising one. Even Hedonists have to admit that insight and wisdom determine their good.

3

Such facts in themselves are, of course, no refutation of Hedonism. Intelligence is required in seeking the good, whether it be of one kind or another. And why may not pleasure be that to which all men in their reason turn? Early and late Plato recognizes the importance of the question. Even in the *Laws* [4] he writes: "We must praise the noblest life, not only as the fairest in appearance . . . but as surprisingly abundant in the thing which we all of us desire—I mean in having a greater amount of pleasure and less of pain during the whole of life." Yet with no less emphasis he points out the differences in the qualities of pleasure. Many such qualities—indeed just those which are most intense—require pain and want to precede them; and often insignificant pleasures are followed by intense unpleasantness. Sometimes pleasure and pain are simultaneous or coalesce.[5] Both can be the result of a diseased state.[6] There are pleasures of hope, memory, replenishment, lust, others of art and learning. Some will satisfy the crowd, others only the cultured few.[7] Cynics who profess acquaintance with both recommend indifference, being satisfied with "relief from

[4] V. 732–3.
[5] *Gorg.* 496.
[6] *Phil.* 46a, 51d.
[7] *Rep.* IX, 584.

pain." Still others feel that pleasure never "arrives," "you seize the flower its bloom is shed," it is constantly "on the move," a mere process of becoming. Not a few have regarded the quest of pleasure as the "greatest incitement to evil." [8] Obviously there is need of some more precise analysis!

This Plato undertakes to do in the *Philebus* where he considers the psychology of pleasures and their relations to man's ultimate desire or highest good. It involves some refined classifications which at first seem rather abstract but later yield very interesting results. From the first he assumes that pleasures make up a "rough material" of good, but that the life of reason, like woof to the warp, alone makes the cloth of satisfaction possible. All pleasures are *mental*—as depending upon our *realizing* them, becoming aware of our experiences, whatever physical background there may be for them. Merely physical, or unconscious, "pleasures" are clearly a delusion.

Now suppose we analyze our experience in the light of the old Pythagorean distinction of the "Unlimited" and the "Limited." By the former we mean the class of whatever can be added to indefinitely, or be indefinitely reduced. So, for example, we put heat and cold into the class of the Unlimited. There is no highest or lowest temperature, no boundary at which heat or cold breaks off. And everything "unlimited" is, accordingly, indefinite, formless, unmeasured. Whatever is "limited," on the other hand, has specific, more or less exact, clear-cut distinctions which enable one to compare, equalize, and sometimes deal with it by numbers. Psychologically speaking, pleasures clearly belong to the unlimited (formless, indefinite, now large and now small) class. By themselves you cannot deal with them, any more than you can deal with temperature by itself—or a jelly-fish which should have no determinable outlines. Concepts, ideas, memories, reasonings, on the other hand, belong to the

[8] *Tim.* 69.

"limited" class. They are specific, meaningful, form-giving, and provide a "grip" upon experience by which it becomes intelligible.

The problem is, of course, how to combine these two classes into a third, or "mixed," one by which vague, inchoate pleasantness may be somehow organized, perhaps even measured through the calculations of reason. In dealing with space (which also belongs to the "unlimited" class) you recognize points of reference, lines, boundaries, to "get anywhere." So too "warm and cold" have to be measured to make them significant. In the same way pleasure, to become valuable, requires the "limit" of fitness, proportion, right degree on a scale. Any good which can be mentioned illustrates the same point. Health requires a rapid beating of the heart. But does one therefore try to make it beat "as rapidly as possible"? Every one desires a good-sized brain. Could one wish, however, for one of boundless size? Music implies measured intervals taken from an ("unlimited") tone material. How foolish he who tried to use the maximum number of all sorts of intervals in his music!

So pleasure, *selected* from a boundless rough material, has limits, fitness, reasonableness, proportion, harmoniousness with our natures, when it becomes a good. A "maximum of pleasure" unadapted to human organs has no more value than the "utmost possible heat" or the "greatest available number of (unorganized) musical tones." The heat must be limited to a certain number of degrees; the music to a certain number of tones. Yet just as a great variety of tones can be utilized in music, so many kinds of pleasure fit into the harmony of life. Analysis again makes clear that particular pleasures are always part of a larger scheme. They are not only associated with *objects;* they also have a "before" and an "after." Those that are most intense, such as drinking when one is terribly thirsty, require antecedent pain and deprivation. And such depletion, want, or anguish, accompanies the disturbance of a healthy balance in every living creature's functions. The maximum pleasures of recuperation thus involve the past, just as the after-effects of other notorious ones involve the future. And the man of ordinary prudence measures in terms of life, rather than by passing moments. Thus he comes to avoid extremes of such types of pleasure, whether the suffering precede or follow. Intelligence as the cause of the "mixture" prevents it from becoming a "mess." Intelligence avoids the violent pleasures which make a man "beside himself," knowing that they, like violent pains, are the cause or effect of disease in body and soul.

But there is also a "pure" type, which neither depends upon earlier cravings nor suffers painful after-effects, as do the greatest of the so-called physical pleasures. It includes many æsthetic experiences, such as the contemplation of pattern or design, appreciation of colors, tones, and most odors. Also the pleasures of science and learning. They are, of course, "moderate in intensity," "measured," and their maximum cannot be too great. If they depend upon repletion after depletion we are not conscious of it. Certainly no pain precedes them, and even forgetting is not at all parallel to getting hungry over again. They are also "true" as being more "genuine," without the adulteration and deception characteristic of some others.

"Mixed" pleasures of the æsthetic and intellectual type also exist. These alternate rapidly from pleasant to unpleasant, or even have contradictory qualities. Pain, for example, sometimes has pleasant tone. Anger indulged can be "sweeter than honey"; and lamentation, a luxury. In tragedy we enjoy our sorrow for the hero, and in comedy we indulge in malice, though we like its object too. The same mixture can be observed in the tragedy and comedy of actual life. So that a Hedonist's quest is indeed a baffling undertaking! No wonder that some respectable thinkers have advocated the avoidance of both pleasure and pain. Plato admits that possibly this might be the ideal of a god. But humans must make the most of their human character, and no man can repudiate his happiness.

Ultimately the problem of Hedonism resolves itself into determining what human functions and objects of desire are harmonious with one another. To "blend" the "water" of reason with the "honey" of pleasure in such a way that the bowl may be a delectable one, and not a nasty "mess," requires a good deal more than just "the maximum of pleasures." The "pure" ones are, of course, poured in without hesitation. So, too, those which accompany our healthy physical life. But no one in his reason would add the self-destructive ones, the frenzied, shamefaced pleasures which have their "before and after," and which everyone thinks it ridiculous or disgraceful even to look at. Obviously the mixture depends more upon intelligence than upon feelings of pleasantness. But reason, too, can be "pure"—as when it deals with exact science and fundamental truth—or "impure," when it "feeds on opinion" or is necessarily guided by rule of thumb. There is no question, however, concerning even "impure" reason in the mixture; for we live not only by dialectic but also by rough observations and everyday "musical guesswork." A man would hardly find his way home by pure mathematics. So *all* the water can safely go into the bowl! We need all the intelligence we can muster as part of human good.

Thus right proportion, beauty, truth return again as criteria of a satisfactory "blend" for pleasures as for every other good. Nor can there be any question as to which is nearer the center of good. As true or genuine reason stands incomparably nearer than "hollow" or "illusory" pleasures (e. g., sex). From the standpoint of proportion, pleasure notoriously leads to wild excess; while science and art are always "measured." There is no uncomeliness in intelligence, while unrestrained pleasures are always unseemly. Far from being first in the series, pleasure is actually last. Measure, beauty, completeness, wisdom, science, all come earlier as "goods." Yet the last is by no means the least! For a life without pleasure would be inhuman.

From beginning to end Plato thinks of success, or the completely satisfactory life, in terms of a work of art. It has unity in variety, balance, wealth in simplicity, exuberance and vitality, yet by restraint of all functions, nothing being overdone or falsified. It implies lifelong progress in proportion, differing for different people, yet for all of them a vigorous, intelligent, healthy, serene quest for perfection, whose flower is the maximum human happiness. He also calls it "the greatest possible likeness to God."

4

A word must be added concerning individual and social values. One might be inclined to suppose that the Platonic ideal implied a selfish doctrine—each man to develop himself to the greatest possible degree without regard to others. But nothing could be farther from the truth. As we shall shortly see, his social theory rather erred in the opposite direction. Suffice it here to note that in the famous allegory of the "cave"—where we unenlightened humans are said to find ourselves, favored only with shadows of the light coming down to us from an "upper world" of truth and beauty—if ever a man of superior insight gains knowledge in the sunshine outside *it behooves him to return to the shade* that his fellow mortals may be helped and enlightened.[9] Surely no "social service" idea was ever more emphatic! Again when complaint is made that the leaders of the state

[9] *Rep.* VII, 514–19.

should have to "mount guard" and perform many other unpleasant and difficult services, Plato answers that the good of the whole and not that of the part must be the deciding factor. Selfishness he also characterizes as the greatest of human evils.[10]

For the man of business whose life is entirely given up to the pursuit of money Plato had unbounded scorn. To subordinate life to the means of livelihood seemed to him like turning a man into a vegetable—living to feed and reproduce itself. The pleasures of gain he put into the class of "unlimited" thirsts, a wild desire destroying man's sense of proportion, justice and honor, and all his nobler functions. The lover of honor he rated higher, as aiming for something more than external power or things. Yet if such a one delights merely in reputation, having his name somewhat bruited about, he, too, is likely to regard the highest human goods—art, science, philosophy—as so much "smoke and nonsense." Only he who discovers the human, as well as the animal and vegetable, in himself can realize how much the lovers of mere gain or of empty honor forfeit.[11]

It would be impossible here to define, or even to enumerate, all the specific forms of right and virtue considered in detail by Plato. They range all the way from pre-natal training and good manners to the making of a will. Economic, æsthetic, physical, recreational, character, and religious values are all taken into account. Even the ethics of treating criminals (aiming not at retribution to the criminal but the prevention of crime), and that of international trade (which should be free and unrestricted), come in for consideration. Suffice it to say that he who has realized the exalted character of Plato's principles is not surprised to hear him maintain that "friends have all things in common,"[12] that it

[10] *Laws* V, 731.
[11] *Rep.* IX, 581.
[12] *Phædr.* 279.

is worse to do than to suffer evil,[13] that "the beautiful is the friend." [14] Nor will he be surprised at the frequent return of the axiom, "The best is the most natural," spontaneously moving toward its own true being.[15]

[13] *Gorg.* 469.
[14] *Lysis,* 216.
[15] *Rep.* IX, 586d.

CHAPTER XVI

PLATO'S SOCIAL THEORY AND CONCEPTION OF GOVERNMENT

Of all Plato's works the *Republic* makes perhaps the deepest impression upon readers of our age. It is an inspired piece of artistry as a human document; it discusses matters very near the center of modern everyday life, and in a way to arouse in all liberal minds a desire to work for better government, better education, a nobler kind of human existence. It is a radical book in the sense of going to the roots—resolutely, fearlessly drawing wide-reaching and thorough-going conclusions when the logic of facts and clear principle constrains him. Like other precious things it is dangerous because so easily misconstrued and abused. Socialism, Communism, the Kingdom of God, Free Love, Militarism, Slavery, Woman's Rights, Public Schools, Puritanism, as well as sundry other movements and projects have construed support from its pages.

It will be well at the outset to inquire as to Plato's general purpose, plan, and presuppositions. The sub-title of the work, *Concerning Justice*, itself suggests legislation, social adjustments, politics, good government, as the central interests. And there could be no doubt of their importance. But the prior question is always ethics. Politics he conceives to be the science and art of expanding individual self-realization to include that of society. Hence the constant dependence of every projected arrangement upon the question: What is human good? The discussion of justice passes easily and naturally from excellence of individual character to what in law or government fosters it. Plato makes no assumptions whatsoever concerning existing laws, constitutions, or sovereign powers as given, necessary, or sacred. Every available fact and relevant principle, whether of history or of nature, is welcomed in the light of disinterested reason, and for the sake of a better humanity. No matter how "established" a tradition or custom, how ancient a precedent, it is examined with an open mind. Monarchy, Oligarchy, Democracy are considered on their merits as one might any plan for a building or a ship, the final question being: How does it serve the cause of human excellence? Not even the spokesman for the tyrant, or the destructive Skeptic who professes to reveal the hypocritical pretensions of humans, could be ruled out of court. All are met on their own ground in utter reasonableness.

The long discussion at the house of the venerable merchant, Cephalus (which seems as though of yesterday), begins with the practical business man's idea that "justice is giving a man his due and speaking the truth"—something everybody ought to be able to know and to do and so fulfill the whole duty of man. Of course the simple-minded old gentleman doesn't last very long. He can hardly see the childlike naïveté of such a principle, and soon retires, not, however, without having given expression to some stimulating remarks on old age. The other members of the company are chiefly: Adeimantus and Glaucon, astute men of the world ever ready to challenge any "idealistic stuff," Thrasymachus the Sophist-superman, and Socrates—a group likely enough to be hard on any dreamer's Utopia!

Thrasymachus leads off by declaring justice to be the sovereign arm of the government, and that power is its essence. He, of course, has little use for the talk of silly billies who think of justice as a moral ideal, the common good, or other high-sounding nonsense. He will be clear and matter of fact. Justice is the interest of the ruling party. People on the inside of a government, whether of one kind or another, democracy or dictatorship, are out for the main chance. They call their own advantage justice and use those who support their conventions and constitutions as tools. Thus the "injustice" which people censure in small matters—not because they shrink from committing it, but from fear lest they may be victims themselves—is in state matters called justice. The successful government must defend its own interests and be guided by the dictum, Might is Right.

Socrates easily confounds the blustering giant out of his own mouth by bringing him to see that the use of power, even to the advantage of its possessor, depends (like the practice of any art) upon intelligence and skill of a certain kind. Skill as a physician means the power of bringing health to a patient; skill as an architect means building with taste; that of the shepherd is to do his best by the sheep. All these men receive pay. But does pay indicate their art? Is it not rather success in attaining particular objects? The practice of justice also has its object, however well or otherwise it be paid. Thrasymachus confusedly admits that its purpose cannot be both good and evil, wise and bungling, measured and measureless, just and unjust. Obviously the question is one of human good writ large. The super-moral advocate of self-assertion and irresponsible sovereignty, who is here compelled to recognize something more than conventional justice, makes no claim, however, that some men are stronger by nature, and hence are entitled to peculiar rights—as does Callicles in the *Gorgias*. But there, too, Socrates easily shows that brute force is no natural right. Natural right is that "the better and wiser should rule and have the advantage over the worse." [1] Only under such conditions can the art of justice be practiced at all. Without the guidance of insight, and some means of measuring the good, it is simply non-existent. Thus from whatever angle you look at

[1] *Gorg.* 490.

it, justice turns out to be an "excellence of soul," beneficial indeed to its possessor, but no less a blessing to all concerned.

But a more serious problem presents itself in the argument that however well this sounds in theory it is not an accepted practice. Glaucon sets forth the commonly accepted opinion that "men practice the rules of right not because they choose, but because they cannot help themselves." If everyone had such a ring as made Gyges invisible in the story whenever he wanted to avoid the penalty for his actions, all men would gratify their desires and passions in a very different way from what they do at present! "Wherever any one thinks that he can safely be unjust, there he is unjust." "If you could imagine any one obtaining this power of becoming invisible, and never doing any wrong or touching what was another's, he would be thought by the lookers-on to be a poor idiot, though they would praise him to one another's faces and try to keep up appearances. . . ." At heart people think of this convention as somehow a bad bargain.

What is still worse, Adeimantus adds, is that the very people who presumably have morality most at heart recommend it, not for its own sake but as a means to something else. They tell you that "honesty is the best *policy*," implying all along that if matters were somehow better arranged you might get on without it. The "broad path" is generally assumed to be pleasanter, more lively and interesting—but alas, convention curbs you. Even the representatives of religion seem to accept this point of view. "No one praises justice except with a view to the glories, honors and benefits which flow from it." The prophets terrify sinners by Hades or bribe them by Elysian Fields, and then (for a small consideration) go through rites and sacraments which easily "bind heaven" and dispose of the unpleasant after-effects of sin. No one praises justice "as invisible to any human or divine eye, abiding in the soul, and its greatest good," to be sought for its own sake. On the contrary, the influence of religion (of the popular sort) seems to be on the side of Thrasymachus. Justice is the arbitrary power of a god, or a human convention, a tool to serve other purposes. How deny such facts? [2]

2

The rest of the Dialogue may be called an effort to meet these questions directly and scientifically, with recourse to all possible evidence. As we have noted before, Plato is convinced that everything good or right has its roots in nature. Justice must therefore be founded on reality, if it exist at all. To call it a make-believe, an appearance, an arbitrary convention, a device of the strong, or even the irrational will of a god is equivalent to calling it a fiction, an unreality. And so he addresses himself to facts. How do states develop as a matter of history? What facts of human nature are back of this development? Under what conditions does one find the healthiest florescence of human life individually and collectively? If there be such a thing as genuine justice valuable for its own sake, one should be able to show how natural it is, both as an expression of human character and as growing out of the very order of things.

And so, with never a tinge of propaganda, Plato describes primitive society, the origins of states and their development, the changes which arts and industries bring into the lives of men. Luxury follows frugality when conditions change, as naturally as a change in diet affects the health of a patient. Customs arise and disappear according to conditions. War is one of them, resulting from expansion of population and the need of greater territory. Very important factors are the religion of a given society and the system of education which obtains in it. Where the gods are capricious, arbitrary, and adulterous beings, who act like Gyges in the

[2] *Rep.* II, 359–368.

story, there will be a reflection of them in the manners and habits of the citizens. In states where martial drill is imposed on children from their early years, or education is based on gaining a livelihood, ideas of justice are very different from those which develop by education around the liberal arts. Even the different sorts of music are potent agencies in determining the kind of laws which govern any given community.

Thus a very simple investigation reveals the interesting fact that certain of these causes are within the scope of man's control. Social organization depends upon climatic, geologic, and economic conditions, but also (and chiefly) upon science, education, religion, art. Efforts in the direction of justice are the creations of man's intelligence, aspiration and energy. The Sophist, of course, can easily point to many and various sorts. Like men, like states. Not a single one quite escapes the stupidity, bungling, and diseases of will which mar all our efforts toward excellence. None the less we can see what it is we are aiming for, and measure our distance from the goal. Like other scientific ideas justice turns out to be an ideal, nowhere perfectly exemplified, but at the same time the criterion of our knowledge and practice—just as ideal lines and figures are for mathematical science.

So Plato assumes as axiomatic the proposition that social justice implies the general good—the maximum richness of life and consequent happiness taken collectively. Justice is very much more than a matter of legal or other *relationships*. It involves the very quality and essence of human existence. The various organs and functions of the social organism must indeed be coördinated and harmonized. But that in turn depends upon the health and well-being of the organs, just as in the individual body. And it follows that, when human lives are cramped, distorted, diseased, ignorant, irreligious, dead to beauty, poverty-stricken or criminal, the responsibility is also a social one.

The *art* of justice, therefore, is learning to utilize as best we can the means and agencies which contribute to the perfecting of our common life. It depends upon the fullest possible knowledge of human nature at its worst—but also at its best. Since states are associations of men their various functions and qualities will show themselves "writ large." Thus the appetitive side of human psychology expresses itself in the economic life of the state, including all common activities growing out of the demands for nutrition and external goods. The executive side—spirit or will in the individual—is found in public agencies of power imposing the common will; while reason, which is back of that authority, is, of course, the highest common function, as it is in individuals.

Plato also assumed as axiomatic that *men are not created equal.* Only ignorant sentimentality could fail to recognize the manifest differences of value in human beings. Only inferior ones desire equality,[3] the envious enemy of distinction and excellence. Where there is no discrimination as between capable, courageous, intelligent citizens and their opposites, no high purpose can be realized. Justice itself depends upon recognition of the various functions and contributions which people of different capacities can make. And we must know what we prize in human life and character before we can work for it. The various organs in the body politic must be helped to function each in its own best way. The nutritive function cannot usurp that of the head, nor the heart, that of the eyes.

He illustrates this by a metaphor. "Citizens, we shall say to them in our tale, you are brothers, yet God has framed you differently. Some of you have the power of command, and in the composition of these he has mingled gold, wherefore they have also the greatest honor; others he has made of silver to be auxiliaries (soldiers); others again who are to be husbandmen and craftsmen he has composed of brass

[3] *Gorg.* 483; *Rep.* VIII, 558b.

and iron; and the species will generally be preserved in the children. But as all are of the same original stock a golden parent will sometimes have a silver son, or a silver parent a golden son."[4] Distinctions of class are therefore both natural and ethical. They are based on facts, as well as on recognition of values in human life.

At the same time one notes that Plato speaks of brotherhood and the common stock. By this he means to advocate a radical equality of opportunity. Justice demands that every child should be given the fullest possible means to develop the powers with which he is born, and that all distinctions of birth among the citizens should be done away with. Of course, Plato recognizes the great importance of heredity. We shall shortly hear him as exponent of a radical eugenics program. But he holds that individuals must be measured by their own qualities and contributions—not by those of their ancestors. Hence his idea of public school education where all may have an equal chance, a free field and no favor. With all its distinctions of persons and positions based upon character and attainment, the *Republic* must be characterized as a radical democracy, because founded upon the idea of brotherhood with equality of opportunity.

The three general classes of citizens are determined by what we have come to call civil service examinations, tests of various sorts of excellence by which men and women are judged fit to undertake particular functions. Education is, of course, recognized as the central means toward the building of the better society. Justice demands that every mother's child should be educated until he demonstrates his capacities and limitations. No young citizen, therefore, will normally be "classified" before his twentieth year. At that time, mental, physical, and moral examinations will decide whether he is to continue his course of formal education or to enter the field of artisan and husbandman. Later on, other ex-

[4] *Rep.* III, 415.

aminations will indicate the candidate's fitness to undertake public offices, whether in the army (at thirty) or among the leaders in the government. Roughly the three groups are: manual workers, farmers, artisans, professional men; then "auxiliaries" or soldiers, policemen and all to whom public power is intrusted; and lastly, the experts, or guardians whose final examination at thirty-five has demonstrated their fitness to direct the common interests.

The development of this class of disinterested leaders, whole-heartedly devoted to the common good and having authority to carry out their plans, is for Plato the strategic center of all our hopes for justice. They alone can make possible that guidance by intelligence upon which every good depends. Yet he is fully aware that intellectual expertness by itself is not the final criterion by which to choose our leaders. A superior knowledge of law, for example, is a frequent incentive to crime. Our "guardians" must possess more than even the widest knowledge of science, or of men and their affairs. They must have attained the "spirit of philosophy," which, because it sees all things in the light of the good, is a spirit of *service*, subordinating personal advantage. So their final examinations are primarily ethical—comprehensive indeed in their intellectual scope, since *all* knowledge eventually comes to Good as its final term—but testing the candidate's capacity to foster the noblest ends by personal sacrifice. The authority of the guardians is power *for*, not merely power *over*.

Nothing arouses the ardor of Plato quite so much as this project of high-minded leadership, the selection and development of the keenest minds of most unselfish devotion, whose insight and authority shall take the place of self-seeking, ignorant bungling, partisanship, disdain of excellence and the higher objects of human life.

"Until philosophers are kings, or the kings and princes of this world have the spirit and power of philosophy, and political greatness and wisdom meet in one, and those commoner natures who pursue either to the exclusion of the other are compelled to stand aside, cities will never have rest from their evils—no, nor the human race, as I believe—and then only will this our state have a possibility of life and behold the light of day." [5]

By philosopher-statesmen Plato means, of course, something more than near-sighted scholastics whose quiddities reflect the nonentities of angelic sophistications. He means men of most comprehensive knowledge, and skill in the use of their knowledge, who are devoted soul and body to the common good. Nor does he suppose that forthwith we shall find them. His purpose confessedly is to determine under what conditions humanity may hope for genuine justice in what direction we must work to attain it, or its nearest approximation. No skeptical cynic of human motives and institutions, ancient or modern, was more thoroughly convinced than Plato himself that such leadership probably would never exist in its perfection. Yet he realized how important it is to have knowledge of the *direction* in which we are traveling, if we expect to arrive anywhere. His temper was not one to cast slurs upon a project because of its unusual difficulty. A good thing for him lost none of its quality by not being immediately available. As an object, a goal, a standard, it provided a "measure to judge our own happy or unhappy condition." The great Idealist, in fact, was more genuinely "practical" than the typical scorner of "Utopias."

His plan for education, "the great business of every man while he lives," is interesting not only as a social, or public school, venture, but on account of its specific content. It is above all education to excellence, not as a means to an end, such as training for trade, or as captain of a ship, but for life itself. Of course it includes professional training, but

[5] *Rep.* V, 473d.

its primary purpose is the enrichment of human existence. Plato is passionately interested in the development of great-souled men and women by whom justice may be made possible for all. But justice in its turn means lives that realize their maximum potentialities. "The most important part of education is right training in the nursery. The soul of the child in his play should be guided to the love of excellence." Thus Plato expresses himself in the *Laws* [6] where his *Republic* plan is sometimes made more explicit. This early education is based mostly on amusement and play of imagination until more formal work begins at ten years. The reason why it is so important is the great influence of environment, examples and their spontaneous imitation, in molding a young person's attitude toward life. Plato projects (as ideal) an environment for children which shall stimulate their æsthetic sense. It should give scope for the free expression of their natural interest in the arts—not as a formal matter of reason, but as play and imagination, of which children never weary. Stories are very strategic here, so too *making* beautiful things in the lesser arts from ceramics to embroidery. By such means children will develop a *sense of form,* propriety, order, nice feeling of fitness, good manners, and in general a love of fine things, which will later stimulate them to work spontaneously at the tasks of reason. Ten years seems to us a late age at which to begin the latter training; but it must not be supposed that the "age of imagination" is wasted.

Ugly sights and sounds are to be kept from the eyes and ears of children; so too looseness, drunkenness and crime of all sorts, whether in fact or in fiction. For all serve as imitative examples. Not even in "religious" books shall the gods be represented as petty, unjust, or adulterous beings. Plato had, in Homer and Hesiod, almost as immoral a group of stories to contend with as we have in the Bible. But he also ruled out certain portions of the dramatic poets, including

[6] I, 643.

Æschylus, as misleading in education. Howsoever exuberant or fanciful our imagination, God must not be represented as vicious or untruthful in our stories. Wholesomeness and cleanliness in them also lead spontaneously to the imitation of these qualities. They who hear classical music in their early years will also develop a sense of proportion in their souls. Relaxed, mawkish, sentimental melodies, insolent and furious rhythms—in short our "jazzy" qualities—go along with angular movements, vulgar manners, flabby, loose and unbalanced minds. In both directions the influence is unconscious.

It is interesting to note that Plato saw no reason for ruling religion out of early training. Along with art it was welcomed into the very kindergarten. But it must be remembered that authority, exclusive divine revelations, heresy-hunting, propagandas, and political chicanery masquerading as religion had not yet done their devastating work in the name of God. Plato could still think of religious cultivation as parallel to that of artistic and scientific training—and as much a common concern. The fact is a commentary on modern integrity.

When, with growing reason, more formal instruction begins, it still centers about the arts, especially music and literature, because of their constant challenge to good form, refinement and excellence in general, as well as their spontaneous interest. Language studies as such, whether foreign or native, were clearly not a part of Greek schooling as it was,[7] nor does Plato recommend them for the new Republic. Such a fact is significant when one considers the difficulty of Greek inflections. Apparently much could be taken for granted with an intelligent attitude toward one's literature—a creative one, rather than a quest for historical or external information. Of course mathematics also figures largely in Plato's program. So, too, the sciences, though little is said of them.

[7] See *Protag.* 328.

A great deal of stress is put upon gymnastics, which at first seems strange when one remembers certain Platonic expressions: how prone athletes are "to sleep away their lives," or to become "mere hardness and ferocity." But students of the liberal arts also become "soft and effeminate" unless their souls are cast in the mold of a vigorous and beautiful body. And physical education can be designed, "for the improvement of the soul." The problem for both girls and boys, and throughout their lives, is to balance firm texture and grace, strength and delicacy. And this is accomplished only by adequate physical work.

There are no distinctions of sex in Plato's educational scheme. From its beginning to the highest ranges of scientific and philosophical studies, women are to have the same privileges as men. As we shall shortly see this is true of all trades and professions. Compulsion in these matters he regards as futile and destructive, however, since education is a process of eliciting one's powers, never one of mere accretion from without.

In brief, the plan begins with training of imagination, under the influence of wholesome art, environment and example. It gradually leads on to the development of reason, creatively concerned with thinking, rather than with information, its tool. It is throughout dominated by intrinsic rather than instrumental purposes; is no less physical than mental, no less ethical than physical, and indefeasibly artistic. It may be called primarily an education of the will to excellence, spontaneously elicited, and hence a lifelong joy. That Plato regarded the Minister of Public Education as the most important officer in the state is not remarkable.

3

The training of guardians and auxiliaries for their life of devotion to the general welfare prompted Plato to propose a system of communism for them. It has very little that is similar to modern proletarian rule or economic interpretations of human life. On the contrary, it is aristocratic in form, and based on the idea that the common good (including, of course, economic good) is best served by leaders who most nearly have overcome their personal and private interests. For that reason the two upper classes are to have "no more property than is absolutely necessary." [8] They are to forego the privileges of a separate home and family, though marriage is not denied them. They will live in state apartments, some for men and others for women, the purpose of this arrangement being to enable women to retain after marriage something of the same opportunity for progress which men enjoy. Other apartments will be given over to children, where they will be partially under the care of trained nurses and teachers, who will thus relieve tired mothers, and save them from a deadening isolation of interests.

This emancipation of educated women from domestic handicaps grew out of the conviction that women should have responsibilities and privileges in every way equal to those of men. Plato, however, does not mean to imply that in general, either physically or mentally, they are the equals of men. In fact he denies it. Yet he insists upon equality of opportunity. Sex should debar no woman from citizenship or from undertaking any profession whatsoever. They should learn to campaign in the open field and compete at the great athletic contests. Many women greatly surpass the common run of men; their characters and attainments should open to them the highest offices in the community. Hence there will be women guardians or legislators, and women policemen, as well as mothers and nursery-maids.

The actual carrying out of the plan is in accordance with the principles of eugenics, marriage being regarded as the concern, not only of the two individuals, but of society.

[8] *Rep.* IV, 416.

Guardians will therefore sanction only such marriages as give promise of healthy children, physically, mentally, morally. Children from their birth are to be the wards of the community. Parents must not be able to discriminate between their own children and others of corresponding age. Thus they will widen their interest in the younger generation and increase the sense of common brotherhood. Children who for any reason may happen to be deformed will be exposed without too great violation of parental feeling, thus safeguarding the future against inferior stock. In these ways personal ties, privileges and private possessions are "as far as possible" to be merged into devotion to community, or non-competitive, goods.

It must be remembered that this communistic arrangement is not proposed for the third class, presumably a majority of the citizens. Artisans, tradesmen, farmers, professional men and others will retain their private property, homes, and other personal privileges. Their interests demand property. They would not be happy without it. Nor can they identify themselves with the wider life of sacrifice for the common good. Hence they will not be legislators or control the general welfare. But they are very fundamental to the state, corresponding as they do to the nutritive part of an individual's life. They need the direction of disinterested intelligence in some such way as the boundless desires and conflicting impulses of a person require the guidance of reason. It is just at this point that Plato's democracy differs radically from the modern conception. Numbers have no sanctity for him. He had no hope for justice, happiness, and excellence of life through majority rule. These depend upon the few who have learned the law of service and sacrifice.

It is very easy to recognize the difficulties of any communistic plan. In the *Republic* Adeimantus raises the question: "How would you answer, Socrates, if a person were to say that you are making the people miserable, and that they are the cause of their own unhappiness; the city in fact belongs to them but they are not any better off for it? . . . Will our citizens be no better than mercenaries who are quartered in the city and are always mounting guard?"[9] But Socrates answers confidently that with all their simplicity of life and freedom from possessions, the guardians may well be the happiest of men. And even supposing they were not, their duty to the state as a whole would take precedence over their lesser satisfactions. Like the beauty of a statue, the general happiness must be proportionate. It would be wrong to concentrate all beauty upon the eyes to the neglect of the hands! We must consider our happiness in relation to that of the whole.

Irrefutable as that answer is, there are still more fundamental objections. Granted that public servants might well be chosen from those who have learned to subordinate economic values, it still remains true that a certain amount of property makes for self-respect, dignity and initiative. To be utterly without possessions is to thwart a very important instinct, which requires proportionate expression in the balanced harmony of our functions. And the same is true of the parental instinct, which depends upon a personal, and not merely a generalized, relation. As human nature is at present constituted, the tender relations of father, wife, child will continue to be something more than solicitation for the common good. There cannot be too much of the latter. But human affections cannot be completely measured in terms of public good, nor can they be isolated from unique and peculiar objects. Plato himself realized this later on in the *Laws*.

[9] *Ibid.* IV, 419.

4

To many modern readers the most interesting part of the Republic is the comparison of various existing types of states with the proposed ideal. The object still is to measure good and ill in human beings as reflected in their states. "Governments vary as the dispositions of men vary and there must be as many of the one as there are of the other." For that reason there is a peculiar directness in the description of the "democratic man" and his type of social organization, based upon head-counting; or of the "oligarchic man" with his deference for riches; or of the "timocratic man," with his estimate of honors and distinctions. And even though the primary object is still ethical, we gain many interesting ideas on government, since states improve or degenerate according to the temper of the people.

Aristocracy, the rule of disinterested experts, is, of course, the most difficult of attainment and most easily corrupted. It lapses when power is vested in men eminent for reasons other than character and wisdom. A military success, for example, can bring distinction to a general in command, quite apart from his qualifications as a superior man. He, a type of the "timocratic man," will profess to be fond of education and culture, without possessing either. His bent for "administration" is strong. He will not therefore be humiliated by his intellectual superiors, and realizes more and more the solid advantages of power and money. The timocratic state, as a result, is an easy prey to inferiority, disorder, and corruption.

And yet timocracy, where some effort is made to recognize excellence of family, or some other preëminence, as the basis of leadership, is higher in the scale than oligarchy, or a "government resting on a valuation of property, in which the rich have power and the poor man is deprived of it." [10]

[10] *Rep.* VIII, 550.

Oligarchy is quite natural among people who think more of making a fortune than they do of character or virtue. "In proportion as riches and rich men are honored in the state, virtue and the virtuous are dishonored." The devotees of trade and commerce look up to the rich man and make a leader of him, with about as much reason as one might choose the pilot of a ship because of his money. And, of course, distinctions between the rich and the poor become acute. Class consciousness takes precedence over the common good. Yet such "government by the interests" is not openly and flagrantly oblivious of good. The oligarchs "coerce their bad passions by an enforced virtue" because they tremble for their possessions. So evil is not avoided among them as evil. When there is a safe way "within the law" of profiteering or making "gentleman's agreements" they forsake their restraints.

But even oligarchy is not the worst. When the poor realize how they have been deceived they begin to regard "the rich and more orderly classes" as defenseless enemies. And the slogan now becomes: Freedom and Equality. They will have a plain-folks' government where no one is better than anybody else and "a man may say and do what he likes." Nowhere is Plato more caustic than in his description of the "democratic man" and his state. Democracy prides itself on a "Don't care about trifles." And these trifles, unfortunately, include such things as beauty and the fundamental excellencies of character. These are distributed without discrimination to equals and unequals alike. A "forgiving spirit" refuses to recognize differences so slight as personality. Democratic "breeding" is insolence; its "liberty," mere bungling anarchy; its "magnificence," extravagant waste; its "courage," mostly impudence. All refinements are looked upon as "high-brow," the commonplace is "good enough." Nobody dares to make distinctions. The democratic man (and state) are pulled hither and thither by every sort of fad and catchy notion. Now it is drinking water only (to get thin), then suddenly gymnastics for a time. Then it is politics for a season, when the democratic man "starts to his feet and says and does whatever comes into his head." [11] Everything is vulgarized. "The father grows accustomed to descend to the level of his sons and to fear them, and the son is on a level with the father, he having no respect or reverence for either of his parents, . . . the master fears and flatters his pupils, and the pupils despise their masters and tutors, . . . even the horses and asses have a way of marching along with all the rights and dignities of freemen; and they will run at anybody who comes in their way if he does not leave the road clear for them: and all things are just ready to burst with liberty." [12]

Eventually comes tyranny—the natural outcome of a sentimental passion for liberty. For freedom is a strong wine in which lurks anarchy. It is but a step from a society in which "citizens chafe impatiently at the least touch of authority," to violent disorder. Then comes the chance for the "protector of the people." Out of the riots and mob-rule some "friend of the workers" will emerge. He is most likely to be from the class of drones "who manage almost everything in democracies," an "informer" ("walking delegate"). He will persuade the distracted people that he is their protector and friend, and then assume command. The next step is a bodyguard obtained by promise of the "abolition of debts and partition of lands." Finally "with unholy tongue and lips tasting the blood of his fellow-citizens" the tyrant proclaims himself dictator. Thus does Plato fear for mere democracy. The extreme of liberty joins hands with that of dictatorship.

We of later centuries who have so often fought for "freedom" and "democracy" hardly share such fears—but for

[11] *Ibid.* 561.
[12] *Ibid.* 563.

other reasons. We are forced indeed to recognize the tendencies which he so pointedly described. History also shows how much of characterless commonplaceness and tasteless indifference may go along with majority standards, how easily license is regarded as liberty, how keen is the race for riches when intelligence is made instrumental to external advantages. But we have come to base our hope as against dictatorships, whether of "proletarians" or of the "interests," exactly where Plato did for aristocracy—a never-ceasing education to excellence, an evaluation of human life at its highest florescence, as superior to every other consideration. If ever we lose contact with ideals such as his we shall likely enough go the way Plato describes.

5

In his later years he set himself the task of working out a second-best, or more immediately feasible, practicable, form of government, one within reach, and yet to retain as much as possible of the Republican ideal. This compromise is elaborated in the *Laws*, his longest work.

The title is itself significant, as emphasizing the importance which law and precedent must have in any state not governed by men sufficiently wise to rule without detailed laws. In such a "mixed" state rulers are subordinate to constitutional arrangements and laws, which they "administer." The government is one of law rather than of persons. Yet Plato would have no arbitrary laws; every statute is to be preceded by a preamble explaining what is to be accomplished or avoided, thus appealing to every man's reason. He still thinks in terms of small city states, and regards a combination of democracy with monarchy as the most promising arrangement. The family is recognized as a necessary expedient for all, in lieu of communism for a few; so also property (whose ultimate ownership is vested in the state, though individuals are to have the private use of it). In the *Laws* no less than in the *Republic*, accumulation of wealth is feared as the cause of destruction to both men and states. Hence he would have an upper limit for possessions, and restrict the use of gold and silver. Marriage still remains a community, rather than a merely personal, arrangement (eugenics); so also education. Punishment is corrective rather than retributory. And slavery retains its place, in some respects superior, however, to modern economic controls. Trade is to be reduced to the satisfaction of simpler needs, and so far as possible given over to inferiors, thus freeing citizens from the shopkeeper's type of life. Free exchange is retained: "Let no one pay any duty on the importation or exportation of goods." [13] Tariffs are recognized as the seeds of war. Even more severely than in the *Republic*, art and religion are considered communal matters, and not to be left to individual caprice and degradation. The Sophist scoffer and irreverent innovator will be restrained and given instruction, lest the belief in mind as ultimate mover in nature and in states be brought into question, and with it the belief in order. A conservative "Nocturnal Council," consisting of the ten oldest directors of education, is to study legislation and recommend amendments in the light of other people's laws and the best interests of the state. Another body called the "Censors" (twelve men chosen by universal suffrage in a series of elections suggestive of our modern proportional representation) watches over public officials generally and impeaches those who are delinquent.

In this combination of representative with monarchical and aristocratic features, Plato seems to have come to realize that ideal rulers, who would combine legislative, executive and judicial powers, were too much to hope for. At any rate he regards a division of powers as necessary in the "mixed" state—an axiom which first appeared in his *Laws*.

[13] *Laws,* VIII, 847b.

There is to be popular sovereignty, but also agencies to prevent the people from bringing harm to themselves. A ruling class or aristocracy, in the sense of official, national recognition of men distinguished for character, knowledge, and science, is a moral factor Plato will not forego. The continuity of the monarchical tradition, as above the changes of party politics, also seemed to him desirable.

It is not improbable that if Plato were alive to-day he would point to the combination of King, Aristocracy, and Commons in the British Constitution as the nearest approximation to his second-best state. The Monarch, a living symbol of permanence and the common good, is superior to all politics and partisan opinion, his personal power being slight. A "ruling class" of great dignity and influence, whose power, at least in principle, rests upon intelligence, traditional excellence, or distinguished contribution to the common good, exists side by side with popular sovereignty and universal suffrage. Thus the preferences of the majority are guided and tempered by men who cultivate a disinterested science of politics, and protect society from mere number-politicians with their ears to the ground. True that this respect for expert leadership is a diminishing quantity there, just as Plato foretold would be the case, if ever fortunate conditions made his mixed constitution possible. The prerogative of the Monarch, or that of the Commons, tends to usurp that of the Aristocracy—this he knew from his own study of history. And doubtless this is one reason for the extreme conservatism of Plato in the *Laws*. He would guard the contributions of the high-minded disinterested few in the mixed balance of powers, where ignorant majority opinion, or the one-man power of king or demagogue, so easily thwarts the common good.

Whatever we think the specific shortcomings of Plato's plans for a just organization of society may be, if we consider his projects as a whole we shall be inclined to prophesy that the future will vindicate more of them than past history already has. Many of his "Utopian visions" are "commonplace facts" to-day. On the horizon of the future day we seem to see eugenics, higher education, especially to non-competitive, æsthetic, moral, and religious ends, the abolition of war, and freedom of exchange. Perhaps, in some more distant time, we shall come to think of governments as existing for the perfecting of life and happiness, primarily of its citizens, but also of humanity as a whole.

CHAPTER XVII

PLATO'S RELIGIOUS CONCEPTIONS

If we except the cults known as "mysteries," the Greeks had no church in our sense of an institution based on certain conceptions of life and destiny, which demand support and propaganda. The classical theater more nearly approached that function. But even there authority was lacking. The poets could appeal only to the reasons and current sentiments of their auditors in maintaining the justice of God or the inexorable laws by which he works. They had no standard books in the sense of "holy men of old spake as they were moved by the Holy Ghost," no court of appeal like the Holy See, no inerrant documents professing, or construed to express, the direct will of God. Homer, Hesiod, and the tragedians were quoted, generally with approval, but as we quote passages which appeal to us from Chaucer, Shakespeare, or Milton. In times of perplexity and difficulty individuals and communities did indeed appeal to the Delphic Oracle. But the astute men who presided over that institution characteristically did not report the exact words of the god, and generally left sufficient ambiguity in their replies to foster further investigation. They were in fact more like political advisers than religious authorities or prophets. And the public ceremonies of religion, like those of the drama and athletic contests, took on the character of great civic occasions intended to please the god as well as human eyes and ears, but with little emphasis on standard dogmas, and considerable scope for the free imagination of artistry.

These facts help us appreciate Plato's method and general point of view. For his is perhaps the highest expression of classical religious aspiration. The "faith" character of religion—as based upon more or less probable imagination—is constantly in his mind. Verbal or personal authority has little scope. The "Varieties" of Xenophanes would indeed have convinced any intelligent man in antiquity that reason, rather than authority, is the court of appeal. So he frequently interpolates his accounts of the creation, or his hypothesis of Immortality, with a "God only knows if what I say is true" or "A man of understanding will hardly suppose that this is literally so. But something like it seems probable." At times indeed he craves the guidance of some divine authority to get him beyond hypothesis. But nowhere does he accept the claim of any assumed revelation. What he was endeavoring to foster, later times have called natural or universal religion.

There are, it is true, other parts in which dogmatism appears to enter in. Thus, in the tenth book of the *Laws*, he would have legislators prescribe severe penalties for certain heretical points of view, which in his later years he esteemed to be of fundamental importance. These are atheism, the denial of providence, and the idea of conniving or bribable gods. On the face of it this looks like intolerance, but we must also remember that Plato could not conceive of religion as divorced from morality, and that he is arguing for belief in the good, as a statesman contemplating the possible rejection of all standards of right and wrong. The Idea of the Good, as we have noted before, is also the basis of science, since its objective is always an interpretation having good as the final term. Plato's heresy hunting (if such it be) is against those who deny the possibility of religion at all, and with it morality and all the sciences. From a philosophical standpoint even this is, of course, indefensible. The absolute skeptic or pessimist may be refuted or pitied, but to punish him as a malefactor is to strike at the roots of disinterested investigation. Plato was so much the lover of all things excellent and good, and felt so secure in the evidence of their reality, that it seemed like treason to human society, and suicidal destruction of a man's own interest to deny the possibility of morality and religion.

The presuppositions and axioms of this philosophical or natural faith will be near to the reader's thought. We may summarize them as follows:

(1) The characteristic quality of mind as we know it is intelligent self-movement. This differs from chance movement, or chance combinations of particles.[1]

(2) Wherever we discover Ideas in nature, and so find interpretation possible, we are tracing mental agencies.[2]

(3) This is true not only of the lesser or artificial products of human art (which no one would think of attributing to chance), but of the ordered movements of the greatest natural bodies. No accidental or "necessary" mixtures of hot and cold, hard and soft weight, and other physical qualities explain the "art" of greater nature, any more than they do of the lesser. These last are conditions, rather than causes.[3]

(4) We may describe as elaborately as we choose, or go as far back as we can in tracing events; unless they are attributed to intelligent causes they remain unintelligible.[4]

(5) Unity must be assumed as the first principle of dialectic. Chaos is always incomprehensible, whether in large or in small.[5]

(6) Science assumes that the organization of the cosmos has the idea of good as its ultimate cause.[6]

[1] *Laws*, X, 894.
[2] *Phædo*, 98 fol.
[3] *Laws*, X, 889.
[4] *Laws*, X, 891–2.
[5] *Rep.* VI, 511; *Phil.* 16.
[6] *Rep.* VI, 508.

More connectedly stated, he assumes that mind can be derived only from mind, the rational from the rational. It is a fundamental error of mechanical interpreters to mistake a *condition* for a cause. Activity takes place *in* matter indeed, but the cause of order is always an intelligent agency. If we went no farther than our own mental activity—which is also a derived cosmic fact—we should be compelled to postulate cosmic mental causes. But this axiom of intelligent causes, as alone accounting for our own minds or for the rational operation of anything else, would of itself be no adequate basis for science and religion if we could not assume a *universal* order. (In modern times we call this the uniformity of nature.) If there were not a unified, rational force, some all-embracing order, there would still be chaos. But science views all things as belonging together. It assumes an organized system of harmoniously coördinating parts, and thus postulates a single intelligence making for *good*, which is another word for the harmonious, healthy, balanced, conservation of the whole.

These ideal presuppositions or projects of completed knowledge are never quite realized, however, in our study of the world about us. We have to assume them in order to have any interpretations at all, as we do the axioms of geometry. Yet our experience everywhere points to disorder, irrationality, chance, and evil. The ideal concepts of the mathematician are nowhere perfectly exemplified in nature. So Plato makes the further postulate that there are limiting and disorderly factors, chance conditions, and even malicious mental agencies at work. Humanity itself provides sufficient evidence for the last-named. But there are also more powerful disruptive forces, clever in their destruction. These are certainly not agencies of reason—which always seeks and fosters the good—but forces akin to our animal or physical urges which, though they are mental, limit the work of our intelligence.

Hence Plato postulates different degrees of reality and power in nature. Changing, evanescent characters or qualities are not so real as those which are permanent. The changing content of the senses is not so real as the fixed conclusions of reason. The power *by* which anything is produced is more real than the space *in* which it is produced. And yet the last is not complete nothingness (though we have neither concept nor percept of it). It is only relatively less real. The primary reality is the universal, unchanging power making for the good; but the secondary (matter, space) is able to condition its activity. Plato agrees with the physical philosophers that nothing comes from nothing, but he also insists that an indefinite, inactive, and seemingly meaningless "something," such as space, can only be thought of as *less* real than active form-giving, significant, ordered and "bounded" portions.[7] Yet the indefinite and inchoate, the unintelligible mass, by itself unformed and meaningless, is none the less a conditioning factor limiting by "necessity" the organizing energies of the world. Thus disorder inevitably conditions order; chance, the products of art and intelligence; change, the relative reality of the visible world; disruptive factors, the conserving, unifying causes of good.

In the process of making his abstract principles more concrete, Plato made no little use of imagination. He tried to build upon the basis of axioms and principles as well as the evidence of "facts"—in short he aimed for what we should call "scientific imagination." But this soon resolved itself (as he well knew) into artistic or creative imagination, which might serve a religious purpose, but must not be thought of as accounts of truth, because sufficient evidence is lacking. Thus he personifies the conserving, unifying, intelligent power as "Demiurgus" and refers to it with masculine gender. He is the "Father" of all creatures, not in any physiological sense but as the ceaseless preserver,

[7] Cf. *Phil.* 23–27.

supporter and friend of all things excellent. As a father is concerned for the happiness (or maximum fullness of life) of his children, so is Demiurgus concerned for the good of the whole world. The part sometimes has to be sacrificed for the whole; but it is of the essence of goodness to put the greater good before the lesser. He is the cosmic artist making the most of the media at his disposal[8] and delighting in his productions, the most beautiful, the most perfect possible.

But as Creator, Demiurgus seems to deal indirectly with the age-old chaos, unformed and unstable matter. He "poured" something of himself into it when by the aid of Ideas and mathematical forms the "boundless" took on definite shapes and motions. But in so doing he gave life to nature, a world-soul dwelling in the body of the universe. And it is through this universal life that the purposes of the creator are being carried out. The world-soul brought into being the "lesser gods," the animating, ordering, conserving powers of the stars and planets, which in their turn gave birth to the forms of life and order which they manifest. Thus the life of the earth (the earth-soul) is "poured from the same cup" whence the life of all nature came; and human beings are the products of the earth-soul. So that we are the "children of God." But as "mixtures" of the divine with the dull, resisting chaos of the unformed, from the world-soul down to the human, there is imperfection, error, chance and discord. Yet the world is the best possible image of the divine Ideas under the conditions and necessary circumstances.

Neither the creation of the visible world, nor that of its ordering invisible life, is the production of something out of nothing. All is conceived as "natural," even though the Deity as unchanging reality is not identified with the changing

[8] *Rep.* X, 596; *Laws,* V, 741; *Tim.* 29.

world of sense. In giving forms to the latter the world-spirit seems to have made use of geometrical shapes and arithmetical means to give character to the various elements. The inchoate, indefinite "boundless" might have been formed into anything—what is now water into air, or fire into air, and earth into water. But the mathematical configurations of their particles now give the elements stability (some of them more than others). Thus we may imagine earth as composed of cubes; air, of octahedrons; fire, of pyramids; and water, of icosahedrons. The last three can apparently still be "transformed" according to the geometric figures which are impressed upon the primitive mass.[9]

Plato seems to have had no objection to the personification of numbers of "divine powers" of higher and lower degree manifested in nature. But this does not limit his monotheism, since all are subordinate to Demiurgus as "sons of God." He is perfectly willing to imagine Apollo as god of light, Athena as goddess of truth, Demeter of the corn, and as many "attendant spirits" (of love, art, the fireside) as you choose. They are different parts or aspects of the divine life, recognized in various ways. One thing, however, he cannot abide in popular mythology. This is the conception of gods as lacking moral character. They must not be imagined as profligate, deceitful, uncontrolled. The stories of Homer, Hesiod, even of Æschylus, in this strain are not only bad for society; they are inherently false. For God is the author of good only, unless the axioms of our science may be discarded.[10] The argument here is chiefly pragmatic, however—the bad effects of evil gods in a state. And elsewhere[11] he writes of "two souls, one making for good, the other for evil," and how "we acknowledge the world to be full of many

[9] *Tim.* 55–57.
[10] *Rep.* II, 379.
[11] *Laws,* X, 896e.

goods and also of evils." The cosmic "battle" is reflected in our own souls, for whom the gods are like good physicians, the pilots of vessels, or shepherds of flocks.[12]

Plato indeed does not solve the problem of evil. The Demiurgus and his subordinate ministers "order all things with a view to the excellence and preservation of the whole." They have created man for the sake of the whole, and not the whole for the sake of man.[13] Yet "every one of us is made pretty much what he is by the bent of his desires and the nature of his soul," and can sink into the abyss of crime, or become divine by following the path of holiness.[14] This freedom depends upon our rationality, whose nature it is spontaneously to seek perfection and the happiness which accompanies it. But the animal is also a part of us, not a condition only but a function of our souls, no less spontaneously urging us to disorder, excess, and crime. And if we are "poured from the same cup" as are the lesser deities, the same problem of their "mixed" natures would seem to apply to them. How then their perfect goodness? To the Demiurgus this problem would not apply. For he is not mixed up with the mess of conditioning matter, a "pure" spirit serenely perfect, unchangingly blessed. His power, too, despite his complete intelligence and goodness cannot be imagined to annul the conditionings of physical necessity.[15] Evil thus seems to be as primeval and inevitable as the good, but the power of reason controls it, in ourselves and the world as a whole.

In considering the destiny of man, Plato's imagination unhesitatingly linked his life both with the animal world and with the cosmos as a whole. The problem of immortality is an issue to be studied as a fact in nature or not a fact, as comporting or not comporting with our knowledge of psychol-

[12] *Ibid.* 905.
[13] *Laws,* X, 903.
[14] *Ibid.* 904.
[15] Cf. *Tim.* 68, 69.

ogy. We have already noted how he considered man's mind as having three main divisions or aspects. Two of these, being so manifestly related to the functions of the body, could by no imagination be supposed to survive its dissolution. (Plato is nowhere tempted to envisage the reassembling of dispersed human bodies.) But perhaps reason, self-active and able to "contemplate all time and all existence," may present another case. Let us consider the evidence.

That our souls do not come into being from utter nothingness at birth seems to him probable from the fact that we have "recollections," which come so directly and are so "ready-made," that it is difficult to assume they were experienced. (Perhaps if we think of Kant's observation that forms of space and time seem to be already in our minds as soon as we begin to see anything in space and time, we shall more readily understand Plato's argument.) There are given, "immediate," data of our minds so highly generalized that they seem to be merely "brought out" of the mind and not the result of particular experiences. Some of these general ideas are equality, similarity, beauty, justice, goodness. How could we ever come to regard two things as equal or similar, etc., unless we already had an idea of equality or similarity? Were we born with them? If so, the probability is that they are evidence of preëxistence. Yet like a true scientist he is "not altogether confident" of this very daring conclusion, and regards it as only the most likely hypothesis in the premises.[16]

The self-activity of the mind, as originating motion and order by its own inherent energy, seems to imply something not produced from nothingness as well as indestructible. Yet this is true of a part and not the whole. For bodily or external conditions also assert themselves. Their motions commingle with and limit the higher work of reason, which in its purity is clearly kindred to the divine. For if unde-

[16] *Phædo,* 75; *Meno,* 86b.

rived it must be immortal. And it further shows its superiority to external conditions and changes by realizing ideal, unchanging causes and realities back of them. The soul that is able to contemplate pure beauty—beauty manifesting itself indeed in a thousand ways in the material world, but none the less above these passing examples—participates in the same activity which that beauty shows. He who knows a goodness undefiled, everywhere making for excellence, is not at all anxious lest its power should cease. He who finds a truth independent of time and circumstance is himself finding and living the life eternal. But it is only in this self-active capacity, when we seem to transcend the limitations of time and place, that we manifest the divine or immortal. Another part of our natures holds us back.[17]

The mixed character of the soul also suggests different degrees of success in realizing a happy, harmonious and reasonable life, not only in the present but also in any continued existence. Our self-ignorance and self-deception stand in the way of reason and its divine Ideas. Men sink as well as rise in the scale and most are little aware of their powers. Only a few in fact are able to lead the life eternal now. So we must assume that in the event of continued existence they will all take places as determined by their development, measured by the impartial justice of God.[18] The ethical side of the problem is emphasized in the further argument that the destruction of anything is brought about only by that which opposes its existence, as disease in the body or rust to iron. That which opposes the existence of the soul, thwarting its activity, is ignorance, cowardice, intemperance, concupiscence, etc. Yet men constantly celebrate victories over vice and internal anarchy. And we can hardly suppose that "anything can perish from without through affection of external evil which could not be destroyed from within by a corrup-

[17] *Phædr.* 245–7.
[18] *Phædo,* 108, 111.

tion of its own."[19] Thus experience seems to confirm the divine life in ourselves as well as opportunity to foster it. Our present ability to "fix the eye of the soul" on the eternal and the perfect, overcoming the limitations of time and place (as well as our petty personal interests), not only points to a natural urge in this direction but to the possibility of more perfect attainment.

We can here do no more than characterize in a general way Plato's imaginative elaboration of the future life. This is not projected into places remote from the world we live in. Rather it is intimately associated with the given cosmos and even with animal life. There is nothing magical or unnatural about it. We continue the interests we have here. The stupid in the world below will get no farther with their leaky vessels than they do anywhere else,[20] and the wise will still have problems to solve. There is work to be done and opportunity for progress. The limitations which condition the cosmos as a whole still show themselves, even among those most blest. There are different places for the wise and the stupid, the lovers of the good, and for criminals. But they who inhabit the Blessed Isles still need their wits about them. Even they sometimes choose tyranny in the cycles of the years and find themselves eventually in Tartarus. Absolute security is nowhere; adventure still beckons in the future. And even the vilest sinner, if he shows himself worthy to those against whom he has offended, may rise to a happier state.

Perhaps the most characteristic passage by way of illustration is the myth of Er in the closing section of the *Republic*. Er, the Pamphylian, is a hero who has been slain in battle and left upon the field for ten days. Upon the twelfth day while his uncorrupted body is lying upon the funeral pyre, he comes back to life and explains how he

[19] *Rep.* X, 609.
[20] *Gorg.* 493.

has been sent a messenger from the nether world to tell of what he saw. So he describes the judges, the newcomers "dusty and worn with travel," others in a glad meadow encamping as at a festival, the happy embraces and inquiries. He tells of the judgments upon tyrants and other criminals, the terrors they have to endure in a segregated place. Five days' journey farther on is a shaft or column of light like the rainbow, where the circle of the universe is held together, and the chains of heaven are visible. Around this spindle all the spheres, including the planets, revolve. There is music in which the Fates, daughters of Necessity, join. Lachesis sings of the past, Clotho of the present, Atropos of the future.

While Er was here the inhabitants of the place were about to choose the type of life they most preferred. Lachesis proclaimed a "new cycle of life and mortality." Each one was to choose his own genius, and his choice was to be his destiny. Nothing was allotted, all was chosen. "Virtue is free, and as a man honors or dishonors her he will have more or less of her; the responsibility is with the chooser . . . God is justified." Among the choices were high and low ones, wealth, poverty, disease, health, fame, power, even animal types of life. So that, there as here, the position of a man depends upon his own soul, whether he can realize how incomparable are the qualities of inward excellence. "Let each one of us . . . then learn to discern between good and evil and so to choose always and everywhere the better life as he has opportunity." Not all of the candidates did so even at the center of opportunity. Orpheus chose the life of a swan; Thamyrus that of a nightingale. Some birds, on the other hand, chose bodies of men; Thersites, the jester, desired to be a monkey. Odysseus, now a wiser man, sought out the life of a private citizen who had no cares. Er saw them for a time by the River of Forgetfulness from which they drank. Then suddenly from their seat by its banks, they, like shooting stars, were driven upwards to new births. . . .

By what manner and means Er now found himself lying again upon his funeral pyre, he had no intimation.

Plato's myths are perhaps his most exquisite artistry, frankly creations of imagination, but guided by all he knew of the world without and the nature of the mind within. Religion as revealer of the ideal could not be divorced from art (whose intuition is also of perfection), any more than it could from the most penetrating knowledge, or from good, measured in terms of what is by nature noblest and happiest. Dissociated from natural justice (even as an arbitrary fiat of God), as at variance with truly scientific knowledge, religion would have seemed to him a worse than worthless thing. But he also realized that without the kindling power of art's vision it would leave the soul cold and uninspired. Beauty gives reality to aspiration. When a man "has eyes to see pure beauty" and "nourishes virtue" he is likely to become the "friend of God and be immortal, if mortal man may." [21]

Yet "as the true order of going . . . is to begin with the beauties of earth and mount upwards from them" so in the traditional conceptions and practices of religion, Plato seems to have found stepping stones to the universal faith. There is never any doubt in his mind that the order of nature is a definite and dependable one. The magical and miraculous are as remote from his faith as the notion of bribing an irate Deity. Nor do prayers divert God from his universal purpose. Yet he finds it "very fit and meet for the good man to offer sacrifice to the gods, and hold converse with them by means of prayers and offering." Nor is there any limit apparently to "finding gods everywhere," even to "private and ancestral" ones.[22] Readers who understand the background of Plato's thought will recognize here a "natural reverence" toward everything making for good. Rev-

[21] *Sym.* 211–212.
[22] *Laws,* IV, 716–7.

erence for living parents is included with that for the Olympians and the manes of a heroic ancestor. We have every reason to suppose that he would have honored the Christian saints or the Oriental deities to the extent that they manifest "the greatest possible likeness to God" as embodying ideals of excellence. We have also seen how he repudiated the Olympians in so far as they lacked this "likeness to God."

Plato's religion in brief is to have confidence in the scientific axioms of an intelligent and good cosmic power; to cleave to whatever, even in imagination, supports the conviction of goodness; and to act accordingly in creating for one's self and others healthy, harmonious, happy lives, serene with the conviction that whatever our destiny it will be for the best—the "justice of him who holds in his hand the beginning, middle, and end of all."

CHAPTER XVIII

PLATO'S INTERPRETATION OF ART

Plato was a great lover of the arts as well as their very severe critic. He knew the thrill of the wingèd word, the delight of figures in marble, the power of noble music, the fascination of terror and pity in tragedy. Yet he was willing for conscience' sake to forego a large part of the arts he knew in the interest of something more important. He found dangerous allurements even in the pages of Homer and Æschylus, something ruinous to the soul in wild Phrygian rhythms, and also in the dulcet tunes of Eolian flutes. For such reasons he would bind a fillet of wool about the head of "our sweet friend, Poetry" to honor him—but also to send him out of the new republic. Whence this poignant division of mind? How could a prince among artists have been so hard on his best-loved occupation, one which he thinks is enjoyed by the cosmic Artist himself?

The wonder becomes even greater when we realize how penetrating were the *aperçus* of this first effort comprehensively to understand the meaning of both beauty and the arts. So great was the interest of the poet-musician-connoisseur and master of superlative prose, that nearly all of the Dialogues have some reference to the arts. So acute is his treatment of beauty in the little work called *Hippias Major* that not a few critics have failed to understand it and called it nonsense—therefore no work of Plato at all! Let us pass in review a few of the main problems which are there discussed that we may better understand the issues.

Socrates appeals to Hippias, the cock-sure Sophist of encyclopædic learning, for aid against the questions of a (hypothetical) friend, who raises all sorts of difficulties on the subject of beauty. "By Zeus, this is but a mite, Socrates, I can teach you to answer much more difficult questions than suchlike ones," answers Hippias. Whereupon Socrates takes the proposed examples of beautiful things—a maiden, a mare, and a soup-tureen—and asks: What is it that these things have in common, by virtue of which we call them beautiful? Surely it is not the substance of which they are made, for it is different in each case. Nor can they be said to act in the same way or to have similar shapes. Moreover they differ in degree. No one would think of equating the beauty of the soup-tureen with that of the maiden. And the same is true when one compares the girl, say, with a god, perfect in all respects. An ape, said Heraclitus, is ugly when compared with man, but a man is ugly when compared with God. What is then their common quality?

The question takes another form when Socrates later compares the arts of painting and music. The first appertains to the eye, the other to the ear. It might seem as though they had nothing in common. Yet we apply the term "beautiful" to both. Does this mean that beauty has nothing to do with our senses, is something wholly superior to them? On such a supposition you face the problem of why there are no arts connected with smell, taste, and touch. We never speak of beautiful smells or objects as touched. We need eyes, and ears, or at least one of these in order to appreciate the beauty of anything. So that it does appear as though our senses had something to do with it. Yet what have eye and ear in common?

Perhaps one may be disposed to answer: Nothing, beauty is in the individual particular thing. Every painting is beautiful in its own way; so too the various sorts of music. They stand independently of each other. Yet whether we deceive ourselves or not, we do in fact compare them. Not only do we say the maiden is more beautiful than the earthen soup-tureen, or this melody more than that one, but this painting as compared with that melody.

Hippias fumbles. He goes back to the starting point and declares that it is the material used in the painting or sculpture which makes them beautiful. "We all surely know that whenever gold is present to a thing, howsoever ugly it may have seemed before, it will appear beautiful when it is decorated, at least with gold."[1] Socrates replies, In that event Phidias must have been a poor sculptor for failing to make Athena's eyes, face, and hands of gold. He used ivory instead; which seems to suggest that it is not the material as such, but the fitness with which it is used, which determines its beauty. Gold would have been unbecoming for Athena's eyes with her face of ivory. It would in fact have been ugly. How then are materials as such beautiful when they depend upon the fitness with which they are used? Imagine (he says elsewhere) a healthy cheek with rouge on it—a repulsive and ugly stuff, and yet lovely enough in the picture of a sunset.

Since it is clearly the fitness with which anything is *used* which determines its beauty, in some part at least, Hippias ventures the shot that actions, behavior, a rational manner of life are the things properly to be called beautiful. Socrates admits that we do so call certain actions, but has difficulty in saying which and for what reasons. He points out that circumstances alter occasions, since what is fitting and attractive in one man's behavior may be ugly and ridiculous in another. Nowhere do we find more disagreements among men than concerning just this matter of which actions are truly beautiful, as compared with those that appear to be so. For the thing is surely not a mere appearance, a passing state or condition. It must be something genuine and real if it exists at all.

[1] *Hippias Major,* 22.

Socrates proposes that usefulness might be a criterion of a thing of beauty, and Hippias assents. One part of a body is beautiful for running, another for wrestling. Musical instruments are so by use, also vehicles and kitchen utensils. A useless thing, a white elephant, a building that serves no purpose whatsoever, cannot properly be so called. It seems to be power, the capacity to do something, which is characteristic of beautiful objects. "But softly, my dear friend, I have a fear about what I am saying," adds Socrates. Power needs *direction*, does it not? It is surely only the *intelligent* use of power, and not mere brute force, which is ever beautiful. So that it looks as though intelligence were more fundamental than merely having power as such. Intelligence, too, means aiming for some good. It expects advantage from what it directs or seeks, which is to say some good. Beautiful things then are good for something.

This looks more hopeful, and Hippias is again impressed, only to be thwarted again by the observation that the cause of a thing is not necessarily the thing itself. A father is a cause of his son but he is not the son himself. Rain and sunshine cause plants to grow but are not therefore plants. Beautiful things may produce good results, but that is very far from making them equivalent to those good results. The beauty of anything is therefore not specified by discovering it to be a cause of good. It would be silly to suppose that a clumsy and ungainly Silenus transforms himself into an object of beauty by turning to good actions.

We seem to come back to eye and ear as very important in this subtle experience! Why is it not the essential characteristic of beautiful objects and actions that they delight either our vision or our hearing? Assuredly every poem or painting does at least that. And ugly things disgust one or the other of these senses. But Socrates quickly points out that pleasure is a very inclusive word. We apply it to all of our senses. And it might seem, if pleasure were the essential thing, as though the delights of eating would also come in for their share of beauty, or that sex pleasures would be called beautiful. But this is far from being the case. We keep the latter as dark as possible. Not even the ignorant would call them, or delicious smells, and sweet tastes, beautiful.

So it turns out that neither the materials of which beautiful objects are made nor their usefulness, neither the pleasure they bring to our senses nor the goodness associated with them, neither the specific sense qualities of vision and hearing, nor the intellectual illumination they sometimes produce, are adequate to explain the wonderful thing. Socrates hopes for more fortunate search at some future time.

The *Hippias Major* is peculiarly interesting for its distinction between beauty in itself and beauty as a cause of good, as well as for its implication that it is not in any object as such, but in the mind which experiences it, that beauty resides. The former point of view, as we shall see, is the most trenchant argument which can be urged against the Moralism so characteristic of Plato's doctrine in general. And the latter foreshadows his fundamental point of view that true art aims to make somehow visible or audible the essence or Ideas of things. Let us turn now to some other interpretations suggested elsewhere.

A very central conception in a number of Dialogues is the assumption that works of art imitate something. Paintings obviously depict objects, characters, of one sort or another. Sculpture does this for a more limited number of objects. Music somehow illustrates human moods and emotions. Poetry "holds the mirror up to life." So that Plato is willing more generally to characterize the function of art as an imitation (mimesis). He does not tell us how this applies to architecture and some of the lesser arts, but makes out a strong case for what are generally called the representative arts.

This point of view is, of course, æsthetic Realism, the

doctrine that a work of art presents truth, something that is worth knowing or realizing—not necessarily as statements of fact, scientific or philosophical investigation, but rather as more direct intuitions of things and their meanings. Now there are many different ways of "imitating" and Plato was far from being so naïve a Realist as to suppose that the artist merely duplicates or copies what he sees or hears. Sometimes, to be sure, the discussions seem to imply just that. In the *Ion*, the rhapsode of that name is shown to be all too ignorant of what he is reciting. How could he appreciate the merit of Homer's lines about charioteers if he himself is not one? And since Ion is no physician, fisherman, prophet, or general he is lacking in knowledge of such passages too.[2] Even Homer is charged with similar ignorance for failing to depict things *as they are*. "Like a painter who will make a likeness of a cobber though he understands nothing of cobbling . . . so the poet ignorant of real men and laws and virtue deceives some who are as ignorant as himself." [3] The defect indeed of all the tribe is that they are thrice removed from truth, i. e., they imitate what is itself an imitation—of Ideas back of the changing world of sense.[4]

This criticism, even though it takes for granted that art is a means of setting forth truth, also implies that, in its better forms at least, it is more than exact imitation or copying of anything we experience by our senses. Art does not falsify or misrepresent. And yet its truth is not the obvious fact we see or hear. There is "something far more deeply interfused" (to use Wordsworth's phrase), a reality whose nature is beyond sensory experience to perceive or depict, and which therefore makes the whole art-venture dubious. Yet in its higher, as well as in its more debased forms, artistry remains for Plato an "imitation." At times he thinks of

[2] *Ion.* 537–42.
[3] *Rep.* X, 601.
[4] *Ibid.* 602.

it as "expression" [5] but without modifying his mimetic conception. To "express" something is also in some way to "imitate" it. There is intellectual content involved. Merely exploiting emotions, even though in the most balanced expression, would not yet be art. In its endeavor to discover and set forth Ideas artistry is kindred to science and philosophy.

But there is another sense in which art-experience is an imitation. When we enjoy a comedy we find ourselves drawn into the situation in such a way that we tend to become like the characters we admire or laugh at. We take home something of the buffoonery we have witnessed, perhaps making fools of ourselves for the family or the neighbors. The rhapsode reciting the sorrows of Andromache finds his eyes filling with tears. The listener too seems to be present, in his ecstasy, among the persons of the narrative. All imagine themselves to be physicians, horsemen, or heroes according to the story. So, too, in painting and music; we tend to become like that to which we listen or gaze upon, when the charm of the artist is upon us.

And here the moral influence of art with its enormous risks impresses itself upon Plato's mind. Sympathetic imitation of the characters in a play, or of the emotions expressed in music, can make for evil as well as good. And the danger is especially great in art because "we are not altogether in our right minds" when we experience its ecstasies. Hence the utmost care must be observed in choosing or permitting only that which is intrinsically worthy of such imitation, to be presented in the arts. In these discussions he tended to confuse that which in the *Hippias Major* was carefully discriminated, namely, a cause of the good, and beauty. Since his Ideal Theory postulated good as the highest Idea, and he was therefore convinced that anything short of good in any representation of reality failed to attain

[5] *Rep.* III, 400b.

complete truth, it was natural that he should conceive of beauty, goodness, and truth as similar if not identical ideals. The true artist does not falsify. He imitates what is genuine, albeit something deeper than the superficial appearance of things. In aiming for this reality he strives to represent truth. And the deepest truth, the final question in every interpretation of reality is: What good?

This is impeccable logic on the Platonic axioms. But he draws the further conclusion that the *means* of imitating or representing good must also be good—which is to abandon the earlier doctrine that a cause is not necessarily similar to its effect. Thus he argues not only that it is morally wrong for Homer to depict the Olympian gods as tricksters and seducers. Homer is wanting in artistry to do such a thing. It is untruthful and hence irreligious to misrepresent God as a petty liar. It is also inartistic as a falsification. Indeed he should not have introduced into the story any characters who are not worthy of being imitated. Similarly in sculpture: it is bad taste to carve in stone a human body which under any circumstances might be misleading to youthful imagination. Music which even for a moment softens unduly one's mood or, on the other hand, loosens one's control over his more primitive emotions, is both morally dangerous and bad art.

The amusing thing in this connection is that in practice Plato introduces not only ideal characters into his own Dialogues, but also succeeds in making evil ones serve a truly artistic as well as moral purpose. In fact he himself would have been one of those who with a fillet of wool about his head would have been sent forth from the new republic. Almost the extreme limit of immorality is embodied in the defiantly brutal superman, Thrasymachus, who appears as the exponent of injustice.[6] And in the *Symposium* he portrays a bantering, drunken Alcibiades. Nor do such descrip-

[6] *Rep.* I, 328–343.

tions preach a lesson or condemn these men overtly. On the contrary, they are rich in the artistry of sympathetic insight and the charm of sensuous detail.

But this inconsistency is not strange. It reflects the wealth and many-sidedness of his thought and sympathy. Indeed few critics of Plato's Moralism to-day are in a position to state wherein its weakness lies. Few probably would question the characterization of great works of art as powerful influences making for inner harmony of life, as incentives to excellence in those who experience them. The fact that art demands one hundred per cent perfection is in itself no small stimulus to perfection in other directions. In fact there are few aspects of life in which the demands of artistry are not applicable. Conversely, the vicious in literature or music is obviously coördinated with a society of similar characters, wherever they prevail. The liberal arts are the best index of a people's progress away from savagery. Assuredly art belongs within the circle of the good. But this is not to say that the moral effect of a poem or sonata is a measure of its artistic excellence. There are so many other agencies of good, that it would be confusing a part with the whole to assume that all good things are also artistic. The latter have their own special character even though they belong within the circle.

Now despite this criticism, we must not suppose that Plato was unaware of the art for art's sake doctrine. In the *Republic* [7] he speaks of judging paintings by colors and figures, and music by meter, "harmony," rhythm, etc. But the difficulty of these formal and sensuous qualities was for him the fact that they can be so misleading. A vicious thing can be decked up in such colors and charm as to upset the minds of those who come under its spell. "Sweet influences" of this kind are like false bloom upon faces that are intrinsically hideous. Much the most important factor for him

[7] X, 601b.

is therefore the content, that to which expression is given, as contrasted with the means or form in which it is presented. He finds difficulty, as a great many people have since, in admitting that technical criteria can be coördinate with the moral one. His anxiety for the latter, together with his fear of seductive forms of pleasure, led him to underestimate the positive value which the formal qualities and charms of sense possess. By them, as we know, even noxious evil, crime and irresistible horror are transformed into a beauty in which we also find spontaneous exultation, even inspiration to excellence of life—and quite independently of any preachments.

The failure of technique, on the other hand, can transform even a paragon of excellence into something ugly and ridiculous, or an unmistakable occasion of evil. Noble objects, characters, and actions are therefore not the primary consideration. The means and manner of representation are more significant, even from a moral standpoint, than are the actions or objects themselves. And yet Plato's fundamental axiom coördinating the arts with human excellence is only reaffirmed by extending their spheres to include sympathetic understanding of evil.

Next to evil subjects, that which gave Plato pause was the seductive possibilities of sensuous pleasures. Most of them are by their nature disruptive, loosening to one's fiber, unlimited in their thirst. That is another reason why in the earlier Dialogues he looked askance at the arts. But it is refreshing and illuminating to find him in a later one, the *Philebus*, analyzing the different forms of pleasure and attributing to the æsthetic ones the highest rank. They are superior because in the first place the pleasures of art have no antecedent thirst or craving, like sex or hunger, which has to be reckoned on the debit side. Neither do æsthetic pleasures have the deleterious after-effects which often follow gratification of others, e. g., intoxication. They are further characterized by right measure, a certain symmetry, and internal harmony which make them more desirable than those which have no balance and no bounds. Hence the pleasures associated with the highest type of human life are those growing out of the liberal arts. They are an index of the soul's health and true success.

It matters little that several of Plato's doctrines have led us to further questions. The richness of his thought is realized when one brings to mind that nearly, if not quite all, of the major interpretations in æsthetics so far made go back to his keen insight.[8] Realism was the starting point. But he was saved from naïve forms of the theory by Idealism. The artist imitates (expresses) the more perfect embodiments or characters of things, those which best exhibit the Ideas everywhere operative in the cosmos. This is held to be a knowledge, or better, a knowing process—an assumption which lies at the basis of all "Intellectualist" interpretations of art. Since this gives the artist and beholder (or listener) intimations of something beyond sensations, it reveals a higher world directly. This is the general presupposition of "Mystical" theories. Plato also characterized art-experience as intuition—to be contrasted with deliberation or dialectical reasoning—a "divine madness." And this is the beginning axiom of "Intuitionists." Art is a never-failing source of pleasure ("Hedonic" theories). But that pleasure is not a criterion of excellence, unless it contributes to moral good ("Moralism"). Though some artists are guided solely by technique, form, and sensuous charm, this—the "art for art's sake" doctrine—must be repudiated. The good which every work of art reveals is not merely external advantage—as "Utilitarians" proclaim. It is the expression of what is inward, a certain quality of soul—which is a first recorded statement of the "Expressionist" doctrine. Whether beauty is solely in the mind, or in external things as well, Plato does

[8] Cf. J. Walter: *Geschichte der Aesthetik im Altertum,* p. 170.

not explicitly discuss. But when he implies that happy, balanced, and healthy movements of the soul are a criterion of true beauty he makes the subject very important. From this point of view "Subjectivist" theories have arisen. Finally, in his doctrine of imitation, the inevitable self-identification, feeling one's self into works of art, he clearly states the (very modern) *Einfühlung* theory.

Students of æsthetics will hardly approve of Plato's supposition that the *means*, tools, or subjects of art must themselves always be moral. And for that reason they will not follow him in his identification of the Good, the True, and the Beautiful. But they will always be grateful to him for his illumination of a difficult and delightful subject.

CHAPTER XIX

ARISTOTLE, THE MAN AND HIS LIFE WORK

Aristotle, who perhaps more than any other person has determined the fundamental concepts, methods of procedure, and interpretations of Western thought, and whose influence upon the future of civilization is still rich with promise, lived from 384 to 322 B. C. He was born at Stagira, a son of Nicomachus who was surgeon to Amyntas, the ruler of Macedonia. For several generations the family had been prominent as physicians to the northern court, one in which the cultural ideals of the southern, or better Ionian, Greeks are known to have been vigorous. But we have no dependable data about the early life and training of Aristotle, beyond the fact that after the premature death of his parents the responsibility for his education was assumed by a benevolent gentleman named Proxenus of Atarneus, a favor which Aristotle could later reciprocate by adopting Nicanor, the son of his benefactor.

At the age of eighteen he entered the Academy at Athens where he continued his studies for twenty years, or to the time of Plato's death. How the master and his great pupil got on together is the subject of many a story, some of them rather damaging to the character of Aristotle. But we know that he had many enemies, a fact altogether natural with his preëminence of mind, and the gossip-grubbers quite obviously contradict each other as well as themselves. It does not seem likely that he should have set himself up in opposition to Plato by starting a rival school, or have maltreated his aged master shortly before his death. However drastically he criticizes some of Plato's doctrines in his own writings, he consistently refers to himself and his followers as "Platonists." And if he had not profoundly respected the Academy it is hardly conceivable that he should so long have remained a member of it.

He broke that relation, however, at the time of Plato's death. Speusippus was appointed to head the college and it is possible that Aristotle was disappointed by not receiving that office. We know that he very much disliked the way philosophy was being turned into mathematics by Speusippus.[1] And Plato himself had called him "the mind of the school." But whatever the reason he left Athens in the company of Xenocrates (who was later to succeed Speusippus) and went to visit Hermias, the ruler of Atarneus and Assos, another pupil from the Academy who had gathered about him a group of "Platonists." He remained in Asia Minor at this court for three years, and at some time during the period married Pythias, the niece of the prince. By her he had a daughter. Later, after the death of Pythias, he married (though without legal ceremony) a native of his home town, Stagira, the lady named Herpyllis, who bore him a son, Nicomachus, for whom the *Nicomachean Ethics* is named. This marriage was both a happy and a permanent one.

After some time on the island of Lesbos, presumably with his friend and fellow student of nature, Theophrastus, who lived there, Aristotle received an invitation from Philip of Macedon in 343 to become the tutor of Alexander, then thirteen years of age. This office he accepted and spent the next eight years of his life in the old family environment. Three years of that time he was training Alexander, and the world would very much like to know what his methods were. But we have only conjectures together with the items that he got out a special copy of the *Iliad* for the future conqueror, and wrote two books for his benefit, one on *Monarchy*

[1] *Meta.* I, 992a, 32.

and the other entitled *Colonies*. These facts are indeed significant. But the relationships between Alexander and Aristotle, even after the Prince in his sixteenth year was appointed regent, are not very clear. Formal instruction probably ceased at that time. It is definitely known that it was the influence of Aristotle which spared the city of Athens from destruction by Alexander's troops, and also brought about the rebuilding of Stagira after it had been destroyed.

The character and motives of Alexander must have been influenced by his teacher. And it is not unreasonable to conjecture that the cultural purposes which inspired his conquests, the desire to bring Greek ideals of science, art, and the conduct of life to the peoples of the East, bore some relationship to the tutor's ideas, even though we know that he was opposed to anything like an amalgamation of Greek and oriental culture. This may also have been true of the fine restraint, the nobility of spirit, the rigorous self-discipline and broad human sympathy which the Conqueror displayed. The fact that he supported Aristotle's college in Athens by munificent grants of money is also evidence in point.

The *Lyceum* was founded about 335 B. C. Twelve years only were left to its head in which to carry out an almost miraculous work. Yet those years were also marked by the closest associations with his students, who very likely helped him in the more mechanical parts of his encyclopædic undertakings. From his habit of walking with his pupils in the grove about the school (sacred incidentally to Apollo Lyceius) he drew upon himself and the Lyceum the name of Peripatetic. He and his pupils had their meals in common. The fervid discussion of Friendship in the *Ethics* is eloquent testimony to the importance he placed upon it in any liberal education. No one, unfortunately, among the Peripatetics made a catalogue of the curriculum studies, nor did any one discuss the methods of instruction there. So we can only make inferences from the texts, which are in large part lecture notes, and from a few casual observations, for example that he taught by the Socratic method of spontaneous discussion as well as by connected lectures. The *Lyceum* had a considerable library, since it was considered a prototype of the Alexandrian collection. There were also laboratories and museums. The many living creatures, so carefully described in the zoölogical works, were obviously studied at first hand. We are told that the royal patron obtained the coöperation of hunters and fishermen throughout the realm in collecting specimens for his old instructor. A great deal of dissection was done there, but we hear little of experimentation. Aristotle's methods were as much inductive as deductive; yet his principle of the uniformity of nature did not, apparently, lead him to put much stress on crucial experiments.

It seems hardly credible that mutual suspicions should have darkened the friendship of Alexander and his master in the later years. But there clearly were misunderstandings, which very probably grew out of situations beyond the control of either. For example, Aristotle had recommended Callisthenes for some royal favor. But the latter turned out to be obnoxious to the king because he opposed certain oriental innovations at the court. He who had commended him also fell under suspicion! Alexander's unpopularity as the destroyer of Greek liberties, in its turn, also reacted on the head of his friend, another result which was natural if not inevitable. Certain story-tellers tried to counteract such impressions and so protect him by inventing a plot in which the great philosopher figures as the prisoner of his royal pupil and benefactor! But when the storm broke in 323 after the death of Alexander, Aristotle found it expedient to withdraw from Athens to his country home in Chalcis, where as we know there was strong feeling in favor of the monarchy. Charges of impiety had also been brought against him, and he is reported to have excused his withdrawal by saying that he wished to save the Athenians from another crime against philosophy. The charge was his "deification of a mortal" in a poem lauding the virtues of his daughter, Hermias, who died about this time. He himself followed her within a year of his flight and almost the same time at which Demosthenes died (322).

If we judge the character of Aristotle by the reports of his enemies he was an ingrate, a petty-minded monster of iniquity. But other sources of information fortunately show him in another light. Chief among these are, of course, his writings. But we also possess his will, and perhaps his portrait-bust. Many students of art are convinced that the marble in the Vienna museum is such a likeness dating from antiquity. If so Aristotle was not of prepossessing appearance. We know from other sources that he was not strong in body, a fact which makes the sheer quantity of his work appear as the product of heroic devotion and self-discipline. The many careful and generous provisions of his will, which included arrangements for the future happiness (by remarriage) of his second wife, Herpyllis, and the setting up in life of faithful friends among his slaves, show a fine sense of justice. His affection for his relatives, the loyalty to his wives, his exquisite feeling for beauty and all forms of excellence, point to a rarely high-minded character, one to whom the life of the spirit on the sides of feeling and action as well as of interpretation was of paramount importance. All who come into contact with his ethical principles realize their noble character. Whether or not one agrees with his estimate of slavery the reader of the *Nicomachean Ethics* realizes the challenge which it presents to the future of humanity.

For sheer intellectual penetration Aristotle stands with Plato. They who undertake the task of reading his works in their entirety never cease to wonder at the power of his intellect, even when, as often happens, he makes the most egregious mistakes. One easily understands why his masterful insight has so often overawed his readers and led them to accept his word as a final one. Yet, in all his grandiose plans and efforts toward a perfected philosophy, common reason is his sole authority. An immense patience for details, acuteness of classification and analysis were balanced by a synthetic grasp of the common and essential in isolated particulars. We miss in him the vision, the poetic charm of Plato. His *aperçus* were less the products of intuition than of painstaking logical and factual analysis. The extant verses from his pen are further evidence in point. But his scientific ideal of complete objectivity, brevity, incisiveness, literalness, exactness has remained ever since an example of scientific writing.

The books attributed to Aristotle make a list of incredible length. Three ancient catalogues enumerate more than two hundred titles of works which have utterly disappeared today. Nineteen more are mentioned by Diogenes Laertius, some of which are quoted by other ancient writers. The extant books vouched for by all possible internal and external evidence themselves constitute no small body of writing. Very likely a considerable number of the lost works were shorter essays. Some of those referred to may have been surreptitiously pawned off as Aristotelian, since we know this was the case with a number of extant essays. Others which we possess bear the marks of being student notes of his lectures. So that, after making allowances, the wonder of his pen becomes at least less incredible. There seems to be clear evidence that his first works were in dialogue form. Their subjects ranged all the way from an *Eroticus* to books *On Wealth*, *On the Poets*, *On Good Birth*, *On Prayer*. Much speculative scholarship has gone into the effort to trace the content of these and other lost books. But this cannot concern us here. Nor can the strangely romantic history of the manuscripts.

Among the undoubtedly authentic works nearly all of the

Organon, or "Instrument" of Knowledge is accepted by Greek scholars generally. It consists of a number of logical treatises, elaborate discussions of the various forms, rules, and pitfalls of thinking, which have remained to this day the basis of formal logic. Among the treatises on physical nature which are genuine belong the *Physics*, *On the Heavens*, *On Generation and Decay*, and the *Meteorology*. His interest in biology is attested by an undisputed and monumental work, *On the History of Animals*, a collection of data for which biologists to-day have only praise, despite its occasional inaccuracies. The theoretical books on biology include treatises on: *The Parts of Animals*, *The Movement of Animals* (2), *The Generation of Animals* (Embryology). The predominantly psychological works include: *On the Soul*, *On the Senses and Sensibles*, *On Memory and Reminiscence*, *On Sleep*, *On Dreams*, *On Divination in Sleep*, *On Length and Shortness of Life*, *On Respiration*, *On Life and Death*. There is some doubt about the book entitled *Problems*, in which a number of questions on physiological, musical, optical and mathematical subjects are discussed. It shows evidences of influences (perhaps additions) from a later period. And yet no small portion of it is distinctly Aristotelian.

A great deal of scholarship has been devoted to the *First Philosophy*, or *Metaphysics*, a mosaic of books forming in part a general introduction to philosophy, in part a discussion of fundamental terms and a somewhat loosely connected presentation of basic principles, especially the problems and difficulties which face anyone who tries to describe substance, or the foundation of reality. That the immensely varied individual things have something in common, a nature or essence which belongs to them merely as being, Aristotle assumed as a beginning intuition of knowledge. And the primary function of metaphysics is therefore to describe Being as such in the most inclusive sense and its most general activities. This *First Philosophy* (which was probably edited by Eudemus) is linked up closely with the *Physics* and parts of the *Organon.* But three books of it (Alpha, Delta, and Kappa) which are possibly later additions, are rather difficult to coördinate with the others.

On Ethics we have three works setting forth the doctrines of Aristotle, the *Nicomachean,* the *Eudemian,* and the *Magna Moralia.* The last was pretty certainly written after Aristotle's day and the other two are very likely stenographic reports of courses on Ethics reported by Nicomachus and Eudemus. There is pretty general agreement between them, but the *Nicomachean Ethics* is commonly regarded by scholars as the more fundamental one. The *Eudemian Ethics* announces at the end of its third book that its next three books are identical with the fifth, sixth and seventh of the *Nicomachean,* a fact which has raised some problems of priority. But close investigation of grammatical peculiarities of style [2] shows that those characteristic of the *Eudemian Ethics* do not appear in the books omitted. So it is very likely that they belong where they now are. The *Magna Moralia* follows the *Eudemian* but introduces Stoic and other later terms.

Aristotle also labored long and fruitfully at the problem of government, as his undoubtedly genuine work on *Politics* and his monumental study of Greek constitutions testify. Most of the latter work, which included a description of 158 constitutions, has been lost. But as late as 1890 an Egyptian mummy brought to light the papyrus containing his *Constitution of Athens,* a first chapter of this much regretted book.

Among other undoubted originals are the *Rhetoric* (whose third book was once suspected but has later been abundantly vindicated) and the *Poetics,* a fragment which no one other than Aristotle could have written. Of other works which

[2] See Eucken: *Sprachgebrauch des Aristoteles,* 10.

claim his authorship there is a considerable number; but content, style, grammar, and especially anachronisms have generally served to show the inadequacy of most claims. In some of the doubtful works, however, such as the one *On Melissus, Xenophanes, Gorgias,* and a few psychological treatises the line is not always certain.

Much painstaking work has been devoted to the effort to determine the likely order and approximate dates of the various books. It seems probable that the Dialogues in the Platonic manner and extant discursive writings, which show considerable dependence upon Plato, should be earlier than those in which there is less of Idealism and more of his own characteristic doctrines. On that assumption the *Organon,* the *Politics,* the *Physics,* and parts of the *Metaphysics* anticipate the biological, psychological, and historical works. But this is all very indefinite. Historical tradition, which is supported by internal analysis, attributes the bulk of his literary work to the twelve years of his teaching at the Lyceum. If this is correct it is evidence of almost superhuman capacity for work.

CHAPTER XX

THE FOUNDATIONS OF LOGIC

To know under what conditions we are safe in trusting the pioneering work of our reasons, clearly is a matter fundamental to all the sciences, philosophy, and religion. Until we have adequate assurance that the products of our thought have relationships to the real world, and hold together as an intelligible whole, they may, for aught we know, be a persuasive dream or a working fancy. At every point Reason seems to bear witness against herself saying, Be sure the conclusion is correct! So that a means of testing the correctness of her instruments becomes perhaps the most important discovery of human knowledge. Unfortunately, it is only by first projecting a thought and *afterwards* testing it, that our thinking takes place, a fact which itself is responsible for several wrong conceptions of Logic. It has misled some modern Pragmatists into supposing that, as an *ex post facto* examination, Logic is unnecessary. In mediæval times the opposite mistake was made—of supposing that the study of processes and methods would itself develop a store of knowledge about the world. Early religion and science alike projected naïve imaginations, unaware of the need of controls. "Practical" Sophists, ancient and modern, profess to find other criteria than examination of the thinking process itself. Their "adventures" in truth pour anathema upon "logic-chopping" and seek to discredit the most elementary means of testing the course of reason.[1]

So it is both important and timely to understand what

[1] See F. C. S. Schiller's *Formal Logic*.

Logic undertakes to do, and what its origin was. Before Aristotle there had been rudimentary efforts to find out under what conditions one might best do justice to facts and find their harmonious coördination. Socrates laid a part of the foundation for the new science by his endeavors to limit, or define, concepts. Thus one might at least avoid the inconvenient evil of unintentionally reasoning about two or more different things at the same time! This was (and still is) a root of many fallacies. If we humans can make sure (Gorgias to the contrary) of thinking about one thing at a time, Socrates held we might go on to Induction. And by Induction he meant what is called in our day a questionnaire, an effort to elicit a consensus of opinion from some larger or smaller group of people. Plato also tackled many problems of method, and tried to discover proper heads of classification, by which the infinitely complex array of facts might be made to yield correct meanings and interpretations. Perhaps his most remarkable contribution was the principle that our success in reasoning depends upon the degree to which we are able systematically to coördinate all the relevant facts of our experience, within and without, into an ordered, actively harmonious scheme. As we have already observed, he regarded this consistency, or harmony, as a mark of what is *good* as well as that of the truth. But it was Aristotle, who first, in a comprehensive way, investigated our thought processes in order to work out the specific conditions and laws of correct procedure.

For this persistent, immense, and thoroughgoing labor, he is justly called the Father of Logic. He for the first time specifically segregated the problem of reasonableness (cogency of thought as such, and as controlled by relation to the external world) from psychological descriptions of how the mind acts, as well as from the metaphysical problem of reason's, or the mind's, ultimate nature. By thousands of examples he investigated nearly all known means of drawing conclusions, and established tests of validity which still clarify the minds of modern students. His work also serves to put us on guard against expecting from Logic more than it can provide. For Logic *tests* conclusions. It does not itself produce them. Aristotle, it is true, did not from the first make this assumption; but he came to this conviction as the result of long deliberation.

We shall hardly be able to present here what is still very largely the content of courses in Logic. But a sketch of Aristotle's researches can perhaps be made more significant if we consider his principles in the light of modern problems and pragmatic difficulties. He did not himself invent the word "*Logic.*" In his studies of reasoning he commonly used the term "*Analytics*" (which implies something *given* for analysis) and designated the collection of these investigations as *Organon*—an instrument or tool. It has been divided into six books. In the *Topics* which seems to be in large part (Bks. II–VII) an earlier work, he discusses argumentation as it were from a Sophistic point of view. How can one most successfully obtain mental gymnastics by arguing with people from all sorts of premises, and thus not only acquaint one's self with a wide range of opinion, but succeed in a debate? The *pros* and the *cons* of all manner of subjects should give one a wide basis for culture and also help in the finding of what is probable. It seems likely that Sophistic quibbles and debates themselves suggested to his mind the thought of a technique for the control of valid inferences! Already he analyzes problems from the standpoint of genus, property, and accident, and sets up ten general points of view from which a subject may be discussed. But in the *Topics* there is still not a little of the Sophist's game [2] of winning the argument without special knowledge. Yet it must also be said that Aristotle never descended to the show or pretense of victorious debate for glory or gain.

[2] See especially Bk. VIII.

In the *Sophistic Elenchi* (Confutation of a Sophistic Adversary) which is a continuation of the *Topics*, he lays bare the various sources of Fallacy. He does this first by *instructing* the Sophist how to invent and make use of deception in leading the argument astray, and then by teaching the seeker for truth how to put himself on guard against these very traps. Some of the chief fallacies arise from language itself. We use ambiguous words (Equivocation), our sentence has a double construction (Amphiboly), we couple words or ideas together which belong so only under peculiar conditions (Composition), or again we separate when normally they belong together (Division). We contort our meanings by misleading emphasis on certain words (Accent); we allow analogous grammatical forms to confuse our thought (Figure of Speech). But the fallacies of diction are not the only ones. We all too often assume that what is generally true of a thing is also true of its accidental qualities, or vice versa (Accident). We find different qualities in different parts of a thing, and forthwith take them all to be characteristic of the whole (*a dicto secundum quid ad dictum simpliciter*). Often enough we go on arguing when our point has been refuted (*ignoratio elenchi*). We argue seriously to prove a conclusion which the argument itself presupposes from the beginning (*petitio principii*). We mistakenly interchange predicate for subject (Illicit Conversion), and often assume that we have disproved very much more than we really have (*non causa pro causa*). In these most strategic analyses Aristotle was a sure-footed pioneer, and later writers on Logic have found it necessary to follow in his steps.

But, on the positive side as well, there were many instruments to be devised. Some of these he invented in the *Topics* but they came to their best use elsewhere. The book called *Categories* discusses the various meanings of the *things* for which words stand, the different *kinds* of being, in so far as we can deal with them by language, or what at bottom are the various *aspects* under which it is possible to look at things. We can perhaps best make clear how important such discrimination is, by recalling the difficulties into which early philosophers got, by their uncertainty as to whether such facts as color, weight, or odor represented an essential or a non-essential aspect of anything. Even yet we are not always sure of what is substance and what is quality in a thing. We are prone to regard a relation between things, e. g., gravitation, as itself something substantial. It was again a strategic aid to human thinking when Aristotle set up his list of categories, and recommended those who would think straight to be mindful of whether their concepts imply one or more of the following heads:

Substance (e. g., man).
Quantity (e. g., two cubits).
Quality (e. g., red).
Relation (e. g., dependence).
Where (e. g., in the market-place).
When (e. g., yesterday).
Position (e. g., sitting).
Possession (e. g., having arms).
Action (e. g., doing something).
Passion (e. g., having something done to you).

Of these, substance is clearly the most important, and generally our chief difficulty is to discriminate between categories which seem to be substantial, or essential characters of things (e. g., qualities), and which yet are perhaps no more than positions or relationships. A good example of this is found in the so-called secondary (or non-essential) qualities which Democritus said depended upon the relative positions of atoms, or which modern chemists say depend upon still smaller spatial relationships and movements. Another rather surprising example is found in the modern effort to regard *quantity* (e. g., velocity in the Einstein Hypothesis) as a determinant of certain qualities in things. The same theory also coördinates *action* (Energy) with substance, by thinking of matter as in large part charges of electricity. Such examples show the importance of knowing under what category one is thinking. When we are studying any form of Life it is not only of great help to us in our investigation, it is necessary, if we expect to reach any conclusions, to attempt to say whether we regard what we are discussing as a substance or a quality, as self-active (Action) or the play of impersonal agencies (Passivity), as consisting of just so much (Quantity), or as possessing real relationships (which also would seem to imply that we think of it as substance). Do we assume that "Life" has a *place* (e. g., some nucleus), or a limited date (a *vis vitalis* of so many years)? These and other aspects of our X make it desirable that we should know which one we are considering, lest we reason about several categories when we supposed that we were discussing only one. This at least is the mistake of a good many efforts to investigate our world. The number of categories in any particular search may be larger or smaller according to the subject under investigation. Aristotle placed no importance upon the number in his list, nor did he regard them (as J. S. Mill seems to have supposed [3]), as a basis for classifying objects. His concern was to get together aspects of things which could appropriately be reasoned about together.

It is sometimes urged that such distinctions of categories are merely *verbal*, a reflection on the forms of language. Thus a modern "Humanist" [4] writes: "His (Aristotle's) categories are among the best illustrations of the formal logician's common assumption that the nature of thought is faithfully mirrored by its expression in language, and that,

[3] *System of Logic,* Bk. I, Chap. III, Sect. I.

[4] F. C. S. Schiller in *Formal Logic,* p. 40.

therefore, a study of words may conveniently take the place of that of living thought." Unfortunately words *are* the tools of our meanings; but, for Aristotle, reasoning concerns itself with the things for which words stand. It suffices to quote his own statement: "A true sentence is by no means the cause of a thing's existence [as, curiously enough, modern Humanism sometimes supposes!] but in some way, the thing appears the cause of the sentence being true, for a sentence is said to be true or false according to whether the thing does or does not exist." [5] Logic clearly borders on Metaphysics here, and we can better discuss in another connection *how* categories reflect the more ultimate aspects of things. *That* they serve to clarify and simplify our reasoning has perhaps been made sufficiently clear.

In the *De Interpretatione* we have chiefly a discussion of propositions, their different types (negative, affirmative, universal, not universal, individual), and how the meanings of propositions are affected by the various changes of form into which they can be turned. Thus we know that if "All A is B" then "*Some* B is A." We also have some information as to not-A. How much do we learn about not-B from the first sentence? And what changes of meaning are involved when we change it to negative form: No A is not B? Such and many other exercises no doubt helped Aristotle's students, as they have helped many another since, to make their meanings precise by all the means that imperfect language permits.

But the matter which chiefly interests us here is Aristotle's earlier conception of truth. It may be called a somewhat naïvely "representative" view of knowledge. That some *correspondence* exists between the terms of a true assertion and the things for which they stand is generally admitted—for example, when I write of a book and its qualities, that the book and its qualities *exist* and can be experienced by

[5] *Categories,* Chap. XII. Last sentence.

others, provided my statement is true. The same is true of the relationship between the subject and the predicate, and that of the "real" relationship for which they stand. Suppose our knowledge to be simply: "A is the cause of B." Then there must be not only a real A and a real B but also the active relationship (and whatever else we mean) by "cause." So much is mere tautology. But Aristotle first conceived of truth as a "copying" of reality, our conceptions or "affections of the soul" being regarded as reproductions, or "likenesses of things," mirrored in our minds.[6] Naturally enough, this led to an interpretation of concepts as more or less "ready-made" as it were, lying about loose in the mind and only requiring the services of Logic to join or separate them. It was this view which lent itself so readily to the word-jugglers of the Middle Ages, when in some quiet corner they professed to make discoveries, and judge the course of nature, by exercises with concepts. These Scholastics could indeed claim Aristotle as their authority, but it was not his Logic at its best. Elsewhere as we shall shortly find he advanced beyond the copy-theory to one which regarded thought as directly concerned with things, one in which words are means to an end, namely, that of asserting or expressing correspondences in reality. Aristotelian Logic must not be thought of either as a unit, or as perfect. Like other sciences, ancient and modern, it has its difficulties, hypotheses, even contradictions. And we must be grateful for the measure of guidance which it can provide. Much criticism of Logic seems to be based on the assumption that, unlike any other science, it must be regarded as perfect and complete. But unfortunately for the sciences that depend upon a perfect Logic, the assumption will not bear investigation. Logic is a progressive science and has developed since Aristotle's day. But the advance has been slow and the Founder still remains its chief investigator.

[6] *De Interpretatione,* 16a and *passim.*

In the *Prior Analytics* the chief matter under discussion is the syllogism as a reliable method of testing conclusions. In essence, it is an analysis of complex inferences into their simplest elements and the application of a form by which to show whether those simple propositions, and the proof which is said to result, abide by the laws which are illustrated in our most secure and unquestioned conclusions. That there are different degrees of certainty, and that we are immediately aware of certain propositions, which serve as the starting points of all investigation, Aristotle took for granted, just as he assumed that we must believe our sensations if we are to get anywhere. We do not demonstrate, we simply apprehend, a color or a word. Similarly, we intuitively know that "All A" includes "Some A." Nobody but Sophists could dispute such axioms. If then we could analyze long and involved arguments into a series of simple steps, and lay bare upon what fundamental intuitions the inferences rest, we should be using the one clear means of arriving at the greatest possible certainty. This is exactly what the syllogism undertakes to do. Aristotle saw that every inference rests upon *two* pieces of knowledge, and that these two propositions (premises) have subjects, or predicates, or *a* subject and *a* predicate in common—the middle term. Thus there are three terms only, and three propositions, in the simplest complete process of reasoning. For example, in the syllogism

All A is B
All B is C
∴ All A is C

the conclusion clearly requires both the first (major) and the second (minor) premise. If one or the other were omitted, the inference would be impossible. True that the premises may be turned about somewhat. We may know only that All B is A and that All C is B. What in that event can we conclude? Clearly very much less easily, but yet certainly, that Some A is C. (This will be readily seen if we represent A, B, C, by circles and draw them in their proper positions—inside or outside of one another.) Much also depends—as we can immediately see—upon whether we have "Some" or "All" in the premises and whether they are negative or affirmative. Two negative premises permit no conclusion at all, just as two particular ("Some") propositions will not. In short there is a natural way to reason which can be described by the position and kind of terms (particular, universal, negative, affirmative) as they occur in a simple, complete, thought-process. The most natural and most cogent way of reasoning (illustrated in our first example) is that in which the conclusion has for its subject the subject of the major premise, and for predicate the predicate of the minor premise, both premises being universal and affirmative.

Now such laws as these are not mere chance, as any one can demonstrate by trying out the various possibilities of combination. If for another example we take these premises: "All A is B," "Some C is B," no one would find it quite natural to conclude from them that: "Some A is C" or that "Some C is A." And the reason is an "undistributed" middle term (B). That is why Aristotle proceeded to the most painstaking investigation of the quantity (distribution, how many), quality (positive or negative), mode (possible combinations of quality and quantity), and figure (derivation of subject and predicate in the conclusion) in endless numbers of syllogisms. In this way he discovered his eight laws governing them, and determined the possible ways in which (by additional information or legitimate change in form) an inconclusive syllogism may be made to yield whatever there is in it. In his *Prior Analytics* he also made an attempt to bring Induction (reasoning from particular cases to the general rule) to the syllogistic tests, but not successfully. He seems here to have supposed that Induction required to be perfect, i. e., to embrace all possible specimens or cases, in order to be fully cogent. Yet elsewhere he also recognized an Induction which falls short of such completeness,[7] as well as other non-syllogistic arguments (e. g., relations of time and place). As we have noted before (*Topics*), he also examined hypothetical and highly problematical syllogisms (those based upon "If" and merely "possible" premises) in order to use and control them.

In modern times we often hear the syllogism criticized for what it cannot do, namely, deal critically with *all* conclusions. But manifestly it can only deal with situations in which it is possible to find certain (and that the most adequate) grounds for our inference, and when the material with which it is concerned allows one to suppose that natural law is operating regularly. Aristotle's famous syllogism,

All men are mortal
Socrates is a man
∴ Socrates is mortal

would not be a correct inference if nature were suddenly to present us with a fountain of perennial youth. But the same uncertainty would also vitiate Induction if we could not bank upon regularity in nature. Assuming, however, that we are justified in accepting a number of axioms, the syllogism presents the most precise and incisive method we possess for testing such conclusions as come within its range.

Again it is maintained that syllogistic reasoning is *petitio principii.*[8] We already know from the original premise (All men are mortal) that Socrates is mortal. So (it is argued) we obtain no new information by such reasoning. But apart from the fact that the function of the syllogism was pri-

[7] *Posterior Analytics,* 100b 31; *Prior Analytics,* 68b 24–37; *Topics,* 105a 13–16.

[8] F. C. S. Schiller: *Formal Logic,* pp. 203–6.

marily conceived to be regulative, i. e., to test conclusions, it is also true that by joining together our facts or reasons syllogistically we often do obtain new conclusions. For instance, in our first example (All A is B, All B is C, ∴ All A is C), it is only by *putting together* the premises that we derive a conclusion. One can hardly say, therefore, that the conclusion is presupposed.

Despite all abuse which has been made of the syllogism in straining it beyond its natural function, it remains our most important means of testing the cogency of reasoning. It lays bare the foundations on which we build; it can discover for us the validity of most of our inferences. It cannot, indeed, disclose for us the truth or fallacy of our primary axioms. These Aristotle saw were the result of Induction [9] and hence not subject to valid argument.[10] Induction is rather a kind of intuition or direct insight, the vision of something common to the members of a species, which is taken to be characteristic of the genus. As simple awareness of things, it lends itself badly to inference. Only in the limiting case of having all the specimens, did he think we could apply the syllogism as a test.

It is also true that the syllogism cannot take cognizance of all the relationships expressed by verbs. As the student of the usual Formal (as distinguished from Symbolic) Logic will remember, such a premise as "Bears attack men" has to be transformed into "Bears *are* animals which attack men." In other words, the syllogism proceeds by subsuming one group under another (or separating them). It cannot deal directly with other relationships. They are subordinated into attributes of a subject or predicate. And this, of course, is a very great handicap. We have as yet discovered no parallel means of testing inferences from propositions such as these:

[9] *Posterior Analytics,* 100b concluding paragraph.
[10] *Ibid.* 72b 25–30.

"Bears attack men."
"Bears rob honey from bees."

Shall we say: "Then bears run rapidly?" or "Then bears climb trees?" or "Then bears fight for their young?" Our conclusions, in short, are unrelated until we see the possible syllogistic basis of the argument. This might be for number two:

All animals that steal honey from bees are such as climb trees.
Bears are animals, etc.
∴ Bears are such as climb trees.

But what shall it be for the third? If we could invent some method of dealing with the many relationships expressed by verbs, as successfully as we lay bare our meanings and test certain conclusions by syllogism, the usefulness of Logic would be greatly enhanced. And this our Symbolic Logicians now seem to be developing without adding to, or contradicting, underlying Logic. They who attack syllogistic reasoning because of its inability to deal directly with the facts expressed by verbs, might, therefore, more profitably try to improve some method which will work as well with them, as Aristotle's invention does within its sphere.

The *Posterior Analytics*, finally, discusses the methods and purposes of science, the conditions which must be fulfilled if it is to have secure foundations, and what is meant by proof. No one has ever maintained more positively than Aristotle does here, that everything we human beings learn is upon the basis of something *given*. Potentially there is something in our heads by way of knowledge at the dawning of our intelligence. Not that we have "innate ideas" or inherited mental *content* of any kind. Rather we (and the animals) possess a *function*, a discriminating power which operates the moment we perceive. We select and join together spontaneously that of which we are simply aware (sensations). But the first stage in the development from sense-awareness to knowledge is memory. The percept remains when the actual sensation is over. Then comes "experience," the framing of conceptions, or what is common in the series of percepts. This is the "universal" with which Induction supplies us and from which we start in every syllogistic reasoning process. Groups of such universals, or axioms, form the foundations of the sciences, and indeed of all our intellectual activity. If we did not have that which we know directly, quite without proof and demonstration, we should know nothing. One cannot go on indefinitely finding reasons for everything. Eventually one comes to something of which we are simply aware, something common in perception, or intuitions such as: Equals added to equals are equal; or (in Logic): Of two contradictory propositions one is true and the other false. Fortunately we possess these primary certainties both as to content and as to method: we believe our sensations, and we know that we must not contradict ourselves.

Now the process of science is to push beyond the primary certainties into a less secure region. By definitions, hypotheses, and experiments, it endeavors to prove certain conclusions which are less obvious than its axioms, even though such demonstrations quite strictly obey the axioms of method (Logic). The various sciences have different starting points; but of all axioms one can say: (1) not only that they are primary, or undemonstrable, (2) more intelligible than the conclusions obtained by their aid; but (3) that they are certainly true, and (4) causally related to what is demonstrated. Here again we see how Aristotle thought of the work of Logic as concerned not only with "formal" validity, but with what later logicians called "material" truth. No one knew better than he how easy it is to reason from false premises to false conclusions (and sometimes true ones!) by quite impeccable argument. Hence his distinction between postulates and axioms. A postulate is an assumption which itself is in need of proof and requires a foundation in sense experience. Mere reasoning from hypotheses and postulates to new conclusions falls short, therefore, of scientific work—however excellent the "form" of the Logic and the cogency of the reasoning as such.

It was none the less a misfortune for the cause of science that Aristotle did not devote more attention to hypothesis and experiment. Mathematics, rather than the experimental sciences, which were then in their infancy, provided him with his patterns. Consequently his Logic stressed *certainty* rather than the *adventure* upon which so much of modern scientific discovery has depended. Yet he laid a good deal of emphasis upon Induction and Examples, even when limited in number. He regarded Induction as clearer to us, more persuasive, more intelligible in terms of sense, and as having a more general appeal than Deduction. And since axioms are for him a product of Induction, it is sometimes a more certain method than the most cogent deductive demonstration based upon such axioms. As a method of reasoning, however, he regarded the going from the universal, or general principle, to the particular case as very much more compelling and intelligible by nature than the opposite, or inductive procedure. And we realize the truth of this when we consider how much more "compelling and intelligible by nature" any piece of scientific work is, which can be expressed mathematically, as compared with one which is purely descriptive.

But Aristotle might also in justice ask whether we are not overestimating the importance of Induction in modern times. Our great discoveries have in part depended upon adventures, chance experiments, or that preoccupation with particulars which he also regarded as central and prior. Nor would he question the wisdom of preserving all possible facts, even the most haphazard and isolated information, statistics and cases. They may all come in useful some day. Like newspaper files they may justify their existence by aiding in the establishment of a true interpretation, the discovery of a cause, the proof of a definite conclusion by specific facts. Yet often enough we have regarded facts as ends in themselves—which is natural enough whenever Induction loses sight of its complement and the goal of its undertaking. For, as Aristotle points out, "*That* a thing is so" is less important than "*Why* it is so." Science is in search of causes, laws, general principles, interpretations of the widest possible scope, insight into the fundamental nature of its data. Particulars are indeed prior and necessary —but as tools whenever such use is possible. That is why he regarded descriptive sciences as less developed than those which can discover the *How* and the *Why*. And we should have to confess that our search for facts as such has often led us into experimentation which a little insight into principles would have shown to be futile. We still enumerate instances in laboratories and elsewhere which are of no greater possible significance than the measurement of geometric figures after the demonstration. So that we can still profit by the advice of Aristotle to make Induction and Deduction reciprocal—testing our conclusions by particular cases as well as by general principles, and making sure whenever we can of the purposes of our experiment.

In another connection we shall consider Aristotle's conception of Cause in detail. Here it suffices to point out that he thought of causes under four heads: (1) That *out of* which, (2) That *by* which, (3) That *into* which, (4) That *on account of* which. The first three aspects—the matter out of which, the *process* or *activity* by which, and the product or result of that activity—are extremely important to know. But our interpretation is not complete until we can explain the *purposes*, the good attained by such causes. Hence the fourth class is called Final Causes—the goal of our endeavor. As the work of the sciences begins with what is undemonstrable (axioms), so also its proof always halts before what is beyond demonstration. Proof occupies a middle ground. At its upper threshold creative reason, a kind of higher Induction, steps in to give us intuitions of reality, those insights of art and religion which, though as far removed from proof as are axioms, are none the less sources of a higher knowledge. Beginning thus with the senses, and never leaving them through all the formal processes of his Logic, Aristotle not only was able to plot the course of natural or cogent reasoning, but also recognized that at the beginning and at the end of our endeavors we find ourselves in touch with what defies analysis and cannot be argued about. Here again he was aware of the limitations of Logic.

CHAPTER XXI

METAPHYSICS (ARISTOTLE)

A librarian in the famous Alexandrian Library in cataloguing the works of Aristotle, placed his "*First Philosophy*" on a shelf beyond the *Physics*. From this circumstance arose the term "Metaphysics" and also the supposition, still commonly held to-day, that this branch of philosophy is concerned with what is above or beyond the physical world, beyond the reach of our senses, and altogether a matter of speculation, in which one man's opinion may be as good as another's. There is some warrant for this conception of Metaphysics, in so far as investigation into the tangible world points to anything beyond the reach of our senses. And it is true enough that an immense variety of conclusions has been reached in the effort to obtain light in these darker places of the mind's work. But that Metaphysics is concerned exclusively with some realm apart or higher than our experiences, or that it depends upon the efforts of a "pure" or speculative reason divesting itself of ordinary sources of information, is an opinion which has done great harm to the cause of human knowledge. It has done more damage than ignorance itself, by discouraging the effort to push our investigations, by processes of thought analogous to those of the mathematician, into the deeper levels of a comprehensive synthesis.

First Philosophy, as Aristotle conceived it, is, in fact, the inevitable goal of every serious investigation. To Metaphysics all penetrating efforts toward knowledge eventually come. We begin by studying particular tangible or visible things, in order to segregate, classify, compare and measure. Knowledge begins with particulars—this object or this memory. It becomes more significant in him who commands many objects and memories. In the experienced man this wealth of detail becomes a means to the recognition of what is essential to these particulars. Technique in turn depends upon the ability of scientific theory to comprehend fundamental relations, to recognize causes and the conditions under which they operate, to be able to determine the essential qualities of things. And Metaphysics is simply an extension of the process, the endeavor to make clear by reference to all data which experience provides, what we mean by the most fundamental terms in that experience. After studying particular forms of life, we face the question: What is Life? After examining a multitude of substances we ask: What is common to them all, what is Substance? And so for Causes, Motions, Time, Space, Virtue, Beauty, God, and many other ideas which the mind of man has invented. To cut ourselves off from this effort to know more comprehensively is to welcome superficiality, with its attendant dogmatism.

At the same time, there is danger lest one generalize without sufficient basis. And here the lesson of Aristotle might have forestalled some of the idle speculations which have passed historically for metaphysics. For Aristotle maintained that all thought must begin with particulars; experience is its foundation. If we discover unseen reality it must be on the basis of what we infer from a seen reality. If certain conclusions are necessary, it must be because clear thought so constrains us by the evidence of all relevant facts. Thus Aristotle was a Realist in accepting what our senses offer as one of the sources of true knowledge. Only in particular things can one find the universal—the essence common to the many, the evidence for the unseen. Such a conception of metaphysics, though it leaves unanswered the Idealist's question of why we believe our senses, should never again be mistaken for the dreams of unthinking fancy.

By taking account of how his predecessors tried to solve the problems with which he deals, Aristotle originated the idea of a History of Philosophy, not as a chronicle merely of past men's thinking, but as an introduction to the problems of his day. In this examination of earlier philosophy his logical investigations gave him immense advantage by way of classifying and defining problems. Merely to ask (as a question of categories): Are we dealing with Substance or Quality? With what moves by itself (Action), or is acted upon (Passion)? led on to many important contributions of his own.

According to Aristotle, the earlier philosophy was dominated by the idea of matter. The Ionians, Heraclitus, the Atomists, even Empedocles, used water, air, fire, atoms or groups of elements to interpret whatever comes to pass. Matter was widely assumed to be the indestructible substance from which all things arise or to which they return. And so they looked to it as the cause of order, the source of life, the center of everything. These interpretations, important as they were for science, did not investigate the problem as to whether or not a variety of causes may be at work, and whether the material cause includes all others.

This analysis of causes (which he had already done in the *Physics*) he then applies to the Materialist hypothesis. If we examine causes more carefully, we find that among the four kinds Material cause—that *out of which*—is undoubtedly of great importance. But we also have to deal with activities, energies, motions, which are no less facts than matter itself. A second kind of cause, therefore, is that *by which* a change is produced. Moreover, when we ask: What is the plan, the order, the design in any course of events? we are looking for still another kind of cause—one superposed upon mechanical agency and pointing to intelligent action. This we find in our own activities, in animals, and vaguely in inanimate nature. And still a fourth kind of cause may be described as one which fulfills a purpose. In addition then to material causes, we find efficient causes (by which), formal causes (into which), and final causes (on account of which).

Now the Materialists are at a loss to interpret efficient causes. At most they attribute motion to matter from the beginning, by necessity, or by chance. And they ignore the other two, just as though goodness, beauty, and intelligence could be attributed to fire or earth, or to the configuration and falling of particles in a vacuum. But whether one element or four, or an infinity of unqualified atoms be thought of as material cause, we still have the problem of the other causes. It was no help in this direction when Leucippus and Democritus broke up the tangible world into an infinite number of tiny indivisible pieces which had been moving from all eternity. For these atoms falling in a vacuum would all descend with equal velocity [1]—there is no "up" or "down" in boundless space—and how then explain development and radical changes in nature? Even to consider them as the sum of very tiny changes is only to push the problem of order and purpose a little farther back.

Other thinkers, to be sure, recognized the existence of this problem. Heraclitus almost neglected material causes themselves, when it came to his doctrine of change. He did not seem to realize that change requires a *substratum*—change must take place *in something.* The Pythagorean idea of Number or Form as back of tangible things presented a similar awareness of more than material causes. So also the cosmic Reason of Anaxagoras and the attracting Love or repelling Strife of Empedocles. Yet the latter seems to have given more scope to chance than to regular causes; and Anaxagoras as though half-ashamed places world reason in

[1] *Phys.* IV, 8, 214b.

the dark backward and abysm of time, a *deus ex machina.*

Plato recognized non-material realities in all their cosmic grandeur, even at the expense of material causes; for matter assumes a somewhat dubious uncertainty in his philosophy. But his Ideas are also difficult to realize as causes. How more specifically do things "participate" or become "copies" of Ideas? How do the latter bring about changes (e. g., movements) in the tangible world, if they themselves do not move? And how can Ideas be thought of as non-sensuous when they include those of particular "somethings"—man, horse, etc.—as well as qualities and relations? Moreover, Plato made the mistake of thinking that Ideas, pure, perfect, and divine, could only exist in some place remote from the dirt and evil of the mundane world.

Those who recall what was written above (in connection with Plato's theory) will realize that probably Aristotle was mistaken in assuming that a transcendental heaven was the only home or sphere of activity for the Ideas. At any rate both master and pupil were aware of the difficult problems which arise when one tries to think out how realities, by hypothesis non-spatial (as Ideas undoubtedly are), can yet act as though they were in particular places. Unless all appearances deceive us, this is what actually takes place in the conscious control of our muscles. But even were this difficulty overcome the problem of understanding the order, relations, limits, and interdependence of these ideal or mental forces would remain. There are so many of them at work apparently, some more important, others less so, that, to find the limits of their operation is no easy matter. Some even seem to be of our own creation (art works). Others have the force of mere adjectives. And none seems to be absolutely *pure,* unmixed with what implies an opposite, e. g., good implies evil; right, left, etc. Even unity cannot be dealt with independently of multiplicity. Moreover, similarity, or the imitation of Ideas in nature, implies in every case a *third*, i. e., a basis for every two that are compared. And this seems to go on indefinitely.

But the curious fact, in connection with all these criticisms, is Plato's awareness of the same problems. One is tempted to suppose the pupil got his criticisms from the master himself. It is not improbable [2] that the "young Socrates" who in the *Parmenides* raises similar difficulties is none other than his ambitious pupil mildly satirized. Be that as it may, we must remember in this connection that Plato tried to conceive how Ideas could be at once perfect and unchanging, and yet of the changing world, and active *in* it. The *Dialogues* show in unmistakable terms an effort to realize mental world-forces as universal *and* particular, as transcendent and yet imminent. They are thought of as active in the generations of men as well as in single persons; in some sense *above* evanescent flowers and blades of grass, but, at the same time, giving them their life and very shape. The point upon which Aristotle here insists is that Ideas must be thought of as *in* particular things. But instead of continuing the use of the word "Idea," he prefers to revert to *Form*, the term of Pythagoras. Form is conceived of as in nearly every respect parallel to Idea. Forms are active, intelligent, designing, purposive agencies, everywhere present in particular things, and in the world at large. At the same time, we must realize that matter is more than the quasi-nothingness of which Plato sometimes speaks. It must also be regarded as in some sense a *cause*, however radically different it may be from efficient, or formal, and final, causes. We cannot, at any rate, separate matter from these three nonmaterial agencies. Efficient, formal, and final causes must be thought of as belonging together. Just as motion in which nothing moves is somewhat of an absurdity, so an efficient cause (a workman at his bench) implies a plan of what he is working at, as well as something to be attained

[2] As J. A. Stewart points out in Plato's *Doctrine of Ideas,* p. 72.

by the completed object. The non-material causes are thus wholly different in character from material causes, but the distinction is one which can be made only in thought. We never find any matter without evidence of active agency in it. No matter is devoid of shape. Conversely, we never discover purposes, plans, activities, hanging *in vacuo*. In our experience, matter, energy, forms, purposes, are indissolubly connected. Yet the distinction between them must be made, if we wish to see clearly at all—the material and the non-material, or Form.

How then is matter to be thought of as a cause? By virtue of the fact that matter *sets limits* to what the Forms attain. It is what gives everything we know its *individuality*, its peculiar character. In nature the driving power of the Forms is held at different levels by material conditions. Not all is realized which might be, if the potentialities of matter were greater. And hence the imperfection of things—as well as their character. To put this into more specific terms: Aristotle would so far agree with the Materialists that what we are is partly the result of what we eat. Intangible factors within us, life-forces giving form to what is received and coördinating what we call chemical activities into a synthetic whole, are indeed primary for him. No amount or quality of food will transform a young ape into a young human. But food, none the less, determines whether either is to come to its characteristic development. Matter and Form (in this case Life), are inseparable parts or aspects of Being, and such they remain in our experience. Whatever the intelligence, design, goodness, or beauty, which Form discloses in its activity, it must not be thought of as "supernatural" (to use our word), as "flowing from some higher realm," but as going along with the very stuff of the tangible world.

More abstractly Aristotle speaks of matter as *Potentiality* and of its combination with form as *Substance*. What is realized when the intangible (Form) completely develops the potentiality of matter is *Entelechy*, or completeness. At the two poles of Being, then, are the limits of formless Matter and matterless Form—but we never experience these limits except as necessary distinctions in Logic, or as mathematical infinities never actually reached. *Pure* potentiality would be formless matter or absolute chaos; its opposite pole, matterless form or pure actuality.

By these principles Aristotle throws new light on other problems of his predecessors. Seemingly hopeless contradictions are approached by the magic question, "Potentially or actually?" In other words, may not both horns of the dilemma have some measure of truth? The seeming contradiction, for instance, of a unified versus an atomic, or as we say "pluralistic," universe might resolve itself into a potentially unified and actually pluralistic, or potentially pluralistic and actually unified, world, according to the principle in whose light we study it. Absolute unity in the sense of Zeno, which has to deny the most obvious motion and diversity, is, like mathematical infinity again, a bare potentiality of thought, unrealized in experience. So, too, are the myriad diversities of Anaxagoras (*Homoiomere*), the endless positions of a line, or moments of time which so troubled the Eleatics, as well as the conception of absolute change by which some followers of Heraclitus thought they could dispense with the idea of anything permanent: these are potentialities of thought which could only attain validity by reference to experience as a whole. Hence their contradictions. The same is true of the question whether the genus or the species represents more fundamental reality. From one point of view, for example, the *race* of man seems to be more certainly *there* than all individual mortals of so short a life. Yet *as realized* in experience human organisms in the singular are the only embodiment of man: the race is but a *name*. The last word has not, of course, been said on these subjects! But henceforward the distinction between potentially there and actually there, what is realized and what is merely a future possibility, is inescapable.

This comes out very strikingly when we consider the idea of evolution. Aristotle recognized how all mundane things are different degrees of a development, whose changes are to be interpreted as the realization of potentialities. Not that something absolutely new is produced by these changes. For this runs counter to our reason and intuition. From the beginning, science and philosophy have resolutely, and successfully, defended the proposition: From nothing, nothing. On the other hand, the course of development has brought into being what cannot be said to have existed before in a *completed* sense. There are degrees of being, from the lower limit of potentiality (which never fades into nothingness, however) to actuality, when being attains its full fruition, its entelechy.

The various kinds of plants and animals (and all individuals as well) are, as it were, so many steps on the ladder of ascent toward their greatest possible perfection. The myriad forms of beauty and design depend for their fruition, according to Aristotle, upon causes kindred to those active in our own minds, though they are also present in every particle of matter. Hence the course of evolution is "spiritual" and yet wholly "natural," the result of intelligible energies, purposive causes, designs of beauty inherent in matter but not themselves material.

Thus the florescence of life in all its variety represents the relative success of the Forms in developing particular portions of matter. Some conditions which are partly chance also enter in. We cannot think of everything as product of intelligence and design. Were such the case all would have arrived at its goal. All life would be perfectly evolved—entelechy everywhere. But not only material causes stand in the way of this. There is a certain amount of contingency in the process. We experience a freedom in willing, and know that a great many things may equally well possess, or not possess, certain qualities. Matter, the great mystery, the ever-pregnant source of individual existence when fructified by Form, is also its corrupter and destroyer—often seemingly by chance in both directions.

What characterizes Aristotle's thought on evolution, however, is not, as in many modern theories, the postulate that the tree of life in all its many species is the product of chance happenings *in time*. He would have recognized, in the survival of the fittest, free sexual selection, chance variations, and other adventitious factors, not a significant basis for knowledge, but rather surds which baffle our calculations. The extent to which pure chance enters into any event or thing is, after all, the measure of our ignorance. Nor does he unload on time the onus of that ignorance. It really serves no scientific object to push a present problem back some ages in time. It only repeats itself there with the same persistent How? and Why? For that reason, time scarcely figures at all in the Aristotelian evolution. The significant thing for him is the discovery of goals toward which the process is tending and their realization in the forms we see—a method hardly less perilous than following chance, as any reader of the *Parts of Animals* will recognize. And yet, in so far as science is thought of in terms of reasons, interpretations, laws, causes, it becomes teleological. Indeed it is open to question whether the ascription of events to time and chance is properly science, however exact the description of those events may be. Evolution, at any rate, will become more definitely intelligible when we discover and recognize its direction—the method which Aristotle strove to realize.

In this way the undertaking called science, or philosophy, provides the foundations for religion in so far as it is rational. Evolution, God, Nature, Mind, Mechanics, Love—these are for Aristotle duly discriminated aspects and facts of our world. But they are not dissociated, as though the process of evolution had nothing to do with God or Mind. How then conceive of God? Simply as the Universal Form or Pure Actuality back of all particular forms, designs, beauty, intelligence. It is only broken up into separate manifestations by matter. Considered in its purity, or essence (which can never be realized in experience, but only in abstract thought), Form is a unity, as the cosmic Final Cause, the Pure Intelligence, back of all particular causes and minds. Yet no particular thing or event can be said to manifest the *essence* of God, since Pure Form is intangible, not to be confused with matter, or any of its motions, or even particular manifestations of intelligence or beauty. These do indeed point to Him and are ultimately caused by Him. But they are not Himself, who as Pure Actuality escapes our matter-bound experience and is realized only by inference.

Deity is thus conceived as the pole of being, absolutely free from the limitations of matter, occupying no space, just as thought occupies no space, yet that by which, for which, and on account of which, the cosmos is and evolves. God is the only pure reality in the world. All else is subject to the vicissitudes of matter. His activity is pure thought contemplation which involves nothing like muscular or mechanical activity. For if God were the mechanism of the world giving forth energy and being affected by it, He would suffer change and diminution—which is to suppose that He could sometimes be less than Himself. But actuality surely remains what it is!

How then can God be conceived as a cause at all if he is not Himself active? The answer is: There are three general types of activity. There is a kind of motion which is *imparted* to a body. The body would not itself move except for the energy applied. A second kind of activity is found in a body which can not only be moved from the outside, but also moves itself, as do many natural objects. The third is produced neither by mechanical impact, nor by moving one's own body, but by influencing things through the power of mind, something akin to what we should call (electric) induction, or perhaps telepathy. Aristotle's concept is Love which draws all things unto itself without compulsion, or itself being externally active. Thus God is Thought, Design, Pure Intelligence, Beauty, moving the universe without being moved, attracting all things by Love, which is active without being at the scene of its operation. At the same time as one passes from the lower ranges of being, from relative chaos and undeveloped matter to the realization of intangible forms in the tangible, one approximates more and more the divine life. It manifests itself more or less in human minds. Very likely it manifests itself in forms higher than human minds, better approximations of the divine life, on other spheres. Sometimes Aristotle thinks of these lesser stellar deities as the agents and co-workers of Deity. But it is difficult to understand what he means by this. If we could think of the Forms as thoughts of God and all things therefore as His fashionings, the problem would be simpler. But Aristotle conceives of God's thought as not at all of material things, but only of Himself, the perfect object of thought. And to assume a *progress* in the thought of God corresponding to the vicissitudes of matter would also challenge its perfection. In fact it cannot be made out quite how Aristotle thought of the relationships between the myriad Forms active in particular things and their great Source. Nor is it clear just how he conceived of mechanical motions as the product of God. We shall shortly see how large a sphere of activity he attributed to what we should call a mechanical order going its way from all eternity without interference. At the same time, like Anaxagoras, he found it necessary to conceive of God as in some sense back of that order. In large and in small, matter has natural, or spontaneous, motions which are none the less coördinate with the attractive power of the Forms. And Forms in their purity are God. Yet even as efficient cause, God does not directly carry out anything. He does not even *will* anything. For this implies a want, a need, which can hardly be true of a being of perfect blessedness. Only thought provides us with an analogue of divine life, thought unruffled by the wars and tragedies of mundane things. Hence God's thought is not of things and yet somehow determines their destiny. He is thought of thought, the sleepless contemplater of perfection toward whom all things are tending.

The cosmic actuality, the ultimately real Being, in whom Aristotle's scientific efforts found their center and goal will hardly be recognized as the traditional anthropomorphic God. The Spirit of pure intelligence without body or bodily passions does not suggest a being "tempted as we are tempted." Nor is He one to suffer our emotions, or be aware of our infirmities, since His thought is ever of perfection. He is above all fear and anger, jealousy and pride. He depends upon no bodily sensations. In referring to Him as to a person we must modify our usual idea of a particular body in time and place. Indeed we have to omit body, sensations, movement, instincts, emotions, volition. The final Reason, in whom all things have purpose, the perfect goal of evolution attracting the universe by love unto Himself has no need of our news or advice. Worship would, indeed, seem to be natural, since not only men but the whole of nature, all plants and the very stars, are spontaneously drawn toward His excellence. But there would seem to be little room for the supposition that men's worship accomplishes results other than their own greater love of perfection, and progress towards it. The advantages and disadvantages of this idea of God from the standpoint of dogmas and offices of traditional religions will be obvious. It should be remembered, however, that Aristotle thought of truth, not in terms of man's convenience or satisfaction, but as interpretation of reality. As such the *First Philosophy* is of vital import to future religion.

CHAPTER XXII

PHILOSOPHY OF NATURE (ARISTOTLE)

The scientific theories of Aristotle were developed without instruments of precision or modern experimental devices. He had no microscope, X-ray, or electric furnace. And yet even investigators who work with these instruments to-day accord him high praise for the penetration which, by sheer reason based on direct observation and the simplest of experiments, nevertheless succeeded in discovering so many of the problems and general principles involved in the interpretation of nature. Many of his conclusions were, of course, vitiated by the naïve or false assumptions incident to a dependence upon direct sensation. For example, he devoted long and patient toil in the manner of a mathematician to an elaboration of geocentric astronomy in terms of "spheres," by which the fixed stars, planets, sun, and moon were supposed to move about the earth. These spheres, hollow and transparent, and having the earth's center as their own, were assumed to move at various angles in relation to the planes of the ecliptic, and thus account for the baffling variety of orbits described by the heavenly bodies. He computed the number of these spheres at 56. One, the outermost, having the "fixed" stars embedded in it, was assumed to account for their seemingly regular motion. The other 55 were divided up among the irregular "wanderers," including, of course, the sun and the moon, whose movements were compounded out of six and two spheres respectively.

It would be possible to make out quite a list of mistakes like this one, mistakes which resulted mostly from a too implicit faith in the direct evidence of sense, or from assumptions current in his day. But the list of correct empirical observations, as well as of important hypotheses and principles, would be a very much longer and more significant one. He made a truly remarkable and discriminating effort at fact-gathering; and most of his general conclusions are of strategic moment today. We shall first consider some of his fundamental concepts.

Motion inevitably plays an important rôle in every interpretation of nature. For Aristotle it served as a means of characterizing nature. All bodies having in themselves whatever determines motion or rest are natural bodies—which in effect is to include everything corporeal. For motion of some kind or other is a determining factor in every natural body, even in the limiting case of rest, or inertia. All changes, all causes, are bound up with motion. It is by motion that the Forms realize actuality in the course of evolution; it is by motion that the mind of man attains its power of knowledge. The term Nature, therefore, did not imply for Aristotle something mean or low, either in contradistinction from a projected "supernatural" or as something "overcome" by the spirit of man. Human minds, like every other reality, are natural facts, though nature presents higher and lower degrees of development.

The motion implied by every process, every change, every cause, every interpretation, has, according to him, a number of kinds. The increase and decrease in size of any particular animal or plant during its life-history is clearly one kind of motion. That involved in the coming into being and destruction of certain substances—what we call chemical change—is interpreted as another form of motion, though related to the first. Simple movement in space is a third form—the one which is most obvious and also most fundamental, since the other two are at bottom developments of spatial motion. In other words, *qualitative* change (as when physical bodies take on new qualities, e. g., water changes into steam or food into flesh) is to be regarded as due to the motions of the particles making up these substances. Qualitative differences between the elements he also refers to differences in their motions. When elements are transmuted this takes place under changing conditions of moisture and temperature.

Motions as determinants of a body's qualities might thus seem to be a more important fact than even Substance itself, since it is hard to think of anything as existent without its qualities. One is tempted here to assume that energy is the center of reality. But Aristotle avoids both the Heraclitean flux (which threatened the material world with impermanence) and the Materialism of the Atomists (which professed to find the complete explanation of all qualities, changes, and developments in the mechanical rearrangements of permanent particles, differing only in shape, order, size, and position). He holds to the permanent substratum or mass, which does not become less real by all its transformations into different elements, being neither spirited into existence, nor out of it by any flux. The reversibility of his simple chemical processes doubtless confirmed him in this hypothesis. But, on the other hand, the many possible shapes of particles, and their complex motions and orders, are not regarded as explanations of the teleological character which every natural body exhibits. Every motion implies a *direction*, and this presupposes *Form*, or purposeful cause. Yet Form is not *superimposed* upon natural bodies. Purposes are inherent in the order of nature, in great and small. This is the famous doctrine of immanent teleology—final causes are manifested in particular things as well as in the order of the cosmos. The true *nature* of anything is therefore its most developed state, when the mechanical motions inherent in (inorganic) bodies are not thwarted, and when the growth and functions of organic bodies have attained their maximum development.

Of course the concept of infinity is variously involved in these ideas of motion, which in their turn involve interpretations of matter, space, and time. Aristotle made a noble effort to resolve the difficulties which Zeno had found so baffling. Motion, he argued, is *continuous* and real. Any movement is mathematically divisible without limit, and no deception is involved in the puzzles of the Eleatics. But we cannot think of motion as made up of units, i. e., sudden displacements and instantaneous positions. As a *process* the flying arrow cannot be said to be precisely at any particular point at any particular time. Rather it is *in passage.* So that a *division* of a given motion into infinitely small portions is only potentially realizable, while an *addition* of endless numbers to indicate these portions is also in reality impossible. The troubles of Zeno are therefore potentialities only, and if one is vexed by the idea of measuring potential infinities by finite numbers, one need only assure himself that finite numbers can measure only finite quantities.

The difficulty of this distinction, however, comes out when we consider Aristotle's concept of space. One might have assumed, from his general use of potentiality and actuality, that space would also be considered in this light. Thus space could be thought of as *potentially* infinite, but actually limited by its content. Real space might then be increased by extending something out beyond the last star in the spheres! But Aristotle, on the contrary, holds that nothing *material* can be infinite in extent. And the "place" of any body—its space—is the inside boundary of whatever limits it. Moreover the universe is a unity and therefore bounded. It is impossible to conceive of the place of anything as without inner limits.[1] For these and similar reasons the (spherical) world is regarded as in a limited "place," and space as everywhere filled.[2]

[1] *Phys.* III, 6.

[2] *De Cœlo,* I, 9, 279a 1–10.

Time Aristotle defines as the "measure or number of motion with respect to what is earlier or later." [3] This implies not only that time involves a change, mentally and physically, but that every change requires a lapse of time. Now, strange to say, no *particular* change among all those that take place in our minds, or out of it, can serve to mark its course. Time goes *its own* definite speed. All events are embedded in it somewhat as bodies are in space. Yet time cannot be regarded as anything real. It is very certain that in a world without motion there would be no time as we understand it. We have "nows" that succeed one another and by their differences give us a realization of duration. But time is not made up of these "nows," or indeed of any minute pieces. Our time is fast or slow; but what seems to be "real" time goes on uniformly the same. Stranger still, some things are not in time—for instance axiomatic truths. Is it because truth cannot change? Again, if we try to think of our world as altogether without any minds in it, there would be no time, even if external bodies did move. Yet Aristotle is sure that time has always been and always will be. For motion and mind (at least that of Deity) are permanent aspects of reality. And yet we cannot say that time is anything but a term of dubious reality! [4]

For these and other reasons one cannot speak of a beginning in time. The continuous processes of nature point to everlastingness. The idea of creation in time finds no place in Aristotle's thought. Nature and her Prime Mover are doing their work and will continue to do so, world without end. The primary matter, of which our various elements are different manifestations, neither comes into being nor passes away. Perhaps one asks: Why is it that through all the boundless reaches of the past that work has not yet attained its goal? Why should not the Forms, with the Prime Mover behind them, have attained at least a greater

[3] *Phys.* IV, 11 *fin.*
[4] *Phys.* IV, 12.

degree of perfection, seeing that matter has also had a spontaneous tendency to respond to them? The answer is that matter *sometimes* reacts in a way to offer resistance. And that is why we cannot speak of a completed process any more than of a beginning. Nature will never arrive at some perfect destination, though she constantly celebrates victories in the creative activity of the Forms. But it is not creation *ex nihilo*. Nor is it the *deliberate* work of a cosmic Artist, as Plato had thought. Natural objects go their individual (purposive) ways, though constantly under the influence of the cosmic Love.

Chance is, of course, implied by such conceptions. There is bound to be contingency when purposive agencies operate along with limiting ones—necessity imposing itself upon purpose and vice versa. Aristotle most explicitly holds that there are exceptions to nature's general rules. But he also insists that chance is not to be regarded as a *cause*, but only the name for a certain kind of connection between events. In answer to Empedocles' doctrine of natural selection by survival of the fittest, he points to the fact that, however much chance is present in the process, nothing definite would come of it except by positive formative agencies.[5]

Aristotle's argument for evolution is based on the continuity of organic forms in nature. All living things can be classified in relation to their neighbors higher or lower in the scale, both as to structure and function. The slight steps which separate the species point to a common basis for the entire scheme. Simpler forms of animal life are hardly to be distinguished from plants, and the higher lead up to man not only in bodily structure, but in mental characters as well. Monkeys form a link between quadrupeds and men.[6] Even where structures differ markedly, they have homologous parts, e. g., hair, scales and feathers; gills and

[5] *Phys.* II, 8.
[6] *Hist. An.* II, 502a, 16–b, 27.

lungs; roots and mouths; arms, wings, claws, and forefeet; teeth and bills.[7]

It is easy to understand Darwin's appreciation of Aristotle's work. He wrote: "Linnæus and Cuvier have been my two gods, though in very different ways, but they were mere schoolboys to old Aristotle." [8] About 500 species of animals were studied by the Stagirite. He undertook the first known comprehensive classification of them on principles which remain fundamental to this day. He dissected 49 species, including an elephant but not a developed human body. A human fœtus he did dissect.[9] The various types of reproduction interested him greatly; his experiments with the egg of the chick are still classic examples of accurate observation.[10] He also practiced vivisection on the heart of a tortoise.[11] Of course, mistaken observations crept in. He accepted spontaneous generation, and drew many curious conclusions as to the purposes of the organs he dissected. But these bulk small when compared with the importance of the correct ones, which range all the way from the recognition of whales as mammals to minute observations on the habits of bees and torpedoes.[12] Such facts help one realize how close is the contact of Aristotle's thought with sense data. Our interest here, however, is less in isolated facts than in general conclusions.

There is, according to Aristotle, evidence of something quasi-living in so-called dead, or inorganic, things. But it is in organisms that we first definitely meet with "souls"—or form-giving, active, purposive movements associated with living bodies. They are the entelechies, or that by which, and on account of which, organic bodies come into being. Plants

[7] *Part. An.* IV, 695b 15, 693b 10. *Hist. An.* I, 486a 5, 489a 26.
[8] *Life and Letters,* III, 252.
[9] *Hist. An.* III, 513b 31–39.
[10] *Hist. An.* VI, 561a fol.
[11] *De Juv. et Senect.* 468b 15.
[12] *Hist. An.* V, 553a 2 fol.; VIII, 605a 6 fol.; IX, 623b 4 fol.

no less than animals exhibit entelechies, though their life-functions are simple, being confined to nutrition (growth) and reproduction. Simplicity of structure goes along with simplicity of function. Plants have no vital center about which their functions are coördinated. They are diffused, so that one can often cut them up and produce new organisms. Animals, on the other hand, die under parallel conditions, because their more complicated organs and functions depend upon a vital center. Of course, this is stated as a general rule. Aristotle, along with modern biologists, knew no absolute way of distinguishing certain forms of life as animal or vegetable.

The rise in the scale of life is thus a complication of structure and centralization of functions. But animals also add *new* functions to those exhibited by plants. Nutrition and reproduction remain fundamental, the basis upon which the more distinctively animal functions develop. These are sensation, appetites, feelings of pleasure and pain, and (in most) the function of locomotion. Moreover, they present themselves in different degrees according to the position of the species in the order of life. Many animals, for example, lack vision and hearing, though all have touch, which is the fundamental sense. Degrees of differentiation are also shown in the greater complexity which the process of reproduction entails among the higher animals, as compared with simpler ones. (Aristotle did not know of sex in plants.) And, of course, nutrition is also much more complicated when, in animals, the heart is a vital center.

Still more remarkable, however, are the degrees of rationality and even rudimentary moral dispositions which animals display. Man's distinctive function is, of course, reason. But he is part of nature, and animals lower in the scale show the foundations of his life of reason and lead up to his distinction. This will be seen more clearly in our discussion of Aristotle's *Psychology*. As organic to nature both in body and in mind, man clearly builds upon all the functions exhibited in plant and animal life.

These conclusions are further supported by the evidence of embryology—the individual's development from conception to birth—and education from infancy to maturity. The first functions to develop in animal embryoes (e. g., chicks) are those concerned with nutrition. The senses and power of movement, appetites, pleasures, and pains come later. In general the order of embryological development is parallel to the degree of the organ's complexity and superiority of function. Of course, "superiority of function" was sometimes measured by Aristotle in terms which are unintelligible to us. But his principle is one which was only "discovered" by von Baer in our own times. He applies it, still more astonishingly, to the development of mental functions. Both the bodies and the minds of young children do not differ from those of young animals kindred to man.[13] Infants, of course, have the seed, so to speak, of reason which later differentiates man from the brutes. In this way body and "soul," structure and function, are conceived as parallel, not only throughout the many species of living organisms, but also in the development of the individual.

Heredity was a subject which greatly intrigued Aristotle and led him to some remarkable conclusions. He thought reproduction was of three kinds: spontaneous, by a single parent (parthenogenesis), and by two parents. Asexual reproduction he conceived to be illustrated in plants and stationary animals. The question which troubled him most in bisexual reproduction was that of pangenesis: Does any new organism represent part for part the actual tissues of the parents? Hippocrates thought the whole body was concerned in this process, that something was transmitted which could alone account for the resemblances even to voice, hair, nails, and gait. To this Aristotle could not assent, though

[13] *Hist. An.* VIII, 588b 1 fol.

he insists that any eventual decision in these matters must rest upon empirical observation. He could not comprehend how anything physical could be held to account for such similarities, howsoever small the transmitted parts were supposed to be. Even conceding infinitesimal particles "represented" every organ, the blood, etc., how could it provide a basis of resemblance? [14] It is rather in functions, activities, motions, that the formative causes must be sought. And he found evidence for this in the motions of the male elements, which he conceivd to be an index of others.

As to the order of development, Aristotle observed that the general always precedes the particular. There is a continuous ascent from nutrition through sensation to reason, the last being somehow no longer connected with the material substratum. Yet the intimate connection of the later stages with the preceding is no less confidently asserted both in the development of the individual and the (non-temporal) evolution of the race.[15] The variability in the transmission of given characters he conceived to be due to chance factors. For example, the *structure* of an eye is the product of final causes. But variations in its *color* may depend upon material causes (e. g., food of the parents). Nature, by immanent teleology, brings about a definite type of life, so far as conditions permit. Finally, and in contradistinction to some present-day theories, Aristotle maintains: "The process of evolution is for the sake of the thing evolved, not this for the sake of the process." [16]

And so the species reproduce themselves from age to age, myriad forms of life that hold their own in varying degrees against the accidents of circumstance. At the same time Aristotle attributes to all a tendency to rise in the scale. Potentiality is a relative term. The Forms are making

[14] *Gen. An.* I, 722b, 1–3.
[15] Cf. *Post. Anal.* II, 99b, 32 fol.; *De An.* III, 429a 10 fol.
[16] *De Part. An.* I, 640a 18.

toward the maximum of perfection. Plants "aspire" toward motion and sensitivity; animals, toward man's reason. Human beings, too, are aware of undeveloped resources which they strive (sometimes) to actualize. But here again, time cuts no figure with Aristotle. For he realizes that millions of years, with which one might glibly deal, would not suffice to develop anything, if a formative active urge were not already there.

This interpretation of nature may be characterized in general as an effort to discover rationality, manifested in order and immanent purposes which build upon mechanical agencies. Complete success in such an undertaking we now see clearly involves omniscience. But the measure of success here is also that of science and philosophy—since no description of a mechanism as such is properly an interpretation of it. And, as we shall later see, every measure of value or excellence, every real criterion of good in human life, also depends upon a real basis in nature. If Aristotle is wrong in his hypothesis of intelligent natural purposes, then all distinctions of good and evil are fundamentally artificial and arbitrary. A world machine (including human automata) would be without significance or value.

CHAPTER XXIII

THE PSYCHOLOGY OF ARISTOTLE

It will surprise some readers to learn that one who knew nothing of the nervous system as such, who had no knowledge of the sense organs and their mechanisms, and who mistook the heart for the center of sensation and the brain as an organ for cooling the blood, should have made important contributions to psychology. Yet from the standpoint of general principles, even as applied to physiological psychology, it would be hard to find more significant material than that derived from Aristotle. It was with good reason that the late exponent of the "new" psychology, Wilhelm Wundt, persistently urged his students: "Back to Aristotle, gentlemen."

The Founder of Logic naturally brought to his investigations a thoroughgoing analysis of problems and methods. The opening paragraph of the *De Anima* pointedly inquires: What is that with which we are concerned when we endeavor to study "souls"? And what premises or fundamental assumptions must we make? Are we to study the functions of the body; and if so, of the body as a whole or in part? And do we think of this "soul" as an aggregate of separate parts or faculties which can be localized in different parts of the body—desire in one part and seeing in another? Or must we think of all the body's functions as bound up with "soul"—which would make it impossible to study any "faculty" apart from the others? Again, can we *reason* about souls as we do in mathematics going from premises to conclusions?

These and other questions, so fundamental as determining what sort of a psychology we are to have, Aristotle discusses in the light of what had been thought before his day. He passes in review the Materialist's hypothesis that souls are a particular kind of matter found in living bodies (somewhat as phosphorus has been associated with "thinking" in our day). He examines the doctrines growing out of the assumption that souls are peculiar combinations, or harmonies of material elements (we should say chemical structures), and, of course, the Atomist doctrine that souls are the round smooth atoms which, by their freedom of motion, impart life to the combinations in which they are found. This last assumption, namely, that life and thought can be explained in terms of little particles in motion, Aristotle compares with the idea of the comic poet, Philippus, "who tells us that Dædalus endowed his wooden Aphrodite with motion, simply by pouring in quick-silver: this is very similar to what Democritus says. For according to him the spherical atoms, which from their nature can never remain still, being moved, tend to draw the whole body after them and then set it in motion. But do these same atoms, we ask in our turn, produce rest, as well as motion?" And do they explain how animals behave *to some purpose?* [1] (No doubt, if Aristotle were alive to-day, he would ask the same question of those who attribute all forms of mental life to molecular motion in neurone fibers or cells.)

His own general conclusions are, of course, intimately related to his fundamental axioms or hypotheses. Among these, perhaps the most important one is that of development or continuity. "Soul" is thought of as continuous with "Life" in all its degrees, from the simplest plants, through the various species of animals to the highest functions associated with the human organism. It is a natural fact to be studied, as other natural facts, in connection with bodies.

[1] *De An.* I, 3, 406b 15–25.

It is the Form of an organic body—i. e., one which has in itself the principle of movement, organizes itself, grows and decays, has sense experience or thinks, according to its degree of life. But the more complicated functions cannot be separated from the primitive ones, since they build upon them as their foundation. Hence even physiological processes (to use our term) are part of soul life, not, of course, conscious parts, but none the less continuous and interconnected with those that are conscious. Life in the individual organism is a coördinated unity having functions everywhere interdependent. So that all the "behavior" of the body is to be taken into account when studying the soul.

At the same time it is a fundamental assumption with Aristotle that bodily motions as such are not "motions" of the soul. Movements in space characterize most organic bodies, but give no clue to knowledge, wish, or perception. The motion in space of a soul is only incidental to that of its body. Mechanisms as such when used to "explain" our minds merely break it up into lifeless pieces. For the mechanisms themselves depend upon the presence of life and rapidly disintegrate when life departs.[2] Soul is therefore the basis of organic unity. Or, to quote the famous definition, it is "the first actuality (Entelechy) of a natural body furnished with organs." [3] "*First* actuality" means endowed with capacity as contrasted with *using* it—just as "having the power of seeing" need not imply actual seeing. Hence life or soul can be present without actively manifesting itself. It is the essence, or fundamental reality, by which the organism functions and that for which the organism exists and has its reason for being. But the Form (life) is not separate from Matter here any more than elsewhere. "There is no need to inquire whether soul and body are one, any more than whether the wax and the imprint are one, or, in gen-

[2] *De An.* I, 5, 411b 6–10.
[3] *De An.* II, 1, 412a 27.

eral, whether the matter of a thing is the same with that of which it is the matter." [4]

Thus Aristotle stresses the continuity of man's organism and its life with those of the lower creation and thinks of their common essence as activity (or "functional" to use the modern word). The differences displayed by these natural bodies depend upon the kind of Forms, or life-functions, which are realized in the (sometimes limiting) matter out of which they are organized. Thus the nutritive function is similar in principle in both plants and men. In both it is to be interpreted not merely as a qualitative (or chemical) change, but as one determined by certain inherent results toward which it tends. An organism "feeds" according to measure, toward a certain general size, a longer or a shorter period of growth and decay. Moreover, nutrition serves not only the individual life; it organizes resources for the future generation. Teleology is thus present in the most primitive function of the soul. Empedocles who tried to explain appetite and growth in terms of "pulls" of the elements in one direction or another (Tropisms we call these in modern times) failed to ask why the pull ceases at a certain point, just as others failed to see that fire will go on burning as long as there is fuel to be consumed.[5]

The unity of the soul's functions, as well as that of body and soul, is emphasized in Aristotle's discussion of sensation. Often enough in antiquity (as also in modern times) sensations have been assumed to be merely the mechanical activity of the external world impinging by different stimuli upon various organs, or sending material particles (cf. Atomists) through them. The senses are then contrasted with reason as being "passive," "material," or sources of error, and the mind divided against itself into various "faculties."

[4] *De An.* II, 1, 412b 6–9.
[5] *De An.* II, 4, 415b 7–416a 18.

For Aristotle the "faculties" implicate each other and differences are mostly relative. Sensation he regards as an *activity* of the soul, only vaguely implying meaning to be sure, and dependent upon changes in the sense organ, which are a form of motion derived through some medium from the external world. But sensations provide the basis of knowledge, even though they give us only particular qualities and the isolated characters of things. The same vagueness of unrealized potentialities which they show is present in all our mental activities. Even reason is at first passive, merely receptive, vague, and only gradually develops the definiteness, clearness, and comprehensiveness of more adequate knowledge. So all functions of the soul illustrate the evolution of Actuality out of Potentiality. Except at the top of the scale (creative reason), and the bottom (nutrition), they can all be both possibility and realization. Sensation is thus the realization (Entelechy) of nutrition, but merely the potentiality of reason. In the same way the higher senses (vision, hearing) develop upon the basis of touch, without which none of the others are present.

Although Aristotle had little knowledge of the sense organs as such, he observed that there are definite ratios between sensations and their stimuli. The change brought about in the sense organ must have a certain intensity: we do not see very small patches of color. If there is too great intensity (violent sounds) we experience merely pain. Contrasts are relative: to be "hot" an object must be hotter than the body at the points of contact. He was aware of what we call thresholds, with a "middle range" between them where alone sensation is possible. He also held to the specific character of each sense by virtue of its having a special organ. If the eye were an organism apart, seeing would be its "soul." But the human soul unites its subsidiaries as it were into a single unit. How is this done? Aristotle's answer (which in principle has dominated all physiological interpretations since) runs: There must be a common (physical) center with which the various senses are connected and by which they are coördinated. Something (we call it "a nervous impulse"—Aristotle called it "pneuma") passes from the sense organs to this center (the heart) and there gives us the possibility of perceiving their data together. It is curious to note this tendency toward localization of function, together with the fact that he associated the soul with the *entire* body.

This center, which Aristotle called the Common Sense, not only synthesizes separate sounds, colors, tastes, etc., into perceptions, but also gives us the *consciousness* that we are thus perceiving. Self-consciousness is a function of the Common Sense. By it we also perceive the "common sensibles," which are not the specific data of any one sense by itself, for example, movement, figure, size, number, duration. These we experience by several senses. Imagination, which he recognized as a child of the senses, was also associated with the Common Sense. Sense impressions (or movements) leave "traces" which can be made to function inwardly. When they do, we have imagination, the faint potentiality of reason. Memory is also closely associated with imagery. All facts that can be presented to imagination can be directly remembered, others are recalled only indirectly, i. e., as they link themselves with images. Recollection, which is a fine example of potentiality becoming actuality, depends upon the three kinds of association: Similarity, Contrariety, and Contiguity. Sleep also is a function of the Common Sense because no one sleeps with a part of his senses, being awake in others! Moreover, dreams are chiefly imagery and only slightly related to our reasons. Finally the central organ is the source of deliberate movement, which involves imagination and desire; and will is defined as any *effort* toward the *good*, thus involving overt action as well as rationality.

At this point we come to the highest function of the soul which is, of course, thinking, the faculty by which we realize intelligible forms, essences, universal qualities, and relationships. Reason is, to be sure, intimately related to the "sensible forms" which we have just been considering. All the soul's functions, from nutrition up, are degrees of potentiality whose goal or entelechy is reason. Every man requires imagination to do any thinking at all.[6] On the other hand, reason has important relations to action. We should have no rational will (active quest of the good) or freedom (the power to be worthy or worthless) without it. And yet, unlike all other functions of the soul, it has no organ, being wholly independent of the body, a realization of pure Form.

Probably Aristotle meant this as an entelechy only partially realized in individual humans. For he has degrees of reason reaching up from the vague "meanings" of sense and imagined associations of ideas, to "passive" reason (which merely *follows*), and "practical" reason (the guide to action), and finally to "creative" reason, where thought is no longer fettered to the tangible world but realizes truth independently of time and place. Again there are the differences of Intuition, when reason apprehends directly and completely, and Judgment, which involves analysis and passage from premise to conclusion. All these aspects of reason represent different degrees of realization, different directions in which it functions, and presumably different degrees of purity. For only as creative is it entirely free. In its lower phases reason is bound up with sensation. It is hampered by bodily conditions which make it more or less passive and dull, until, like light which elicits colors out of a gray dawn, self-active apprehension appears. Not, of course, as a creation *ex nihilo*, any more than matter is created out of nothingness. For intelligence is immanent in

[6] *De An.* III, 7, 431a 16.

human souls; once more it is a case of realizing potentiality, the higher Form bringing up the lower to its fuller life. But here, as elsewhere in evolution, it is the higher Form which elicits progress. Creative intelligence would never develop as a *product* of sensation however closely the senses are connected with the work of reason.

The fact that Aristotle thinks of Creative Reason as a function entirely free from the body, not subject to its changes, whether of growth and decay or joy and suffering, seems at first thought to imply a doctrine of immortality. Creative Reason is indeed a permanent Form immanent and active in the soul of man to bring its potentialities into their fullest florescence. But Aristotle was no less convinced that all activities dependent upon bodily organs cease at death. Not only nutrition, but movement and sensation, imagination, and memory no longer function when they disintegrate. So that from the standpoint of personal immortality the question becomes: To what extent is an individual as such dependent upon Nutrition, Sensation, Memory, for an awareness of his existence? There could be only one answer to this from the standpoint of our present life. Nevertheless, we are all thought to participate in an Eternal Reason which enters into human life, an immanent yet universal and divine force inspiring and informing intelligence as far as individual circumstances will permit. Whether persons retain self-consciousness as disembodied Creative Reasons under new conditions is a question of experience about which he does not express himself. He neither affirms nor denies.

CHAPTER XXIV

ARISTOTLE'S MORAL IDEAL

Virtue according to Aristotle has its roots in nature. Human beings are endowed by nature with judgment, intelligence, and intuitive reason. "We are just, temperate, courageous, and the like from our very birth . . . natural moral states exist even in children and lower animals." [1] The excellence of life which morality seeks is, therefore, something more than artificial or arbitrary arrangements imposed upon creatures who are at heart averse to them. It is founded on the very essence of our being. Whatever is unnatural in human life and conduct is, in fact, evil, and whatever is genuinely good is in conformity with human character. Thus good pleasures are natural pleasures,[2] and, conversely, natural friendships and natural love of one's self make for excellence.[3]

Aristotle is very far, therefore, from assuming that "the natural man is at enmity with God." Such phrases as "rebirth" and "total depravity" would have seemed to him a disastrous libel on humanity. Not that he was blind to the incontinence, brutality, perversity, and crime which mar the lives of men. His knowledge of what so many have described as "human nature" was surely second to no other. Only he preferred to call brutality, vice, and the rest unnatural, not the expression of man's essential character. And the difference marks the contrast between a basis of excellence founded on reality, the very nature of things,

[1] *Eth. Nic.* VI, 13, 1144b 5.
[2] *Ibid.* VII, 13, 1153b 14.
[3] *Ibid.* IX, 8, 1169a 2.

and one which by hypothesis is at variance with nature as "overcoming the world," the "flesh," and the "Devil," or even "crucifying" the natural man.

The Aristotelian point of view is, of course, that of evolution. There are different levels of development morally as there are mentally; one finds rudimentary parallels to our conduct, as well as to our intelligence, among animals lower in the scale of life. He was as firmly convinced of this as was Darwin. Nor was he less certain that men stand on different levels of life according as they approximate their distinctively human character. Men share a number of functions with the lower creation. But no one could reasonably maintain that these are the central, or human, ones. A good digestion, an excellent eyesight, important as they are as means to ends, provide no criterion of moral character. Our excellence is one which differentiates us. It must, therefore, depend upon functions which we do not share with other animals. And here again Aristotle was one with Darwin in maintaining that man alone can be said to have moral character, since his behavior (at times) is determined by deliberate choice in relationship to an ideal plan of action. Hence the distinctive excellence of man is centered in his reason. Animals are non-moral, despite their quasi-moral conduct, just because they lack reason. Again, when a man has lost his reason he has lost his moral character. And when he acts immorally it is by crippling his reason and so stultifying his essential nature.

That is why reason (and especially that part which is creative, form-giving, or synthetic) has in man a value above all other functions. He would not *be* a man without it. He could not *act* as a man. Being a man in itself implies self-active intelligence—knowledge for the sake of knowing, as in science and philosophy—contemplation of God and his loving purposes as in religion, artistry in productivity according to right reason. To lack these utterly is to be not yet human, to forfeit a birthright. To exercise them is to cultivate the most distinctive human excellence. These functions in themselves are self-justified and disinterested, even though truth, religion, and art are sometimes made to serve ulterior purposes. Hence the disinterested work of creative intelligence is a special kind of virtue. Aristotle calls it dianoëtic virtue—an activity which is always good, so little need be said about it. Dianoëtic virtue is simply the exercise of our highest and most distinctively human functions for their own sakes.

When reason undertakes the regulation of *behavior* it is called practical. And practical virtues are those which grow out of good conduct, especially in relation to our fellow men. These are the moral virtues and, of course, are also fundamental and indispensable. But they are less exalted than dianoëtic virtue. For we often meet men whose conduct may be good, but who fail to realize the richness and meaning of our world and life, or are blind to beauty. Moreover, practical virtues involve functions which we share with the lower creation, for example, desires and emotions. And though reason is still the strategic factor, it is not the only one. Socrates was surely correct in maintaining the centrality of knowledge for every action having good for its objective. But he was mistaken in assuming that sin is *only* ignorance. Habits, emotions, pleasures and pains help to determine our conduct just as they do in the case of animals. Man, in other words, is rarely perfectly rational in his behavior. He can only approximate it when he aims for what is good.

We need nurture, therefore, as well as nature for the attainment of both kinds of virtue. Nature gives us our capacities for virtue; intellect (which is also a gift) helps us realize them in actuality—here again giving form to what is otherwise potential. And dianoëtic virtue, no less than moral virtue, grows by instruction and exercise—thanks to the law of habit. It is one and the same intelligence in both. But in moral virtue it supervenes upon other functions to modify, coördinate, or give form to their otherwise non-moral activities. Thus we have animal passions, many desires and emotions, which are parts of our natural being. In the absence of reason these are neither moral nor immoral. But when reason comes it uses and regulates, rather than destroys, them—just as life itself makes an organism out of inorganic matter. Even our animal nature in this way attains to moral virtue. It is, therefore, neither in defiance of spontaneous natural tendencies nor in simple acquiescence to them that we attain excellence. Desires, passions, emotions, physical pleasures and pains, all have their place in the perfected life. Nothing is "rooted out," be it a vegetable, animal, or human function.

What are the indications, the marks of assurance, that we are behaving like human beings? Aristotle rarely hesitates to affirm as a matter of experience that the results of virtue, both dianoëtic and practical, are happiness. The higher the approximation to *human* life and conduct, the greater the degree of happiness. Here again dianoëtic virtue shows itself supreme: for there is no blessedness comparable to that of the creative thinker, or "the worship and contemplation of God." But it is also generally true that the nobler the conduct the greater the product of inner happiness. Conversely, immoral conduct brings only misery to him who is conscious of what he does. So, too, the stupid, or merely nutritive, man (who is but partially human), has only inferior pleasures. Which facts all seem to be based on a general law. "Most men," says Aristotle, "find a sense of discord in their pleasures, because their pleasures are not such as are naturally pleasant. To the lovers of nobleness natural pleasures are pleasant. . . . Happiness, then, is the best and noblest and pleasantest thing in the world.[4]

There are, of course, external conditions of happiness as

[4] *Nic. Eth.* Welldon's Trans. p. 20.

well as these internal ones. Men are blessed or cursed by the gifts of birth, family, possessions, ugliness, good or bad children, opportunity for political power, etc. A low-born, solitary, or childless person is limited in his happiness, though his actions may be noble and his creative reason large. Both good fortune and virtue are implied in the higher type of life. In this way Aristotle recognized once more the given natural situation; environment, heredity, power, and social background, as, in part, determinants of human good. And that is another reason why he thinks of it in terms of *common* good. Politics, as the science and art of realizing for every citizen the greatest possible fullness of life, aims to attain its end primarily by education in both types of virtue. But it also takes cognizance of external conditions which, even before our birth, help to determine a noble and happy form of existence.

These very general conclusions will seem to one who conceives of excellence in terms of mathematics as hard to measure by. To such critics Aristotle says quite frankly that it is a mark of intelligence to expect a degree of accuracy commensurate with the matter under discussion. When one has to take account of so many variable factors an exact definition of a course of action for particular people at particular times and under peculiar circumstances is, indeed, difficult. But it is also unnecessary. For the individual reason is a court of last appeal, and individuals vary. The peculiar virtue of A and its corresponding happiness can no more be identified with those of B than can their respective faces. Virtue is not a thing to be realized by all people in the same way. Courage in one man has a very different aspect from what it has in another. And yet both may be equally courageous. So, too, for generosity, temperance, self-respect, and the rest, they are relative to the person and his given situation. To gauge a rich man's generosity in terms of a poor man's gift might well be a measure of meanness. But this does not imply (as we shall shortly see) the absence of a standard. It means that we must always take account of the great variety of human beings, their different levels of culture, their limitations or advantages of environment, fortune, and heredity. It would be preposterous to demand the same refinement of virtue, either moral or dianoëtic, in an uninstructed Ethiopean that one does in a Sophocles. Yet the difference is one of degree and not of kind. Human life has common functions and qualities through all individual differences. Only some men develop more essentially human character than do others.

To resume these general points of view we may characterize Aristotle's doctrine as Naturalism. It assumes that man's life in all its functions is organic to nature. From the operations of digestion to those of his limbs, senses, and intellect, natural forces proclaim him part of the cosmic reality. Hence his virtues are neither unnatural nor supernatural. True that the form-giving, purposive activity of mind is superior to mechanical operations—what we should call reflex or instinctive action. In its highest phases creative reason is even independent of bodily functions. But that does not make it supernatural, either in its deepest insights or in making possible the most exalted conduct. In other words, man's essential, characteristic nature is the criterion of virtue. Perhaps we shall best appreciate the meaning of this Naturalism (which should not be confused with the Nineteenth Century Naturalism reducing everything to matter and motion) if we compare Aristotle's conception of virtue with the assumed standards of divine decrees, supernaturally revealed and arbitrarily enforced, e. g., the Second Commandment of the Decalogue.

His, again, is a doctrine of Evolution, but not in the (modern) sense of *deriving* man's moral character and reason from what is non-moral or mechanical. Aristotle *relates* man's equipment in mind and body to the structures and functions of the lower animal kingdom. But he also recognizes man's distinctive character: animal potentialities realized as an animal, plus human potentialities actualized by his reason—and a suggestion of the divine in creative thought.

As aiming to realize the maximum fullness and richness of human life both in quantity and quality, it is a doctrine of Perfectionism. It is Activism,[5] since it describes that perfection as one of activities and functions rather than as *existing* in a certain way or as *possessing* something, e. g., pleasurable mental states. The sleeping man (or one who approximates complete inactivity) exhibits no form of excellence. Nor does he who merely *possesses* anything whether it be internal or external. Perhaps the meaning of Activism will be made clearer if we contrast it with those doctrines of *merit* which conceive of so much moral capital, as it were, possessed by individuals. Or perhaps more clearly still, if we compare it with the quasi-material conception of sin as something to be gradually reduced or passed off entirely upon some (innocent) scapegoat. For Aristotle good and evil are displayed in action inwardly and outwardly. In action we find the index of moral disposition and purpose by which to measure guilt or virtue. Practice, therefore (rather than the later "grace" or "forgiveness"), is the basis of development in either direction.

Psychologically Aristotle's doctrine may be described as Intellectualism. Reason determines ethical values. Superficially it might seem as though any action which produced good results must be virtuous, whatever its motive might have been. But closer inspection shows that such results must have been intended, and hence understood as such, before the action can be regarded as good. On the other hand, feeling is certainly indicative of moral disposition. He who does not take delight in virtuous actions is hardly virtuous. But feeling by itself—anger, appetite for pleasure, fear—

[5] Or "Energism," as Paulsen prefers in his *System of Ethics,* p. 224.

is far from being a criterion. It is only when associated with deliberate choice (and hence understanding) that feeling becomes significant for character and action. The same is true of any capacity or inherited tendency: it is virtuous only when guided by reason, either directly, or indirectly in the form of habit growing out of intelligent practice.

Since happiness is the natural outcome of excellence, the theory is further to be described as Eudæmonism. Every healthy life-function has its attendant pleasure, the higher the function the greater the pleasure both as to quantity and quality. But human happiness implies a certain form, balance, rationality in pleasures, which means that the function having the greatest pleasure associated with it (intelligence) must dominate the rest. Animals and children cannot be called happy. For the former do not realize what their pleasures are about; and children are rational only prospectively. These facts, and the one mentioned above—namely, that feelings as such are neither good nor evil—show the absurdity of Hedonism. Pleasures are always derived through activities, mental or physical, and cannot be attained directly. But even if they could be secured by themselves they would give us no means of knowing what is good. Human perfection in character and conduct none the less promises the maximum happiness. If the sensual and the stupid man are in doubt concerning this, it only proves that they have not experienced the distinctively human sources of pleasure.

By insisting that virtue must be measured from the standpoint of particular persons and their peculiar character and fortune, Aristotle was an Individualist. In morality you cannot demand *exactly* the same conduct from one man that you do from another. Goodness is relative and always has, so to speak, its local flavor. But this Individualism must not be identified with that which, in our day, stands for the self-assertion of the individual—in its extreme form, "each man for himself and the Devil take the hindmost." Aristotle's insistence on the social nature of man, the social conditions of virtue and happiness, the superiority of political, or general, well-being over particular, sufficiently emphasizes this point. But the locus of moral value is always the individual.

Coming now to more specific descriptions of virtues we are ready for the famous definition: "Virtue is a state of deliberate moral purpose consisting in a mean that is relative to ourselves, the mean being determined by reason, or as a prudent man would determine it." [6] The central idea here is the *mean* which is regarded as strategic in evaluating moral virtue: "nothing overmuch." It is an expression of the æsthetic character of the Greeks in general and of Aristotle in particular, that life itself should have been regarded as so like an art. Excellence implies *harmonious* development of all the parts and functions which make up a human life, no one of them being deprived of its healthy activity, no one exaggerated. Suppression, whether of the body, of natural affections, or of the desire for knowledge,[7] would have been to Aristotle the marring of life's beauty, as well as partial suicide. To realize, on the other hand, the maximum abundance of life implies attaining the qualities which an artist secures in his work: proportion, richness, balance, pleasantness, variety, vividness, originality (individuality), unity. Moral virtue is itself a kind of music, the thrilled expression of a full life in contact with perfection. How strange the contrast when one recalls how many arbitrary or destructive commands and odiously inhuman claims have passed as "right" and "duty" since!

When applied to particular virtues the mean is described as the avoidance of excess on the one hand, and of defect on

[6] *Nic. Eth.* II, 6, 1106b 36.

[7] As among early Christian saints, see Lecky's *Hist. of Europ. Morals*, II, p. 101–124.

the other. Thus courage lies between the extremes of rashness and timidity. Both the foolhardy man and the coward lack courage—the latter, of course, to a greater degree. Friendliness is a mean between obsequiousness and quarrelsomeness; high-mindedness, between vanity and lowliness (little-mindedness). Temperance lies between the excess of licentiousness and the defect of insensibility. *Where* it lies depends always upon the individual. One cannot reckon in the case of temperance in food that six units of beef would be a "happy medium" because ten proved excessive and two insufficient for a certain number of people. Ten might be inadequate for Milo, the wrestler, and two sheer license for a beginner in gymnastics. So, too, with modesty (as opposed to bashfulness and shamelessness), or gentleness (between passionateness and impassivity). The mean will lie where a prudent man would put it, a man who realized the external results of actions in general, but especially the way in which the particular action suited the particular person, and made for greater perfection of character. In this way emphasis is thrown upon education, practice, progress—again strangely contrasting with some modern conceptions of morality, as made up of ready-made, standardized, perfected norms which every one, whether instructed or not, ought to know and obey in the same way.

Of course, not a little criticism has been directed against the Aristotelian mean. By those who aim for fixed standards it is urged that, since all men are equal before the law, their virtues must, in general, be equivalent. As theft can hardly be a crime for Peter and a virtue for Paul, so telling the strictest truth must be virtuous for both. Such an argument, however, fails to comprehend both the nature of a moral standard and the facts of human well-being. Standards are means to ends. "Man was not made for the Sabbath." Right, Law, Duty—all reduce to Good as a final term. Morally speaking, there is no venerable duty, no divine law, or eternal right which runs counter to human good. If there were, its abolition would become itself a duty. And secondly, the well-being, good, character, life, of no single individual is quite identifiable with that of another. Consequently his moral rights and duties are not either, however large the common ground, which all men share, may be.

The recognition of these fundamental facts offers perhaps the most hopeful means of overcoming our present-day confusion in these matters. Consider the cases of theft, or of truthfulness cited above. The assumption of fixed unalterable standards by which all men's virtue may be judged, often produces inferior, if not ignoble, criteria. Theft, for example, may be thought of as "appropriating the property of another person without due process of law," be it no more than a penny's worth. Now a man of low degree who has avoided taking the penny's worth will very likely count himself virtuous with respect to stealing. Even some who profess a horror of robbery have been known to be oblivious of how a scandalous story might well cost its victim position, home, reputation, and financial ruin into the bargain. And similarly with truthfulness—which commonly passes as *verbally* correct statement, however otherwise misleading. Only the prudent man whose insight recognizes differences such as these can hope to rise superior to the lower "standard." Education (whether by one's self or by another) alone can bring a man to see that injury to a neighbor's soul is no less a theft than injury to his pocketbook. The Law, perhaps necessarily, is guided by moral *minima*. Even the Decalogue (in so far as it is moral) forbids only the crudest crimes, and commends the primitive or obvious virtues. Moral progress therefore depends upon flexibility of norms made amenable to human good. But these variations (under the guidance of reason deciding as a wise man would) are clearly not in the backward ranges of morality; rather they are where the lines of virtue are making new advances.

A more radical criticism of the Aristotelian mean is represented by arguments such as those of W. D. Ross. He writes: "It is not always the case that the right action is a mean. . . . There are occasions on which a particular feeling should be entirely suppressed and others on which a particular feeling should be followed to the uttermost. It seems to be an accident, though a very frequent accident, of right action that it should be intermediate between extremes." [8] This seems to imply some misunderstanding, since Aristotle himself points out that there are actions and emotions which do not admit of a mean state. "There are some whose very name implies wickedness, e. g., malice, shamelessness, and envy, among emotions, or adultery, theft, and murder, among actions. . . . They are always sinful. Right or wrong in such actions as adultery does not depend upon our committing them with the right person, at the right time or in the right manner; on the contrary, it is sinful to do anything of the kind at all." [9] And so, of course, for other extremes, which vary all the way from little-mindedness to murder in their degree of inhumanity. You cannot get a virtue out of any extreme by taking more or less of *it*. You get virtue only by avoiding extremes altogether. And there cannot be *too much* of it. Virtue implies a habitual balance of one's inner life and conduct, so intelligently adjusted as to make extremes impossible. If there are "feelings which should be entirely suppressed" (perhaps Prof. Ross means anger) there are none—not even love—which do not need the check of intelligent insight. And surely it remains an open question whether any instinct and its attendant emotion—from anger and fear to emulation and positive self-feeling—should be *entirely* suppressed. The present writer holds that even jealousy has its place in the economy of human good—always, of course, under the

[8] W. D. Ross: *Aristotle,* p. 195.
[9] *Nic. Eth.* II, 6, 1107a 9.

reins of right reason. At any rate, the fact that so much excellence of character and conduct can be described as a rational mean is surely more than "accidental." The principle does not serve to delimit or to make specific all the particular virtues. But it is significant enough to point the human way as between the fanaticism of arbitrary duty and the *laissez-faire* of pleasure or animality.

In his more specific description of practical virtues, Aristotle includes some which contrast markedly with certain later-day conceptions. Thus good temper, which is a mean between irascibility and phlegmatic or slavish spiritlessness, is described as "growing angry on the right occasion and with the right people, and also in the right manner, at the right times and for the right length of time." Entirely to suppress anger makes people foolish and pusillanimous. At the same time the good tempered man is more inclined to forgiveness than he is to revenge.[10]

Very characteristic is the description of high-mindedness, great-souledness, or perhaps better, proper pride. The high-minded man is occupied with matters of great import and worthy of being so occupied. He is to be contrasted with the conceited man who regards himself as worthy of high things but is in fact unworthy; and with the mean-minded or little-souled man who underrates his deserts, however great or small they be. Because high-mindedness depends upon true honor, and not mere appearances or reputation, it cultivates all the virtues. True honor, therefore, is a touchstone of the highest human qualities. Indeed the high-minded man rates excellence so highly that he has only mild pleasure in honors even from the highest sources. As for trivial ones, he disdains them—and disregards dishonor as impossible. Power, birth and wealth contribute to high-mindedness in their possessor, if he be virtuous. But in those who lack the love of excellence gifts of fortune are sources of in-

[10] *Nic. Eth.* IV, 5, 1126a 2.

solence, lawlessness, and contempt for their fellow men in general. The high-minded man prefers giving to receiving; he is ready to do a service for anybody but hardly ever asks a favor. He is stately in his bearing toward people of dignity, but unassuming toward the middle class. To act otherwise—toward inferiors—would be "like a display of physical strength at the expense of an invalid." His performances are rare, but great. Because he does not fear the light he avoids every kind of secrecy, with his friends as well as with his enemies. He does not hesitate to speak his mind, but avoids gossip, says little of himself, seeks no praise, overlooks injuries, speaks no evil—unless to insult his enemy. He is the last to set up a wailing over what is inevitable or insignificant. He is not easily given to admiration, calm in his manner, above all noble in action.[11]

Meekness and poverty of spirit form no part of such a picture. Aristotle regarded "little" or "mean-mindedness" as very specially culpable in those who are really worthy of high undertakings. It prejudices their own position by self-depreciation and self-ignorance. Since our aims always depend upon our estimate of our own deserts, little mindedness deteriorates character by making people abandon the hope of noble actions and pursuits from a feeling that they do not deserve them. Such a thwarting of high aspirations Aristotle pictures as "a more common and a worse defect" than conceit.[12]

One does not find self-sacrifice among the Aristotelian virtues. In itself, independently of some good attained, it probably would have seemed to him unreflective, and hence merely pre-moral, or non-moral, emotion. But this does not imply the absence of Altruism in Aristotle, or in the civilization of which he was so characteristic an exponent. In his day Greek concern for the common welfare—and sacrifice even

[11] *Nic. Eth.* IV, 2, 1122a 19 fol.
[12] *Ibid.* 1125a 33.

to death for its attainment—compares very favorably with our own. The fact that they regarded themselves as shareholders in the state rather than as taxpayers will shortly be evident from the *Politics*. But indiscriminate sacrifice, like indiscriminate loving, Aristotle probably would have regarded as in need of no discussion among grown-ups. One must give, be helpful, forego—but to the right people, at the right time, for good purposes, etc. Generosity he describes as making the best use of one's means, a virtue (which like others) prefers to be the *author* of benefactions rather than their recipient. It is difficult, therefore, for a liberal man to be rich, for he values wealth not for its own sake but as affording an opportunity for giving. Mere giving, however, is not generosity. It is giving to the right objects.[13] In the same way true love or friendship implies moral purpose—the disposition to serve the friend's good for its own sake.[14]

Aristotle has another name for the virtue whose aim is the good of others. It is justice. Justice, we have heard Plato say, encompasses all other virtues. His pupil agreed, but not from Plato's argument of proportionate adjustments of classes in the state and individual "peace, health and harmony of soul." Aristotle was more inclined to equality—though, as we shall see, he recognized different types of constitutions and their justice. In our day it may appear somewhat strange that he for whom justice was a thing so wondrous in beauty that "not the morning and not the evening star" can equal it, should have thought of it primarily in terms of law. It argues high praise to law-givers! There were, to be sure, many aspects of justice for him. But in its most general form as perfected virtue, it is *never* disobedient to the laws of the land. Among its particular forms

[13] *Nic. Eth.* IV, 1, 1121b 3.
[14] *Nic. Eth.* VIII, 5, 1157b 32.

is, firstly, "distributive" justice, which proportions rewards for services and adjusts duties to rights in such a way that there may be neither too little nor too much for anybody. This seems to him an expression of the mean once more. Too much, or too little, wealth may ruin particular individuals. The just state makes both extremes impossible, and also distributes honors and rights in proportion to merit. "Corrective," or remedial, justice he considers from the standpoint of gain and loss to culprit and sufferer. How, is not made clear.[15] But it should be observed that Aristotle expressly repudiates the idea of "an eye for an eye and a tooth for a tooth."[16] He also distinguishes between "natural" and "conventional" law and asserts the supremacy of the former, an interpretation which has had wide-reaching effects upon modern ideas of equity. To be sure it has not even yet been generally recognized that all legal arrangements, civil and criminal, national and international, are ultimately derived from this more fundamental equity, which in man somehow reflects the very order of the cosmos. But we are growing in this direction.

The discussion of friendship and love in the eighth and ninth books of the *Ethics* is one of the great passages in literature. Friendship, or the mutual attraction of two people for each other, is there considered in its relations both to the baser and the nobler aspects of life. Love is so natural and indispensable that certain kinds of friendships exist even among criminals. In its higher ranges it supervenes upon other virtues—itself presupposing all the rest. Even states attain something of this relationship when they are just one to another. "Indeed it seems that justice in its supreme form assumes the character of friendship." The essay as a whole is a remarkable commentary on the al-

[15] *Nic. Eth.* V, 4, 1131b 15 fol.
[16] *Ibid.* V, 5, 1133a 2.

truism of the age, but nowhere more strikingly so than near its beginning: "We may observe in travelling how near and dear every man is to his fellow-men."

The supposition that there is only one kind of love, or mutual attraction between two people (an idea which has so often beclouded the thought of later times, when love has been advocated as the "fulfilling of the law") Aristotle considers in the light of the evidence. He analyzes first of all the conditions and motives which make love possible, the kinds of people between whom it exists, what is implied by an ideal friendship, the meaning of "self-love," and the love of God. His first classification of friendship divides them into those of mutual usefulness or utility (more likely among old people); those based upon the somewhat higher plane of mutual pleasure, which decay, however, when the pleasure is no longer provided (characteristic of young people); and thirdly, friendship in which the good of the friend is sought for the friend's own sake. The last are often useful as well as pleasurable but they do not decay when such advantages cease. Again there are equal and unequal friendships—the latter between persons who differ from one another in power or dignity, for example parents and children, ruler and subject, husband and wife. The love of a son for his father is different from that of the father for the son, as that of the wife is different from her husband's love. Nor do worthless people expect to become the intimate friends of noble characters. When the distance is too great—as between God and man—there cannot be intimate friendship at all. Suppose you could exalt your friend into a god, asks Aristotle, would you not lose him as a friend, even though you adored and worshipped him?

Loving rather than being loved is the heart of friendship, yet there must be reciprocity, both must know of its mutuality.[17] The benefactor, however, enjoys a keener satisfaction

[17] *Nic. Eth.* VIII, 1159a 26.

than the recipient because taking trouble for another is itself a stimulus to one's affections.[18] Friendship is in its essence altruistic: one wishes the good of the friend not for one's own happiness' sake but for the other's greater perfection of life.[19] "Commercial" friendships (based on exchange of advantages), or even the more liberal ones which grow up by exchange of pleasures, are therefore impure kinds. The higher love involves a moral purpose. And like other virtues it is more than mere emotion. Unless the affection is based upon mutual recognition of excellence it degenerates into commercial or even lower forms. When people grow apart in their moral character even the longest friendship goes to pieces—though he who has once been a friend can never become altogether as a stranger. Good-will, the germ of friendly relations, may abide; but good-will is far from being adequate for friendship. It is distant and need not be mutual.[20] Unanimity in matters of science or opinion is not at all necessary among friends—but it is when it comes to ideal purposes.[21]

Thus Aristotle finds the social nature of man a central fact in our moral disposition. Self-realization itself is impossible without recognizing the primacy of the good. Even dianoëtic virtue requires others with whom it may be exercised; nor can moral virtues be developed in isolation from human society.[22] On the other hand, nature places a limit on the number of close associates—just as time is required for friendship to mature.

What then is self-love and how would Aristotle describe the disposition we call selfish? His answer is perhaps the most interesting part of the essay. Self-love (he holds) implies the same disinterested and sympathetic relation of a

[18] *Nic. Eth.* IX, 1167b 30.
[19] *Ibid.* VIII, 1157b 25 fol.
[20] *Ibid.* IX, 1166b 30 fol.
[21] *Ibid.* IX, 1167a 21 fol.
[22] *Ibid.* IX, 1170a 14–b 19.

man to himself that he has to his true friend. For the man who is just to himself cultivates his higher faculties for their own sakes, just as he cultivates the good in his friend. When, on the contrary, he values the irrational or animal part of his being—mere money, honors, or external pleasure—he is censured. And because most people do estimate this side of themselves so highly, self-love has come to be a term of reproach. What we call selfishness is thus for Aristotle the cultivation of a mean and petty self. To develop the nobler part of one's nature, to have pride in valuing it highly, to seek preëminence in doing justice, and so forth, is another (and unselfish) kind of self-love.[23]

Though it be true then that "a bad man has an eye to his own interest in all that he does, and all the more so in proportion to his greater viciousness," [24] on the other hand, when a man comes to develop what is more distinctively human in him, the line between self and others breaks down. He cultivates disinterested and non-competitive ends. The other's good becomes essentially a part of his own. His life is thus indefinitely extended. And the old cleavage between altruism and egoism is merged with the more fundamental one of degrees of excellence which rise above the distinction. It is only in "goods that are fought about" that one man's gain is another's losing. The higher self-love spends such goods that friends and fellow-citizens may have more. This is altruism; but it also involves the good of the giver; he still has the better of the bargain. Even the giving of one's life —for a noble cause—is self-love in its proper sense. Thus Aristotle provides a *positive* meaning for sacrifice and unselfishness.[25]

A word must be added here on his doctrine of the will. Action is voluntary, according to Aristotle, when it is not

[23] *Nic. Eth.* IX, 1169a 6–1169b 3.
[24] *Ibid.* IX, 1168a 30.
[25] *Ibid.* IX, 1169a 18–26.

imposed upon the agent, and he knows the circumstances under which it is done. But to choose is not the same thing as to act voluntarily. Animals, children and even grown-ups, on the spur of the moment, do things voluntarily but without real choice. Choice is not mere desire, appetite, emotion, opinion, or even rational wish by itself. Wishes are not horses; nor is the blow of anger generally chosen—though it may be voluntary. Choice is the "deliberate desire of things in our own power." And, of course, it is only for *choices* and their evidence in action that we are morally responsible. Yet every choice is the outcome of our character and habits. Aristotle was thus a determinist, though he did not formulate a principle of general causation. On the other hand, our characters are determined by our choices. It is no excuse for licentiousness that one has formed the habit of such actions. We hold him responsible even though choice is only partly in his power because of previous decisions. "When a man has thrown a stone, it is no longer in his power to control it." So with some choices leading to moral and physical health or disease. The central fact is reason-becoming-desire in a self. Without, therefore, describing internal causes (reasoned desires) as contingent, or bringing them into coördination with external causes, Aristotle conceives of the will (or more strictly, choice) as free. Choice is to be called free in proportion to the intelligence of our desires.

The modernity of the *Nicomachean Ethics* is probably apparent by now to the reader. It is still the most important book on the subject. Its general points of view are those to which modern writers (including those on "Christian" Ethics) are increasingly turning. This is not because of its perfect adequacy or finality on any subject. Many later refinements of thought probably never entered Aristotle's mind. But the importance of his fundamental principles becomes more and more impressive when one realizes how they are based upon an extraordinarily high ideal of human life and conduct, as well as upon views of nature (within and without), which derive their force from the evidence of science and history.

We have seen how his doctrine is one of evolution—but not a degradation of higher values to lower ones, or derivation of the rational from the irrational. It is throughout natural in taking no account of external, supernatural, or arbitrary authority. Yet it recognizes higher and lower degrees of nature and finds in humanity itself something of the divine life. In this way right and duty are imbued with reasonableness. The fanaticism so easily possible in the form of "duty for duty's sake," as well as the vested rights of legality and tradition, are brought into the discriminating light of human good. Obligations are seen to derive their ultimate authority not from compulsion, power, or precedent, but from the fact of making more excellent human lives.

That excellence is found in nothing formal, negative, or what could be externally possessed. It lies in *functioning* as the most perfectly developed human among humans. The characteristic activity of men, as distinguished from vegetable and animal life, is mental; yet this involves no snubbing or destruction of the vegetable and animal in us. Since they form parts of us by nature, the problem of ethical thought is to coördinate them into a balanced whole. Hence asceticism plays no part, however important that of restraint and self-control. Nor does reason suppress the emotions, which are recognized as important factors in determining right conduct. Since man as a social being finds the excellence of his own life dependent upon an identification of his interests with those of his fellows, self-sacrifice is given a rational motive. The harsh antithesis of egoism and altruism is overcome by referring both to a common matrix—the communal good which, in the life distinctive of humanity, becomes disinterested. The altruism of seeking the friend's or the community's good is also a heightening of one's own. On the plane of human life, giving does not impoverish, nor does withholding enrich. "Mine" and "thine" are emphasized on the lower plan of nutrition, bodily pleasures, and possessions. But in this fierce struggle reason also looks to advantages for the life of spirit. The human in another is preferred to the animal in ourselves.

Another marked advantage is Aristotle's realization that morality is not the dreary business of making "Blue Laws" and new ways of saying "Don't." Since excellence is the basis of happiness, the quest of virtue is the very highest source of human pleasure. Yet he recognizes that the pleasures of the animal and vegetable in us, if uncoördinated with the human kind, can be destructive both to themselves and to those that grow on the higher level. All pleasures in their maximum fullness are thus made possible by moral insight. Its nice balance of our various functions, like the creation of a work of art, is assuredly a difficult, but also a joyous, undertaking. The frequent assumption in modern times that morals make for dreariness would have been regarded by Aristotle as proof of their perversion.

The limitations of the "Golden Mean" are obvious. Not every virtuous action can be described in terms of steering between the evils of excess and defect of a quality. But as descriptive of an ethical attitude of mind it is of very great importance. It means intelligent decisions; the product neither of passion nor of indifference. It implies progress —since no man quite attains, and always has the problem of steering away from his particular excess or defect toward "heroic and divine virtue." It makes life itself an art, with all the inspiration of creation, an art which also includes the community as something to be molded to a proportionate and beautiful whole.

Again it applies not only to man's distinctive or noncompetitive values. Even among the instrumental or egocentric values—e. g., economic goods which are chiefly responsible for human depravity—he could use his norm. How much wealth should a man possess? "A mean conformable to his nature"—one which helps him to realize his powers of mind and body to their fullest and happiest activity. But how much is that? A dollar might be too much for a lazy Ethiopian; and a million inadequate for one active in his country's good! Moreover, this applies in states no less than in individuals, as we shall shortly see. Too great prosperity ruins communities, when it takes away men's human character by transforming their minds into mere instruments of money-making.

These terms imply quantitative distinctions. And Aristotle has been charged, by Kant and others, with making the difference between vice and virtue merely a quantitative one. But it should be noted that the mensuration involved here bears no analogy to arithmetic or geometry, being rather a "fitness" or "beauty" which our minds and actions display at their best. Surely rational generosity ("right cause, right way, right amount, right time, right person") is *qualitatively* different from irrational generosity! [26] And nowhere does Aristotle put us on guard against a deficiency of vice or an excess of virtue! Kant's rigorous, ironbound Duty, with its relentless Maxim or Law, is, of course, absent; but not the grace and joyous reasonableness of noble living.

There are obvious similarities between Plato's and his great pupil's Ideal of Life. They are founded on the same general axioms. But there are also striking differences. Aristotle does not bring theology or metaphysics into his discussion of human good. Indeed he raises questions concerning Plato's Idea of cosmic good (back of all existence) as relevant to decisions concerning particular human actions and virtues. He is, to be sure, constantly aware of the "divine" in man; but he insists that we cannot attribute *our*

[26] *Nic. Eth.* II, 1109a 26.

moral virtues to God.[27] Nor does he connect the character of our present life with its fate in some future existence. Instead he subordinates the religious motive, with all its fervor of "being made like to God through becoming just and holy," to the more practical and mundane one of cultivating certain qualities of character and good relations with our fellows. This, to be sure, is also Platonic ground. But the ideal unity of the four cardinal virtues (which are really different aspects of a single one, Justice, whereby the very stars are also kept in their cosmos) is by Aristotle broken up into an indefinite number of particular, specifically human, virtues. And these are cultivated for their own sakes.

There are advantages, however, in a more scientific and everyday conception of human excellence free from theology. Perhaps the best example of this (on its negative side) is found in the way moral training is made impossible in our American public schools because of its supposedly "sectarian" character. It is the function of the state, says Aristotle, to develop in its citizens ideals of moral excellence. And we know that this high purpose can be fostered among intelligent youth neither by exploitation of emotions, however fanatical, nor by imposition of arbitrary laws, legal or theological. Here the great Stagirite comes to our aid with his alternative of a natural, progressive, happy-faced, open-minded examination of what we consider good and why. It will yet come to its own as a strategic factor in human welfare! Its center will be Good rather than Duty. And once sectarianism is vanquished, a scientific attitude will not be antithetical to Plato's delicate humor, poetry, and reverence.

[27] *Nic Eth.* X, 1178b 7–23.

CHAPTER XXV

ARISTOTLE'S POLITICAL SCIENCE

In his *Politics* Aristotle deals with the life of a state conceived as a community having for its object the highest good of the group. All community organizations aim for some good. The state, however, shows its supremacy by a comprehensive concern for the best good of all. For that reason he takes account not only of powers and rights, constitutions, legislative and judicial arrangements, but of property, marriage, slavery, revolutions (the pathology of states), and the best forms of public education. His method is throughout empirical and historical, supported by constant reference to cases in point. The reader will remember how he got together 158 constitutions for the study of government. Yet through all this inductive procedure he never lost sight of the principle that states have an ethical function to perform and are to be measured by the success with which they attain that purpose.

We shall better understand this teleological point of view if we contrast it with some others. Aristotle, as we have learned before, considered that everything must be judged by its most developed form, that which most nearly succeeds in realizing its perfected function. A man is not judged by what he shares with the animal kingdom but by his specific excellence, what is characteristic of him as a man. A state in the same way is not to be judged by its commercial arrangements and economic successes, for these are not the characteristic functions of a state—the highest good of men as men, which includes more than nutrition and self-preservation! States, again, do not *happen;* they are the outgrowth of men's wills and intelligence. The Sophists, as will be recalled, were so much impressed by this fact that they looked upon all given states, from despotism to democracy, as arbitrary conventions, and hence more or less unnatural. The Cynics for other reasons extolled the man without a country, the citizen of the world. Oriental despots, like some modern kings, conceived their power as derived from God. Anarchists ancient and modern have regarded the elimination of states as something to be attained in the future. Others going part way in this direction propose to limit the state's functions just as far as possible.[1]

Aristotle, taking account of all the states he knew, recognized a tendency in men to get together for the common good, no less natural than reproduction, no less spontaneous than self-preservation. The state indeed is an outgrowth of the family, which in the various relationships of its members already foreshadows the types of authority illustrated by different governments. A group of families in a village exemplifies a natural demand for more than everyday wants, the satisfaction of more varied needs; while a group of villages forming a community rises still further above bare existence, "for the sake of good life," the more perfectly realized human life. "He who by nature and not by mere accident is without a state, is either above humanity or below it. . . . The individual when isolated is not self-sufficing. . . . He who is unable to live in society, or who has no need because he is sufficient for himself, must be either a beast or a god. . . . A social instinct is implanted in all men by nature." [2] Only in communities, of which the state is the highest, does man attain the development of his powers and the satisfaction of his cravings. This is true even of economic needs. But it is still more striking in his intellectual life.

[1] Cf. Alex. Humboldt and Herbert Spencer.
[2] *Pol.* I, 2, 1253a 2; a25.

States then are not the products of arbitrary power, nor can they be described in terms of power at all. The state as supreme community has sovereign power; but the possession of sovereign power does not make a state. Its functions are better described in terms of coöperation than of compulsion. And, of course, there are higher and lower degrees to which its functions are realized. Aristotle had no standard form of government suited to all sorts and conditions of men—as some people think of "democracy" today. With the great differences in men's intellectual, moral, economic development, he thought it natural to expect that monarchy and aristocracy would suit some people better than democracy. Yet the good of all is the touchstone, and states can be measured in terms of how nearly they approximate making possible the richest and happiest life. Those based on unreasoning power, with little or no ethical insight (tyranny), are obviously lower in the scale than the rule of a few rich men (oligarchy) who have, at least in some degree, to consider the common good. The rule of an enlightened unselfish minority is greatly to be preferred to that of an ignorant majority.

In this way Aristotle comes eventually to consider the ideal form of commonwealth. But he finds it necessary to trace its roots in human nature and therefore raises some very incisive preliminary questions. Are some men intended by nature *to be ruled* and others to rule? What are the marks of this distinction if it exists? There could hardly be any question that in the family community there are these differences. It is fitting that the children should be governed by the superior knowledge of their parents, and that power should not be vested in domestic servants. The contribution of the latter is physical toil; that of their masters insight and guidance. But the good of all concerned is insured by this arrangement—assuming of course its reasonableness, that is, the competence of the masters and the suitableness of toil for the servant.

In this connection the question of slavery is raised. Is it ever justifiable? Aristotle considers both alternatives: that nature recognizes no distinctions, and that it is normal and natural for the superior (in knowledge and good motive) to rule the inferior. The first he answers unhesitatingly. "From the hour of their birth some are marked out for subjection, others for rule." [3] That all men are by nature equal would have seemed to him a statement wildly at variance with facts, physically, intellectually, ethically, artistically, religiously. And there could hardly be any question that just as mind must direct the body, so the superior in every group should, in the interest of the whole, direct its affairs. Now the slave can contribute domestic work (note in this connection that Aristotle takes no account of industrial or agricultural slavery) but not much more if he be truly a slave. And under these conditions slavery is an ethical arrangement in which the slave profits by superior guidance and the master by the physical toil.

The difficulty for us in modern times is, of course, the question: Who are these slaves? Are there human beings so lacking in the characteristic human functions that they are predoomed to little more than animal existence? Aristotle characterizes them as "living possessions," "instruments for the conduct of life." And he does not admit that any Greeks can be so regarded. Nor does he hold any brief for slavery based on force, e. g., capture in war. It must be a reasonable, that is ethical, subordination realized by both master and slave as contributing to their mutual advantage. And hence it is a *friendly* relation. The slave is an integral part of the family, serving its physical needs but none the less eating at the family table and otherwise enjoying the family

[3] *Pol.* I, 5, 1254a 22.

life. The arrangement is not to be regarded as permanent; he must ever have the prospect of freedom before him. Nor are his children necessarily slaves. . . . One immediately thinks of modern domestics as well as of industrial and agricultural servants with the question whether, apart from terminology, this is not the kind of subordination Aristotle meant. In some respects Greek slavery was superior to it as involving greater community of interests and even friendship in a single household group. But, on the other hand, we realize that it is difficult if not impossible to say who is solely (or even characteristically) the "living possession" or tool of any person or group. Nevertheless, it is of the very essence of political morality to recognize Aristotle's principle of subordination. The interests of the whole must take precedence over those of the parts, mind over body, the intellect over appetites, the more disinterested human excellence over selfish and petty mentality. Differences here are differences of degree, however, and not of kind.

Economic questions also come in as a preliminary to the problem of better government. Property, trade, the basic conditions of mere existence, anticipate the problem of good living and are matters of importance to every legislator. In this connection Aristotle presents a number of economic principles which we can hardly consider here. Suffice it to say that he tried to distinguish between natural or justifiable, and unnatural means of acquiring wealth, and that among the latter he included financial operations (e. g., usury) growing out of the peculiar and unjustifiable advantages of money in itself. He recognized the convenience and utility of money but observed that (unlike the pursuit of goods for necessary life purposes) the quest for money is boundless. For that reason the law-giver will do what he can to set limits to this pursuit, the mean business of getting all one can from his fellows, or of devoting all one's time to shopkeeping. He will strive to realize for all citizens the "most liberal life in which there is the greatest need of excellence"; they must not lead the life of mechanics or tradesmen, for such a life is ignoble and inimical to virtue."[4] It need hardly be pointed out that Aristotle's condemnation of all interest fails to appreciate the uses of credit. But his realization of the unethical advantages made possible by the invention of money is given point by the endless "operations of high finance" even to our day.

Property can be of three kinds in his judgment: (1) the soil may be privately owned, the produce commonly used; (2) the soil may be common and produce divided for private use; (3) the soil may be common and the produce also.[5] Here Aristotle sets forth the relative advantages and disadvantages of Communism by showing that common ownership of property generally presents no end of disputes, which are attributable to indefinite ownership, while disputes about private property are traceable to other causes (human wickedness). Moreover, every man is most efficient "on his own," and his sense of property not only gives him pleasure, but greater opportunity for the exercise of virtue. The chief argument against Communism, however, is its unethical equalization. Men are not equal in their gifts or characters, and the failure to recognize differences only tends to remove the incentive to excellence. Aristotle is thus an Individualist on both economic and ethical grounds. But he views property and all the undertakings connected with it as means to ends. He unhestitatingly condemns not only industries which make for human deterioration, but the increase of wants (especially capital) beyond the point where they contribute to human welfare. Thus his Individualism is also fundamentally social. The good of the community is fostered not by Communism, nor by *laissez-faire*, but by each man's concern to make his life and possessions congruent

[4] *Pol.* VII, 9, 1328b 39.
[5] *Pol.* II, 5, 1263a 3 fol.

with the most nearly human form of existence. And this is attained in part by due restraint of one's desires. Aristotle had much fear of that prosperity in which men's wants wax to the uttermost and life is subordinated to livelihood.

The Communism of wives and children as set forth in Plato's *Republic* he also condemns in this connection, and for similar reasons. He does not here do justice to Plato in assuming that the *Republic* aimed for the maximum degree of unity as best for the state. After all Plato had various social classes and advocated Communism only for the higher ones. Yet Aristotle's arguments against this Communism are fundamental. "Mine" and "thine" are bound to play an important rôle in every community, however social be its point of view. "Our" children are indeed of the group. But it would be a logical, as well as psychological, error to say that "each" is the child of "all." The father, moreover, of a thousand "children" can have but a watery affection for each. This is human nature—to crave intensity of affection—and human nature on its nobler side. "How much better is it to be the real cousin of somebody than to be a son after Plato's fashion!" [6]

Before we consider Aristotle's discussion of the various types of constitutions it will be desirable to take account of his conception of citizenship, because it is so closely linked up with his idea of government. The fundamentally democratic nature of his assumptions comes out in the fact that he speaks of *citizens* rather than *subjects*, and regards the community itself as the sovereign power. Citizenship, however, is for him a very much more important matter than anything implied in our modern conceptions of popular sovereignty. For not every one born in a given district, or resident there, or having the power of suing and being sued, or the son of a citizen, is necessarily one. To Aristotle the privilege of voting would also have seemed a watery form

[6] *Pol.* II, 3, 1262a 12.

of citizenship. He regards it as a definite *function*, an actual participation in community interests, which, being the highest to which intelligence can direct itself, calls for more than the gifts of Tom, Dick and Harry. "He who has the power to take part in the deliberative or judicial administration of any state is said by us to be a citizen of that state; and, speaking generally, a state is a body of citizens sufficing for the purposes of life." [7] A state is therefore no geographical conception, nor does it depend upon the identity of its inhabitants.

This very high ideal of citizenship of course commits Aristotle to the smaller type of state as best. If all the citizens are to have power to deliberate and legislate, there cannot be millions of them scattered over a large territory. Now the tutor of Alexander was acquainted with both nations and empires, which he had abundant opportunity to study. He thought that, if the various Greek states could be brought to unite, they might easily rule the world. Yet he held tenaciously to his conviction that the small city-state is the best form of government. When all the citizens may take their turn in fostering the common good, this is more likely to be attained than by indirect, or representative, government. Moreover, the better forms of states will regard citizenship as a privilege to which only those who are qualified will be admitted. Farm-laborers, artisans, and others who have little aptitude at discriminating the higher forms of human excellence are hardly worthy of citizenship. All such will be excluded if the state has the maximum richness and happiness of life as its object.[8]

Here Aristotle seems to have so much confidence in intellectual and moral power that he all but ignores the physical power of those who may be disfranchised. He also disregards the alternative of permitting the ignorant and

[7] *Pol.* III, 1, 1275b 18.
[8] *Pol.* III, 5, 1277b 33 fol.

ethically obtuse folk to vote for suitable delegates to represent them, and seems to have assumed that discriminating votes required not only intelligence, but acquaintance with the characters of the candidates. Our own practice has shown the force of the latter point of view, and perhaps justified as an ideal both the qualifications for citizenship and the more direct form of government proposed by him. But our larger groups, as well as the increased importance of naval and military force in connection with the life of modern states, have made both of these ethical ideals subordinate in practice. Perhaps in time we shall succeed in combining the direct form (in local affairs) with the representative (in national and international). But the success of the former will clearly depend upon high qualifications for citizenship.

Aristotle knew well enough that in practice such citizenship is rare. So guided by his principle that the most perfectly developed form is the standard of reference, he proceeds to examine the various types of constitutions exemplified in existing or historic states. For his purpose he divides them into six main kinds according to the seat of authority and arrangement of the highest officers. These are: Monarchy (which would be ideal if a royal person incomparably more gifted than any other, a superman wholly devoted to the common good were to appear and receive recognition), Aristocracy (the rule of those few most capable and disinterested), and Polity (the rule of the middle class) among the better forms. Their perversions are respectively: Tyranny (arbitrary power of a despot), Oligarchy (power vested in a group of the rich, who may also be of good birth and education), and Democracy (domination by the poorer and lower classes). Tyranny, as the perversion of the best form, is, of course, the worst—a government of craft and violence instead of distinguished virtue. But Democracy is very far from being "safe for the world" if justice is to obtain. Everyone must admit that justice means equality for equals and inequality for unequals, that is to say, good men rather than scoundrels, capable rather than bungling, and honorable rather than mean men should determine the life of the community. Wealth in itself is no standard. But in so far as oligarchs are likely to be men of better birth, and amenable to honor, they are preferable to the ignorant mob dominated by demagogues. Thus extreme Democracy is kindred to Tyranny. The spirit of both is the same. "The decrees of the demos correspond to the edicts of the tyrant; and the demagogue is to the one what the flatterer is to the other." [9]

Of course there are many varieties of Democracy, Aristocracy, and the rest. There is a form of Democracy, "said to be based strictly on equality," where the poor should no more govern than the rich, and no one be esteemed superior or inferior, the opinion of the majority being decisive. In other forms there are property qualifications, for citizenship as well as for offices. Some may be said to be governed by *law*, while in other forms the multitude discards the law and substitutes its own decrees. This in fact is the line along which the better Democracies degenerate into something like Tyranny. They can hardly be said to be a constitution at all. "For where the laws have no authority, there is no constitution." [10] Yet it must not be supposed that Aristotle failed to appreciate the fundamental principle of Democracy. There are no better arguments than his for the sovereignty of the people. Abraham Lincoln would have recognized here something better than his own. It may be that a community can boast no one who is wholly competent to rule. And yet the contributions of the group, like lunch-baskets pooled at a picnic, provide a better result than any individual's wisdom. Again: a number of people are much less likely than a single one to be carried away by a fit of passion, just as a

[9] *Pol.* IV, 4, 1292a 19.
[10] *Ibid.* a 30.

larger body of water is less easily polluted than a small one. Again: those who wear the shoe know best where it pinches, and if those who are ruled can have a hand in the choice of their rulers there is much less likelihood of discontent.[11]

Yet this, he knows, is not the whole story. The difficulty with the advocates of particular forms of government is that they see only a part of the facts or have only a partial notion of justice. The nobles think constantly in terms of heredity as the sole basis of excellence. Oligarchs whose position depends upon their wealth, measure everything in terms of money. Nothing else counts. In Democracy political equality is the thing. And those who boast this equality forthwith think themselves equal to anybody in every respect. But the state is surely something more than a means of providing equal status. It is more than an instrument to aid business, more than police-power against crime, more than a guarantor of "liberty." Some communities of animals would have to be called states if their functions included no more than providing for the bare conditions of life and self-preservation. The constantly recurring question then is: Does the given form of state, monarchical, oligarchic, or democratic, provide for the maximum richness and happiness of life, the free choice of noble action? When a more comprehensive conception of justice is realized, one sees at once that power should go neither to the free as such, nor to the well-born, nor to the rich, but to the intelligent lovers of virtue.[12]

The general status of the community also will determine what form of state is best for it. Some people are better fitted for Monarchy, others for Democracy. In the rare, if not impossible, case of virtue and ability so extraordinary as to be incomparable or godlike being exemplified in a certain

[11] *Pol.* III, 10, 11, 15, esp. 1281b 1.
[12] *Pol.* III, 9, 1281a 2.

man, it would be to the common good for him to possess absolute power. In general "a people who are by nature capable of producing a race superior in virtue and political talent are fitted for kingly government."[13] But again there are varieties of Monarchies. In the better types the king is above the desire to transmit the power to his descendants, above the temptation to use his (necessary) guards improperly. When he sets the pace by his own superior excellence and constant regard for the public good, Monarchy is likely to be the state in which the higher form of human life best flourishes. But alas, this is rare among kings!

A somewhat more feasible form than ideal kingship is Aristocracy—when a people submit to be ruled as freemen by a group, or ruling class, specially gifted for political command by their virtue. In some respects it has advantages over kingship as based upon a number of high-minded men instead of a single one. But it too is rare and difficult to maintain, just because of the inequalities which are introduced by all incentives to excellence and the superior claims of education and virtue. Much more easily possible than Aristocracy is Polity, a state dominated by a powerful middle class, individually distinguished neither for wealth, nor virtue, nor noble descent, but aggressively able by numbers and acumen to hold the balance between the very rich and the very poor. They allot offices to the well-to-do according to their deserts. They stand between the excesses and violence of those who by gifts of fortune have been prevented from learning self-control, and the petty slavelike roguery of the proletariat. Without them the state would be one "of masters and slaves, the one despising, the others envying." But the middle class will have the confidence of both extremes and need not fear a coalition between them. Happy, therefore, the state having a considerable proportion of middle-class citizens! Polity based on their power is the

[13] *Pol.* III, 17, 1288a 7.

best way of avoiding Oligarchy on the one hand with its standards of wealth, and Democracy on the other, "which claims equality without regard to merit" and "liberty to do what it pleases." Polity promises most among human beings as they are.

Very interesting is Aristotle's discussion of the causes which ruin and preserve states, causes which, he declares, have repeatedly been exemplified in history. Obviously of first importance are erroneous ideas of justice, aggrandizement of one class at the expense of others, feuds between the rich and the poor. In Democracy, where the poor have power since they are everywhere in the majority, the persecution of the rich is a frequent cause of disaster; or the politicians learn to compete for the suffrages of the mob; or some demagogue succeeds in attaining an important military office. The most likely conditions for successful Democracy are found among an agricultural or a pastoral people. Accumulations of property are less likely; people bother less about politics; they feel none the less that they have a part and can call officeholders to account. They can "live as they like" and have as little government as possible. Among an industrial people Democracy is far less likely to succeed. Mechanics, traders, and laborers have not the character and stamina of a pastoral or an agricultural people,[14] and accumulations of wealth upset the desired equality and liberty. Hence the easy disintegration of an industrial democracy into lawlessness, revolutions, and tyranny.

Of course other states also disintegrate. Aristocracy easily drifts into Oligarchy when the ruling class becomes selfish or arrogant. Monarchy is perhaps the most stable form of all when moral ideals prevail, but Democracy of the better sort and especially Polity also promise stability. To preserve the state one must constantly be on guard against the growth of the spirit of lawlessness and oppression of one

[14] *Pol.* VI, 4, 1318b 9.

class by another. Offices must be a source of gain to nobody and good feeling must be preserved between rulers and the ruled. Especially difficult are minorities. For, although it is true that in every state the majority ultimately rules,[15] those in which the minority has no power are most unstable. Hence, in the arrangement of offices, executive, legislative, and judicial, that constitution is best which, whether it be dominantly monarchical or democratic, allows for the representation of all groups. Government by law is greatly to be preferred to one by men. It is more stable as well as more likely to attain disinterested justice. Lightly changing the laws from old to new inculcates disobedience—for habit, which requires time, is the foundation of loyalty and obedience.

In the later (unfinished) chapters of the *Politics* Aristotle gives us his conception of education which, like Plato, he considered of fundamental importance in every state aiming for better human life. And it is interesting to note how the problems of what subjects, what methods, whether useful or disinterested studies, what kind of moral training, etc., presented themselves to his mind. He argues that education should be under state control, the same for all citizens, developing them to the fullest life activities. Physical education comes first in the natural order of development, then education of the appetites and emotions, finally disinterested reason. Only by obedience and self-discipline in youth can one attain to any power of command later on. But the Spartan emphasis on valor, physique, and external discipline is at the expense of the mind, the nobler virtues of peace and leisure. The Spartans do not know what to do with themselves when they are not externally active. But the useful arts, like the arts of war, are always means to ends, namely, peace and the liberal studies of a noble leisure.[16]

[15] *Pol.* IV, 4, 1290a 30.

[16] *Pol.* VII, 14, esp. 1333a 30 fol.

A primary condition of attaining this florescence of life is practical reason—education to noble action. Hence from the earliest years Aristotle would have the affections of young people directed toward beauty, which by its very nature spontaneously appeals to the desire for excellence. The arts therefore, and especially music, have a very important place not only as primary sources of pleasure and inclination, but as spontaneous and character-forming disciplines, activities of creative reason itself. But there is very great danger too from the abuse of the arts by those who indulge in sentimental, relaxing, unbalanced melodies, stories and pictures, or wild and uncontrolled rhythms. The controller of education is a very important officer in the state! The rites and ceremonies of religion—which Aristotle also considers a community matter—he would have performed by older men who in their prime had held dignified offices of leadership. The possibility that dogmatic authority and ignorant passions might prove embarrassing here seems never to have presented itself to his mind as likely in an intelligent community.

There are some aspects of the *Politics* which strike one as simple, if not naïve, when one considers the size and complexities of modern states. The ideal city-state, with inhabitants not too numerous to be homogeneous, its limited territory, and trade only large enough to supply the citizens with moderate livelihood and abundant leisure, may seem parochial. We think in terms of world-states and ever-increasing commerce. Our complex governments cannot possibly be classified under any of the forms described by Aristotle. Yet it is precisely in the directness and penetrating simplicity with which he meets fundamental issues that the value of his thought lies. In our much talk of Democracy as source of everything good it is helpful to inquire: What *is* Democracy? and What do we consider the purposes for which states exist? Are they unavoidable evils to be reduced to the minimum (a dominant conception to-day), or are they collective expressions of an indefeasibly moral community aiming for more distinctively human life? If we answer with Aristotle we realize a new faith: one based on the naturalness of an ethical state, a social will superior indeed to individuals but finding its purpose in those individuals. The fetish of sovereignty, whether in the form of divine right and arbitrary force, or in the majority of seven million over six and three-quarter million votes, is henceforward shorn of its magical powers. Natural equity based on the quest for the highest possible excellence of life as discovered by disinterested intelligence takes its place and displays a new ideal of citizenship. We need not agree with all the recommendations or even the observations of Aristotle. But his principles challenge our thought and will inspire the future actions of statesmen who look forward to better government.

CHAPTER XXVI

ARISTOTLE ON POETRY AND OTHER ARTS

The Stagirite was no poet. He had neither the exuberance of imagination nor the exquisite sense of form which we found in Plato. He saw little with that "fine frenzy" which stirs the spirit of an artist. His was an analytic mind. Yet to him must be attributed some of the most illuminating observations on the nature of art, and more particularly poetry, which have so far been made. His keen interest in the arts comes out in the treatises all the way from the *Metaphysics* to the *Politics*. In the *Poetics*, he devotes himself chiefly to an analysis of epic and tragic poetry, but in so penetrating a way that, although the book is but a fragment and its principles are not always clear without their larger context, it remains of first-rate importance. A whole library has been written around the ideas it presents, and their interest is ever fresh.

Let us consider first some of its general points of view. The various arts according to Aristotle have their roots in a spontaneous natural tendency, an instinct to imitate. Men of all sorts, children and philosophers, find delight in copying or representing things they see and hear. It matters not whether the objects are of one kind or another, whether dead and ugly, or living and beautiful; merely to imitate them successfully "gives the liveliest pleasure not only to philosophers but to men in general." [1] They derive insight and knowledge by it as well as the pleasure of recognition: "So this is what it is like!"

[1] 4, 1448b 4. Where not otherwise indicated, numbers in these notes refer to the *Poetics*.

Though the process begins with simple imitation, it becomes not only more elaborate, but a different thing as it develops. Thus comedy grew out of mimicking people, lampooning them and finding satisfaction in the mere fact of imitating them. Painting developed from this instinctive tendency to make likenesses of anything and everything and so know things better, as well as to find a new delight in seeing them a second time. But art did not develop by the process of imitation in itself. Another factor, also having its roots in human instinct, a natural tendency for man to use "harmony, rhythm, meter," came into play.

In fact the mere imitation of anything, reproducing somebody's action or passing emotion, a tree or a face, is not yet art. Nor can one say that a larger assemblage of such particulars attains it. Homer in writing the *Iliad* chose certain personages and events of the Trojan War and had no use for most of the historical details. When he wrote of Odysseus he told but a little of what he might have reported. Art means the imitation of—not just anything and everything.

What then is its content? Aristotle answers: "Poetry tends to express the universal." [2] And here a little difficulty presents itself, for elsewhere [3] he describes the work of science as the discovery of universals, "what is common to a number of particulars." This, of course, is the most usual meaning of the term. Does he intend to say that the artist also undertakes to discover, depict, set forth in some way "what is common to a number of particulars"? Is he one to give us insight into the essential nature of things and the pleasure that comes from knowledge—is he, in short, a kind of scientist? Is art a higher—or lower—form of philosophy?

The answer seems to be: No, and yes. As example of a universal in poetry he cites "how a person of a certain type will

[2] 9, 1451b 5.

[3] *Meta.* XI, 1059b 24; *De Interp.* 17a 39.

on occasion speak or act according to the law of probability or necessity."[4] Such a person will, in other words, speak or act in a way to show character and consistency. There will be point in that content. It will show internal coherence. There will be no chance particulars. Nothing can be added or substracted without doing damage to the work. It will have a definite beginning, a middle, and a conclusion.

Now this is clearly something more than what the historian gives us. Nor is the scientist bound by just this kind of necessity. He will assuredly have logic and order, system in getting at "what is common to a number of particulars." But this will develop out of those particular facts themselves. The artist, on the other hand, follows a "necessity" which grows out of his own mind. This is a more explicit statement than any which Aristotle makes. Yet it is implied in a considerable number of passages.

For example, we are told that Zeuxis painted such men as can nowhere be found in reality.[5] Sophocles "drew men as they ought to be."[6] It very often happens that a poet's stories are neither higher than fact nor true to fact.[7] Yet all of these are examples of universals. Their "necessity" or inner bond of connection—whatever makes Zeuxis' or Sophocles' men real types—is certainly not an average of men's characters but something which the artist's mind imposes upon the facts. The poet may even "describe the impossible" and thus be "guilty of an error." Yet "if the poem is in this way rendered more striking" such an error is justified.[8] Generally speaking, however, the painter does not give men the shape of satyrs, nor does he depict fawns as possessing antlers.

Artists assuredly take into account, then, the given types

[4] 9, 1451b 7.
[5] 25, 1461b 12.
[6] 25, 1460b 33.
[7] 25, 1461b 13 fol.
[8] 25, 1460b 23.

or universals of science, and do them not too great violence. But their own universals are not obtained by abstracting common or essential qualities and discarding differences. They are the result of selecting what is necessary for a particular purpose. And very definite principles become manifest when you examine the works of artists. Thus epic poets use only one kind of meter and nothing but the narrative form. Tragic poets admit nothing by way of character, emotion, or action that detracts from the feelings of fear and pity inspired by such pieces. They try to make the action of the plot throughout an inevitable development of the characters in the plays. Examples could be multiplied from the other arts, all of which have definite internal coherence, a certain course of events, or colors, characters, tunes, which suit the work in question. Such are the "probable or necessary" universals which are clearly different from scientific universals and are yet related to them, since all the fine arts have their roots in the soil of reality.

From this it is clear that Aristotle would have had no sympathy for those modern realists who copy whatever is next to hand. This is the work of mere, or haphazard, imitation. And he would have called the symbolists who, on the other hand, utilize particulars for the purpose of rendering types as such (that is, conceptual truth revealing "what is common to a number of particulars"), by their proper name of scientists. Otherwise put we may say that "man" in terms of the artist's universal is indeed *homo sapiens*, but neither the passing individual nor an "Everyman" who is no one in particular. The dramatist creates an Œdipus, an Agamemnon, an Electra, with distinctive characters, emotions, and actions, who do indeed serve as types, but whose purpose is to contribute to the action of the play. In this way scientific, or objective, reality is caught up and transformed into universals which also satisfy subjective necessity. Of course there is something of Mysticism in such a point of view. The artist in imitating universals gains insight *directly* and not through scientific data. The means he employs in giving expression to his art are also utilized *instinctively*.

More specifically, what are the means by which artists imitate the richly variegated world without and within, so full of possibilities and impossibilities, probabilities and improbabilities, necessity and chance? The answer is: by movements, tunes, rhythms, language, colors, etc., ordered in such a way by their significance, coherence, naturalness, and completeness, as to give some semblance of a universal. Thus the dance, making use of but one medium (motion), and one mode (rhythm), gives pleasurable insight into something deep-lying in human character, feeling, and movement which would never appear in unrhythmic motions having no beginning, middle, or end. What that universal is, can, of course, be realized only by one who appreciates the art. Since it is not an art of language it is not something to be put into language.

Music adds "harmony" (probably our melody) to rhythm, and illustrates the same "necessity," which Aristotle would probably find lacking in some modern forms, namely, consequentialness, each note dependent upon what has preceded and related to what is to follow, all forming a significant whole with definite beginning and ending. The fact that he regards music as the "most imitative" of the arts throws additional light upon what he meant by imitation of universals. For, like anyone in his senses, he knew that music cannot possibly undertake the functions of painting or sculpture. The universal of which music gives us very direct intimation is clearly within the soul itself and is brought out, imitated (we are accustomed to say "expressed") most successfully and pleasurably by that art. Others use language, colors, visible shapes to attain a similar purpose, and by analogous laws.

The means employed by the poetic arts are language,

rhythm and tune. Prose as art is rhythmical language with words appropriate to the content and characterized by coherence, naturalness, perfection and other qualities belonging to the arts in general. But, of course, it makes no use of meter. When that content calls for the heightened feeling associated with meter so that its use seems natural, as in epic poetry, then, and then only, is it to be employed. Thus hexameters seem to be the only measure appropriate to Homer's narratives; while lyric and dramatic verse-forms are numerous. Lyrics and, in part, tragedies are also sung, at which times "harmony" is appropriate. No one is more emphatic than Aristotle, however, that metrical language is a means to an end. One might put Herodotus into excellent verse, and still have history. Empedocles' metrical philosophy is still philosophy—and presumably would have been better if devoid both of meter and rhythm. A poet, on the other hand, can create from historical and even philosophical subjects. Mimes (the fictitious sketches of character widely enjoyed in antiquity) can also be genuine poetry though entirely devoid of meter.

"Content" thus seemed to be of first importance. But we must remember that Aristotle made no such distinction as is sometimes made to-day between "form" and "content"—as though a work could be excellent in one of these and not in the other. What the artist wishes to give us will quite "naturally" take one form or another if it be art. Content thus presupposes appropriate forms, and *vice versa.* To separate them is impossible.

Yet Aristotle classifies different kinds of poetry according to the characters, emotions, and actions with which they deal. Thus under dramatic poetry one group of works presents characters in general above the level of ordinary human nature—but not so far above us as to forego our sympathy. Another group presents men worse than the average but not in any and every sort of fault. Their inferiority is of a particular kind—"the ridiculous, which is a species of the ugly." It is defined more specifically as "a mistake or deformity not productive of pain or harm to others." [9] These two kinds of works are, of course, tragedy and comedy. Epic poetry is like tragedy in being an imitation "of serious subjects in a grand kind of verse." [10] This distinction of noble characters, emotions, and actions from their opposites suggests that the moral will play an important rôle with him, as it did with Plato. But of this later. Here we can only note that Aristotle would have depraved characters figure in a tragedy only when there is an inner necessity for introducing them.[11] And then they can only be subordinate. A Satan or a Macbeth as hero in an epic or a tragedy would have been to him quite unsuitable. His reason will later appear.

The most famous and most disputed sentence in the whole realm of æsthetics is Aristotle's definition of tragedy. It runs as follows: "Tragedy is the imitation of an action that is good as well as complete in itself and of a sufficient magnitude; in language with pleasurable accessories, each kind brought in separately in the parts of the work; in the form of action not that of narration; with incidents arousing pity and fear by which to effect its purgation of such emotions." [12] Most of this will already be clear to the reader. The action of tragedy as "complete in itself" implies of course the absence of redundancy as well as of any loose ends. "A thing whose presence or absence makes no appreciable difference is not an organic part of the whole." [13] "Pleasurable accessories" refers to the singing of the chorus and the different verse forms in their appropriate parts. A "sufficient magnitude" implies something monumental in

[9] 5, 1449a 34.
[10] 5, 1449b 9.
[11] 25, 1461b 19.
[12] 6, 1449b 23.
[13] 8, 1451a 34.

size, if action, characters, and the poet's treatment warrant it. Every work of art is neither too long nor too short! A great work will delight and interest the "better sort of audience" for relatively the longest time. Bad tragedy quickly fatigues, even a little is too much.

Action, it will be noted, is the first term in the definition. A little later the *Poetics* adds: "Tragedy is an imitation not of men, but of an action and of life, and life consists in action." Incidents and plot are thus the chief thing, character comes in as subsidiary. Character indeed determines men's qualities, but it is by their actions that they are happy or unhappy.[14] For that reason he regards a play with a good plot acted by less significant characters as greatly superior to one with an ordinary plot done by remarkable characters who may use the most perfect diction and express the most interesting thought. "The plot is the soul of a tragedy; character holds the second place."[15] This point of view is, of course, the formulation of the best Greek practice. And it must be admitted that in point of sheer dramatic quality the fateful course of events in *Œdipus Rex* or *Antigone* is superior to any tragedy of modern times. The reasons probably are: firstly, the inevitable nature of the action, and secondly, the fact that it is so closely linked up with the (fixed) characters of the play. When a hero *develops* in the course of action and one has a sense of contingency in the outcome—as sometimes in Shakespeare—the essentially tragic feeling is less strong.

Pity and fear for the hero are the specific emotions involved—pity for his past and fear for the inevitable future. Of course there is something of "in-feeling" implied in these emotions. Everyone will intuitively find parallels between the sufferer and himself. That is why Aristotle would have noble but *not superhuman* characters with whom we could

[14] 6, 1450a 16.
[15] *Ibid.* a 37.

not sympathize. As to the action growing out of these characters, it will not show us "a good man passing from happiness to misery," which is simply "odious," eliciting very little of either pity or fear. Nor can a bad man be shown rising from misery to happiness, the most untragic action imaginable. Again an extremely bad man falling from happiness into misery may elicit moral reflection; but such action produces little fear or pity. The best hero, therefore, is "a character midway between extremes"—neither a saint nor an incorrigible sinner—"a man who is not exceptionally good and just, yet whose misfortune is brought about not by vice or depravity but by some error or frailty." He must, however, be renowned and prosperous, more than a plain average man.[16]

Thought is of third-rate importance among the objects of tragedy. It is never introduced for its own sake and always serves the purpose of delineating character, which in turn is subordinate to action. Singing or chanting he esteems as the finest "accessory," the most pleasant "sweetening" of tragedy—a sweetening which probably had little in common with modern opera or with our ecclesiastical chanting. The stage-setting, or "spectacle," he also regards as subordinate and all too easily overdone, as when elocutionists, concentrating on voice-effects, put the contemplation of universals—man in the grip of destiny—quite in the background. Even stage paraphernalia can be discarded without sacrifice of dramatic quality. Reading a tragedy can be more poignant than stage production. As to diction, or perfection of style, he regards it as depending chiefly upon clearness and distinction. The poet will create no riddles by over-brilliance, no jargon by his new words. He will often deviate from normal idiom, even lengthening or altering words, but his large agreement with common usage will guarantee perspicuity.

[16] 13, 1453a 7.

The "Unities"—of time, place and action—about which so much discussion raged in later literary criticism, reduce to one upon a closer reading of the text. That tragedy "endeavors so far as possible to confine itself to a single revolution of the sun, or but slightly to exceed this limit," [17] is obviously a statement of current practice. As to unity of place the only reference in the *Poetics* is to "several lines of action going on at one and the same time." Of these we are obliged to confine ourselves to what is going on upon the stage.[18] In other words, you can't be in two places at the same time in tragedy any more than you can in physics. Unity of action, internal cohesion, consistency, this is what the Aristotelian unities reduce to.

The doctrine of *katharsis* is less easily dealt with. "Incidents arousing pity and fear by which to effect . . . purgation of such emotions" seems on the face of it to imply that the purpose of tragedy is to eliminate these pities and fears making us no longer subject to them—and thus in the end taking away all *raison d'etre* for tragedies as well! By this reading, pity and fear are undesirable emotions which we should put behind us. Tragedy has the ethical purpose of helping us so to do.

But such an interpretation hardly agrees with Aristotle's fundamental points of view in ethics. The suppression of any function, as we observed before, was by him considered unnatural and a distortion of human nature. Anger, fear and the other emotions all have their suitable occasions, objects and appropriate measures. "There are things which we ought to fear" and be angry about, at the right time and manner, and for the right length of time—in short, according to the prudent mean. Is it conceivable that Aristotle should here have become an ascetic for whom virtue lay in the elimination of certain emotions?

[17] 5, 1449b 13.
[18] 24, 1459b 23.

Again, as a psychologist dealing with habit, he remarks on the wholly obvious fact that indulgence in any opinion, emotion, or action tends to strengthen it. Can we assume that he here conceives of pity and fear as exceptions to this law of habit, that their exercise tends to weaken or eliminate them?

Both assumptions are impossible, so that we are constrained to look for some less simple meaning in the passage. In the last chapter of the *Politics* where he considers the ethical effects of various sorts of melodies and rhythms he also uses the word *katharsis* and describes its result as lightening and delighting the souls *both* of those who are especially susceptible to these emotions and those who are deficient in this respect. Thus sacred melodies restore the souls of those who abound in such feelings and—to a lesser degree—of those who are more phlegmatic.[19] The language here is clearly medical so that it seems somewhat strained for Lessing [20] to assume that the *katharsis* of art "depends upon nothing else than the transformation of the passions into promptings to virtue." Aristotle repeatedly presupposes the moral effect of painting, sculpture, music, and poetry. But it is a different thing to say: Such are the natural results; or, Such are the purpose and essence of art. Tragedy "heals the soul" by providing an outlet for certain emotions which may be excessive or morbid in some people. Something very like the meaning of our word "sublimation" was probably in his mind here. Heavier and more stolid people, on the other hand, are aroused by it to a fuller realization emotionally of life's meanings, assuming they have pity and fear in their hearts for anything. In both cases what is primitive, or even brutal and diseased, is in fact made more essentially human, harmonious, happy, and healthy. But it is only a certain kind of exercise, a gratification by means of art enjoyment

[19] *Pol.* VIII, 7, 1341b 32 fol.
[20] *Hamb. Dram.* 74–8.

that this takes place. We are given an outlet for our emotions and passions which raises us above their brutal gratification, heals their abnormality, and restores us to peace with ourselves. Yet this "delight" in the "innocent pleasures" of art does not tell us what art is.

It seems probable, therefore, that Aristotle meant rather to free the arts from the moralistic straight-jacket which Plato had imposed upon them than to make them means to ends. He certainly considered them amenable to moral judgment by their strategic influence on the course of civilization—all the way from the rhythm of a dance to the *katharsis* induced by a Sophocles. But such judgment is clearly not of their essence. For not only good men and good actions figure in them, but evil as well. Comedy laughs at inferior men, thus instructing and also delighting the mind—as well as purging it of bad humors—but only by the media, modes, rhythms, etc., appropriate to its "imitation of the universal."

It is a pity that we have lost the second book of the *Poetics*. In it Aristotle treated of comedy, and very likely elucidated further his conception of *katharsis*. Possibly he had more to say here on the subject of Beauty as related to Art, upon which he is strangely silent elsewhere. All lovers of lyric poetry would also have been grateful for what he might have said about it. Yet the little we possess is no small contribution toward intelligent appreciation of the arts.

CHAPTER XXVII

THE ACADEMY, PYRRHO'S "SCHOOL," AND THE LYCEUM

The history of educational institutions is often an unenlightening one. To carry on a great tradition with established doctrines is indeed important work. But from the standpoint of progress in thought authority is depressing to human initiative. Not that investigators can, or ever will, be free from the accumulated wisdom of the elders. Every man in his senses craves all the light that the past can supply. But institutions which merely rehearse established doctrines—even in the most scholarly way—without creative participation in new undertakings are not primary agencies in the life of reason.

Plato's Academy and Aristotle's Lyceum were not in their better years colleges of this character. They were inspired by the great doctrines of their founders. But they were also communities devoted to the progress and extension of learning. For a time the scholarship and zeal of the succeeding teachers were as keen as those of their great masters. When creative insight became rarer among them, the work of philosophy, which above all others demands intellectual initiative, suffered a decline. By some it was declared to be impossible. Others implicitly followed the authority of the founders. The more vigorous among them, who yet lacked the power of seeing general principles, took to fact-gathering and by their collective work amassed an immense amount of scientific data. This scholarly erudition characterized a number of schools, e.g., medical and astronomical, which continued to exist for centuries. In this chapter we are concerned with two schools of philosophy, and chiefly as they illustrate the fortunes of great intellectual movements in a time of decline.

1

When Plato, in 347 B. C., designated Speusippus, his nephew, as head of the Academy, he probably did not anticipate that for 874 years his school would be a center of intellectual and religious interests in Europe. Nor could he have suspected that so soon his doctrines would be incrusted with the fancies of the number-mystics, or that the work of philosophy and all its parts would from his seat be declared a self deception. Speusippus was a man of no mean ability. His critical insight is shown by an idea of evolution which incidentally seems to reflect his discussions with Aristotle. Time, he declared, is necessary for the forces of good to develop in the order of nature. Hence we must look for good not in the beginning causes of things (as Plato did) but rather in the more developed stages. The divine itself is in process of development. God is that toward which time points in the future—not in the backward reaches of eternity.

Both he and Xenocrates, who succeeded him, were men of marked religious fervor. Speusippus sought in all possible ways to make concrete and particular what seemed to him abstract in Plato's teaching. Thus he tried to make certain laws of mathematics and astronomy the basis of piety, as teaching men the eternal proportions by which God orders the world. He also allowed his imagination wide scope in inventing a whole series of intermediate beings between God and mankind, who were destined to play an important rôle in later religious speculations. Xenocrates further specified that these developments were *emanations* of the Deity. By a strange mathematical mysticism he tried to explain how the *one* God and Father evolved the many minds through the feminine double or *Dyad.* God also made possible the communion of man with himself through spirits—many of them saintly, others, alas, renegade, who often deceive humanity. Three, the Triad, or Trinity, was his most sacred number, however, and best manifested Deity. Three parts of the Godhead correspond to three parts of the universe. Everything in fact is divided into three. Knowledge itself is divisible into three stages, corresponding to the three kinds of realities—the intelligible, the sensible, and the mixed. These are somewhat different applications of mathematics from that of Heraclides, another member of the Older Academy, who by calculation confirmed the rotation of the earth from west to east!

Perhaps there is some connection between this number theology and the succeeding or "Middle" Academy, which took to doubting everything. Arcesilaus (d. 241 B. C.) is said to have set up as his principle: Not ever to express his own judgment but to note what could be said against it.[1] Cicero further reports how this same head of the Academy taught not only that we cannot know, but that we cannot even learn that we cannot know.[2] With Plato there was always a certain wholesome Skepticism in scrutinizing his data. That after a hundred years his successor should have denied the possibility of knowledge is indeed anomalous, but it bespeaks the spirit of the age. Carneades, who, another hundred years later (d. 129 B. C.), sat in his seat, declared philosophy to be wholly impossible. There is no criterion of truth. Nor can a false statement be distinguished from a true one. Proof is a self-deception, for it always goes back to what can't be proved! The faint gleam of a positive tendency does indeed show itself later in his theory of probability. Some statements are at least more probable than

1 Cicero: *de Orat.* III, 18, 67.
2 *Acad. Post.* I, 12, 45.

others, according to whether they are conceivable and uncontradicted, or confirmed by plausible evidence.

Decay is discouraging anywhere but most of all in science and philosophy. After the Skepticism of the Middle came the Dogmatism of the "New" Academy, basing its philosophy upon the authority of the Founder. One must get back to the pure teachings of the Master! They cannot be improved upon. Or, in the opinion of a man like Antiochus of Ascalon, who was the teacher of Cicero 79–78 B. C. at the Academy, the philosopher was one who "chose the best" from among the doctrines of earlier thinkers. Such Eclecticism commingled with varying proportions of Skepticism and Dogmatism seems then to have continued down to the time when the propagandists of the faith closed the Academy, after having themselves appropriated many of its most fanciful theological speculations.

2

Extreme Skepticism is usually characteristic of a decaying civilization. Its milder forms, on the other hand, are a great stimulus to philosophy and science. Socrates in the Periclean age, although he professed to know nothing, inspired nearly all with whom he came into contact with an ardent desire for a certain kind of knowledge. Even the challenges of the Sophists, fundamental as they were in the case of a Gorgias, urged more persistent and penetrating minds to new discoveries, the gratification of important intellectual interests.

The Skepticism of Pyrrho of Elis, a contemporary of Aristotle, who seems to have come into contact both with the Megarians and the Atomists, was one which tended toward very different results. The reason for this was a very practical one. It is not necessarily a form of intellectual suicide to challenge conventional ideas of beauty and justice or accepted truth. This is indeed the motive of progress in science. But Pyrrho, attracted by the pragmatic ideas of Stoics and Epicureans who were then coming to the fore, justified Skepticism on the basis of one's individual mental peace. Tranquillity of soul requires that one should withhold assent or denial to each and every troublesome issue. Philosophers present no true source of happiness with the uncertainties of their speculations, the endless and often contradictory propositions which their inquiries have produced. Heated discussions are no source of inner content; they lead to an interminable thirst. *Ataraxy*, freedom from passion, calmness, requires that one should make one's mind as much of a blank as possible so far as these vexations are concerned. In intellectual vacuity is peace.

Yet it is one of the most paradoxical tributes to the vitality of human reason that Pyrrho's school should also have maintained itself for several centuries, rehearsing its proofs about the impossibility of proof, elaborating its knowledge about the non-existence of knowledge. There is no point for us in rehearsing the names of these successive teachers, except in the case of Timon, a friend of Pyrrho. Timon made use of the skeptical argument growing out of the idea of "things in themselves" or what our world really is considered independently of our senses and intelligence. Of course the very presupposition of such "things in themselves" assumes by hypothesis our impossibility of knowing them. But probably it was intended as a challenge to the *homo mensura* doctrine of Protagoras. In other words, we experience how things affect us but not what they are. Our every starting point (other than this) is a bald hypothesis, and they who indulge in speculations based on them abandon their happiness.

Peace and tranquillity thus become the final quest of intelligence; suppressing the wonder, which Aristotle held to be the source of all philosophy, is the best species of "philosophy." One can understand with what eagerness later centuries, intent upon discrediting human intelligence in the interest of divine revelations, made use of these and kindred reasonings. The chief source for our knowledge concerning Timon comes from the *Preparatio evangelica* of Eusebius (266–349 A. D.), one of the early Christian apologists.

3

The Peripatetic School also had its best years in the decades following its Founder's death. Theophrastus, who succeeded Aristotle as head of the Lyceum, was indeed a remarkable man. Merely the titles of the books he wrote are a commentary on his scientific undertakings. Those which have come down to us in whole or in part include: *Signs of the Weather, Winds, Fire Rocks, Opinions on Physics, On Sense Perception, On Logic, Perspiration, Fainting, Paralysis, Plant Lore, Causes of Vegetable Processes, Ethical Characters.* But these are only a small portion of the treatises he wrote. We know of seven books on Animals, three on Vision, three on Water, two on Petrifaction, others on Intoxication, Insanity, Plagues, Hibernation, Spontaneous Generation. He compiled a Lexicon of Law, wrote ten books on Political Theory, three on Æsthetics, another on Piety, as well as an amazing number of treatises on Education, Friendship, Marriage, and other ethical subjects.

What is still more remarkable is that ancient critics and modern specialists give very high praise to these books. This is especially true of his work in Botany in which he brought together a vast amount of information, gathered by various scientific expeditions, including one which accompanied Alexander in his Oriental campaigns. The ideal of Theophrastus seems to have been wholesale fact-gathering by collaboration of experts from many fields, a motive which long dominated the Peripatetic School. With this empirical work, so necessary for both science and philosophy, came specialization and an emphasis upon particulars, which more and more tended to push general principles into the background. With it, of course, went a decreased interest in philosophy and eventually also in science. For particulars by themselves are means to ends. The greater the array of facts unenlightened by interpretation, the greater the erudite impotence of our intelligence. Theory was ever its lifeblood—even when facts were scarce.

Theophrastus did not lose sight of laws, causes, and general principles. But so great was his reverence for Aristotle that he seems nowhere to have essayed any great improvement upon those set up by the Founder. He raised many problems, and fundamental ones. Thus he questioned Aristotle's principle that motion is the natural tendency of the heavenly spheres. *Why* should motion rather than rest be more natural? He points out many difficulties connected with the conception of immanent purpose, as well as that of a *First* Cause, or Prime Mover. He wonders how fire can be elemental, since it is always *in* something else; and how one can distinguish between active and passive reason, especially since man stands so closely related to lower animals, who seem to have imagination. Yet very rarely does he venture his own creative insights and generally returns to the authority of the Master. Nevertheless, Theophrastus enriched in no small measure the data upon which interpretation builds. Even the dust of his specialized minutiæ added a certain glory to the declining sun of philosophy.

Strato, who succeeded Theophrastus in 288 B. C., went a little farther than his predecessor in questioning the doctrines of Aristotle. He challenged the conception of a Prime Mover, or Pure Form, as transcending particular things. All is to be explained in terms of natural inherent qualities and the movements shown by the smaller particles—the method of Democritus. Yet Strato also held that the Atomic Doctrine needed modification in its conception of indivisible particles qualitatively the same and differing only in the way they are "hooked up." He conceived atoms to have differences of quality, and characterized the idea of a single elementary substance as a "dream." His "void" in which the atoms move suggests our conception of the ether. By it alone can we explain how light penetrates solid bodies, how magnets attract iron, or torpedo fish can succeed in giving one a shock when they are harpooned. By the void—which also is yet *something*—we can also comprehend how elasticity is possible in a body.

The causes for the being and order of things are thus inherent in themselves taken as a whole. Chief among these causes to which changes are due are heat and cold. Something very like our modern conception of gravity also plays a rôle: All things have a tendency to move toward the center of their mass. This was, of course, intended to supersede Aristotle's idea of particular places and spheres, toward which the various elements were assumed spontaneously to move. Yet Strato was not a mechanist nor a materialist. He recognized the purposive aspects of Nature. God, the world-energy, is not "outside," but manifested in Nature itself. It goes without saying that he would have agreed with Xenophanes in his criticism of biological and anthropomorphic gods.

Strato had no inconsiderable influence upon the development of natural science. Aristarchus of Samos, who developed the first heliocentric astronomy, was his pupil. He is often quoted by Archimedes the mathematician. In psychology he tried to establish the unity of life-processes—a unity which tended to break down Aristotle's distinctions between vegetable, animal, and human functions. Characteristic in this connection is his identification of creative and practical reasons, both being brain-activity in the part covered by the forehead and between the eyes. Except in degree one cannot distinguish between an act of reason and one of sensation. Something of reason is present in every sense-perception; and, on the other hand, reason requires sensation. In point of quality animal and human mental functions are identical. It follows that both have a similar destiny. Plato's arguments for immortality are, of course, regarded as inconclusive.

Such was Strato, the "Physicist," whose philosophical acumen and independence of judgment no one will bring in question. But he was the last of the Peripatetics so far as these interests are concerned. Just as in the Academy the second generation of leaders marked the advent of other times, so in Aristotle's college the "practical" and factual henceforward took more and more precedence over the scientific and philosophical. True that even in Aristotle's day, Eudemus had preferred the *history* of arithmetic, geometry, and astronomy to these sciences themselves; and Aristoxenus had found place in his learned theory of music for a discussion of its important uses as healer of mental diseases. But, after Strato, theory became subordinate to practice; intellectual interests were more barely empirical. The descriptive sciences flourished. All possible data for history were gathered and classified. Literary criticism abounded; so too the writing of books on geography. The investigation of ethical principles gave way to popular preachments, anecdotes, and biographies of admirable men. The Alexandrian age of erudition for which no fact was too insignificant to catalogue and preserve, when scholarly learning was encyclopædic and creative thinking rare, was at hand.

The Peripatetic School continued its existence until well into the sixth century A. D. But our chief reason for gratitude is the work of Andronicus of Rhodes (fl. 70 B. C.) and that of Alexander of Aphrodisius (200 A. D.). These are scholarly textual criticisms and exhaustive commentaries on Aristotle.

PART THREE:

The Quest for a Way of Life

CHAPTER XXVIII

THE STOICS

The "practical" tendency which we have noted in the decline of the Platonic and Aristotelian schools is exhibited in all others of the later period. The Academy tried to make philosophy the handmaiden of religion, and when that failed took refuge in Skepticism and later in Dogmatism. The Peripatetics made philosophy subservient to science, which in its turn was to serve a useful purpose. "Mere theory" became more and more otiose, as the fact-gathering process made it increasingly dangerous for any one to express a general conclusion. But this uninterpreted, albeit encyclopædic, information also took its revenge upon the theories of science—which are nothing if not more specialized philosophical interpretations. And the outcome here, as we saw, was textual criticism and the authority of the Founder.

A somewhat different history is presented in the school founded by Zeno (336–264 B. C.), a merchant from Cyprus who after suffering shipwreck found himself in Athens at twenty-two years of age. Here he decided to give up his business after he had heard certain teachers. These were Polemo of the Academy, Crates the Cynic, and Diodorus Chronos of the Megarian School. After a number of years' study at Athens, Zeno set up a school of his own, which, because of the fact that he taught in a magnificent covered colonnade or porch (Stoa), was called Stoic. Here near the Athenian Agora in a place already famous for its paintings by Polygnotus, the lean, short man gathered about him a numerous company whose influence has gone through all the Western world. Even to-day any one who has the faintest glimmer of light on the history of human thought has heard of this popular philosophy and what it means to take at least some experiences "Stoically."

Two other men distinguished themselves as his successors here: Cleanthes, a prize-fighter, and a "hard nut" intellectually, but also a hard worker, succeeded Zeno in 264 B. C., and in the third generation his pupil, Chrysippus, a brilliant debater and voluminous writer, who greatly extended the popularity of the Porch. Like the other Greek schools it continued for hundreds of years, and had numbers of eminent men among its students and teachers. In the days of imperial Rome, it included among the latter: Seneca, the slave Epictetus, and the emperor Marcus Aurelius. Here we are less concerned with the external fortunes of the school than with its primary doctrines.

Let us begin with what is best known and will therefore best serve to make the rest significant. Broadly speaking, we may put it thus: The most important subject with which thought can be concerned is human character. What matters in our philosophy is not so much a theory of astronomy or of God as how to make this knowledge relevant to our quest of virtue. Philosophy, in other words, is the handmaiden of the good life. Natural science, psychology, logic, these are the servants of a noble master, namely, Ethics of the Grander Humanity. The servants must indeed be considered, the good life requires their presence, just as a jewel requires a setting. But the setting by itself is to no purpose. Knowledge (as later-day pragmatists put it) is not a useless thing, mere theory for theory's sake, but an instrument to serve human life.

And yet ethics, as we have before observed, requires a background of interpretation and, of course, the Stoics also had theirs. One has to give some answer to the question, What more specifically *is* human good and what are the means of realizing it? Their own answer perhaps best illustrates that necessity. Following the Cynics, Zeno and his successors declared the good of man to consist in living "according to nature." But one immediately inquires, *What* then is nature? Is the "dog" life, devoid of refinements, arts, families, states, as advocated by Diogenes, "natural"? Where does one find nature; is it in the passing emotions of the individual, or in what science can observe of the outside world? We are already familiar with the Cynic answer, which found the life of reason in the simpler, more primitive, human existence. Plato and Aristotle on the contrary regarded the most highly developed form as standard of excellence. Unless both of these are mere opinions, they will be grounded upon a satisfactory interpretation of human life in relation to its total environment. Nature will be both within and without.

So also the Stoic philosophy did not fail to develop conceptions of the physical world as well as of psychology. Their intellectual plant would not have grown at all without roots in the soil of logic and physics. This would have been necessary, even independently of their fundamental conception that the individual man is an offshoot, a "spark" of the wider life of nature. For our wildest crimes as well as noblest actions are the results of at least partly observable conditions and causes. Values of every sort, ideals, as even Plato saw, have their occasion and evidence in the "language of facts."

Now the Stoic leaders generally accepted the evidence for their convictions from the thought of earlier investigators. And among these Heraclitus was of primary importance. His doctrine of the Divine Fire or Energy as the basic fact, a dynamic reality back of all the ceaseless changes of phenomena, together with his Logos-doctrine and its immutable law determining the course of the Flux, the manifestations of the Logos attributed to human minds, and the traditional conceptions of periodic world-destruction and rehabilitation by fire were all incorporated into the framework of their system.

Another conception very fundamental for them was Materialism. Nothing is real unless it have corporeal form. All the changes, physical and mental, which we observe in nature are due to physical causes. The world-energy itself, God, and whatever existing thing one may choose to name, are all parts of the one substance, Matter, eternally going through its cycles of change and repeating itself from age to age. Invisible "realities," anything beyond the senses of men, Platonic Ideas, Aristotelian Forms, they denied as nonmaterial. Only as matter can something be said to exist. All causes are material, only by impacts and mechanical motions does anything take place.

Another one of their adoptions was the doctrine of Teleology. The course of nature indicates a providential purpose making for the welfare and advantage of rational beings, as well as the order and harmony of the universe as a whole. The designs of Deity are everywhere being carried out down to the smallest decision or event in the life of a moth or a man. Even in a man's choice of the evil course and resultant crime Providence is fulfilling its ends. The little suffering of the parts accomplishes a greater good. Nowhere in the most "accidental" or trivial event is anything not subject to the law of Zeus. Winds, earthquakes, diseases, even omens and men's prayers are effects of causes whose origin must be traced to the mind of God.

This Teleology is combined with unconditional Optimism. Everything being the result of perfect reason, events happen in the best possible way and to the benefit of rational beings—which in terms of the current theology were specified as men and gods. Evil is either incompleted good or its necessary foil. When we fail to see this we must remember that God's thoughts are not our thoughts. What we conceive to be calamity or human baseness may from His point of view be fundamental good. Chrysippus illustrated this by explaining how the Creator designed human beings to be healthy, but in order to insure other advantages along with this, found it necessary to introduce diseases. He made the bones of the head of very thin material in order to have them light. But this makes it extremely easy to crack a skull. Vice comes in by a similar necessity. You cannot have virtue without it.[1]

Still another choice was the doctrine of human freedom. Men have the power to choose the way they go. They are responsible for their actions, and are able to follow or not to follow the way of the Logos. All men have the "seeds" of the Logos (*Logoi spermatikoi*) within them, and it is natural for them to follow that divine light. But many do not choose to do so. Even in that very choice, however, they are fulfilling the purposes of the Logos. Thus human choice has three aspects: It is the inevitable result of given causes (which are ultimately material) ; it is the free activity of the agent; it is part of the providence of God.

Thus the Stoic account of nature combined a number of widely different and sometimes contradictory interpretations. Pantheism appealed to them as postulating the presence of God in every part of the universe and tracing all its activities to divine agency. They liked the idea of cosmic mental energy as presented by Plato and Aristotle. But being "hard headed" practical men they preferred to take the evidence of direct sensation, which vouches only for material things. Hence they identified every agency, mental and physical, with the one world substance, which is at once God and matter. Matter, to be sure, has different qualities, as well as degrees in which it manifests the "breath" of Deity. Some elements are relatively passive, others more active. It is the latter which best display divine power and reason, and especially in organic forms. Matter is, indeed, infinitely

[1] *Noctes Atticæ,* VII, 1, 7, Von Arnim Collection No. 1169.

various. No two leaves of a tree or least particles of anything are identically similar each to any other. Yet all are one substance embracing within itself all particular things. All forms of energy, every individual thought and emotion, every winking of an eyelid, are part of a single scheme. The cosmic unity not only holds together the various parts in an unbroken chain of causes and effects; it actually repeats itself detail for detail in the infinite series of worlds which have been and will be built up and destroyed.

Yet Materialism and mechanical necessity were for them no obstacle to a completely purposive and providential guidance, ordaining such events as make for the good of rational beings. The latter have independence, freely choosing their actions; and their every act is likewise the inevitable result of cosmic necessity. Individual rational beings can commune with, pray to, Deity; their little "words" (*Logoi*) are indeed part of the world reason and consciousness. At the same time this free creative activity is an evanescent aspect of reality. The individual soul (*Logos spermatikos*) may survive death for a time but cannot continue beyond the next world conflagration. He will, however, have the prospect of being repeated identically an infinite number of times in the new cosmic cycles.

The mechanical world order is a moral one. But it is also "beyond good and evil" as we understand these terms. No particular action can be certainly designated as good from a cosmic standpoint. And every action is good regarded from the standpoint of unconditioned Optimism; it is part of the world purpose. If our reasons cannot comprehend this they are not following their *logoi spermatikoi*, the divinities in ourselves. But of Stoic ethics later.

There could hardly be a better example of Eclecticism and of the difficulties growing out of a free choice of doctrines which appeal on one basis or another, and are also mutually contradictory. One asks, By what logic did they come to such conclusions? Or did they in their love of the "practical" esteem logic to be of no use? We may answer the first question in part by saying that they attributed to sense-perception the source and validity of all our knowledge. Our minds, said Cleanthes, are blank tablets at birth upon which the motions of outside particles, acting through the sense organs, imprint changes in the body. These imprints get clustered together in certain ways and are "recalled" in imagination. And thus, in some unexplained way, general concepts result on the markings and protuberances of the material substance from which mind is made. Chrysippus used slightly different terms. He spoke of "modifications" and "impressions" instead of imprints. But the arguments remain the same. The mind is made up of sensations which are the product of the external world. Minds are the passive recipients of motions which originate outside of it and continue on the inside. In short they are mechanisms—matter in motion under special conditions. This, it need hardly be pointed out, was also an adoption.

The difficulty with such a conception of knowledge and of the mind is that one does not know what to do with what at least appears to be self-activity—choice, the forming of alternatives, whatever is "subjective," e. g., feelings, which also help to determine our opinions and our actions. If we had only sensations there would be more point in the Stoic criterion of truth: the sensation or group of sensations which forces itself upon us, that is to say, compels assent. Yet even here the problem remains, What is the "us," or the "assent," and why should the latter be necessary at all if sensations are imposed upon us?

Of course the Stoics also recognized this inner activity, even though they described minds as passive, the products of sensory motions. It is difficult to gainsay ideas, assents, comparisons, conclusions, intuitions! The Stoics could not do so despite their Sensationalism. In fact, they found another criterion of truth in the active side of the mind, parallel to the sensory (or imagined) presentation which compels assent. This is the stock of common ideas generally entertained by human beings, a standard which theologians later called the *consentium gentium.* In other words, opinions on such subjects as What is God? or What is beautiful? are true if they are widely popular or universal. Comment would be superfluous here.

The logic of the Stoics, which professed to be a simplification of Aristotle's *Organon,* could not sidestep the question as to what these general concepts are. In what sense are ideas realities, actively determining the course of things? We have already noted that in their purposive conception of the cosmos they adopted and even extended the Platonic interpretation of Ideas as causes. They rejected it, however, in insisting that matter, operating by mechanical necessity, is the only reality. If these Ideas are real, they should, by the latter criterion, be larger or smaller pieces of matter. But here the Stoics adopted still another point of view. They denied all reality whatsoever to general ideas. Only individual concepts have anything back of them—this fig tree, this day, this place, Chrysippus. The genus *Ficus*, Time, Space, Mankind, are non-existent. They are mere class names, breath standing for nothing real. Hence the term "Nominalism" by which this doctrine was later designated. Its logical tendency is to deny real existence to anything but absolute atoms going their independent way in the void. But the Stoics apparently did not like Atomism. And the "individuals" which they recognized were themselves highly generalized collective concepts. They knew, for example, that an egg is made up of parts, and that a particular man is an organism. Yet these parts collectively constitute an "individual" for them, and the "race of men" stands for nothing at all.

Perhaps we can illustrate this still more pointedly by a brief account of the Stoic psychology. Human nature was, of course, another primary interest and, in view of their Nominalism, one wonders what for them could have constituted the basis for so highly complex a class name as mind or soul. Assuming that only individual events or particular states are real—*this* sensation, *this* prevailing imagination ("*phantasia kataleptika*"), *this* passing choice, —what, if anything, is back of all these particulars holding them together, so that one can speak of Socrates' nature or more generally of human nature? Now the Stoics save "you" and "me" from being resolved into a series of particular mental states strung together on nothing. They find a reality back of the fleeting individual emotions, perceptions, choices, thoughts.

That reality is sometimes characterized as "warm breath," sometimes as "upbuilding fire or energy," or again as "creative (*spermatikos*) logos," which is part of the cosmic reason. Soul extends throughout the body, but its "center" is the heart to which all sensations go. They are transmitted thither by the contacts of physical particles. The mind's functions are of one fundamental kind. Emotion, desire, thought, sensations are only relatively different. They are the same rational, or knowledge, function, considered from various angles or aspects. To feel about something is also to acknowledge and judge it. To will to do is also to know what you do. No thought without sensations, and so forth. The soul is a single function even though eight can be distinguished relatively. These are the five senses, speech, reproduction, and the "controlling power" (*hegemonikon*), the center to which all the other functions are subordinate.

The distinctions between rational and irrational, active and passive, vegetative, animal and human functions, or parts of the soul as worked out by Aristotle, seem to have had little significance to the Stoics. Qualitative distinctions were for them merely degrees of intelligence, rationality, or the extent to which *hegemonikon* maintains its hegemony. This again is difficult as implying a *continuity* of man's mental life with that of the lower creation when Stoic writers distinguish quite sharply between "brutes" and men. Rational beings are specified to be men and gods, who first and last remain the center of their interest. Yet this Eclecticism is curiously instructive. Like some "newer" psychological interpretations it combines a number of contradictory points of view. Mental facts are physical facts brought about by the contacts, motions, energies of matter. They are the passive results of sensations and combinations of particles, which latter also transport them through the body, e. g., from periphery to center. What is sensed is in direct, spatial contact with the center (*hegemonikon*). All is mechanism. On the other hand, the mind is a purposive, self-active agency directing the motions, contacts, energies, of which it is said to be the result. It develops ideas inwardly which are a criterion of truth. It operates according to fixed laws which are everywhere rational. It is often irrational in choosing what is not in accord with these fixed laws. It suffers from emotions (passions) which its own activity is able to overcome.

We are now in a position to appreciate the grandeur as well as the difficulties of the Stoic ethics. Life according to nature implied, for Chrysippus, not only a harmony of human nature with itself, but also a conformity with the cosmic order, which is everywhere rational as well as necessary. This at first raises the question of how in a world already thoroughly orderly, good, and rational there can be any moral problem at all. "Whatever is is right," as Pope expressed it. The Stoics waive this Monism, in their ethics, however, and assume, as all in their senses must, that not a little in human nature and society could under certain conditions be improved upon. The unbounded Optimism of their theology gave way to no little Pessimism on the score of human conduct and institutions.

Perhaps the most characteristic of all Stoic principles is the doctrine that virtues, as consisting in the mind's complete rationality and unity with itself, are one and not many. We have met with this before in Plato, when he argued that to understand justice you must also understand courage, temperance, and so forth. But the Stoics contended that, since all of these depend upon what we should call an attitude of mind, they are intrinsically identical. To be brave is to be pious and to be temperate is to be brave—because all depend upon being rational. Similarly with vice. The irrational man is as likely to slander as he is to steal. Anything may be expected of him if his attitude is wrong. Consequently, it is the spirit with which an act is performed, rather than the action itself, to which value is attributed. Conduct having terrible consequences for the doer or his friends may yet be noble, if done with good will. Loving one's enemies is virtue, though one reap scorn from it.

The Stoic emphasis is thus entirely on the side of motive and not at all (as with Plato and Aristotle) on results. To act irrationally is to act badly, and, conversely, goodness is rationality—in action. Of course the contemplative life by itself had for them no virtue. And, since one factor and only one is the touchstone of virtue, it follows that any given action is just as good as any other, assuming it is done rationally. The cardinal virtues (which following Plato they name as four) are of equal importance. They differ only in their direction, or application of the same intelligence. Vices (being the absence of rationality) are all equally bad. By this criterion it might appear as though the Stoics divided mankind into "sheep" and "goats," the wise and the foolish. But since they quite generally refused to admit the existence of thoroughly wise men, the effect of the distinction was to make a single class of all mankind, no one person being theoretically better than any other, since all are irrational and hence vicious. One sees in these doctrines the blighting shadows of others, not yet explicit for the Stoic, but of terrible import for later days.

The practical Stoic did not, of course, take this theory seriously. Chrysippus himself wrote of *progress* and moral discipline, advance on the road toward the ideal wise man. Later Stoics made much of the same idea. In effect this resulted in a fine moral Idealism—a striving toward the qualities exemplified by the perfectly rational being. Though no one was actually supposed to attain this perfection, it was not thought to be beyond human power. First certain heroes and later the Founders were thought to have approximated it. So that viciousness was, in practice, thought to be less marked in some people than in others!

The picture of the Ideal Sage as painted by Stoic writers has always commanded a great deal of admiration and enthusiasm. The Wise Man is, of course, independent, above the "slings and arrows of outrageous fortune." He has an inner criterion of value, something in his own soul incomparably beyond the price of any external good, untouched by any external evil. Aristotle had said that a certain amount of wealth, good birth, friends, children, and good name were necessary for a happy life. The Stoics rigorously denied that any of these concerned the good life at all. Its criterion is right reason, good will, obedient attitude toward the will of Zeus, the Father of all mankind. And this is wholly *inward*. For the Stoics—in the earlier day before the conceptions of Roman Law influenced them—conceived of this obedience as wholly without compulsion. It is simply fitting one's self into the divine order wisely. There is no duty in the sense of meeting an obligation or command of superior power. Rather it is the deliberate voluntary choice of what one earnestly desires, independently of rewards and punishments, with no one in Heaven or earth to bring any compulsion to bear. It is the product neither of fear nor of pleasure. As Kant later said (speaking, however, of duty) it is like a jewel which shines by its own light.

What then is the Wise Man's attitude toward what seem to be "natural" pleasures and pains, desires and fears? Is he the Apathetic Man, one who is absolutely unaffected by emotions, wholly "objective" in the light of his "pure" reason? The popular error which answers this question affirmatively is ignorant of the fact that, far from trying to eradicate their emotions, the Stoics cultivated them, in so far as they were harmonious with right reason. The instinctive side of man, e. g., self-preservation, constitutes a "fitting" guide to our conduct in the earlier years before reason asserts its hegemony. And as our minds develop, emotions remain integral parts of this reason, just as does also the will. But that which constitutes the *essence* or center of mind is reason, and only that which is in accord with it is therefore *natural*. Hence the Sage will overcome morbid and vicious emotions which upset his reason, and cultivate sentiments expressive of harmony with himself and with the "Ruler of the universe," namely serenity, joy, contentment, peace.

Now it is exactly pleasure-seeking and avoidance of pains which the Stoics regarded as "perturbations" of our reasons, beclouding it when we try to make intelligent decisions. It is distinctive of *right* reason that it sees things in the light of wide horizons—not a particular moment of time, or any passing pleasure, but rather from the standpoint of one's life as a whole and as related to the rest of men. This is what is meant by "taking things philosophically." The Wise Man will not allow a great value to be subordinated to a petty one. He will find his joy in what outlasts the moment's gratification; he will keep his reason superior to sensuous physical desires, necessary and involuntary though these be. He will fear nothing save what is truly to be feared —namely, to have his reason perturbed. He will desire with all his heart to be true to himself, to be an *integer*, to be harmoniously tuned to the world Reason. The problem then is not so much how to suppress emotions as how to maintain your reason with emotions as its necessary part.

There were, of course, many specific applications of these principles to particular virtues. We can mention but a few of them here. Resignation, "accepting the universe," applies to the trivial as well as to the great events of life. To mourn the loss of fortune is irrational, just as it is to bewail the loss of a friend. Seeing events in the light of causes and effects, or as the will of Zeus, takes away their sting. Even one's own death should be viewed fearlessly, even welcomed when it is clearly reasonable that it is better for one to die. (Consonant with the principle, a number of aged Stoics are said to have passed this judgment on themselves and acted accordingly.) In contradistinction to the Cynics, they respected traditions, holding that conventional morality, though not yet reasonable, is "fitting" as a stage on the road to something better. Hence the Wise Man is a family man and participates in community affairs. He makes the most of the established religion. But he looks forward to the time of universal brotherhood, a single world-state, and a world religion based on the will of God as manifested in rational, which is also natural, justice.

Purity of life, fidelity, magnanimity, tranquillity concerning all that is not within our power, endurance, unselfishness, persistent activity, cleanliness, and of course many other qualities characterize the rational life, which is also the happiest one. So the Wise Man treats his enemies justly—which is never to avenge himself and, so far as he can, to do them good. He is the benignant well-wisher of every man, the friend of the wise between whom alone a deeper friendship can exist. Pity, as softening the fiber of its object, is irrational. Self-discipline in enduring hard things produces firmness of inner texture.

This ideal of the Wise Man will hardly spend its force

while humanity continues to exist. But a man's motive must surely learn to take account of results and be guided by them, as well as by a right attitude. Otherwise the danger of fanaticism presents itself. Rationality will also progressively break down the separate compartments into which Stoics (and others) have been content to leave their chosen doctrines, many of them flagrantly contradictory. Stoic "rationality" is in fact dominantly emotional. Very little scientific evidence or proof figures in their philosophy. Like some other "practical" men, they cared little for consistency and were willing to dissociate their intelligence from their practice. In fact the Greek Spirit is very impure in Stoicism. This is further evidenced by the parentage of the founders, which seems to have been partly Greek and partly Semitic in Zeno, and Phrygian in Cleanthes.

CHAPTER XXIX

EPICURUS

The subordination of theory to practice took another turn in the projects of Epicurus (341–277 B. C.), who, following the lead of the Cyrenaics, founded a school devoted to the study of the blessed life, and the means of attaining it. Its doctrines are not complicated by a succession of teachers as with the Stoics. The Founder was also the final authority, and perhaps more highly esteemed as such than any other philosopher. Even the Roman poet Lucretius (98–55 B. C.) in his remarkable "*De rerum natura*" writes as the mouthpiece of his doctrines. Epicurus was an Athenian citizen, the son of a colonist who had gone out to Samos in the capacity of an elementary school-teacher. At 18 he went to Athens to do his two years' military training. Meantime his poor father had been expelled from Samos and gone to Colophon, whither Epicurus followed. Little is known of his youth, except his friendship for the poet Menander and his own statement about having been self-taught. In his thirty-second year he opened a school at Mitylene, and soon became the friend of several men of wealth and influence, who remained his lifelong patrons and correspondents.

Five years later he transferred his school and numerous followers to Athens, where for thirty years he taught in his Garden to the great delight of his pupils, both men and women, among the most enthusiastic of whom were his own three brothers. He wrote an incredible number of books, despite his lifelong delicate health. "Pain and torture I have had to the full," he wrote to his friend, Idomeneus, on the last day of his life, "but there is set over against these the joy of my heart at the memory of our happy conversations of the past."[1] He was a generous, genial, frugal, and abstemious man, as remote as can be conceived from the "epicure" unjustly associated with his name. Cities actually had his teachings inscribed upon their walls (e. g., Oenoanda) and his native country honored him with a statue. Some of his writings have been recovered from the lava of Herculaneum; but the many fragments we possess are not distinguished for literary quality.

His teaching can be briefly dealt with, since there is little of the nature of a contribution, and his precepts looking toward the pleasant life interest us chiefly as pointing the way to a scientific and philosophical Lethe. "Vain is the discourse of that philosopher by which no human suffering is healed"[2] well illustrates the pragmatic temper of the Founder. "We should never have had any need of studying natural science had it not been for our imaginings about death, the alarms of atmospheric changes, and questions as to how to deal with our pains and desires."[3] And his philosophy does away with these fears and alarms, as well as with the problems of pain and desires. If any other philosophy could do this more effectively it would be preferable. Better to adopt legends concerning the gods than the fixed necessity of cause and effect as advocated by natural philosophers, if thereby one attains "health of body and tranquillity of mind," which is "the sum and purpose of a blessed life."[4] Feeling is the criterion of such a life, since all our choices and aversions depend upon feeling; pleasure is its alpha and omega.

Yet it must not be supposed that Epicurus advocated what would ordinarily be understood as pleasure-seeking. The

[1] Usener: *Epicurea,* Frag. 138, p. 143, 16.
[2] *Ibid.* p. 169, 14.
[3] C. Bailey: *Epicurus,* p. 97, XI.
[4] Usener: *Epicurea,* p. 59 (Trans. R. D. Hicks: *Stoic and Epicurean* p. 167 fol.

thirst for new titillations of sense, ever increasing in quantity, was, on the contrary, regarded by him as an evil. The state of mind in which these unsatisfied demands hang constantly over it is far from one of peace and tranquillity. One must learn rather to curb these desires and with the Cynics reduce one's wants to a minimum. "Give me barley-bread and water and I will vie with Zeus in happiness" well expresses this temper. Like the Buddha, Epicurus would stop these endless cravings at their source. So that "pleasure" has something of negation in it as "the absence of pain in the body and of trouble in the soul"—trouble which the vicious circle of new wants only augments.

The Epicurean way of life was, in fact, more simple and severe than that of the Stoic. At its source at least, it cut off the individual from marriage, from participation in state-affairs, from wealth, from the usual social relationships, from objective scientific investigation, from the performance of religious exercises—because on the whole these disturbed one's tranquillity of mind. Epicurus stressed friendship as a source of blessedness, but only the kind involving less responsibility than advantage. "No one," wrote Epicurus, "loves another except for his own interest."[5] Nor is this intended in the sense of including one's own interest in the wider good of society. A thoroughgoing egoism pervades the doctrine. Friendships are based upon mutual utility. (The reader will here recall Aristotle's class of "economic" friendships!) Marriage is the source of more trouble than tranquillity to the partners. Hence it is better not to marry. Pain is indeed often necessary, even desirable, but only in case the sufferer himself ultimately attains greater happiness. Life in the country as a private citizen, undisturbed by business or state affairs, which are inevitably the source of much vexation, is the ideal. The state is an invention, a social contract to enable men to get on to-

[5] *Epicurea,* p. 324, 16 (Trans. Hicks *l. c.* p. 182.

gether, who could not otherwise do so. Why not do the better thing of avoiding altogether these disturbing contacts, except, as in friendship, they contribute to one's inner peace?

Wealth is likewise a care. The Epicurean will not burden his soul by its anxieties. And having resolved all his fears about death—which concerns neither the living while alive, nor the dead who know nothing of it—he will trouble himself no more about natural science and the vexatious problems of other philosophy. His senses show him that some things happen by necessity, others, by chance, and his personal actions, by his own free choice. Let it be at that! The superstitions before which most men quail in their religious fervor should be calmly dismissed. True religion is whatever ideas and practices contribute to serenity of mind. Let us assume that the gods are mindful of our affairs, if such legends make us happy. Possibly they are better suited to that purpose than the Stoic ideas of a fixed order and necessity.[6] In the matter of death Epicurus wrote: "Learn betimes to die, or, if you like it better, to pass over to the gods." [7]

"If you like it better"—here is the strategic phrase about which this philosophy moves. And the "you" is the individual, in all the variations of his milder feelings and experiences. The logic of such a point of view would seem to be: My soul's tranquillity is the touchstone of truth for me; yours, for you—or whatever else you prefer. This is a reversion to Sophistic rather than a continuation of the scientific tradition, a fact which is further confirmed by the Founder's remarks concerning logic. All perceptions are true and beyond contradiction, said he. Truth is simply agreement with perception. Investigations of inference, syl-

[6] Letter to Monœceus, *Epicurea,* p. 59. (Cf. Bailey's Trans. *Epicurus* p. 83.)

[7] *Ibid.* p. 162, 18. (Hicks' trans. *Stoic and Epicurean* p. 191.

logisms, definitions, and so forth, may all be dispensed with.

What is then to be thought of an Epicurean "Physics," intended as a means of freeing the mind from the fears of superstition? It is, in fact, very much more than that, being a resolute effort to think through the Atomism of Leucippus and Democritus, to a consistent account of physical, as well as of human, nature. As we have just noted, Epicurus was a sensationalist. His criterion of truth was simply: what agrees with our sense-perceptions. For that reason he repudiated mathematics. Its lines, planes, surfaces, points, can nowhere be observed in nature, they lack the sensory basis upon which all true knowledge builds. Yet he adopted atoms, which, by hypothesis, are invisible, inaudible, intangible, odorless, and tasteless. And having committed himself to this faith in reason, he worked out a really remarkable defense of the theory.[8]

There are few deviations from the doctrines of the Atomists. Everything in heaven and earth consists of imperceptible, inelastic, no-further-divisible particles, everlastingly moving, singly and as groups, bounding and rebounding in the infinite void, having manifold shapes and projections by which they get hooked up together into the great variety of objects we perceive. Gases, fluids, solids, all the different states and qualities of matter are ultimately to be referred to the orders, positions, and shapes of infinitely numerous atoms.

To this Epicurus adds, or makes more specific, that the basic original motion of the atoms is *weight*. They all have a tendency to fall downwards. He realizes that "downwards" is ambiguous when taken in a smaller compass. In that case it may be true that "the way up and the way down are one and the same" at different times. But he insists that downward has a very definite meaning when applied to the universe as a whole. In this original motion all atoms fall

[8] Diogenes Laertius: *Lives and Opinions,* Bk. X, 24.

with equal velocities, but the (chance) deviations of some from this perpendicular line produced, and produces, collisions, from which arise reboundings in all directions, and also circular motion, around an axis, by which world systems arise. Our earth and all the visible stars form such a system, which, however, is only one of an infinite number existing in the boundless void.

Epicurus thus modified the absolute Mechanism of Leucippus by introducing deviations from the necessary movements of atoms. In fact, the whole organization of the universe seems to be attributed to these "exceedingly slight" and imperceptible chance changes. For otherwise atoms would have continued their parallel courses during infinite time. Are these spontaneous changes due to the soul atoms commingled with the mass of the world? Epicurus retained these soul atoms, which are spherical, the smoothest and smallest of them all. But he denied that they are a cause of order in external nature. Soul atoms in our minds have free choice and originate motions. But this is due to the peculiar conditions of their being associated with very special collections of atoms. There is mutual interdependence between the soul atoms and the bulkier ones of the body. They permeate the body as a whole, mediating between sensation and thought, will, pleasure, and pain. They are inhaled and exhaled, increased and diminished, and at death broken loose from their organization, leaving no trace of anything mental behind. All psychological facts, from sensations to deliberate choice, are the configurations (*eidola*) or "films" of atoms. But in human beings they are also purposive, spontaneous, free.

One suspects these variations from the strict Mechanism of the Atomists! They seem to be connected with the avowed purpose of saving man from depression by exempting him from the idea of fixed laws, inevitable in every consistent Materialism. In the external world Epicurus rejected the idea of mental causes, Platonic ideas, Aristotelian Forms, God, whether as soul atoms or non-material agency. There he regarded such conceptions as the basis of fear and superstition. But in the mind of man he accepted them and for the self-same reason—his own peace and tranquillity. Thus can a prepossession work in contradictory directions, "if you like it better." But the satisfaction must be small, even to him who conceives of truth as merely a means to his own happiness.

Curiously enough, after denying all activity and significance to mental agencies in the world at large, Epicurus postulated another unseen reality, in addition to the atoms and the void. These are the gods, who exemplify in everlasting blessedness, superior to all the concerns of the world, the ideal life of peace and tranquillity, which it behooves us humans to seek after. They dwell in the voids between the great world-systems, oblivious of all events, unaffected by prayers, entreaties, or praise from any quarter, intent only upon what a good Epicurean should be—his own simple satisfactions and painlessness. Thus did devotion to the practical also make of no avail the theoretical basis upon which religion has generally built.

Many noble sayings concerning the pleasurable aspects of ethical progress have come down to us from Epicurus. These are fine sources of illumination to those who suppose that the life of virtue makes for dullness and misery. The cause of greater human excellence is surely a spring of the highest happiness! Yet few, in their reasons, will subordinate their intelligence to feelings, as measures of good and evil, much less strive to eliminate all feelings other than those characterized by gentle, half apathetic indifference, the tranquillity of painlessness. Surely the richer human life demands more pleasures than Epicurus would allow! The identification of ourselves with family, community, state, disinterested science, philosophy, art, and religion brings with it much of vexation, yearnings that remain a perennial thirst, a discontent, a disturbance of our tranquillity. But poor indeed the individual life or community in which all these are sacrificed to any other objectives.

CHAPTER XXX

HELLENISM

Progress in the arts and philosophy has sometimes been assumed to be the flower of economic power and political éclat. Some modern historians have even attributed the florescence of Athens, after the defeat of the Persians at Thermopylæ and Salamis, to the spoils of these victories and the heightened prestige of the city which followed. Æschylus, Sophocles, Euripides, Phidias, Socrates are said to have been raised to their height by this external glory; the foundations of the Periclean Age were laid in a great expansion of material resources.

Yet the long career of Plato began during the Peloponnesian War. Philip of Macedon was gradually overpowering the Greek allies, working toward Chæronea (338 B. C.), during the lifetime of Aristotle. Indeed the fourth century was a time of deep political humiliation and material subordination for Athens. But it was also the time of Praxiteles, Scopas, Demosthenes, and other names of the first order. Fourth century Athens, despite the lessening of her external power and the decline of her political prestige, was still the undisputed intellectual and artistic center of the world.

In the course of the third century B. C. all this was changed. Not that Athens ever failed to be a town of importance for the human spirit. Even through the terrible vicissitudes of her sieges, tyrants, demagogues, after her subjection to Rome in 146 B. C. and the sack of her chief treasures of beauty by Sulla in 86 B. C., she remained a city of light to those who cherished lost causes. But no such names as these just mentioned came in the third and second centuries. The strong serene splendor of her fifth and fourth century art gradually gives way now to clever technique and sentimental exaggerations; her philosophers have yielded to Skepticism or narrow Empiricisms; her scientists undertake descriptions with little interpretation; her pride is in a vanished age. No doubt the loss of the old civic ideal was in part responsible for this. The ethical conception of the *polis* and every citizen's participation in its life fostered a natural, spontaneous love of excellence. If, on the other hand, material resources and political power as such were really the basis of a great age, the Alexandrian period should have ushered in a florescence of all things Greek eclipsing the earlier centuries.

Alexander's conquests of Persia and India brought immense resources into the hands of those to whom Greek culture was the glory of the world. Cities which surpassed Athens in external magnificence—Antioch, Pergamum, Alexandria in Egypt—were built with the deliberate purpose of expanding the influence and achievements of the tiny homeland and giving them world-wide scope. Lesser Alexandrias arose in Mesopotamia, in Carmania, in Parthia. The Antigonids, Seleucids, and Ptolemies, who succeeded to the world-power of Alexander, were, in general, enthusiastic patrons of Greek culture, and some of them had prodigious economic resources. They founded libraries, attracted men of learning to their courts, and lavished money on their intellectual projects. They founded elaborate "homes of the Muses"—Museums—to enlarge upon the Academy and Lyceum. They spent millions on temples, which surpassed the Parthenon in size and splendor. Botanical and zoological gardens, astronomical laboratories, and medical clinics abounded.

The dominant center in the Hellenistic period was, of

course, Alexandria, founded by Alexander in 332 B.C. and rapidly developed by his successors, the Ptolemies Soter, Philadelphus, and Euergetes (305–221 B.C.) into the most important commercial city of the world. It was laid out on a magnificent scale with "modern improvements," including a lighthouse 400 feet high, a mole something over a mile in length, endless baths, and palatial houses. Grandiose proportion was clearly a passion of the times. Another was an abounding pride in educational institutions. It seems to have been the ambition of the Ptolemies to possess for the Museum library every book extant, to have professors of every conceivable subject, and investigators of any and every thing suitable for research. Alexandria abounded in students of languages, grammars, textual criticism, philology, who aimed to get out definitive editions of the classics and to make available the literatures and knowledge of the most distant lands and peoples. There were anatomists, botanists, geologists, astronomers, engineers, historians in all branches, philologists, students of *materia medica*, mathematicians.

A general conception of these scholarly researches will perhaps be best obtained by more particular mention of a few individuals, some of them from Alexandria, others from lesser centers about the Mediterranean where similar studies were cherished. We have already noted at Athens itself this development toward descriptive, empirical science among the successors of Aristotle at the Lyceum. In the Pythagorian schools the period brought out the heliocentric astronomy of Aristarchus (Samos cir. 310–230 B.C.), also his treatises on the sizes and distances of the sun and moon as determined by geometric means. Timocharus in 283–2 B.C. made observations concerning the position of the star *Spica*, with enough accuracy to enable Hipparchus to discover the precession of the equinoxes by comparing them with his own observations in 129 B. C. Hipparchus also measured the length of the mean lunar month to within a second of our present accepted figure (29.53059 days). He catalogued 850 "fixed" stars, estimated their brightnesses, and tried to give their exact positions (by coördinates), that later times might be able to discover their possible movements. The school at Syracuse could boast an Archimedes (287–212 B.C.) who investigated hydrostatics, and worked out the principles of the lever and the endless screw. He was also famous for his study of optics and astronomy. His devotion to science is illustrated by the heroic manner of his death. When the city of Syracuse was being stormed, a soldier broke into his work-room. Archimedes forbade him to disturb his models; whereupon the soldier struck him down.

Euclid, author of the *Elements,* easily the most famous book on mathematics, so famous that not a few people identify his name with a book rather than a man, lived and wrote other treatises at Alexandria, during the reigns of the earlier Ptolemies. Another characteristic Alexandrian *savant,* contemporary of Euclid, was Herophilus, the anatomist. He made very painstaking researches on the human nervous system, lungs, liver, and organs of reproduction, by *post mortem* dissection. He was particularly interested in the ventricles of the brain, and distinguished cerebrum from cerebellum, as well as motor from sensory nerves. Vivisection of condemned criminals, which is charged against him by some writers, attests not only his own resolute interest in science, but that of the authorities as well. How much experimental and empirical character medicine had in those days is further illustrated by a *materia medica* written by Heraclides of Tarentum, and containing, as he said, nothing that he had not observed himself.

The translation of the Hebrew Scriptures into Greek

(the Septuagint), which was begun in the time of the early Ptolemies, and elaborate textual studies of the older poets and philosophers illustrate another phase of this age of scholarship. The names of quite a few of these professors have come down to us, also some of their original works—Alexander Ætolus, Lycophron, Zenodotus of Ephesus, Apollonius of Rhodes, Callimachus, Eratosthenes, Aristophanes of Byzantium—but we are chiefly indebted to them for their texts of the classics. Eratosthenes, perhaps the most characteristic prose writer of the times, was more interested in history, geography, and mathematics than in literature. He was enough of a scientist, however, to calculate the circumference of the earth (at 28,000 miles), by observing the positions of the sun exactly at noon both in Alexandria and Syene, at the time of the summer solstice. In poetry the most characteristic figure was Theocritus, whose praise of simple country life breathes the desire to escape the learned artificialities of his age. Yet these pastorales and bucolics are themselves full of the most sophisticated, clever, and superficial sentiment. In the other arts the period was characterized by parallel tendencies. The quest for bigness and theatrical efforts is illustrated by the statue called the Colossus of Rhodes (which stood 105 feet high), also by attempts to carve the figures of great leaders on mountain-side or promontory. Exaggeration, display of technique, sheer cleverness are illustrated in such works as the Farnese Bull and the Laocoön. But it must be observed that in sculpture the genius of a better age preserved itself longer than in any other of the arts. The Dying Gaul, the Venus de Milo, and Victory of Samothrace remain sincere, restrained, harmonious expressions of vital intuitions.

To religion, the Alexandrian Age attained considerable indifference. The ancient ceremonies were, to be sure, continued. Their value to the state was recognized by Alexander and his successors. The conqueror himself went on a splendid pilgrimage to the priests of Amon at Siwah, that he might undergo the age-old Egyptian rite of deification. Probably with some modification, for the Pharaohs had, from time immemorial, been thought of as *physically* sons of the god Amon by the successive queens. But, whatever these convenient changes may have been, Alexander became a Son of God, a divine vicegerent on earth; and his successors likewise undertook this office, one which provided both a higher sanction for their decrees, and a symbol of unity for the various races gathered together under their sway. Alexander looked forward to a "marriage of East and West," and whatever could be accomplished in that direction by religious synthesis was welcomed. So we hear of the Ptolemies not only as Amon-Re but also Theos Euergetes, Theos Philopater, and so forth. As "Benefactor," "Saviour" (Soter), the ruler tried to do a political service such as might indeed be prayed for from a god—rescue of the state from oppression, external distress, or destruction. But except for the conventionally faithful, these were apparently external forms.

Of interest in religion, viewed as the expression of individuals vitally concerned with their relation to cosmic power, intelligence, or goodness, these services, gorgeous processions, and rituals, of course, gave little evidence. But they indicated the abundant political power and resources of the priesthood. In this great melting-pot of the faiths most of them became quickly "historic" and their data largely mythological. The cults could be changed like a uniform to suit the occasion, and all had their color to add to the rich display. Alexander had some preference for Amon-Re (probably as the oldest cult), but Isis and Osiris, Zeus and Dionysus, Jahweh, Amenophis, Serapis, and others had their place, and were distinguished mainly by their paraphernalia and mythology. To the common people of the various races, these deities were associated with mysterious occultisms, and sometimes delirious fanaticisms, which led to terrible excesses. But to the Hellenistic intelligentsia, religious interests, like those in the arts, were subordinate to empirical science and practical affairs of the moment. Some, no doubt, sought and found salvation in the mystery-cults of Adonis, Mithras, Dionysus Zagreus. These deities died for the sake of their followers and rose again as revealers of immortality and blessedness. We know that they (especially Mithras) had a numerous following in the centuries preceding the new era. So too the tender Serapis, with whom the worshiper could enter into intimate mystical union. A fundamental tenet of Judaism was that religion must be revealed—which, of course, resisted mere wisdom and knowledge. There were also those who abstractly universalized the faiths and distantly recognized Zeus-Amon-Jahweh-Ahuramazda-Jupiter as the Highest God. But one cannot call the Alexandrian a religious or an artistic era.

Neither can one say that philosophy flourished then. There was plenty of scholarship applied to philosophical texts, but little creative thinking in Aristotle's sense. No doubt the thoroughgoing Skepticism of the Middle Academy had much to do with this. When those who sat in the seat of Plato, and presumably knew most about the teachings of the great masters, themselves proclaimed that only one thing could be truly known: namely, the impossibility of philosophy, it was bound to have some weight. But even Carneades and Arcesilaus were exceeded by the followers of Pyrrho in their thesis that this, too, could not be known. Later on, Alexandria became a center both of philosophical and scientific Skepticism. Not only inference but even true observation is impossible, said Ænesidemus (probably first century B. C.) who set up no less than ten arguments to prove the impossibility of reaching conclusions. No two people can so much as *see* the same thing; how then can they argue about it? Souls are different, eyes are different, distances, colors, sizes, interrelations of all sorts, in short all experiences are relative, nothing is so or so without qualification.

Two centuries later Sextus Empiricus came to similar conclusions, by attempting to show that every inference is reasoning in a circle: you start with what you suppose you have proved. Induction, likewise, was held to be absurd, since it requires the complete enumeration of all possible cases. So too every idea of cause as such: if a "cause" precedes the effect it has not yet become a cause, for the effect must be there if the cause is; if the two are simultaneous there is no reason for calling either of them the cause or the effect; and it is idiotic to assume the effect can precede the cause. Arguments parallel to these were also potent in religious discussion. The idea of Providence is absurd, since Deity either cannot, or will not, oppose evil. And neither alternative is permitted in any concept of Providence. The work of Sextus Empiricus is significantly named "Against the Mathematicians," they who claim to have the most secure of all knowledge, but in fact represent the final refuge of dogmatism and metaphysics. The contradictory nature both of our sensations and ideas destroys not only logic, ethics, and the philosophical sciences in general, but also astronomy, physics, and geometry. Mathematics, for example, is helpless even in trying to justify its fundamental concepts. Thus a line is thought to be extended and yet made up of points which have no extension!

Such Skepticisms were, of course, cognate with other "practical" movements, like Epicureanism and Stoicism, in the matter of recommending neutrality in all such perplexing questions. But a chief reason for the decline of philosophy in Hellenistic times was undoubtedly the fact-gathering specializations, which by their very nature were opposed to generalizations. "Why's" were subordinated to plain "That's." It was sufficient to know that a given measurement or other empirical relationship was "there." The questions, By what laws?, Or reasons? To what purpose? became more and more futile and otiose.

But in one direction an exception must be made. Philosophy could still be used as a very practical agency when its conclusions might be interpreted as support of previously chosen causes, and especially as handmaiden of religion. Among the many "foreign colonies" in cosmopolitan Alexandria, the Hebrews were among the most influential. A characteristic tenet of their faith was the supposition that the Law and the Prophets had been divinely ordained by special revelation. The teachings of these sacred books did, indeed, require interpretation. And in so far as philosophy could provide a means of making them more acceptable, it was cultivated as an admirable propaganda for the faith. This was especially true of the deeply religious character of Plato's fundamental conceptions. But Stoicism and the pre-Socratics, as well as Aristotle, were also called upon for arguments.

From this union of Hebrew theology with Greek philosophy the very characteristic theosophy of Alexandria took its rise. As early as Aristobulus (flourished about 175 B. C.) the attempt was made to synthesize Plato, the Stoics, and Moses, as a means of making more intelligible the nature of God. The method of Aristobulus was to find support for the words of Holy Writ from Greek sources. But the latter in their turn were supposed to have obtained their wisdom from a very ancient translation of the Pentateuch. Greek thinkers were thus, indirectly, the mouthpieces of Deity, as giving expression to Hebrew revelation in a different form. The synthesis had its difficulties; also the historical assumptions. But Aristobulus seems not to have been too sorely tried by such matters. He could use allegory along with divine revelations and retranslate the seven days of creation in terms of Greek evolutionary ideas, always maintaining, none the less, the Hebrew origin of all these conceptions.

But far more remarkable as a synthesizer was Philo (b. about 25 B. C., d. 41 A. D.), an Alexandrian priest of noble family. He retained the fundamental thesis that Greek philosophy (or chosen portions of it) was indirectly, through the Hebrew scriptures, a revelation from God. In this way its wisdom could be regarded as interpretation of the sacred writings, which constituted the final authority. No inconsiderable latitude in the employment of allegory, as well as of one's own ideas, was implied by this. But a pragmatic use of history, as well as of philosophy, had been discovered, which was destined to be of no small influence in the world.

Perhaps the most remarkable of his ideas was the conception of an intermediary between God and man, the Logos, or first-born son of God. Deity, said Philo, is invisible, inaudible, and without body. He is realized, only by our inmost reason, as the most universal of all beings, better than knowledge, better than virtue, above even perfect goodness or absolute beauty. God is eternal, unchangeable, forever the One and the Simple, a Being existing by and for Himself. He is not to be confused with nature, for the world is his creation. The latter, the finite, is, moreover, bound by necessity. God alone is free. He has no contacts whatsoever with matter, which would sully his purity. In his character he is beyond our reasons: we can know only that he is, not what he is. We see his activities indirectly, not his real presence. Every name we might employ to characterize him is inapplicable to his pure (Eleatic) Being, for all our terms imply attributes, which cannot be ascribed to something beyond all attributes.

Hence the necessity of an intermediary, one who dwells with God and yet has attributes comprehensible to us. He is the Logos, or divine wisdom, with whom the (Platonic) Ideas are at home, by whom also the thoughts of God are revealed in the tangible, visible, world. The Logos in turn divides himself into partial, limited agencies of wisdom, immortal souls, demons, angels, who carry out the divine will. Plato's Ideas are thus identified with the thoughts of God, the Logos being the Idea of Ideas, the most universal except for God. Yet, as the Son of God, the Logos came into being in the course of time. He is not co-eternal with Deity. By the Logos too the world was created—a younger "son of God"—almost *ex nihilo*, that is to say, out of matter which before the creation was "devoid of all properties." The first-born Son of God takes the place of Deity for us imperfect humans. He reveals Divinity to us, gives us wisdom and also represents us in the capacity of a Priest and Paraclete before God.

Both knowledge and virtue come to us, therefore, as divine gifts. They are for the greater part beyond the attainment of our unaided reasons. Philo did not want to fall into the dangers of Fatalism here, and so made the lower ranges of the process accessible to man's native intelligence and choice. But we attain true enlightenment only by becoming the "temple of God," a place where higher inspirations may raise us above the weakness and foolishness of our own opinions. When the Logos dwells in us we are virtuous, otherwise not. Only by denying ourselves can we attain to both duty and our highest joy, which is the worship of God. The higher ranges here involve the suppression of conceptual thinking and the loss of one's individual selfhood, the attainment of a purely passive condition similar to the ecstasy, or madness, of Corybantic dancers. Then one becomes aware of laying hold directly on intangible Deity, the true Being who is higher than all thought, all action, all virtue and all beauty. For such a Mysticism, everyday mundane affairs, of course, stand in the way of divine illumination. Not only business and politics, but the natural sciences, logic, history, mathematics, and similar efforts of unaided reason, become of passing moment. They are also dubious and dangerous undertakings.

We do not know what Philo may have thought of his people's Messianic hopes. But it is interesting to note that he nowhere identifies the Logos with any historic or prospective human being. His low opinion of matter and of the "flesh" seems to have restrained him from such speculations.

Two centuries later, another synthetic movement, called Neo-Platonism, originated in Alexandria. Its founder was Ammonius Saccus, and his pupil, Plotinus, its greatest exponent. But since the former left no writings, and the latter wrote and taught in Rome, this last afterglow of Greek thought can best be considered in the next chapter.

CHAPTER XXXI

GREEK IDEAS IN ROME

It goes without saying, that the practical Roman was not one likely to distinguish himself in metaphysics. Ontological speculations, mathematics, astronomy, theories of art, of evolution, or of psychology, physical science and epistemology, were never necessary for his happiness. Government, business, organization, war, law—these were his passion. From the time when the Latins emerge into history (Seventh century B. C.), through the period of their early kings (until 498 B. C.), and the republican era (498–27 B. C.), as well as during the early centuries of the Cæsars, the growth of Roman power, prosperity, and external éclat was almost continuous. But we hear very little of philosophy, literature, science, and art, until comparatively late in that history. And when these interests came at length, they were not spontaneous and indigenous, but the echo of another people's life.

In the year 240 B. C. Livius Andronicus, a Greek slave, somehow succeeded in having a drama which he had translated, accepted on the Roman stage. For once the Saturnæ, or variety-shows, which heretofore had held sway there, yielded to a piece having literary qualities and a regular plot. This is said first to have awakened the Romans to the significance of Greek literature; and although the story is probably exaggerated, it is evidence to show the lateness of their development. In the succeeding decades other writers, Nævius, Plautus, Ennius, Cato, Terence, followed this successful example, either translating *verbatim* or adapting Greek authors to the Roman taste. The latter alternative generally meant changes in the direction of somewhat more practical, moralistic, satirical, or commemorative forms. Of course works on agriculture, medicine, the building trades, etc., abounded; also chronicles and handbooks of law. Somewhat later, in Cæsar, Sallust, Livy, Tacitus, history attained remarkable interest as literature. But even the great poets of the Augustan age, Virgil, Horace, Ovid, were largely dependent upon Greek sources both for their matter, and their inspiration.

Neither were the Latins creators of great religious ideas or ideals, unless we so designate the work of Numa Pompilius. Here again the Olympian gods, and the other Greek conceptions, were destined to play important rôles. This influence was much earlier than the literary one; but it, too, assumed larger proportions, after the Romans, in the Third century B. C., had conquered Tarentum and other colonies in Magna Græcia. It was generally characteristic of Roman policy to respect the religious forms and feelings of the conquered as a means of amalgamating them. Gradually Rome became a pantheon, to which all cults were welcomed, provided they were not subversive to the state. Among them were not a few Oriental forms, of which Judaism and Mithraism were of considerable importance during the late Republic and early Empire. The subordination of Alexandria to Rome in the Second century B. C. hastened this growth. And when the Cæsars came they also adopted the Pharaonic-Alexandrian conception of deification, by which they became not merely vicegerents of Deity, but veritably divine persons. The *pontifex maximus* from an early day had presided over the auspices, and professed to interpret the will of the god, by observing the flight or the entrails of birds. Now, the greatest power of earth, he himself received divine honors—doubtless as a matter of political expediency. Institutions were of vastly more concern to Roman leaders generally, than the items of any inner, personal conviction.

Philosophy was also imported to Rome. We first hear of such interests at the capital when Panætius of Rhodes (180–110 B. C.) and Posidonius from Syria (d. 91 B. C.) came over to teach Stoicism there. They must have been very successful, for the doctrines took strong root in Roman minds. Doubtless this was due to their easy practicality and pragmatic temper, the seeming universality of Stoic Electicism and Cosmopolitanism. A facile Skepticism springs up wherever philosophy takes even superficial root. And one quickly realizes why it, too, found expression in Rome, amid the many occultisms and authoritative faiths, whenever difficulties arose in the reasonings of their devotees. Skepticism based on religious assurance was destined, in fact, to give many deadly blows, during the later Roman empire, to the major projects of human reason. Yet dogmatisms, on the other hand, also professed to continue the philosophic tradition, in the form of authoritative old masters. Neo-Pythagoreanism was, perhaps, the best example of this. Epicureanism found a noble exponent in the poet Lucretius (99–55 B. C.), who gave it, indeed, its classic expression. But in the decadent days of the Empire, Epicureanism drew upon itself an evil name, a reputation which, despite its injustice, has not even yet been overcome. Neo-Platonism, because of its far-reaching later influence, was, perhaps, the most significant historically, of these various movements. In Plotinus it became a bold, sustained effort to create a mystically religious conception of the world. Based as it was on an old-time faith in the power of human reason, it represents a kind of apocalyptic afterglow when the sun of Greek philosophy had been for some time set.

We shall probably gain a better insight into the intellectual backgrounds of the times if we begin with the Neo-Pythagoreans. This school claimed to be the authoritative vehicle of teachings which had been "revealed" to Pythagoras and Archytas. The Roman Præter, P. Nigidius Figulus (d. 45 B. C.), is mentioned by Cicero as the new founder of the order. It claimed, however, to have been continuous with the original movement, when, in the first century B. C., it became prominent in Rome. Very likely the ancient Pythagorean brotherhood had transformed itself, as early as the fourth century B. C., into a religious mystery-cult. Be that as it may, when it reëmerges as a revival movement, it is dominated by the idea of a divine revelation, vouchsafed to these saints of old. Their words became authoritative, even as Moses and the Prophets for the Hebrews. Yet (just as with Aristobulus and Philo) a wider philosophical foundation was sought in those parts of Plato, Aristotle, and the Stoics, which could be made to fit in with their presuppositions. Characteristically enough a considerable literature sprang up in the new florescence of the school—literature which was also attributed to the divine authority of Pythagoras and Archytas.

One notable figure in this movement will serve as example of many others, who by preaching and writing expressed these occult tendencies of the times. This was Apollonius of Tyana, who, in the time of Nero, claimed, and received, honors as a divine person. Apollonius had schooled himself in his youth to the most extreme penances under Euxenus, a Neo-Pythagórean, and thereupon traveled widely east and west, as a preacher of the only true God. If his fellow-traveler and biographer, Damis, could be trusted, we should believe that Apollonius reinforced his teachings by numerous miracles. He taught that God is a spirit, who is to be sought not by rites and external sacrifices, but inwardly by silent prayer and conscientious action. And, to demonstrate the superiority of spirit over matter, he healed the plague, and drove out unclean spirits, by his own word of command. Matter he regarded as unholy and corrupt, the source of man's pollution. Confined in the prison-house of his body, man's spirit can attain its life and freedom only by overcoming the "flesh," by penance, which is the godly life. To suppress one's senses is a chief moral and religious purpose. God, the controlling power of the universe, avoids all contact with matter and makes use of the "demiurge" to mediate between Him and the world. Such lessons Apollonius is said to have reinforced by foretelling earthquakes and raising the dead. His own death, which seems to have been at a great old age (possibly 60 A.D.), his biographer refers to in the following terms: "Here ends the story of Apollonius the Tyanæan, as written by Damis. Concerning the manner of his death *if he did die*, the accounts are various."

Neo-Pythagoreanism had a considerable number of lesser spirits, dæmons, and angels, along with its Monotheism. In addition, it seems to have been on the lookout for man-gods, or perfect men in whom God had revealed himself. Apollonius was one of these. Temples were erected to him and the Romans placed his statue among those of the gods—which they would hardly have done if his following had been an insignificant one. Later on the Number-mysticisms increased. There was fertile soil for this in Rome. From an earlier day the triad, Jupiter, Juno, Minerva, had had peculiar significance in religion. Seven too had some holiness. Numinius, who was clearly familiar with Philo's teaching, came over from Syria in the second century and laid great stress upon three in relation to Deity. First came the Supreme and Suprasensible; then, the Demiurge who gave form to material things; finally, the Universe thus created. The second member is, of course, the mediator between God, as pure spirit, and the world. Platonic Ideas came to the Romans as the thoughts of the divine spirit. When these religious purposes required some philosophical support recourse was also had to selected parts of Aristotle, or the Stoics. But we are indebted to the Neo-Pythagoreans for setting up in Rome that terrible source of human misery: authority in the form of divine revelation.

There was some tendency toward Skepticism, and the consolations of a religious faith, among the Roman Stoics also. But generally speaking, it was subordinate to confidence in the legitimacy of practical, or moral, reason. The Greek Stoics were appealed to for authority, but never in the sense of a divine, inerrant, source of truth. The first to give a Roman expression of Stoicism was the Spaniard, Seneca (b. Cordova 3 B. C., killed 65 A. D. by order of Nero, whose tutor in philosophy he had been). Seneca turned away from this world of corruption, vice, and misery, of which he doubtless saw sufficient, to the consolations of a blessed immortality. "Death is the birthday of eternity," wrote he,[1] "and in its attainment lies man's salvation." The eternal peace of the future life is inspiration to a wise man's devotion. Such faith supervenes upon philosophic disputation to bring its peace and calm. For true philosophy instructs us *how to act, not how to explain;* and faith is its foundation. Perhaps the most characteristic notes in Seneca's many and varied expressions of this practical reason are his commands to love one's enemies, and to act as a unit—like Horace's "*Integer vitæ*"—if one wishes to act in accordance with reason. He also wrote: "It behooves you to live for others, if you would live for yourself." [2]

That Epictetus, the Phrygian slave of one of Nero's body guards (last half of the first century), and Marcus Aurelius (Emperor from 161–180) should both have been influential leaders, is a commentary on Roman Stoicism. The influence of both these men in modern times has also been considerable. For Epictetus, philosophy's sole excuse for being is the improvement of humanity. Theory is not, indeed, scorned. It simply becomes uninteresting and otiose.

[1] *Epistle* 102, 25.
[2] *Ibid.* 48, 2 fol.

The Cynicism of the older Stoics, which had expressed itself in their doctrine of independence, is developed by Epictetus into a touchstone of morality. For the first consideration of human life is knowledge of what *is* and what is *not* within our power. To be able to rise superior to the latter is criterion of excellence. We attain this superiority by self-denial and endurance, by finding the good of life in our own wills. This is to find the god in our breasts, the portion of Deity within, which the older Stoics called *logos spermatikos.* All humans are brothers, as sons of God; to do good unto others is the noblest pursuit of man. Love, patience, and gentleness are both its seeds and its fruits.

Marcus Aurelius was, in spirit, kindred with Epictetus. His was the same emphasis upon the practical, which included, however, frequent meditative communion with one's "dæmon," or reason, the divine soul in ourselves. In striking contrast with Seneca, he conceived the world in very optimistic terms. The gods arrange all things for the best, according to their foreknowledge and wisdom. It behooves us, therefore, to fear them, and to do their will with respect to our neighbors—which is to love and cherish all, including even our enemies, ingrates, and the vicious. Combined with this is the characteristic (Cynic) doctrine of keeping free from external entanglements, at least in mind, and endeavoring to fill our place in the scheme of things, as in obedience to the will of a loving father.

Roman Stoicism thus shows itself as a purely ethical movement. Even the subordinate position which Zeno and Cleanthes had given to natural science, mathematics, logic, and the rest, is, by the Romans, reduced to nothingness. Philosophy has become the means of helping us act a noble part. Yet as such it found noble exponents both in the slave and the emperor. After Marcus Aurelius, Stoicism seems to have lost its identity in other movements.

Roman Epicureanism never attained any very fervid religious character. Nor did it lose itself in skeptical doubts. Confidence in a dependable universe seems to have been its characteristic attitude. The gods continue their life in the pure ether of the cosmic vacuum,

> Where never creeps a cloud nor moves a wind . . .
> Nor sound of human sorrow mounts to mar
> Their sacred everlasting calm.

But meanwhile the great play of atoms goes its course. For Lucretius, prayers, sacrifices, prophecies are quite foreign to religion. So too the ascription of meteors, clouds, winds, hail, the "rapid mumblings and loud threatful thunder-claps" to divine agency. Only such joyous reverence as the human mind, quite free from fears of hell and hopes of immortality, could disinterestedly and spontaneously offer to ideals of excellence, seemed to him worthy either of gods or of men. Thus, although Epicureans early and late maintained their search for "peace and tranquillity of mind," their appeal to reason and nature did more than any other movement, in late Hellenistic times and the early centuries of our era, to keep the scientific spirit from disappearing utterly.

Lucretius was probably the most potent individual force making for sanity, in these times of mystifying miracles and paralyzing superstitions. His poem "*On the Nature of Things*," by its incisive thought, its keen analysis of traditional fears of imagination, its clear-cut descriptions of natural phenomena in terms of atomic movements, descriptions which often rise to magnificent artistry, must have been a strong and positive factor in a world of intellectual negations. In point of theory there was little advance upon Epicurus. Perhaps the most significant modification was the conception of slight, chance variations, in the fall of atoms. These irregularities gave Lucretius a means of explaining the peculiar prerogatives of soul atoms in "wresting from the fates the power by which we go forward whither the will leads each one of us; by which likewise we change the directions of our motions neither at a fixed time nor fixed places, but when and where the mind itself has prompted." Will is thus made the spontaneous originator of some bodily motions, though in general these are coördinated with atomic motions (II, 251–260).[3] Something of this same "innate power" is characteristic, indeed, of the mind as a whole—just as it is of seeds. But ultimately all are at bottom thought of as atomic mechanism.[4]

Whatever one may think of the atomic theory, of Lucretius' rejection of evolution,[5] or of design [6] and Providence,[7] his work will be recognized as a noble effort to maintain the naturalistic scientific tradition. He persistently argued for the uniformity and regularity of nature, even challenging Time as a world-factor, and appealing for experimentation.[8] It seems a little incongruous that this should, confessedly, have been linked up with the primary motive of gaining mental peace and tranquillity. But it cannot be gainsaid that Roman Epicureanism contributed much toward such health and sanity as could prevail against intellectual hopelessness and obscurantism. How long the school maintained itself in Roman days cannot now be made out with any certainty. The ignorance of those unknown persons who linked the luxurious living and licentiousness of the decadent empire with the restrained simplicity, and even severity, of an Epicurus and a Lucretius, should at length be corrected. It has done grave injustice to these men. If the former manner of life had been Epicureanism, one would have to find another name for Epicurus.

Neo-Platonism was brought to Rome by Plotinus 205–269 A. D.), who after long studies in Alexandria with Am-

[3] *De rerum natura,* II, 251–260.
[4] *Ibid.* II, 284–293.
[5] I, 763.
[6] I, 1021.
[7] II, 174.
[8] I, 174.

monius Saccus, and wide travels in the east, came thither, in his fortieth year, to start a school of philosophy. He was clearly a man of personal impressiveness, as well as of learning, for he soon found favor in royal circles, and had the Emperor Gallienus among his pupils. The latter for a time considered the possibility of having Plotinus found a philosophic colony in Campania to be called Platonopolis and modeled after the *Republic*. This scheme ultimately fell through. But the philosopher seems to have found consolation in literary undertakings. Six *Enneads*, which his pupil, Porphyry, edited posthumously, have come down to us. These give expression to a deeply religious purpose. But their author conceives religion neither in the widely current terms of a skeptic's refuge and renunciation of the world, nor of authority, miracles, and special revelation. Rather it is the realization and appreciation of ultimate reality, the rediscovery and return to the fountain and source of all the world's life and being.

Plotinus aimed to justify the philosophy of Plato to his age. But he was himself a man of marked analytical penetration, and acquainted with the Greek schools as a whole, including, of course, the later developments in Alexandria. As a consequence, he expands the conceptions of Plato into a philosophy of his own which has no little originality. It is dominantly metaphysical, in the special sense of endeavoring to interpret the background of our experience as related to certain concepts, which he deems to be of primary importance. These are, indeed, mostly Plato's. But he also derives inspiration from Aristotle, Zeno, and even Philo. If we call his school Spiritualism it must be with a careful use of that term. If we characterize it as Mysticism, again there must be reservations; for Plotinus was very much more than a mystic.

The problem of the one and the many, which had aroused so much thought in Parmenides and Plato, was a crucial one for Plotinus. Both unity and multiplicity seem real, and at the same time are contradictory. How do the many qualities and properties of things hold together in all their variety? They come and go according to circumstances, a continuous flux, as Heraclitus observed. Yet we also assume a genuinely stable, unchanging reality which remains what it always was. We are also constrained to think of it as *one*, underlying all the manifestations of things. Must not thought and its object, widely different though they seem, have something in common? In fact, are not all events, whether in the mind or outside, all bodies, qualities, motions, whatsoever seems to be "there," revelations, manifestations, of a single, that is, unified, reality? On the other hand, it does not seem to be possible to point to any particular property, color, thought, extension, or anything imaginable, as the underlying foundation of that unity—something which everything shares in common. No wonder it appears to be unknowable, an X devoid of any known properties, something defying both our senses and our thought!

Yet Plotinus, following the lead of the mathematicians, endeavors to discover what negative conclusions can be drawn concerning this X in terms of what is assumed to be known. He can think of no better word than the *One*, to designate that which is opposed to multiplicity, and which yet, somehow, binds all things together. He concludes (since nothing comes from nothing) that this multiplicity must have been contained in the One, and never derived from it. Again, the One is simple as transcending all distinctions—such as extended or non-extended, heavy and light, subject and object—none of which are characteristic or essential to it, and all of which can be thought of only as derivatives or manifestations of the primeval One. Hence we must assume that a process of division, of emanation like that of light from the sun, is continually taking place. By it, nature as we know it, is becoming indefinitely diversified, and its potentialities developed. Only we must not suppose (as some evolutionists do) that this process represents an ascent in the scale of being. It is, on the contrary, a degradation for what is pure, simple, and self-contained, to manifest itself in these variegated, impure, and changing forms. The farther anything is from its source the lower it stands in the scale of being. The question: Why does the primeval One send forth these many emanations—the various individual humans, flowers, and stars?—has no satisfactory answer in Plotinus. It remains an ultimate datum, or miracle. But he agrees with Plato that the One is somehow (even for him, of course, indefinably) good.

He could not answer this question in terms of an ultimate world-reason, because he conceived all forms of reason to be derivative, as dependent upon the distinction which we call subject and object, and which he called thinking and what *is* thought. Even the cosmic Reason, the first emanation of the One, represents a duality; it depends upon objects. Hence the original One, or ultimate reality, is superior to reason itself, though the world Intelligence is close to its great Source. It is made up of Ideas which together constitute a world Intellect, from whom all the lesser manifestations are derived. Descent in the scale brings further limitations. For example, human minds, or souls, even though they are all emanations ultimately of the cosmic *Nous* (Intelligence), are so far removed from their source, that, unlike the Intellect, which finds in itself, as its very substance, world-fashioning Ideas, souls have to ascend and search for them by reflection, as well as content themselves with inadequate notions. Lower still in the scale are sensations, which taper off again into ever duller and less intelligent manifestations of life. So that psychic life finds itself midway between Ideas and sensations, easily tempted to descend toward the latter, but occasionally rising to the former.

The material, tangible world is also an emanation from the ultimate One, produced by its overwhelming power as light flows out from the sun. This does not mean creation out of nothingness. Potentially, matter has always been of the All, the infinite One, but without its present specific qualities, such as extension, solidity, being an object, having color, and the rest. Only when Ideas, Forms, came from the great Source, and a world Intelligence manifested itself, did matter become differentiated, the great stage upon which the glorious play of Intellect could be reflected. It provided, and provides, the objects upon which all intelligence depends. But originally—very much like the One itself—matter was devoid of any qualities we know. You cannot say it was this, or that. You have no terms in which to describe it.

Plotinus finds an analogy for this in the way our individual lives give form to physical bodies. A particular life (which also acts as a unity, though always part of the larger whole) organizes what before was inchoate, relatively non-existent as vague and indistinct. But we must be careful to say relatively so or so. For all the examples of matter with which we are acquainted bear some trace of the divine Ideas. Forms, as Aristotle saw, are involved in all the fluctuations of matter, and represent what seems more real. But we must not assume that, because of this vagueness, matter is nothingness. It is reflected, through all the levels of being, right up to the cosmic Intelligence. In ourselves not only sensations, but the highest ranges of our intellects, are bound up with matter in some form or other. It appears in all our conceptions. Indeed if we were entirely free from it we should have attained the unity of the absolute One in which there are no distinctions—and no thought. So that instead of reducing the material world to a creation or emanation of a "spiritual" something, Plotinus really makes it coordinate with all other emanations of the One. In point of value it is, of course, subordinate, as representing a less organized, less intelligent, less good, and less beautiful, development in the course of things.

These interpretations give us the key to his ethical and religious conceptions, which are, of course, the ultimate object of his thought. To turn away from the lower, material, ugly, stupid, manifestations of nature, back to the pure, unmixed serenity of the divine Source—this is wisdom and religion. But our souls, being intermediate between intellect and body, are dragged down by the allurements of sense on the one hand, and invited to visions of glorious thought on the other. The power is physical necessity; yet, as souls, we have freedom of choice, because we participate in intelligence and can direct our course back home. Many have attained something of the exquisite happiness, even that of the World-Soul itself, by obeying divine reason, forgetting their petty selves, and overcoming the limitations of their separateness. This is, above all, training in the direction of (Neo-Platonic) philosophy. The quest for beauty conducts one thither by making one seek for Ideas in the sensible world. Love also; for the lover seeks them in the soul of the beloved. But the philosopher seeks Ideas in their pure, disembodied form, and in this way rises above both beauty and love to the delights of meditation.

Our present condition is thus a fall from an earlier, more blessed, state, when we were not conscious of ourselves, not bound up with the physical sources of our degradation. This fall was a wholly natural fact, that is, determined by our own natures. But our incarnation is not to be considered as unmitigated evil. Plotinus was indeed ashamed of his body, and tried to forget the day of his birth. But he also held that certain advantages were derived from our descent into the flesh. For we can transform these bodies and discipline our souls to ascend heavenwards as quickly as possible. The contacts help us to recognize evil and to discover latent powers. When we succeed in the highest degree, we attain once more the blessedness of peace and changelessness. Memory and anticipation have both been dissipated; so too all hopes and regrets, for the perfect life admits neither fear of what is worse, nor expectation of what is better. In that life, freed from the limitations of matter as we know it, freed also from awkward self-consciousness, eternally beyond all wants, cravings, pains and passions, in ecstasy one with God and realizing His Ideas, we shall have lost our petty individualities and be merged with the Absolute.

Earlier in this chapter, Plotinus was spoken of as an apocalyptic afterglow of classical Greek philosophy. The figure might be misleading in two directions: if it minimized the originality of the last great "pagan" philosopher, or if it assumed a comprehensiveness as great as that of Plato or Aristotle. Plotinus, by his faith in intelligence, his optimism, his love of order, form and beauty, his devotion to theory for theory's sake, his subordination of economic and other practical interests to those of the mind's inner life, was essentially a Greek of the great age. But he lived in a time when religious interests, varying all the way from superstitious occultisms, miraculous revelations, and suicidal asceticisms, to Stoic serenity and "confidence in the universe," were the chief consolations of a moribund world. And his own thought became dominantly religious, not by skeptical limitation of itself, but as the outcome of his new interpretation of Plato. He found all nature rational and purposive, in varying degrees, according to the distance from its Source. So that for all his deprecation of evil or ugliness, and its embodiment in irrational things, he remained an optimist. There is always the possibility of a return homewards. Even the lowest expression, or emanation, of the world-process bears the marks of the divine, and can be transformed into something better. Nowhere did Plotinus deem it necessary to prostitute intellect to practical advantage.

He did, however, maintain that a time arrives when, after utilizing all our resources, we may take a step beyond reason. This is, of course, the mystic's ecstasy, the stage when the distinctions upon which reason depends have been superseded. That of thought and its object is now transcended, just as sensation is superseded by thought. The separation of the individual as a piecemeal portion of a larger whole is broken down, and he realizes, feels, has contacts, with the life of the great Source. All these expressions are, at best, symbolic, since language is itself the tool of reason. The experience can be compared to that of finding the sovereign, and forthwith forgetting the palace. It is inspiration, motionlessness, harmony, a choral dance, a rising to the perfectly good, a finding of the center in one's self and in existence, an ascent from *Nous* to the One. Particularly striking in this mystic exaltation of Plotinus (which he professed to have experienced only four times in his life) is his argument that it does not imply other-worldliness, in the sense of alienating one from the beauty and goodness of our natural life. The whole experience, indeed, is quite natural, only more rare and on a higher plane. One does not find in the *Enneads* that condemnation of the world and all that it contains, which, already in that time, was playing so destructive a rôle. And Plotinus expressly puts all on their guard against miraculously ordained codes of morals, or merely "looking to God," as though the rest could be taken for granted. Discipline, knowledge, making use of whatever resources are at hand, in short, finding the divine through nature, is the true way of religion. By our natural enlightenment and virtue God is revealed to us. Without it he remains an empty name.

Neo-Platonism maintained a rallying ground for intellectuals in Rome, in Alexandria, and in Syria (whither certain pupils of Plotinus went), until Justinian in 529 closed all the schools of "heathen" philosophy. By that time, Greek science, literature, and art had already become obscure memories. Henceforward "the wisdom of this world" was doomed to be "made of no avail" for many succeeding centuries.

CHAPTER XXXII

EPILOGUE

The drama of "Lost Causes" continued even after the closing of the schools, the burning of many books including the whole Alexandrian library, and much punishment of heathen heretics. It continues its course to-day with ever-increasing interest and significance. But its sequel in the Middle Ages and later times is not to be a part of this book. We have come to the end of a trilogy. If, in retrospect now, we contemplate the action from Thales to Plotinus, imagining ourselves writers of drama for an hour, we shall easily recognize our three chief movements, three contrasting "acts." Each of these implicates the others, yet (to one who surveys them as a whole) they lack the unity which would make a tragedy of them. Our closing scenes have much too much pathos of helplessness for that. And our leading actors early and late do not seem to appreciate many inherently dramatic conflicts among themselves, or in the sequels of their own plots and projects. But in our imagination the poignancy of the piece will perhaps be heightened by this.

How confident was the movement of the first act, which came to its surprising climax in vortices of invisible atoms! What bold, youthful security seemed to live in the early Ionian plot, which did not hesitate to include itself, the plot, together with every other device, aspiration, thought, and feeling, among the configurations and motions of these particles! Here was no faintness of heart, no search for comforters! Here indeed was tragic magnificence. All unaware of what the wooden horse of their building might yield in the citadel of their inner life, these heroes of science manfully toiled that the mechanism might be ceaselessly improved. And how nearly perfect was the structure! It challenges the admiration of the most ardent devotee of mechanical science.

Yet in the climax of this movement, in his world of robots all determined by cogs of the infinite machine, Democritus smiled as though unmindful of them. He planned his life as in accordance with the wishes of some god, superior to all this paraphernalia, himself being that god. He gave kindly, gentle advice, replete with tenderness, to the robots. Was this grimly sardonic? A joke on the irretrievable necessity of the dancing atoms and *eidola?* Exquisite new applications of ancient Pythagorean number-fancies might indeed be imagined here: circles as inspiration to love, the fear of death as shadows of icosahedrons. . . . Or did something new develop somewhere between Plenum and Vacuum, something not determined by angles of incidence, sizes of particles, configurations and motions? Such a negation of his science Democritus at no point admitted, so far as the record goes, himself thus expressing once for all the inevitable purpose of mechanical science—which is to find no purpose.

The second "act," the Quest for Purpose, was no less vigorous or dramatic. The pragmatic Sophists began it by calling upon the universe to obey the measures of their minds, a behest ludicrous enough to a consistent scientist, yet no less arresting than his own machines, and assuredly not pathetic. It was indeed disconcerting to hear Gorgias throw doubt on all these "measures," even to the very last syllable. But his, and other Skepticisms then, were only like questions from a chorus giving zest to the primary actors of the piece. Socrates, in gymnasium and market-place justifying the ways of God to man, linking human hopes and irrepressible desires with the pulse of cosmic life, discovering meaning even in his own death, was at no time a pathetic figure. Plato, with the fervor and balance of a Sophocles, construed the "long and difficult language of fact" into a cosmic vision of Mind itself—no apologetic stranger in the familiar scene, but the confident source of rationality, the basis of science as criterion of reality. Aristotle, the Indefatigable, applying his master's intuition to ten thousand examples of common things, rejoiced, so far as his calm, judicial temper could, in the same cosmic love and thought—facts even more invisible than atoms, no less remote from what appears to be, prodigious for imagination.

But the search and discovery of the cosmic Ideas was also replete with tragedy. Socrates' providential arrangements, which forever and forever govern the course of events, Plato's hierarchy, with Good as its all-determining Idea even more fundamental than Being itself, Aristotle's immanent purposes, inherent in every situation, howsoever mechanical or humanly planned it might appear, all alike seemed to involve themselves in the Wheel of Necessity. It mattered not whether God, or Ideas, or events themselves, were described as purposive. Such knowledge of a definitely ordered cosmos once again resolved the "best-laid plans of mice and men" into parts of the general scheme. How could they be at variance with it?

Now a dramatist might conceive of a third act in which a conflict of mechanist and teleologist goes on to a bitter end, when both meet their doom, Prometheus-like, defying Fate. But philosophy after all is not tragedy. It had a beginning, but has no middle, and will have no conclusion. The actors never die, and the piece goes on as though in eternal recurrence, without dénouement. Yet what we called the Search for Practical Wisdom characterizes a third period, which is also of no small dramatic interest.

Greek thinkers concerned themselves, as we know, with the problem of the one and the many, which, on the side of individual choice, also reaches to the foundations of human life. But, except at Megara, they seem to have avoided the implications of a fixed Determinism. Plato and Aristotle, quite like Democritus, worked out plans of human living based on the assumption of real alternatives, choices that are not foredoomed. This was fortunate. For their ethics, at once natural and exalted, progressive and definite, personal and social, flexible and exacting, broad-minded and high-minded, positive and unbigoted, bid fair eventually to overcome our present paralyzing negations. But the great alternative, as between the cosmic machine and the cosmic mind, was left for future generations. And hence too the problem of how to link up our knowledge of the way of life with a ground in reality.

But even the quest for a practical wisdom (fitted to help men find their way home through the streets), continued to intrigue intelligence into more fundamental problems. The third act gives us Stoicism, that most dignified of Pragmatisms, with its cosmopolitan outlook in business, politics and religion, its noble conception of everyday life, its seeds of the Logos. For all their increasing practicality, from Zeno to Marcus Aurelius, these men, albeit indirectly (and sometimes ineptly), aided and abetted the great Interpreter. Epicureanism, too, was no mean help to the cause of creative intelligence even in its search for peace and tranquillity. Nor are the little fellows called Empirics, patiently gathering minutiæ as a miser gathers his pennies, to be disesteemed among these later *dramatis personæ.* How many a better insight depended upon their obscure toil! How many an error, overlooked by the great masters, was corrected by their concentration upon a narrow field! They should have odes rather than elegies, in this our imaginary play, even though their miserly love of facts often blinded them to the only value of their treasure, which is after all in use. Philo and his group should have no praise for their falsification of history in the interest of the Chosen People's religion. This kind of Pragmatism only confounds the work of reason, and leads to such sentimental maundering on the stage as sickens every honest beholder. But let Philo be praised for his intuition that in the second act lay the cues for a conscientious religion based on intelligence and integrity—despite his genuflections before a jealous idol. And to Plotinus let a greater meed of honor be given! For he, in a time of deepening obscurity, paralyzing anarchy, and blind dictatorships, kept alive the faith in mind and nature, in cosmic justice and rationality. He knew little of physics, mathematics, astronomy. His thought concerned itself chiefly with the rational basis of natural, or universal, religion. His terms are difficult of application to our concrete world of variegated things. But whatever we may think of his emanations and degradations, or his conception of a return to a universal Source, we see in him a heroic figure, a defender of intellect, ready indeed for what may lie beyond intellect, but steadfastly holding to mental integrity in his search for a unifying cosmic Idea.

The chorus, however, and the great majority of actors in the long twilight of Greek philosophy, speak of the impending night as though it had no to-morrow. "Behold, we know not anything," is the burden of Ænesidemus. "Let us proclaim this knowledge to the whole earth," answers Sextus Empiricus. "All is relative, nothing is so or so, except as we make it so," his pupils, Saturninus and others, intone from the farthest recesses of the stage. A group from the older chorus solemnly chants the *Ipse Dixit* of Pythagoras and Archytas, declaring this revelation to be the authoritative word of God. "Follow Mithra and be saved" we hear from among the many promises of physical resurrection, combined with prophecies of destruction to the world by a consuming fire. The dominant choral antiphonal declares that Reason's work has been confounded. Only Faith can see the miracles now being enacted before the eyes of all. Only Faith can believe them even after they have been seen. Mysterious forms appear upon the stage bringing revealments of the upper and the nether worlds. Curiosity yields to fear. Mystification drives metaphysics with all her arrogant claims into the cell of a monk. "Let us pray," resounds from various groups.

This was not the confident prayer of Socrates, not Plato's reverent quest for excellence—as human enlightenment and science may reveal its divine reasonableness. It repudiated the faith of Aristotle in axioms coördinating daily experience and intellect, or expanding them in terms of creative imagination and coherent intuition. It explicitly rejected human sources of insight, save as these might be construed in support for whatever oracles or accepted divine pronouncements could be made effective to human credulity —and then erected into fear-inspiring institutions and authorities. In short the Epilogue brings us back to the Prologue among the gods.

This was, of course, no sudden turn in the action. Nor was God ever absent from the thought of Greek philosophers. But all the way from Thales to Plotinus no Deity asserted himself as dictator by possession of physical power, as authority to decide what men should think, as determiner of justice by the arbitrary fiat of his will. Such terms were remote from that free and unrestricted knowledge, that spontaneous endeavor toward natural, or intrinsic, virtue (and sometimes mystical meditation), which characterized their tentative, honest efforts in this direction. Nor must it be supposed that this motive wholly disappeared, even through the age-long quiescence of the Greek spirit that followed. And yet, by the time the various theosophies, systems of magic, and miraculous authorities had yielded priority to Christianity as official state-religion in 325 A. D., not only mathematical, astronomical, biological theories, and scientific undertakings in general, and independent philosophy, but all efforts at a realistic or mundane evaluation of human character, institutions, and conduct, were quite thoroughly discredited.

The fourth act (had we included it) would have required an unearthly light, a kind of *aurora borealis* in which the outlines of the stage itself and all the spectators should merge into the "insubstantial pageant" of a resurrected world. Greek actors have become slaves and stage-hands. The burden is salvation, salvation from this world of "natural depravity," "at enmity with God," and "under a curse," a world given over to the devil and his agents. No one of the "elect" is at home in it, or concerns himself much with its affairs. Its wisdom is confounded "out of the mouths of babes and sucklings," its art is the "lust of the eyes," its education an estrangement from God. Here indeed was a challenge to heroic action if one's neighbors were to find a way of escape! Perfect bliss or endless torment—what an alternative as the outcome! Yet many and diverse are the doctrines which proclaim the way of salvation. And few commend that of worldly learning, or "vain philosophy" and science. Virtues cherished by the natural man present no hope whatsoever, nor do any goods of our merely mundane life. From the Pauline chorus comes a note of tragedy unapproached in its sublime inevitableness. The "elect" are said to have been chosen irrevocably by divine sovereignty "from before the foundations of the world." Others telling more intimately of the dazzling New Jerusalem proclaim as final revelation: "Whosoever will, let him take of the water of life freely."

The fifth act would be one of heart breaking disillusionment with the newly arising sun. The distant glories of the life to come, like waning stars, give way to the "light of common day." The old landmarks are no longer recognized. A new reality-sense questions the visions of the night and the very authority of the old torch-bearers. The story of the divine plan—all the world a stage whereon the redemption of man is played from generation to generation—is itself brought into question. So too miracles, the creation, the fall, the flood, the shepherds, the star, the resurrection—all the sublime and tender tales that had heartened the "pilgrims of the night." Man the center of the universe, albeit in sad depravity with which the whole creation groaneth and travaileth together in sympathy, the utter helplessness and hopelessness of those who had not heard the story of redemption, the jealous love of a Father for his chosen few—these and many more of the "sweetest tales that e'er were told" are examined as the growing child reconsiders the accounts of Santa Claus.

Yet these losses—beginning with the Renaissance and still continuing to-day—are not without their recompense. A new faith takes the place of a somewhat forlorn acquiescence in the futility of one's unaided vision, or the falsity of one's ideas and virtues unillumined by divine authority. A venturesome, sometimes audacious, even impious, spirit of discovery challenges these very sources of authority. The curious studies of Copernicus rediscover the pagan astronomer. The flat earth is circumnavigated, and removed from its once proud position. History is traced to a period anticipating the creation of the world. Observations of rocks, plants, men, lead to convictions that nature is no longer the embodiment of evil and corruption, the peculiar domain of Satan, but a manifestation of reason and order. The claim is made that here and now, amid the new glories of a colorful and bejeweled earth, is man's local sign and habitation. Artists find pigments and marble; writers delight in human nature, with all its quaint, and not always wicked, variety; even preachers recall how the Galilean had said: "The kingdom of God is within you." Once more we see healthy human bodies rejoicing in all their functions, embracing ideas of natural excellence, beauty by harmony, happiness too in mundane success. The worldly interests of stable and just governments, unqualified science, and especially the quest for reality interpreted without privileged assumptions—in all these the Greek Ideas are playing important rôles. Nor does the play seem likely to end a tragedy, howsoever far the stars of faith may again tempt man's imagination.

A SELECTED BIBLIOGRAPHY

FOR GENERAL REFERENCE:

Joh. Ed. Erdmann: *History of Philosophy*, Vol. I. Trans. W. S. Hough, 1899.

Wilh. Windelband: *History of Ancient Philosophy*, Trans. H. E. Cushman, 1901.

Uberweg-Heinze: *History of Philosophy*, Vol.I. Trans. G. S. Morris, 1903.

Theodor Gomperz: *Greek Thinkers. A History of Ancient Philosophy*, 4 Vols., 1901–12. Vol. I, Trans. Laurie Magnus; II–IV, G. E. Berry.

Robert Adamson: *The Development of Greek Philosophy*, 1908.

Alfred W. Benn: *The Greek Philosophers*, 2 Vols., 1882.

G. Lowes Dickinson: *Greek View of Life*, 1906.

James Adam: *The Religious Teachers of Greece*, 1908.

F. A. Lange: *History of Materialism*, 1877, Trans. E. C. Thomas.

T. L. Heath: *A History of Greek Mathematics*, 1921.

J. I. Beare: *Greek Theories of Elementary Cognition*, 1906.

A. E. S. Chaignet: *Histoire de la Psychologie des Grecs*, 5 Vols., 1893.

Max Wundt: *Geschichte der griechischen Ethik*, 1908.

Leon Robin: *Greek Thought and the Origin of the Scientific Spirit*. 1928.

PRE-SOCRATICS:

Eduard Zeller: *Pre-Socratic Philosophy*, 2 Vols. Trans. S. F. Alleyne, 1881.

Hermann Diels: *Fragmente der Vorsokratiker*, 1923.

John Burnet: *Early Greek Philosophy*, 1920.
Greek Philosophy. Part I. Thales to Plato, 1924.

A. Fairbanks: *The First Philosophers of Greece*, 1898.

Charles M. Bakewell: *Source Book in Ancient Philosophy*, 1907.

Robert Scoon: *Greek Philosophy before Plato*, 1928.

B. A. G. Fuller: *History of Greek Philosophy. Thales to Democritus*, 1923.

Jos. Neuhäuser: *Anaximander Milesius*, 1883.

G. T. W. Patrick: *The Fragments of the Work of Heraclitus of Ephesus*, 1889.

Ferdinand Lassalle: *Die Philosophie Herakleitos des Dunkeln von Ephesus*, 2 Vols., 1858.

A. Ed. Chaignet: *Pythagore et la Philosophie Pythagorienne, contenant les Fragments de Philolaus et d'Archytas*, 2 Vols., 1873.

Aristotle (?): *De Xenophane, Zenone, Gorgias.* Published in the English Translation of Aristotle's Works. Ed. by W. D. Ross, 1908.

Th. Davidson: *The Fragments of Parmenides*, in *Journal of Speculative Philosophy*, Jan., 1870.

John Burnet: Article "*Pythagoras*" in *Hastings' Encyclopædia of Religion and Ethics*, 1908–1921.

W. E. Leonard: *The Fragments of Empedocles Translated into English Verse*, 1908.

E. Dentler: *Die Grundprincipien der Philosophie des Anaxagoras*, 1897.

H. C. Liepmann: *Die Mechanik der Leucipp-Democritischen Atome*, 1885.

A. Dyroff: *Demokritstudien*, 1899.

SOPHISTS:

George Grote: *History of Greece*, Vol. VIII, pp. 474–544.

H. Jackson: Article "*Sophists*" in *Encyclopædia Britannica*, 9th Ed.

F. C. S. Schiller: *Studies in Humanism*, Chapters II, XIV, 1907.

SOCRATES AND HIS FOLLOWERS:

Ed. Zeller: *Socrates and the Socratic Schools*, Trans. O. J. Reichel, 1885.

Xenophon: *Memorabilia*, Trans. H. G. Dakyns, 1897.

A. E. Taylor: *Varia Socratica*, 1911.

J. T. Forbes: *Socrates*, 1905.

M. M. Dawson: *Ethics of Socrates*, 1924.

George Grote: *Plato and the Other Companions of* Socrates, 4 Vols., 1888.

K. Joël: *Der echte und der xenophontische Socrates*, 2 Vols., 1901. (Especially for Cynicism.)

PLATO:

Ed. Zeller: *Plato and the Older Academy*, Trans. S. F. Alleyne and A. Goodwin, 1888.

The Dialogues of Plato, Trans. Benj. Jowett.

A. E. Taylor: *Platonism*, 1924.
Plato, the Man and his Work, 1926.

J. A. Stewart: *Plato's Doctrine of Ideas*, 1909.
The Myths of Plato, 1905.

P. Natorp: *Platons Ideenlehre*, 1921.

R. L. Nettleship: *Lectures on the Republic*, 1906.

Wilh. Windelband: *Platon*, 1901.

D. G. Ritchie: *Plato*, 1902.

R. C. Lodge: *Plato's Theory of Ethics*, 1928.

W. Lutoslawski: *The Origin and Growth of Plato's Logic*, 1905.

E. Barker: *The Greek Political Theory. Plato and his Predecessors*, 1918.

P. E. More: *The Religion of Plato*, 1921.

W. Pater: *Plato and Platonism*, 1893.

(For commentaries on the individual dialogues of Plato see bibliography in Uberweg-Heinze: *Geschichte der Philosophie*, Vol. I, pp. 159–171.)

ARISTOTLE:

W. D. Ross: *Selections from Aristotle*, 1927.

Aristotle's Works. English Translation edited by J. A. Smith and W. D. Ross, 1908–1930.

The more important in this series follow:

Metaphysica, W. D. Ross, 1908.

Parva Naturalia, J. I. Beare and G. R. T. Ross, 1908.

Historia Animalium, D. W. Thompson, 1910.

De Generatione Animalium, A. Platt, 1910.

De Partibus Animalium, W. Ogle, 1911.

Atheniensium Respublica, F. C. Kenyon, 1920.

Meteorologica, E. W. Webster, 1923.

Analytica Priora, A. J. Jenkman, 1926.

Analytica Posteriora, G. R. G. Mure, 1926.

Problemata, E. S. Forster, 1927.

J. Barthélemy Saint-Hilaire: *Physique D'Aristote*, 1862.

W. A. Hammond: *Aristotle's Psychology*, 1902.

J. E. C. Welldon: *Nicomachean Ethics*, 1906.

W. L. Newman: *Politics of Aristotle*, 4 Vols., 1902.

R. E. Jebb (Ed. J. E. Sandys): *The Rhetoric of Aristotle*, 1909.

S. H. Butcher: *Aristotle's Theory of Poetry and Fine Art*, 1907.

W. D. Ross: *Aristotle*, 1928.

A. E. Taylor: *Aristotle*, 1919.

Ed. Zeller: *Aristotle and the Earlier Peripatetics*, Trans. B. F. C. Costelloi, J. H. Muirhead, 2 Vols., 1897.

George Grote: *Aristotle*, 2 Vols., 1880.

J. L. Stocke: *Aristoteleanism*, 1925.

T. E. Lones: *Aristotle's Researches in Natural Science*, 1912.

John Burnet: *Aristotle on Education*, 1905.

E. Barker: *The Political Thought of Plato and Aristotle*, 1906.

STOICS, SKEPTICS, EPICUREANS:

Ed. Zeller: *Stoics, Epicureans, Sceptics*, Trans. O. J. Reichel, 1880.

A. C. Pearson: *The Fragments of Zeno and Cleanthes*, 1891.

H. von Arnim: *Stoicorum veterum Fragmenta*, 3 Vols., 1903–5.

A. Grant: *The Ancient Stoics*. Essay VI in Preface to *The Ethics of Aristotle*, 1884.

G. Long: *The Thoughts of the Emperor M. Aurelius Antoninus*, 1886.

R. M. Wenley: *Stoicism*.

E. V. Arnold: *Roman Stoicism*, 1911.

E. Bevan: *Stoics and Sceptics*, 1913.

M. Heinze: *Die Lehre vom Logos in der griechischen Philosophie*, 1872.

A. Dyroff: *Die Ethik der Alten Stoa*, 1897.

R. D. Hicks: *Stoic and Epicurean*, 1910.

N. Maccoll: *The Greek Sceptics*, 1869.

M. M. Patrick: *Sextus Empiricus and Greek Scepticism*, 1899.

The Greek Sceptics, 1929.

Cyril Bailey: *Epicurus, the Extant Remains*, 1926.

H. Usener: *Epicurea*, 1887.

H. A. G. Munro: *Lucretius. With Notes and a Translation*, Ed. W. A. Merrill, 1907.

H. Diels: *Lukrezstudien*, (Proceedings of the Berlin Academy, 1916.)

W. Wallace: *Epicureanism*, 1880.

J. Masson: *Lucretius, Epicurean and Poet*, 1907.

HELLENISM, NEO-PLATONISM:

Philo's Works, Trans. C. D. Yonge, 4 Vols., 1900.

The Enneads of Plotinus, Trans. S. Mackenna, 3 Vols., 1917–24.

Apollonius of Tyana, Life and Epistles, Trans. F. C. Conybeare.

T. Whittaker: *The Neo-Platonists*, 1918.

W. R. Inge: *The Philosophy of Plotinus*, 2 Vols., 1923.

P. E. More: *Hellenistic Philosophies*, 1923.

T. R. Glover: *The Conflict of Religions in the Early Roman Empire*, 1909.

G. Kafka und H. Eibel: *Der Ausklang der antiken Philosophie und das Erwachen einer neuren Zeit*, 1928.

INDEX

(The following abbreviations are employed below: Gr., Greek; Soph., Sophist; Soc., Socrates; Pl., Plato; Ar., Aristotle; St., Stoic; Epic., Epicurus; Skep., Skeptic.)